The Joy of Philosophy

The Joy of Philosophy

*Thinking Thin versus
the Passionate Life*

Robert C. Solomon

New York   Oxford
Oxford University Press
1999

Oxford University Press

Oxford New York

Athens Auckland Bangkok Bogotá Buenos Aires Calcutta
Cape Town Chennai Dar es Salaam Delhi Florence Hong Kong Istanbul
Karachi Kuala Lumpur Madrid Melbourne Mexico City Mumbai
Nairobi Paris São Paulo Singapore Taipei Tokyo Toronto Warsaw

and associated companies in
Berlin Ibadan

Copyright © 1999 by Robert C. Solomon

Published by Oxford University Press, Inc.
198 Madison Avenue, New York, New York 10016

Oxford is a registered trademark of Oxford University Press, Inc.

Library of Congress Cataloging-in-Publication Data
Solomon, Robert C.
    The joy of philosophy : thinking thin versus the passionate life /
Robert C. Solomon.
       p.   cm.
    ISBN 0-19-506759-2
    1. Philosophy. I. Title.
B72.S654   1999
100—DC21   98-50825

9 8 7 6 5 4 3 2 1

Printed in the United States of America
on acid-free paper

PREFACE

> I suppose I am especially susceptible to the magic of games.
> Vladimir Nabokov, *Lolita*

He was forty-five years old when I met him. He had been a jock in college (track and field). He had tolerated his classes with good humor (and not much else), as punctuation between fraternity parties and Saturday football games. After college, he became a successful business-man, an excellent tennis player, a society person of some importance, an embodiment of the American dream. But now his backhand starting to fail, and in the midst of another acquisition, he would catch himself asking questions he could not articulate. He came to realize that his life was full, but what? "Hollow and superficial," he said to himself. Then he discovered the joy of philosophy. It wasn't an intellectual pretension, much less a required course. Like a child, he displayed almost unlimited enthusiasm for his new toy. He got his hands on a few books (what most academics would dismiss as "popular" or "secondary" reading), a few lecture tapes to play in the Porsche, a few names to drop here and there, and more than a few ideas. But what he had really gotten hold of was a lifetime love, an open-ended sense of wonder and fascination.

After thirty years, philosophy remains for me, as for many people, a source of considerable joy and delight. But "joy" and "delight" are not respectable terms in professional philosophy. Nietzsche, who celebrated philosophy as a "joyful wisdom," is still dismissed as "not a philosopher," despite his popularity in many circles. His prose is too shimmering, too full of sarcasm and wise-cracks, too personal. He has too much fun. (Too many exclamation points!)

He is a dancer, a philosophical prankster, an ironist in the grand tradition of Socrates, a jokester and a comic who includes everything in his philosophy—health hints, recipes, gossip, bumper stickers, nursery rhymes, advice to the lovelorn, pop psychology, popular physics, a bit of the occult and esoteric, social commentary, mythological history, contentious philology, family feuds, political diatribes, libelous insults, declarations of war, petty complaints, megalomania, blasphemies, bad jokes, overly clever puns, parodies, and plagiarisms. Professionalized philosophers complain about the lack of rigor, even the absence of a consistent thesis. But why ruin such a rich feast with the fibrous tendrils of mere argument? Nietzsche knew how to get joy out of philosophy, his "gaya scienza."

Although I have no pretensions about competing with Nietzsche or mimicking him, either in his depth of passion and insight or in his wonderful, notorious "style," I do share with him his sense of joy in philosophy. In opposition to a good deal of current philosophy, this is neither the love of argument nor the love of the elegant put-down. It does not imply what the postmodernists call "play," that is, provoking and enjoying the consternation and confusion of other people. What it does mean is going beyond the thinness of arguments to the richness that is philosophy, trying to add to our experience rather than to "prove a point." Points, we learned in plane geometry, have no dimensions and, consequently, no texture, no color, and certainly no depth. This book, accordingly, is not an argument, much less does it embody a "theory." As some readers will note, with increasing exasperation, I often go out of my way not to make "points" and offer "proofs," but rather to shift perspectives, even topics, in the hope of finding something new to explore. My main concern is to break down some old walls, between academic philosophy and its lost audience, between thin logic and thick rhetoric, between philosophical reason and philosophical passion, between "analytic" and "continental" philosophy, between philosophy and everything else.

Philosophy has become too "serious," a "profession" with its insiders and "experts." It is no longer—if it ever was—for Everyman, with its technical demands, its specialized but nevertheless intractable problems and puzzles, its academic hierarchies and sectarianism. The problem, as I see it in this book, is that philosophy has gotten too "thin," attenuated, emaciated, anorectic (to use a properly pathological term). In too many quarters, it has been reduced to logic and the criticism of arguments, to "deconstruction," jargon-mongering and the thin air of metaphilosophy. Concrete experience and scientific research, religion and spirituality alike are rejected as irrelevant or patronized as mere "objects" of study. Questions that require actually looking at and living in the world are dismissed with a patronizing chuckle and "but isn't that an *empirical* question?" What used to be called "speculation," not to mention "the vision thing," is no longer in fashion. The old ideal of philosophy as all-embracing, as thick, fat, and omnivorous, has been sacrificed to the new philosophy of lean and mean, whether in the form of linear arguments or of postmodern cynicism.

One of my colleagues was giving a lecture at one of our more prestigious universities in (southern) California on this narrowness in philosophy. He mused that recent philosophy had become rather like the proverbial blind men feeling around an elephant. One of the most prestigious of the several prestigious philosophers in attendance proudly conceded that he was "solely interested in the anatomy of the trunk and didn't much care if the elephant died."

In this book, I would like to attempt a glimpse of the living elephant, or at least grasp more than dead trunk and tusks. Many philosophers today insist on "pure" philosophy, that is, philosophy stripped of all but its skeleton: logic and argument and the bare bones of philosophical history (sometimes beginning with the formalism of Frege, at the end of the nineteenth century). I offer instead a volume filled with "impure philosophy," as the great Chilean poet Pablo Neruda once said (of his poetry): "as impure as old clothes, as a body with its foodstains and its shame, with wrinkles, observations, dreams, wakefulness, prophesies, declarations of love and hate, stupidities, shocks, idylls, political beliefs, negations, doubts, affirmations, and taxes."[1]

In the following pages, I do not claim anything more than to explore some alternative perspectives on some perennial philosophical problems. The book is not, in the sense that is so often invoked with moralizing righteousness, *serious*. I would rather have it read as "just playing around with (serious) ideas." That (dare I say?) is what philosophy is. Not serious, just having fun with ideas, ideas that really mean something. This is not to say that I will provide chuckles, much less belly laughs, throughout. I am afraid that my expressions of joy will be limited to a few epithets, adverbs, sarcastic comments, and bad puns. But the current notion that joy is to be found only in the vacuous, orthodonic smiles of lean, sun-drenched, wind-swept twenty-somethings is not the whole truth. It is also to be found in the fat lifelong broodings and musings of philosophers.

Thanks to the Philosophy Department at the University of Auckland, New Zealand; the Philosophy Department and the Humanities Research Institute at Australian National University; my good friend Roger Ames, editor of *Philosophy East and West*; my editor Cynthia Read, at Oxford University Press; and my subversive friends Bernd Magnus, Arthur Danto, Jay Hullett, Paul Woodruff, Alexander Nehamas, Richard Rorty, Peter Kraus, and Frithjof Bergmann, who, more than anyone, taught me the joy and richness of philosophy.

And, above all, to Kathy Higgins, for the joy she continues to bring to me and to philosophy.

REPRINT CREDITS

Chapter 1, "The Passionate Life," was originally written for a Center for Social Policy conference, "Virtue and Vice," at Bowling Green State University in September 1996. The essay, "The Virtues of the Passionate Life," was subsequently published in the journal *Social Philosophy and Policy*, 15, no. 1, (1998) and in a book, *Virtue and Vice*, Ellen Frankel Paul, Fred Miller, Jeffrey Paul, eds. (New York: Cambridge University Press, 1998).

Chapter 2, "The Politics of Emotions," is based on my essay of the same name in *Midwest Studies in Philosophy*, Vol. 22, *The Philosophy of the Emotions* P. French, H. Wettstein, eds. (Notre Dame, Ind.: University of Notre Dame Press, 1999). Portions of the chapter are drawn from my chapter, "The Philosophy of Emotions" in *Handbook of the Emotions*, M. Lewis, J. Haviland, eds, (New York: Guilford Press, 1993) and my "Beyond Reason," in *Revisioning Philosophy*, J. Ogilvy, ed. (Albany: SUNY Press 1993).

Chapter 3, "Rationality and its Vicissitudes," is based on a talk at a conference, "Culture and Rationality," at Mount Abu, Rajasthan, and subsequently published as "Existentialism, Emotions, and the Cultural Limits of Rationality," in *Philosophy East and West*, 42, no. 4 (1992): 597–622. My thanks to the editors for allowing me to use and considerably amplify parts of that essay here. This version is dedicated to my good friend David Zimmerman.

Chapter 4, "Justice, Sympathy, Vengeance," is based on a series of lectures and papers I have given over the years, including a Memorial Lecture at the University of Massachusetts, Boston, for the late Shula Sommers in April 1989; a presentation at the I.S.R.E. meeting in Paris in March 1988; a presentation at the conference of N.A.S.S.P. at Oxford University in 1988; and in the essay "Justice as Vengeance, Vengeance as Justice: A Partial Defense of Polymarchus," which was originally published in *Morality and Social Justice*, J.

Sterba, ed. (Lanham, Md.: Rowman and Littlefield, 1995). Parts of the essay are also adapted from my book *A Passion for Justice* (New York: Addison-Wesley, 1990; Lanham, Md.: Rowman & Littlefield, 1994). My special thanks to Nico Frijda for his encouragement and support.

Chapter 5, "Philosophy and the Tragic Sense of Life," was written for this volume.

Chapter 6, "Thinking Death in the Face," was written for a conference in the Bay of Islands, in northern New Zealand, in January 1996 and published as "Death Fetishism, Morbid Solipsism," in *Death and Philosophy*, Jeff Malpas and Solomon, eds. (London: Routledge, 1998). My personal thanks to Peter Kraus for hosting a delightful conference and for his friendship. This chapter is dedicated to him. Peter described life on the breathtakingly beautiful Bay of Islands as "a holiday from death." I'm not very good at holidays (my honeymoon was a "working honeymoon"), but the idea hit home. I'm now thinking of my life as a "working holiday," and writing about death is (for a philosopher) an essential part of it.

Chapter 7, "Recovering Personal Identity," first appeared in *Self as Person in Asia, Theory and Practice*, ed. Roger Ames, Wimal Wissanyake, Thomas Kasulis, (Albany: SUNY Press, 1994). Excerpted by permission of the publisher. All rights reserved.

Chapter 8, "Deception, Self, and Self-Deception in Philosophy," is based on two essays, "Self, Deception, and Self-Deception in Philosophy," in *Self and Deception: A Cross-Cultural Philosophical Enquiry*, Ames and Wissanyake, eds. (Albany: SUNY Press, 1996) and "What a Tangled Web: Deception and Self-Deception in Philosophy" in M. Lewis, C. Saarni, eds., *Lying in Everyday Life* (New York: Guilford Press, 1993).

The Afterthought, "Has Analytic Philosophy Ruined Philosophy?," is adapted from *A Short History of Philosophy* (co-authored with Kathleen M. Higgins) (New York: Oxford, 1996).

CONTENTS

The Joy of Philosophy

Introduction

PHILOSOPHY THROUGH THICK AND THIN (BEING, AND NOTHING LESS)

[G. E.] Moore took the lead in the rebellion, and I followed with a sense of emancipation.... We believed that the grass is green, and that the sun and stars would exist if no one was aware of them. The world which had been thin and logical now became rich and varied.

Bertrand Russell

The history of philosophy has many ironies. One of them, surely, is Bertrand Russell's self-congratulatory observation about the origins of "analytic" philosophy. Against Hegel, who incorporated virtually every facet of concrete human experience into his philosophy, Russell, following Frege and Moore, "rebelled." Misinterpreting German idealism, which he took (wrongly) to be the conviction that the world is made up of ideas and not of good, solid matter, Russell made his comment "the world which had been thin and logical . . . became rich and varied" in his own philosophy.[1] So began a hundred-year "analytic" movement that would render philosophy thin and logical indeed.[2]

We might agree with Russell, that the joy of philosophy is its richness and variety. But how sad, then, that as a "discipline" it has narrowed itself to a set of conceptual skills, declared war on richness and variety in favor of a "thin" and all but exclusive preference for argument and logical analysis, and dismissed Hegel's "speculative" imagination and his all-embracing conception of experience ("totalization," in the equally thin jargon of the postmodernists[3]). Philosophy now requires "specialization," technique, narrow focus, and rigor rather than vision, curiosity, and openness. Hegel's ideal was all-embracing "comprehension." Today, some of the most prestigious articles in philosophy are sequences of symbols and strings of impenetrable jargon, of interest only to a few fellow travelers. The dominant aim of philosophy, as political philosopher John Rawls announces at the beginning of his epochal *Theory of Justice*, is ever to raise the level of conversation "to a higher order of abstraction."[4] But philosophy (as Hegel argued) does not need to be abstract. There is concrete philosophy that lives in the details, in the flesh-and-blood dialectic of ideas, something more than mere bones and sinew. It succeeds, in the words of Wilfrid Sellars, by "seeing how things hang together." It thrives on making the ordinary, remarkable and the unremarkable, mysterious: time, life, mind, self, how we and the world "hang together."

Philosophy is, or should be, a kind of magic. It is not an escape from but rather a new window—or many windows—onto our lives. It is not so much abstraction as insight and vision. Great philosophers, from the earliest Vedantins to the existentialists, have offered dazzling and disturbing insights and visions, ideas that make our heads spin and make us lose for the moment our everyday orientation and concerns. I hate to think that sense of magic and joy has been lost or abandoned. Philosophers today are too often killjoys, too quick with objections, too obstinate to understand (or to listen to) imperfectly stated alternatives, too anxious to belittle both insight and enthusiasm. When I was in graduate school, a superbly talented and creative young woman, one of my exact contemporaries, handed in a quite creative philosophy paper. It was brutally trashed by her teacher, who exclaimed to her with Old Testament indignation, *"Philosophy is not supposed to be fun!"* (Today she is a leading academic, but in another field.) The most enthusiastic and talented graduate students are still chased out of philosophy with the same reprimand. Philosophy is not supposed to be fun!

In my travels around the country, I often meet people—successful businesspeople, artists, and others, as well as academics—who without any prompting regale me with a familiar confession. It begins "I had a philosophy class once, but. . . ." I know what is coming. I cringe from the opening syllables. Sometimes it is something innocently annoying along the lines of "but I don't remember a thing." Too often it is "but I hated it," typically followed by a most unflattering portrait of an uncaring, pompous teacher who was obviously too clever by half and intent on displaying this. I ask, Who is this bad apple? All too often the *who* turns out to be one of the more distinguished members of our profession. He (almost always a *he*) has a distinguished publication record, and his lifework is to inspire one or two students (out of hundreds or thousands) to go on in philosophy to inflict similar damage on the next generation. The idea that the fate of philosophy depends on one thing and one thing only, our collective ability to inspire joy in philosophy, is an idea that is too often treated with disdain. The very suggestion inspires heated condemnation of philosophy as "entertainment" and a renewed insistence on professional competence and "the integrity of the discipline."

What is the joy of philosophy? I, too, used to say that it is the thrill of seeing how all sorts of ideas fit together. But now, I would say that it is, rather, the thrill of seeing other people's eyes light up when they start seeing how all sorts of ideas fit together, in their own terms.

"The joy of philosophy." That phrase should not seem odd to anyone who has taken the time to philosophize. My philosopher friends are among the most devoted—not quite to say obsessed or addicted—people I know. Some find joy (along, perhaps, with some angst) in trying to grapple with "the big questions." Others are chopping their way through inexcusably obscurantist texts. Many more are now working their way through ever more intricately puzzling "brainteasers" dealing with logic and the peculiarities of philosophical language. I know lots of artists, musicians, politicians, other academics, businesspeople, and moneymakers—all of them devotees, but none so devoted as my philosophy friends. And this is not just those at the top of the profession. Indeed, they tend to be more defensive and far less enthusiastic than the hundreds of excellent and enthusiastic teachers I meet at small colleges and even in high schools. For the latter, the joy of philosophy is the joy *of philosophy*, not just the joy of a professional made good.

The most buoyant, vital people around (not only, of course, those who get paid for it) know the joy of philosophy. Even those who have otherwise empty, pathetic lives sometimes find a vibrant life in philosophy (and not just by way of "consolation"). Ambitious philosophical tomes—most of them unpublished and unread—have been written in prisons and flophouses, in lonely rooms and on the cluttered desks of frustrated clerks and disillusioned lawyers. No lack of speculation and enthusiasm there. Such tame phrases as "the life of the mind" and "the world of ideas" fail to capture the dynamism, the excitement, the joy of philosophy. It's not quite the joy of cooking, and it's certainly not the joy of sex, but it is joy nonetheless.

Portrait of a Philosopher

> What can be said at all [in philosophy] can be said clearly; and what we cannot speak thereof we must remain silent.
> Ludwig Wittgenstein, *Tractatus Logico-Philosophicus*

Here is a portrait of the philosopher in the late twentieth century. He (the example is still almost always a he) is standing in front of a small audience. He is in agony. His eyes, although intense, are looking at nothing; perhaps they even are turned in on themselves. There is a deep furrow on his brow, a frown—no, a scowl—and one hand grapples at his forehead, as if to keep his head or his brains from exploding. For those who enjoy classical references, he resembles no figure so much as Rodin's famous *Thinker*, or perhaps, rather, the twisted, most unhappy father and priest in *Laocoön*, the most convoluted and woeful depiction of suffering in all of antiquity. His speech is broken, almost stuttering, betraying the traffic jam of ideas and the intensity with which he tries to get the words right. He paces feverishly, compulsively, erratically, along a well-worn track, from corner to corner, never once making eye contact with his rapt and utterly perplexed audience. His free hand alternately covers his mouth, then his eyes, pulls on his nose, grapples with the scruff of his neck, caresses an armpit, nervously picks up, circumcises, and releases one piece of chalk after another, occasionally gesturing as if to write something, but no more emerges than an occasional "x" or an oblong. There are excruciating (pregnant) pauses. It is a performance that demands the attention of Dr. Oliver Sachs, the great neuropsychiatrist. It is a living theater of neurosis, of narcissism, of thought turned against itself, of language desperately needing a holiday. This is philosophy, and here is the philosopher. Suffering, and suffering because of philosophy. Philosophy as a disease, the only cure for which is . . . more philosophy.

The portrait I have just sketched belongs to an easily identifiable historical person, Ludwig Wittgenstein, whose philosophy is becoming eclipsed but whose biography has emerged as one of the more enduring icons of twentieth-century philosophical life. Although few of Wittenstein's students shared his genius or his morbid Viennese view of life, many, many of them borrowed his gestures, his style, and put on the face of his seriousness as if, indeed, his turmoil were their own. The result is two generations of philosophy students and teachers who perform philosophy as if it were a public self-exorcism. They perform for introductory college classes, and those students who are predisposed to join in the performance (as opposed to laughing at it) are encouraged to join them. The topics for the most part remain tediously the same, but the style, the performance, the seriousness, has turned philosophy—as Wittgenstein himself complained—into a kind of psychopathology.

In the movie *Rain Man*, Dustin Hoffman (in his brilliant performance as autistic Raymond) responds to stress by trying to solve—over and over—the puzzle of Abbott and Costello's classic routine, "Who's on First?" In exasperation, his brother (Tom Cruise) yells at Ray, "It's a riddle, it's a joke. If you would see that, maybe you'd get better." Psychiatrically naive, perhaps, but profound all the same. It is a pathology that is not at all unfamiliar to anyone who has watched many of the most brilliant and prestigious philosophers at work today. The fact that philosophical puzzles are notoriously difficult, even intractable, is taken as evidence of their profundity.[5] But intractability may also be a sign of intellectual masochism or, more innocent and innocuous, intellectual masturbation. The awareness that philosophical puzzles are both intractable and inconsequential is good reason to insist that they are ultimately pursued only "for their own sake." Which is to say, for fun, for the sheer joy of it, however we may struggle and grumble on our way. Wittgenstein himself once wrote that an entire book of philosophy might contain nothing but jokes. He himself never wrote it, of course.

In philosophy—let's clear away the pretensions and just be clear about this—*nothing is really at stake*. When doctors, engineers, members of the Federal Reserve Board, or experts on the bomb squad get it wrong, there are very real consequences. When a philosopher gets it wrong, no one dies; nothing crashes, explodes, or collapses; there is no increase in poverty or unemployment; the stock market doesn't take a nosedive. To be sure, some bad interpretations of a few good philosophers have been calamitous in history, both ancient and modern. But these are the exceptions, not the rule, and, even so, it is hardly the deskbound philosophers themselves who put the world at risk. Indeed, there is a feeling of liberation that comes with the irresponsibility of philosophy. However gloomy their personalities, and whatever violent sentiments they may have expressed or inspired in the world, even such sourpusses as Marx and Rousseau clearly had a lot of fun.

Most philosophers, I would guess, came into philosophy as rebels, searching for a profound kind of freedom. How ironic, then, that we have become the prisoners of a self-imposed authoritarianism, under the banners of "professionalism" and "the integrity of the discipline." Freethinking and wild ideas have become out of place; "discipline" is what it takes to be a philosopher. Except in undergraduate recruitment brochures, philosophy is no longer described as "thinking about life" or "self-examination," much less the joy of ideas. As one of its foremost practitioners has said, with considerable authority, "logic and the philosophy of science is philosophy enough." With that absolute lock on what counts as philosophy, freedom, imagination, accessibility and, worst of all, sensitivity have gone by the wayside.

On Philosophy as Criticism

Seriousness is the only refuge of the shallow.

Oscar Wilde

Philosophy, like most academic and intellectual disciplines, has become largely the domain of criticism. The salutary effects of this are obvious: critical acumen is clearly essential to a democracy and it is the essence of good science. It creates a dialectic in which the truth (or, at any rate, better understanding) emerges from half-baked or one-sided ideas. It makes theorizing interesting, not to mention more responsible. In theory, at least, it helps to eliminate a good deal of fraud and foolishness. And, one should add, it adds a competitive edge, which for many of the combative personalities that are attracted to the life of the mind can itself be the source of a lot of entertainment. But criticism can be overdone. Philosophy, in particular, is now conceived by many of its professional practitioners as nothing more than the examination of arguments and the production of counterarguments. Ideas and visions? They are just targets.

First-year undergraduates are initiated into the discipline of philosophy by being taught to gun down the arguments of the great philosophers, as if in a sideshow shooting gallery. ("Plato said P: What's wrong with that?" "Kant argued Q: Give a counterexample." "John Stuart Mill made this inference: Isn't that a 'howler' "?) More advanced philosophers ply their skill in articles that inevitably begin, "So-and-so has argued X, but I will show that s/he has failed." In a time of "publish or perish," philosophy thus becomes the skill of nit-picking. It employs increasingly "tighter" arguments involving decreasing perspective, knowledge, and interest. To avoid smuggling originality with all of its vulnerabilities into the argument, philosophers rely on the most unoriginal examples (often the same ones that Frege, for example, used back in 1900, or that Kant employed a century before that, or that Aristotle used over two millennia ago). The scope of the concern becomes more narrow and more formal—less tender flesh to be bitten and bleed, and no personal feelings to make things messy. The joy of philosophy becomes largely destructive, the fun of "tearing apart" and destroying, not to mention "deconstructing" arguments. The Hegelian joys of constructive ("speculative") vision, of appreciating the ideas of one's predecessors even in ways they did not appreciate them themselves, of using philosophy to generate new ideas, not to mention extraordinary experiences, are pushed out of the picture.[6] Arguments and refutations: What more does a philosopher need to know?

When I teach, I now aspire to what has been called the principle of charity. Crudely put, it says that even if an idea sounds like nonsense, we should try to figure out what the author might have had in mind, or what good idea might be hiding beneath the uninviting surface. (This is, of course, an essential pedagogical skill when fielding students' questions.) How often I have heard my colleagues dismiss an article, a whole book, or an entire career because of a single mistake, a factual error, a misinterpretation, or (worst of all) a logical fallacy. Whatever is of value there, they missed. In practice, of course, I only sometimes succeed in upholding my own principle. A hint of some crackpot political view, a bit of New Age or postmodernist pretension, a combative counterclaim to some precious idea I have defended, almost inevitably throws me back into my professional gunfighter mode, so ably taught to me by my gunslinger teachers in Philadelphia, Ann Arbor, Princeton, and Dodge City. But at least I see the error of my ways. There may be fun in a philosophical put-down, but the joy of philosophy lies elsewhere, in the cooperative development of ideas, in the exploration of new perspectives, in the creation of visions in which the everyday becomes interesting, even fascinating. Criticism has its place, of course, but criticism is, or ought to be, only a tool for shaping ideas, for expanding our vision. It is not, or ought not to be, an end in itself.[7]

In this book (which itself is all too critical), I want to return to an older, more "romantic" mode of philosophizing. It will not be devoid of arguments—indeed, one might look at the entire book as an argument against "thinness" in philosophy—but the structure of the book has much more to do with the complexity of the ideas than the standardized analytic campaign.[8] Quite frankly, I often do not know where my explorations have taken me. That is the difference between passion and proof. Indeed, my revolt against logical "thinness" is very much a celebration of the passions in philosophy and the richness they provide. But at least since Plato, philosophers have been wary of the passions, and certainly since the logical positivists (who had their own good reasons), philosophy has warned against romanticism. There is danger in speculation and passion, in trying to delve into human experience as opposed to just tearing bad arguments apart. *Postmodernists/empiricists*

It is surprising, given the strong "nothing but" bias toward empiricism in the past century, that there is in the same quarters such strong resistance to talking about experience and especially about feelings and the concrete details of life.[9] The focus instead is on "logical form." Perhaps this emphasis goes back to a misreading of Plato, the most imaginative of all philosophers, and his fascination with the Forms. It certainly traces back to Kant, who celebrated the *a priori* (but in doing so did not mean to demean the empirical). Hegel, despite his insistence on all-inclusiveness, nevertheless flirted dangerously with "the Concept," the nineteenth-century version of "a higher order of abstraction," and so he is sometimes read (and attacked) not for his richness but for his all-encompassing thinness.[10]

In Anglo-American philosophy today, the insistence on thinness is the continuation—indeed, the rejuvenation—of the Frege-Russell-(early)Wittgenstein fixation on logic and formal analysis. It also continues in the postmodern puff of meta-philosophical weightlessness, which in its (often formal) insistence on pluralism and fragmentation remains oblivious to or disdainful of any ordinary human experience.[11] But the net result of the emphasis on criticism and deconstruction has been a thoroughgoing skepticism bordering on cynicism regarding "interesting ideas" and a compensatory fascination with the purely formal, with inferences and arguments, with finding the fault lines of others' positions but abstaining from taking any position oneself.[12] With this cynicism, there quite naturally comes a deep suspicion of enthusiasm—indeed, of any passion or sentiment. However weighty its origins, philosophy has become light as a feather, virtually without substance, without content.

Of course, even the thickest philosophy is still pretty thin, a mere veneer, only the surface (and not the "depth") of things. "The truth is on the surface," insisted Mark Twain, one of America's greatest philosophers. What is "profound" in philosophy is more likely a broad sweep, a matter of seeing, not of digging. Philosophy isn't argument but discernment, contemplation, vision. If philosophy is thick and rich, it is because life is thick and rich. And philosophy is about life. It may even be essential for life (at least, for the examined life), but philosophy is not life, from which it only borrows. Neither is philosophy the skeleton around which life fleshes out, as if philosophy is the foundation and all else merely meat. Philosophy cannot live as one-dimensional reasoning, but even at its fullest, philosophy will still be, without apologies, thin even if not logical. The grass, with or without philosophy, is a luxurious green.

Perhaps because philosophy has gotten so ominously thin, a great deal has been written about the end of philosophy, playing on that now tiresome ambiguity between "end" as linear goal or purpose and "end" as terminus. Some writers are less coy, announcing the "death" or "exhaustion" of philosophy. Others are more evasive. Cornell West and John Rajchman tried to start an avalanche when they announced the arrival of "postanalytic philosophy," but any change has remained undetectable.[13] The move to "postanalytic" philosophy (or what is now misnamed "pragmatism") is no more than a slight shift in a few strategic plays, carried out by the same familiar players. The technocracy remains intact, proudly displaying the same "dryness" that Iris Murdoch warned against several decades ago when the field was still moist. But the "thinner" and better-defined the problems become, the more intractable they seem to get. "Truth," for example, has been reduced to a nonsense term, and many philosophers have convinced themselves that they would just as soon be rid of it, at least in philosophy.[14] So, too, the notion of "self" has become so thin that it is unrecognizable, not to mention insignificant.[15] The central concepts of life are reduced to logical paradoxes and puzzles, and then philosophers are reprimanded (but only by themselves): Philosophy is misconceived. We have been chasing "pseudo problems" all of these years, they say, and their prestige, their salaries, and their lock on the profession increase considerably.

The Perennial Problems
of Philosophy

Sooner or later, life makes philosophers of us all.

Maurice Riseling

Against the cynical ("ironic") view that insists philosophy is nothing but what gainfully employed philosophers happen to be doing at the moment, I want to insist that there are very real, palpable, and universal human problems that provide the impetus and the motivation for philosophy. This is not to deny, as Nietzsche suggested, that there is also a curious "will to truth," a fascination for puzzles and paradoxes that, once stimulated, may keep chugging along for years, unmotivated by anything else. But philosophy is not this. It is an engaged wrestling with the perennial problems of life. We are all philosophers, and we have to democratize philosophy, in spite of its long elitist roots. Philosophy is not a speciality, a profession, an exclusive club with its own rules and passwords. Philosophy is nothing but thinking about such matters as passion, justice, tragedy, death, self-identity, and, of course, philosophy itself, which is by no means the province or the privilege of any small number of university-trained professionals.

Philosophy, in the most important and politically incorrect sense of the term, is intrinsic to our very human way of being. We think. We feel. And there are some matters—we might think of them as "preexisting philosophical conditions" (aka "the human condition")—about which we have no choice but to think and feel. These matters include, not surprisingly, the nature of the good life, the place and rationale of our most powerful passions, our place among other people, questions of justice, explanations for tragedy, the apparent finality of death, one's own identity, and the point and purpose of thinking, of reflection, of consciousness, of philosophy, however these may differ in detail or conception from culture to culture.

These are (some of) the perennial problems of philosophy. There have been philosophers (Richard Rorty, to take the most prominent example[16]) who have said that there are no perennial problems of philosophy. That, I think, is just plain wrong (and Rorty elsewhere makes that quite clear). Of course you can take such a "thick" description of these problems that they turn out to be, not surprisingly, peculiar to a time, a place, a people, or the American Philosophical Association membership in 1973. But life has its problems quite apart from any particular philosophical tradition, for instance, our awareness of our own vulnerability and eventual death. Whether or not there is any correct "logic" for thinking about death, death nevertheless looks awfully like a universal "fact" about us ("our most necessary possibility," wrote Heidegger). Of course, there are any number of ways of conceptualizing life and its meaning(s)—and, accordingly, the meaning and the nature of death. But I think that the awareness of death, for one, counts as a "preexisting philosophical condition," something not in any way invented by philosophers but, nevertheless, shaped by (and giving shape to) philosophy.[17]

To say that there are perennial problems in philosophy is, in a way, just to point, perhaps to grunt, at something that even in its "thinnest" descriptions is already provincial, perspectival, and therefore something less than "perennial." (As Nietzsche would put it, there are no facts and there is no urtext, only interpretations.) There is a good argument, for instance, that what is now referred to as the mind-body problem is, in fact, peculiar to a particular moment of learning and hope in the convergence of the exciting subjects of neuropsychology and computer science, coupled with the Christian bifurcation of body and soul, Descartes's (Cartesian) philosophy of "two substances," some inventiveness at the professional intersection of the philosophy of language and the philosophy of mind, and some peculiarities of the English language. In Japan, in ancient Greece, among the Yoruba of Nigeria, there is no such distinction and thus no such problem.

But what does this mean? It is not to deny that there are other problems, other "splits," that cause equal consternation. (Nor is it to say, what is absurd, that other cultures could not accept the findings of neuroscience.) In Japan, for example, the tension between the "face" that one shows the public world and unshowable private feelings is a source of continuous concern. The Yoruba, like most people, worry about the nature of the soul, which they distinguish, in several senses, from the body. But there is no mind-body problem, in the strict sense, if only because (in Japanese and Yoruba) there is no word for (no equivalent of) "mind." (*kokoro*, the best approximation in Japanese, clearly embraces all sorts of features that would be located on the "body" side of the Cartesian divide. Aristotle had no sense of an *anima* distinct from an organism, and the Yoruba *ori* means something more like "head" than "inner mind," and the contrast is with the rest of the body.) What we call "mind," one might surmise, is the "thinnest" description available of certain aspects of first person experience; it is then contrasted with "the body," which in turn is very thinly described in purely physiological terms.

It would be nonsense to think that the mind-body problem is *nothing but* a cultural peculiarity of one very particular epoch in one very regional philosophical tradition. How to provide a sufficiently "thin" description of the problem so as to include all cultures and all such oppositions is not my concern here, and such a thin presentation of the problem may be so attentuated that it becomes a matter of indifference to us. But what I want to pursue here—very much against that postmodern line that Rorty on occasion endorses—is that core of concerns that cannot be matters of mere irony or indifference to us and deserve recognition as quintessentially human, whether or not they are recognized as such by philosophers and whether or not they ever appear free of any particular cultural and philosophical perspective. To be sure, some perspectives apply only in some cultures and, not in others. But to insist that there are some concerns that are essentially human is not to commit either of the postmodern sins of "essentializing" and "totalizing." Nor is it to deny that if human beings were very different kinds of creatures (for example, invulnerable or immortal), the perennial problems would be very different. To talk of "perennial problems" is simply to say that there are some questions, in some form, that for us (that is, for all of us, as far as our limited and necessarily provincial imaginations will carry us) are inescapable.

It was Gabriel Marcel who distinguished puzzles from mysteries and complained that philosophers (midcentury) had lost sight of the mysteries by distracting themselves with puzzles. I would put the matter a bit differently, but the distinction he was drawing seems to me to be unavoidable. He was writing before his time. In the sense he was reaching for—that confusion regarding matters of deep concern for every thinking being—philosophy has all but disappeared in the best universities in America. Philosophy is not the introduction of new esoteric concerns. It is more concentrated attention on those concerns that are already shared by everyone, and in particular by bright-eyed hormonal undergraduates and forty-five-year-old professional men and women. But the "best" philosophy departments have become those that are the most technically brilliant and have the least to say to most students, which is why so many good students leave philosophy for religious studies and literature departments. Off campus, the same students pursue New Age philosophy with the enthusiasm one might have expected in our philosophy courses. Instead of being indignant or dismissive, we would be much better off if we tried to understand where such impulses come from and how they might be satisfied.

Philosophy is a genuine need, and the problems it confronts are real, not pseudo, problems. Philosophy surfaces several times in life, most predictably during childhood, before it is quashed by unresponsive parents and teachers; during late adolescence, when the questions of identity and one's place in the world are in tumultuous play; and in the various crises of life—divorce, serious illness, the death of a loved one, personal failure, political upheaval. And if professional philosophers are not willing to respond to the heartfelt questions that alone, in most people's eyes, justify the philosophers' (publically supported) existence, then alternative sources of philosophical solace are bound to pop up. Check the extensive self-help shelves of any bookstore. For a great many intelligent people these days, better the libidinal fantasies of Shirley MacLaine than the tedium of the professional skepticism that finds fault with every argument, confusions in every insight, foolishness in every good feeling, an intractable paradox hiding beneath every figure of speech. Ms. MacLaine, at least, seems to find real joy in what she does.

Celebrating Socrates

Laughter is the language of the soul.

Pablo Neruda

It is often quipped that Socrates never published, and so he perished. Neverthless, he has become our hero, the philosophers' inspiration and ideal.

Indeed, although there were philosophers before him (somewhat dismissively referred to as pre-Socratic philosophers), it is hard to imagine the growth or development of philosophy without him. What would Plato have written about? From what intellectual pad would Aristotle have been launched? Would we know what to do with Augustine or Aquinas? Nietzsche's ravings (and his envy) would have been short-circuited (though small-town Protestantism still would have given him a turn). Socrates' personality—as well as his wit and brilliance—charms all of us. It is with his example (and Plato's presentation) that philosophy gets sharply divided from (and against) poetry, rhetoric, from public politics, and becomes splendidly isolated as the discipline of self-examination.[18]

And yet, the truth is that Socrates was a self-styled charlatan. He knowingly insisted that he was ignorant, and on that basis declared himself the wisest man around. He employed atrocious arguments, when they would win. He would wheedle and tease, confuse and cajole. He would ridicule ad hominem, one of the many informal fallacies he routinely committed. He was a man of pleasure who was, or could be, strikingly indifferent to love and pleasure and even life itself. He died for philosophy, or so he would have had us believe. But he died for himself, for "the good of his soul," and even the political principles for which he sacrificed himself seem now dubious, inconsistent and perhaps insufferable.[19]

It seems, from the various accounts we have of him, that Socrates was never alone, rarely contemplative, and rarely all that serious. So much for our image of the philosopher as solitary, somber, and purely pensive thinker. Socrates was a compulsive party goer, a symposiast, a non-stop talker, a gadfly who wouldn't stop buzzing around the issues and, of course, the boys. Whatever else we may say of him—that he was wise, that he was courageous, that he was ugly, that he was, after all, merely mortal (as in the requisite syllogism)—he had a good time. His dialogues are filled with wisecracks, charming insults, philosophical slapstick. One can read even now the sparkle in his eyes as well as the crackle in his wit, the joy with which he pursued his subjects and his willing victims, and the not wholly immodest glee with which he would make his point, seal the argument, end one part of the discussion to make way for another. Perhaps, as Nietzsche—in awe and envy—argued two millennia later, he was really a buffoon. But what a buffoon! He charmed the youth of Athens and within a few years after his death charmed the ancient world. Two thousand years later, he charmed the new philosophers of the Renaissance and the newly pagan modern world. He taught philosophy as conversation, as enlightened kibitzing, by teasing, by cajoling. He taught philosophy as joyful wisdom, philosophy *as fun*.

Later philosophers may have sipped alone by bourgeois fireside with pen in hand, but Socrates drank his fill at gala symposia and died, appropriately, by drink. He was condemned, as we all know, for "corrupting the youth of

Athens," a charge as vague as it was unprovable, and for rejecting the gods of the city, a charge he denied but that was no doubt true. He flaunted his activities to the jury that condemned him, suggesting that he deserved a pension rather than a sentence. He was unjustly condemned to death, but only at his own provocation and with great hesitation on the part of the jury. (No doubt some of those jurors already suspected what history would make of such a verdict.) He turned down his friend Crito, who offered to spring him from prison and help him escape. Why? Because of several notoriously bad arguments. But perhaps he, too, had an inkling of what history had in store for him. That is the fantasy of all martyrs, but it rarely (except for one other) meets with such success. (Cf. Aristotle, who à la Falstaff declared, "Athens will not have a second chance to sin against philosophy." Wisdom is the better part of valor.)

Socrates was and is a paradox, the singular personality from whom all of the subsequent confusions and compulsions of philosophy originate and flow like the conversations from his ever-moving mouth. He insisted on reason, but it was the art of rhetoric in which he was champion. He established himself, with pure charisma, as a man of passion rather than contemplation. He always had the quick response and the ready question rather than the thought-out theory. Indeed, it's not clear that he had a theory about anything, much less an answer to his own questions. Even his great *Republic*, which got the West arguing about "What is justice?" for the next two thousand years, comes to no clear conclusion and suggests, at least, that there may be none.

Socrates insisted on *definitions*, necessary and sufficient conditions that would cover every appropriate case and exclude none, but he himself was much better at the clever counterexample and the deft refutation. And when he had refuted every proposed definition, he would take his turn not with another doomed effort but with a tale or a fable, a make-believe city or a portrait of the psyche as a team of wild horses and driver, recollecting an imaginary meeting with a muse or indulging in speculation about the immortality of the soul. He was, in fact, a mythmaker, the sculptor of myth and countermyth—the world of the Forms, of true Being, the escape from the cave, the ideal of true integrity, the immortality of the soul. He suggested that poets be thrown out of the republic as liars and charlatans, but he was the greatest poet, liar, and charlatan of them all.

Thus there are two Socrates, the flesh-and-blood enthusiast of twenty-five hundred years ago, and the name attached to the bloodless logical construction of a handful of dubious arguments and wild otherworldly theories. We have grabbed hold of Socrates' fascination with puzzles and paradoxes but lost sight of both the deep personal concerns and the irrepressible sense of humor that motivated him. Worse, philosophy has taken on an exclusionary self-righteousness that simply dismisses the heartfelt concerns of most students and other fans of philosophy. Socrates had it right: philosophy can and should be a joy, not a burden. This is not to say that it is easy. Or that anything goes. But Socrates faced his death with far more equanimity than most philosophers simply face one another and their students in the seminar room. Not for Socrates the anguished grimaces of today's deep thinkers.[20] A giggle and a chuckle of delight were the most appropriate expressions of wisdom.

Principle of Respect —
Utility —

1

THE PASSIONATE LIFE

What remains of life, except having loved?

Victor Hugo

Tell them I had a wonderful life.

Ludwig Wittgenstein (last words)

Life is rich, fat with possibilities and passions. But philosophy, including philosophies of life, are all too often thin, reduced to skeletal principles, reductionist concepts, single-minded theories. Ethics, which ought to serve the philosophy of life, is notorious in this regard. Throughout much of the twentieth century—and the preceding century as well—there has been a conscientious effort to reduce ethics to a single perspective, even a single principle, "the principle of utility" or "the principle of respect." Or, more dismissively and disastrously, ethics (along with politics and social philosophy, aesthetics and religion) has been pushed to the margins of philosophy, "not real philosophy." It is dismissed as "soft," as "merely subjective," as "strictly speaking, meaningless."[1] The fat, messy richness of human life and passion is reduced to its single most celebrated attribute, so-called rationality, what Bernard Williams has called "the featureless subject."[2] "Man [sic] is a rational animal," said Aristotle, twenty-five centuries ago. And modern philosophers have taken him up with a vengeance, reducing the "animal" to mere biology and limiting "rationality" to logic and language. Aristotle, no doubt, would be appalled.

I want to defend a "thick" conception of life that has often been ignored or dismissed in philosophy, and with it a set of virtues that have often been ignored in ethics. To begin with, I would like to defend what the philosopher Sam Keen called, in a book of the same name, *the passionate life*.[3] It is neither exotic nor unfamiliar. It is a life defined by emotions, by impassioned engagement and belief, by one or more quests, grand projects, embracing affections. It also is sometimes characterized (for example, by Goethe in *Faust*, by Kierkegaard, and by Nietzsche) in terms of frenzy, vaulting ambition, "sickness unto death," essentially insatiable goals, impossible affections, I want to contrast this conception of life with ordinary morality and "being a good person," although for obvious reasons I do not want to say that one must give up the latter in pursuing the former. This is a mistake that Nietzsche often suggests with his "immoralist" posturing and warrior metaphors, but I am convinced—on a solid textual basis—that he intended no such result.[4] Nor do I want to dogmatically assert any superiority of a passionate, engaged life over a life that is more calm and routine ("bourgeois," in the now standard cant of Bohemian rebellion).[5] But, on the other hand, I do want to raise the question of whether mere proper living, obedience to the law, utilitarian "rational choice" calculations, respect for others' rights and for contracts, and a bit of self-righteousness is all there is to a good life, even if one fills in the nonmoral spaces with permissible pleasures and accomplishments. The meaning of life is not reserved for those who are merely "good," and the vision of a life that burns out brilliantly rather than rusts inexorably, a vision shared by the ancients, the Romantics, and contemporary rock-and-rollers is not to be so easily dismissed, even by those of us now well over thirty.[6]

On a deeper level, many philosophers—including Socrates, Spinoza, Schopenhauer, and the Stoics as well as the Buddha, Confucius, and Chuang-Tzu, even Adam Smith, to name a few—have defended some variation of "peace of mind" or "tranquillity" (*ataraxia, apatheia*, nirvana, tao, *an*) as the highest good. This, too, I want to call into question. It is not as if these thinkers and their traditions have encouraged or defended the complete absence of emotion, to be sure. (Adam Smith was a firm defender of the moral sentiments, for example; and varieties of compassion, even bliss, are essential to many Asian traditions.) But they have all been more or less staunch in their insistence that strong, violent emotion—the sort that is said to "sweep us away"— is at best untoward and often disastrous, even fatal.

In this chapter, by contrast, I would like to promote the legitimacy of that Dionysian temper of life suggested by dynamic rather than static metaphors, notions of "energy," "enthusiasm," "charisma," even "mania."[7] It is also the erotic conception of life suggested by such poets as Homer, Byron and (Allen) Ginsberg, occasionally weighted down with despair and Weltschmertz, perhaps, but buoyed by joy and exuberance as well. Closer to home for most philosophers, the admittedly neurotic but admirable life of Wittgenstein serves as a startling example (and not just for his genius). Indeed, rejecting the ultimate distinction between happiness and suffering ("good" and "evil," respectively) might turn out to be part of the perspective I want to defend, although this exotic thesis is beyond my scope here. (But see chapter 5 for a fumbling attempt at it.) The more modest point is that a virtuous life might be something more than becoming the congenial neighbor, respected citizen, responsible colleague, and affective zombie that many philosophers and contemporary moral pundits urge us to be.

To put the matter in a still more sober philosophical fashion: In this book, I want to promote, among other things, the importance of an often neglected dimension of ethics: the passions and, more generally, the emotions.[8] So-called virtue ethics, which places the emphasis in ethical evaluation on the agent and his or her character, is now recognized as a viable alternative to act- and principle-centered and consequentialist theories. To be sure, the concept of a virtue has also been sliced intolerably thin by some philosophers, but the virtue of virtue ethics, as I see it, is both the enriching of moral description and the enrichment of moral life.[9] Principles of duty and of utility are notoriously thin. Focussing on virtue and questions of character tends to take in the whole of the person, the history, the circumstances, the culture, the overall significance. There is considerable disagreement concerning what is to count as a virtue, of course, and exactly how virtues relate to character, to principles, and to action. But to this list of issues, I want to add how virtues and character relate to emotion in ethics.

It is obvious that many, if not most, of the virtues most often cited involve some concern for the emotions, but too often in a negative way. Courage, for example, has much to do with overcoming fear, as Aristotle argued at some length in his *Nicomachean Ethics*. Philippa Foot has famously argued that the virtues are "correctives" of emotion, keeping in check the more vulgar, self-interested emotions.[10] Most of the traditional vices (avarice, lust, pride, anger, and perhaps envy, though notably not sloth) are readily defined as excesses of emotion. Too often, however, the absence of any such emotion is counted as virtue (abstinence, chastity, modesty, etc.). Thus Nietzsche warns us (in various places) against identifying the "eviscerated man" with the good man.

In a more positive light, the moral sentiment theorists Francis Hutcheson, Hume, Shaftsbury, and Smith, as well as Schopenhauer, argued that all of ethics is founded on such emotions as sympathy, pity, or compassion (*Mitleid*), but such emotions (or sentiments) have often been considered wimpy, merely sentimental, or worse. (Nietzsche, of course, takes them at their worst, shot through with smugness, a bullying superiority, and hypocrisy.[11]) In the case of courage, the virtue is a modulator of emotion (as in also "a good temper" and "being reasonable"). In the case of sympathy, the emotion *is* a motive. Being compassionate or having compassion, accordingly, might be argued to be a virtue in its own right, and not just insofar as it is a durable "state of character," as Aristotle and most virtue ethicists argue. (Imagine an otherwise callous person who is compassionate just once, but when it really counts.)

Aristotle nevertheless recognizes some emotions as virtues, for example, in his inclusion of pride as a virtue (albeit his pride is considerably different from our notion of pride) and in his somewhat awkward and apologetic inclusion of shame as a "quasi virtue." (A person incapable of shame presumably is also devoid of pride, or, as an Ethiopian proverb has it, "A man without shame is a man without honor.") In other words, an emotion may itself be a virtue, subject, of course, to various contextual constraints and considerations of intensity and appropriateness.

This is the claim I want to pursue here, that passions *as such* can be virtues. (They can also be vices, of course.) Aristotle asks in *Ethics*, book II, whether virtues are to be considered passions or, rather, states of character; he argues firmly against the former and for the latter. I do not deny that virtues are typically states of character (or, for that matter, that passions can be states of character), but it seems to me that passions (such as love) can also be virtues.

Aristotle assumes that passions are fleeting, a common assumption. The truth, I would suggest, is that "passions" (as opposed to transient bouts of emotion, fits of temper, crushes and the like) are typically durable—indeed, "intractable."[12] Passions, in particular, seem to refer only to durable as well as intense emotions. One cannot make much sense out of a claim that one "loves passionately, but only for a few minutes at a time," except, perhaps, as a biting joke. Accordingly, I would like to challenge the now standard characterization of a virtue as (in Bernard Williams's phrasing) "a *disposition of character* to choose or reject actions."[13] Passions and emotions are not mere "dispositions of character," except in the trivializing sense that they do, of course, tend to make one or another choice or course of action more likely.

But an emotion is not a disposition; it is, first of all, an experience and a way of being-in-the-world. As such (in the jargon established by Gilbert Ryle[14]) it is episodic, not dispositional. This is not to deny that a passion can go on for a very long time—even a lifetime—and include any number of dispositions, including dispositions to have other emotions. (I have often heard it argued, on these grounds, that love is not an emotion but a disposition to have emotions.[15] This, like so many arguments in this area, seems to me to oversimplify what it is to have an emotion—as well as to get very wrong what it is to be in love.) Moreover, a passion as a virtue not only need not be a disposition of character; it may even be "out of character" and quite contrary to anything that one might usually expect of this person.[16] "Falling in love" and stress-induced acts of heroism often exemplify such "lapses." Indeed, such examples are more than convincing reasons to seriously consider passions, *rather than* as dispositions of character, as virtues.

I want to begin by confronting several standard objections to the primacy of what Kant called "the inclinations" in ethics, according to the Kantian tradition—though not, one might argue, according to Kant himself.[17] I then want to pay attention to one particular emotion, love. This promiscuously broad term might include everything from filial affection to saintly devotion, but only some of these would count as passionate. Among these would surely be the love that we call "romantic," the love that "burns" (as Jane Austen's Marianne describes it in *Sense and Sensibility*, or as June and Johnny Cash sing it in "Ring of Fire"). Millennia ago, Plato defended the passion of *eros* as such a virtue. Aristotle, perhaps being more discreet, defended the virtue of *philia* (indeed, it is the longest single discussion in his *Ethics*), but it is not altogether obvious to what extent this is a passion and not more what we would call "affection." I will not here consider the so-called love of humanity (*agape*, *caritas*), and I will save compassion, sympathy, and the like for a later chapter (chapter 4), although these have a long-standing role in ethics, not only in Christianity, Confucianism, and Buddhism but also in the "moral sentiment theories" that populated the reason-oriented European Enlightenment in the eighteenth century.[18] Here, I am going to take a more difficult route and defend what we now call romantic love, erotic love, as a virtue—indeed, as an exemplary virtue. My aim here is nothing less than to turn our entire picture of the virtues (and with them, the vices) on its head, or, more appropriately, to envision them some distance from the head. (Some would say "the heart," but that is physiologically dubious.) I want to defend what one might call enthusiasm as a virtue, the enthusiasm born of love's attachments being the most obvious example.

At the risk of being overly reasonable, let me qualify my defense in an important way. When I say that I will be defending the passionate life and the passions as virtues, let me make it quite clear that not any passion or any emotion will do, and emotions, even if they are virtues, may not *always* be virtues.[19] I am extremely wary, for example, of certain sorts of collective emotions: war hysteria, racism, and the sorts of passions that result in genocide. (I am not sanguine about the role of those kindred "sublimated" or "displaced" passions that are so inescapable in sports arenas. The unconstrained joy of sports fans, who otherwise have little to cheer about and who themselves have done nothing other than buy a ticket or sit home and watch television, will forever remain a disturbing mystery to me.) There are emotions that are out of the range of virtue (for instance, envy), and there are degrees or intensities of emotion (although I would challenge this quantitative characterization) that are by no means virtuous.

Regarding love, for example, there is a delicate line between passion and obsession (often ignored by *parfumiers* and jeans makers), and I am not defending obsession by any means (although the difference may have more to do with the reciprocity of the recipient than with the passion itself). There is misplaced love, foolish love, overly possessive love (which may be better characterized as jealousy); these are not virtues or virtuous, although even a foolish love may display more virtue than no love at all. But it is particularly important to note the distinction and the affinity between passionate love and obsessive love, including sexual obsession, if only to make one crucial point about the nature of the virtues. It is often said that virtue is concerned with what one can control, and being "out of control" is the very antithesis of virtuousness. (Consider the term "virtuosity."[20]) But it is the very nature of love that it is not, or is not wholly, in control. It is firmly tied to fate as well as to the whims and well-being of the other person. We find that passion and desire wax and wane, quite indifferent to our hopes and commitments. What is called an obsession may just be the firm attachment that is necessary in the churning seas of a changing life together, and what is called passion is in part due to the uncertainty that goes with that attachment. What I want to argue is that it is that passion, that excitement in the face of uncertainty, the acceptance of that lack of control, that constitutes love's virtue.

Finally, I would like to generalize this philosophical somersault in the work of the most adventurous and exciting modern virtue ethicist, Friedrich Nietzsche. Nietzsche sometimes calls himself an "immoralist"; that overwrought self-description points, however, not to the rejection of ethics but rather to the rejection of one conception of morals and morality, that defined most famously by Kant and (historically) by the Judeo-Christian tradition. In contrast, Nietzsche also defended a version of "virtue ethics" (he would not have liked the ugly label) in which not only virtue but also passion would take a primary place. Ethics, to put it bluntly, is not an external imposition, whether by God or the Law or the "herd," nor does it consist of those calculations and states of character that tend to directly promote social welfare or the public good as usually construed. Neither does it consist of obedience to the internal rational promptings of the Moral Law or "conscience," nor, for that matter, of that generalized love that is often celebrated by Christians as agape. "What is good?—All that heightens the feeling of power," Nietzsche writes at the beginning of his obviously polemical *Antichrist.* I take it that "feeling of power" has a good deal to do with emotions and passion.

In Nietzsche's earlier book *The Gay Science*, the very title would indicate a defense of the passionate life: *la gaya scienzia*, the life of the troubadours, a life of longing (*languor*) and love. Nietzsche's "immoralism," accordingly, has often been taken to rather be akin to aestheticism, that is, the thesis that ethics and ethical judgments reduce to or can be translated into aesthetics and aesthetic judgments.[21] That is not my position here, although I think that there is a great deal of truth to it. Instead, I want to pursue Nietzsche's emphasis on the passions and, in particular, his vigorous and spine-chilling notion of "the Will to Power," which emphasizes not aesthetics but something else: "energy," "enthusiasm," "strength," as well as "self-mastery," which does not mean the conquest, but rather the cultivation, of the passions. This obviously is opposed not only to Kantian practical reason and utilitarian calculation and hedonism but also to those more benign conceptions of emotion in ethics defended by the moral sentiment theorists and (closer to Nietzsche's heart) by Schopenhauer. But let me also say, before I go on, that I think the role of the Will to Power in Nietzsche is often misunderstood and much bloated and has been elevated to a status it should not have in his philosophy. I will not argue this here.[22] I will only argue that there is a plausible ethics of virtue and vice that looks very different from the standard accounts of "virtue ethics" and, more broadly, from the various ethics of "practical reason." With apologies to Goya, I suggest that it is not only the sleep of reason but also its hegemony that produces monsters.[23]

Love as a Virtue: Against the Kantian Paradigm

> Love out of inclination cannot be commanded; but kindness done from duty—although no inclination impels us, and even although natural and unconquerable disinclination stands in our way—is Practical, and not Pathological love, residing in the will and not of melting compassion.
>
> Kant, *Grounding of the Metaphysics of Morals*

> It [love] does not hesitate to intrude with its trash. . . . It knows how to slip its love-notes and ringlets even into ministerial portfolios and philosophical manuscripts. Every day it brews and hatches the worst and most perplexing quarrels and disputes, destroys the most valuable relationships and breaks the strongest bonds. . . . Why all this noise and fuss? . . . It is merely a question of every Jack finding his Jill. (The gracious reader should translate this phrase into precise Aristophanic language.) Why should such a trifle play so important a role?
>
> Arthur Schopenhauer, *World as Will and Idea*

Schopenhauer was among the Kantians who turned against their mentor. As steeped in the Kantian worldview as the Great Pessimist may have been, in ethics he rebelled. Compassion (*Mitleid*), not practical reason, was the heart and foundation of ethics. But when it came to sexual love, Schopenhauer was hardly more enlightened (though undoubtedly more experienced) than Kant. "Trash, noise and fuss," he says, with more than a dribble of sarcasm. Of course, virtually everything in human life—art, Buddhism and his own philosophy excepted—was of negligible value to Schopenhauer. Love, for him, was clearly not among the salvations in life. Indeed, passion in general was just so much floundering about of the Will, that singular metaphysical purposelessness that defines and dominates all of us. Besides compassion (which Kant, too, recognized as "beautiful"[24]), Schopenhauer also discounted "the inclinations," and dismissed the passions in particular as just so much irrationality. Like Kant, he clearly dismissed romantic affection as wholly irrelevant to moral worth. *Schopenhauer*

Kant's paradigm of moral judgment and rationality has maintained its hegemony in ethics since the Enlightenment. However the sharpness of Kant's rationalism has been softened and his concept of moral judgment broadened, the primary focus remains undeniable, and in his followers, unabashedly obvious: Moral philosophy remains nothing if not objective, dispassionate, based on principles, exclusive of particular self-reference, and independent of personal "prejudices." For instance, in his *The Moral Rules*, Bernard Gert dismisses feelings as morally worthless and insists instead that "feelings are morally important only insofar as they lead to morally good actions."[25] What is shocking is what the paradigm leaves out, notably, most emotions, and love in particular, except insofar as these might help motivate duty or, perhaps, serve "the greatest good for the greatest number." Bernard Williams points out that it would be insane to prefer an act of kindness born of principle rather than personal affection, as Kant recommends. Whether or not this is genuinely Kant's recommendation, one can imagine taking the same claim and transposing it into the realm of passionate love. The very suggestion is appalling. (The language of "conjugal duty" comes to mind.) One thinks of the myriad delights, affections, and felt obligations in love; instead of insisting that love is amoral (at best), we should rather treat love as a virtue and give up the overly impersonal "Kantian" notion of morality.

It is tempting to say that what makes love and other "feelings" admirable is, as Gert suggests, their consequences, the fact that they tend to result in "morally good actions." It may or may not be true that love "results" in praiseworthy actions, but the worth of our feelings does not depend on the desirability of any resultant actions or their consequences.[26] Love is the most persuasive example: In love, the worthiness of our actions depends on the feelings they express. Generous and even heroic actions may follow from love, but the virtue of love stands quite on its own. (Socrates criticizes Phaedrus in the *Symposium* for just this reason. Phaedrus praises the consequences of love [good behavior] rather than the virtue of love itself.) We may think Marianne foolish (in *Sense and Sensibility*) but one can still admire her passion, while Edwardian literature is filled with Kantian gentlemen acting on their principles who are utterly repulsive. Not only is it desirable to love, but those who have not loved (whether or not they've also lost), or fear they cannot love, rightly worry not only about their character but also about their completeness as human beings—quite apart from any questions about action or performance. We (their friends) worry about them too. Love is admirable in itself, quite apart from its effects and consequences.[27]

The opposition to love and other feelings as essential ingredients in morality is inconsistent with the emphasis on love (even if agape, not eros) as the supreme virtue in the New Testament, where the intent is surely not utilitarian or Kantian. It is just this oddity that Kant is trying to explain away in the passage on "pathological love" quoted at the beginning of this section. He seems to believe that only that which can be "commanded" is morally obligatory, and love as a passion cannot be commanded. This particular claim has often been disputed, for instance, in Edward Sankowski's paper on love and moral obligation, which argues that we at least hold people responsible for fostering or evading the conditions that breed love.[28] One might challenge as well the claim that only that which can be commanded is moral (even obligatory); much of what goes into "good character," while it can be cultivated, cannot be commanded. One might also argue—as I often have—that the emotions are far more voluntaristic and under our control than we normally believe, and not just in the sense that we can foster or avoid the conditions in which they typically emerge. This is not to say that an emotion such as love can simply be produced by an act of will or volition, as one might produce a thought or a movement of one's finger. There may be, in a Dantoesque phrase, no "basic action" where love is concerned.[29] To insist that love (or virtually any virtuous action, for that matter) can be produced ex *de nihilo* is surely a misunderstanding.

Kant may appear to be in agreement with New Testament ethics in his insistence that it is always the universal that is central to morality, but virtues are always particular.[30] And on most interpretations of Christian love, love is emphatically the love of particular persons. An exemplary Christian will love every particular person. His or her affection and respect are not reserved only for the universal (God, humanity). Indeed, even Kant insists that we love humanity *in a person*. Moreover, love—especially erotic or romantic love—is not only particular; it is selective, even exclusive. It is the elevation of one otherwise ordinary person to extraordinary heights with extraordinary privileges. The idea of a "categorical imperative"—a univeral "ought"—in such instances is laughable. On the Kantian model, the particularity of love would seem to be a paradigm form of irrationality—a version of our tendency to make exceptions of ourselves, in this case making exceptions of the persons closest to us. A lover who insisted on treating everyone, including his or her lover, impersonally and dispassionately would strike us as utterly repulsive.

It is sometimes said that emotions in general, and love in particular, are irrational, and therefore cannot be virtues because they are capricious.[31] They simply come and go. They are all contingency, without rational necessity and the constancy of reason. But consider, in the same light, the accusation of "intractability."[32] It is notoriously difficult, when one has been in love, to purge that emotion, even though it now has become an intolerable source of pain. More positively, love tends to build on itself, to amplify with time, to find—through love—ever more reasons to love.[33] This is not, I would argue, an argument against the emotions, but rather an aspect of their virtue. It is passing fancy that we criticize, not unmovable devotion. It is sudden anger that we call irrational, not long-motivated and well-reasoned animosity (which is not to say that sudden anger is always improper or inappropriate, or that long-term rage is not sometimes irrational and even insane). It is true that the emotions are stubborn and intractable, but this—as opposed to ultimately less dependable action in accordance with principle—is what makes them so essential to ethics. A person fighting from passion may be better depended upon than one fighting for an abstract principle. Intractability is a virtue of the emotions as rationalization is a vice of reason. Indeed, we might even say that the truth of emotions is (in part) their intractability, their resistance to change.

It is also said that love and other emotions confuse or distort our experience and therefore are not virtuous. But consider: A homely lover looks longingly at his equally plain beloved and declares, "You are the most beautiful woman in the world." How are we to understand this? Self-deception? Insanity? Surely not blindness, for the problem is not that he cannot see. Indeed, he might well claim to see much more than we do, or more deeply. Impolitely pressed, our enraptured lover may resentfully concede the point, perhaps making a phenomenological retreat to "Well, she's the most beautiful woman in the world to me," but we know how such qualifications are treated in philosophy—with proper epistemological disdain. But wouldn't we do better to consider such privileged vision part of the virtue rather than a vice of love? (Obviously this argument cannot be uncritically generalized to other emotions.)

Objectively, love may be contrary to everything that philosophical ethics likes to emphasize—objectivity, impersonality, disinterestedness, universality, respect for evidence and arguments, and so on. And yet, it seems to me that such "irrationality" constitutes some of our most important *moral* features. We care about each other apart from any evidence or arguments that we ought to. We find each other beautiful, charming, and desirable, seemingly without reference to common standards. We think less, not more, of a lover if his or her love "alters when it alteration finds," or if he or she bends to the opinion of friends. Many people even think it admirable, if also foolish, to continue to love someone who has proved him- or herself utterly undeserving of that love. (The popular press seems to confirm this unapologetic opinion of love, for example, in the cases of women who fall in love with and marry incarcerated criminals or, in a recent movie [*Dead Man Walking*], a convicted killer on death row.) Love (or loving) itself is the virtue, a virtue so important that rationality pales in significance.

The Virtue of Eros

That is why I say Eros is the eldest of the gods and most honored and the most powerful for acquiring virtue and blessedness, for men both living and dead.

Phaedrus, in Plato's *Symposium*

The spirituality of sensuosity is called *love;* it represents a great triumph over Christianity.

Nietzsche, *Twilight of the Idols*

Most of what I have argued above would hold for virtually any variety of love (as well as other affections), but it is erotic love or eros that provides the exemplary case for the defense of the passionate life. One might argue that there are any number of virtues to be found in parental or filial love, for instance, but nevertheless question whether these are also present in the notorious anxiety and arousal surrounding eros. Note, in this regard, the distinction between eros and agape, "sexual" love and selfless, sexless love. It is a distinction that, through the centuries between Plato and the solid institutionalization of Pauline Chrisianity, has been drawn with increasing crudity and much to the disadvantage of eros. Eros has been taken to be purely erotic and reduced to sexual desire, which it surely is not. Agape has been characterized as selfless giving, in opposion to eros, which thus becomes selfish taking or craving. Agape has been idealized to the point where it becomes an attitude possible only to God, thus rendering it virtually inapplicable to our human fellow feelings. Eros, by contrast, has been degraded to the profanely secular and denied any hint of spirituality.

To think of love as a virtue is first of all to expand (once again) the domain of eros. One need not deny the desirability (or the possibility) of altruistic agape in order to insist that eros shares at least some of its virtues. Eros differs from agape in the prevalence of self-interested desire, but it is not thereby selfish and the desire is not just sexual. It includes a much more general physical desire to *be with,* such personal desires as "to be appreciated" and "to be happy together," such inspirational desires as "to be the best for you," and such "altruistic" desires as "to do anything I can for you." But notice how the language of morality breaks down in such thoughts, not because we have retreated to the realm of the pre- or amoral but because the very distinction between "yours" and "mine" has started to dissolve.

One key ingredient in the derogation of eros has been the deprecation of sex. It is a common mistake to think of the other person in sex as a mere "object" of desire, which leads to the idea that eros, too, is degrading and seeks only its own satisfaction. Consider Kant on the matter:

> Because sexuality is not an inclination which one human being has for another as such, but is an inclination for the sex of another, it is a principle of the degradation of human nature, in that it gives rise to the preference of one sex to the other, and to the dishonoring of that sex through the satisfaction of desire.[34]

But surely the question (as Plato raised it 2,300 years earlier) is *what* one desires when one sexually desires another person. In the *Symposium*, Aristophanes suggested that one desires not just sexual union but also permanent (re)unification with the other; Socrates insisted that one really wants the Forms. Even if we consider such goals too fantastic for eros, it is clear that the Greeks—as opposed to Kant and many moderns—saw that sexual desire is much, much more than desire for sex, and not at all opposed to virtuous desire. At the very least, it is clear that sexual desire is some sort of powerful desire for the other person through sex. The question is: A desire for what? And by no means should we assume from the outset that the answer to this question has anything to do with sexual objects. Indeed, taking our cue from Hegel and Sartre, we might suggest, rather, that it has everything to do with the sexual subject, the person as an agent of sexual activity and as the recipient (or cocreator) of sexual experience.[35]

The passionate attachment of one person for another is a virtue, in other words, because it embodies a form of respect, although this is, to be sure, very different from the abstract, attenuated form of respect promoted by Kant and the Kantians. To think that sexuality and respect are mutually opposed may be a typical teenager's nightmare. (One might add that teenage status is easily thrust upon anyone who suddenly finds him- or herself thrown back into the dating game.) It is hardly the voice of either experience or wisdom. Sexuality is the most intimate form of attachment, wholly involving both mind and body. Indeed, one wonders how much of the exclusion of the sexual from the realm of the moral (except, of course, for all of those rules and prohibitions) has to do with the fact that it is unavoidably bodily, involving some of the messiest, most vulnerable, and most tender parts of the body. How far this is from the purified "subject" that inhabits the Kantian "intelligible" world! To answer Kant's objection, we might say that in sex in love (which is emphatically not what Alan Goldman has called "plain sex"), one passionately loves the other person *as such*.[36] This seems to me to be the ultimate form of that sense of respect that we most admire, not just respect for the law or the abstract respect that one has for others insofar as one leaves them alone, but that thoroughgoing, all-embracing acceptance and the joy of thus accepting another person.

One aspect of this respect that is often ignored or denied is the prerequisite of equality between lovers. This may seem odd in the light of modern accusations against love as a vehicle for the degradation and oppression of women, but in historical perspective it becomes clear that—however far we may be from real (social, economic, political) equality—romantic love emerges only with the relative liberation of women from traditional subservient social and economic roles. Romantic love emerges only when women begin to have more choice about their lives—and about their lovers and husbands in particular. One thinks of John Milton's Adam, created early in the era of romantic love, who specifically requested from God not a mere playmate or companion or mirror image of himself, but an equal, for "among unequals what society/ Can sort, what harmony or true delight?"[32] Or, paraphrasing Stendhal, we might say that love tends to create equals where it does not find them, for equality is as essential to romantic love as authority is to parenthood—whether or not this is adequately acknowledged or acted upon.

Perhaps most important for our purposes here, however, is the fact that love, unlike most of the virtues that are touted (amiability, trustworthiness, fairness, modesty, temperance, even courage) is *exciting*. Some of this excitement is sexual, of course, and I have taken some pains in the preceding pages not to suggest that sexuality as such is a virtue. Neither, however, is it a vice, nor should it be degraded, although obviously sex is a medium that can be used to express all sorts of vicious and obscene messages. But the sense in which sex is exciting should not be reduced or restricted to what is commonly (and ambiguously) referred to as "arousal." Physical arousal, like sex "as such," is morally and hedonically neutral; its role in our lives depends on context and, in particular, on the emotions that accompany it and the relationships in which it comes to count as "expression." But much of the excitement of sex might better be understood in terms of our vulnerability, our openness to others in an obviously more "basic" way than is specified by many of the recognized virtues. Some of the excitement of sexual love is the uncertainty, particularly at the beginning of a relationship, but I would certainly want to argue that the excitement of newness should not be confused with love.[38] Kierkegaard described the openness of love in general (although he was cynical about sexual love) as "a leap of faith," as "subjective truth," as "commitment in the face of objective uncertainty." What is especially to be noticed in this is that sexual love involves the question of choice (however much it might seem a matter of fate), and choice—continuous choice—readily leads to existential angst, even when the outcome is pretty well decided.

Desire is Suffering.

The ultimate reason for the excitement of sexual love, however, might best be put in the philosophical terms of self-identity. Passions are often distinguished from ordinary emotions, and emotions from dispassionate beliefs or judgments, in terms of their "intensity,"[39] but I think a better explanation might be put in economic terms, what one might call emotional "investment." Passions define the self, they are the heavy "investments" of the self, in a way that most emotions do not and are not. Love, notably, might be defined (in part) as *defining yourself in and through another person.* This is very different, needless to say, from Schopenhauer's view of love as sexual lust plus philosophical confusion. It is, rather, an updated version of Plato's original "Aristophanic" language of love as "the completion" and "merging" of two halved souls.[40] I cannot go into this analysis here, but it suggests that the "intensity" of love (and other passions and emotions) is something much more profound than mere neurological and hormonal agitation.

The excited commitment and attachments of love stand most at odds with all of those philosophies of *apatheia,* those celebrations of peace of mind, for whatever joys and securities love may provide, dispassionate indifference is not one of them. Thus the Stoics from Chrysippus to Spinoza warned against the frenzied, easily frustrated passion of love even while they defended some larger cosmic attitude. Here Freud and the Buddha join hands in their agreement that "desire is suffering," and only the cessation of desire ("the death instinct," nirvana) brings release. Here the wisdom of "maturity" is forever badgering the young: Beware the thrills of love, for there one can only be disappointed. From such views, whether defended out of prudence or in the name of virtue, one could not possibly expect a defense of the passionate life or the view that love is a virtue. But here is where the change of perspective, initiated by our general consideration of emotion and our specific look at love, comes full circle. Suppose we were to look at life not through the calm eyes of eternity but as we live it: as all too short, as an urgency, not a puzzle or a mystery to be unraveled by reason.[41] Suppose we took passion itself as the highest good—not any passion, of course, but the life defined by such passions as love rather than the life defined by tranquillity and peace of mind.[42] Here, as always, we have to beware of sophistry and "persuasive" definitions. If giving up peace of mind only means living with a sense of failure, with frustration, with a guilty conscience, or in humiliation, for example, then the passionate conception of life has little to recommend it. But if one of the virtues of love is its ongoing excitement, and this excitement is not just punctuation for an otherwise peaceful, "satisfying" life (although the notion of "satisfaction" can be gerrymandered to fit philosophical preconceptions), then we ought to take seriously a vision of life in which "agitation" rather than the lack of it is our ultimate desideratum. The vision of such a life is nowhere better depicted—and enacted—than in the vigorous prose of Nietzsche.

The Will to Power as Virtue

> What is good?—All that heightens the feeling of power, the will to
> power, power itself in man.
>   What is bad?—All that proceeds from weakness.
>   What is happiness?—The feeling that power increases, that
> resistance is overcome.
>   Not contentment but more power: not peace at all, but war; not
> virtue but proficiency (virtue in the Renaissance style, *virtù*, virtue free
> of moralic acid).
>
> Nietzsche, Antichrist

Nietzsche, of course, overstates himself. Overstatement (as well as overreaching) is not an unfamiliar symptom of enthusiasm. Accordingly, generations of good rationalist philosophers dismissed Nietzsche outright ("not a
philosopher!") on the basis of one or two of his more hyperbolic aphorisms.
(The distinguished Yale philosopher Brand Blandshard reportedly threw a
copy of one of Nietzsche's books across the room, thus acting out a reaction
to Nietzsche that was very common until fairly recently.[43]) Nietzsche overstates his reactions against morality, which he variously calls "slave morality"
and "herd morality," and in rebellion calls himself an "immoralist." In fact,
Nietzsche insisted that he himself had "a more severe morality,"[44] and I have
already suggested that what Nietzsche really meant is that we should understand morals and morality from a different "perspective," namely, what we
now call virtue ethics. He similarly overstates his reactions against religion
(starting with "God is dead"), when he can be argued to be defending what
he found best in the Lutheranism of his childhood and in the spirituality that
he thought had been foresaken by the Germans (in particular, by his onetime
friend Richard Wagner). He famously overstates his (inconsistent) view that
"there is no truth" (while insisting on total honesty). But nowhere does he
overstate himself so remarkably and misleadingly as in his comments concerning "the Will to Power," which begin in full force in *Daybreak* (1881) and
culminate in the clearly outrageous overstatements (above) that begin his last
philosophical work, *The Antichrist* (1889, published 1895).

This is not the place to launch a full-scale investigation of Nietzsche's
philosophy, nor even of the various intricacies of his notion of "the Will to
Power." But I should make it clear why I want to take Nietzsche, not Aristotle,
as my ultimate mentor in the area of virtue ethics and the champion of the
passionate life. I will therefore (briefly) outline what I take to be a Nietzschean
virtue theory. I cannot produce a list of "Nietzsche's Virtues," as one can
easily do for Aristotle (although one might note that Aristotle's list, despite
his supposed criterion of "the mean between the extremes," never escapes the
suspicion of being ad hoc). For one thing, to begin with the obvious, Nietzsche

was not a systematic thinker. For another, Nietzsche insisted that each of us has his or her "own virtues," that even to give names to one's virtues is to make them "common" and deny their uniqueness. One now popular post-modern argument against any such analysis of Nietzsche's philosophy is that Nietzsche did not have an ethics, did not make assertions, did not give "moral advice." Even the briefest reading of any of his many texts will surely show such claims to be unsupportable.[45] Nevertheless, such readings have attracted some of the very best Nietzsche scholars, including Bernd Magnus and Alexander Nehamas. But I do not want to tackle these issues here.[46] Rather, let me heuristically suppose that Nietzsche does have some advice to give (in fact, everything from nutritional guidance to how to save the world), and try to say something about what a systematic view of that advice—or, rather, of Nietzsche's virtue ethics, under the rubric of "the Will to Power"—might look like.

What Nietzsche means by "power" (*Macht*) has been widely debated. This is partly owing to Heidegger's elaborate and most implausible analysis of Nietzsche as the "metaphysician of the will to power," partly to the attention Walter Kaufmann gives to the concept in his classic *Nietzsche: Philosopher, Psychologist, Antichrist*, and, especially, partly to the ominous "jackboot" connotations of the term, which readily appeals to protofascists and rightly appalls liberals. But Nietzsche quite clearly rejects the idea of power as power over other people (including political power, or *Reich*); and although he certainly approves of competition, he is adamant about the primacy of power as self-mastery. It is not implausible to suggest that what Nietzsche has mainly in mind is creative power, the power of the artist, the poet, the occasional philosopher. Nietzsche equates power and "spiritualization," although always with the warning that much of what passes for "spirit" in both religion and philosophy is unworthy of the name. What makes the German "spirit" in particular so unworthy is the fact that it has become so thoroughly and self-consciously weakened, burdened by the wrong virtues (notably such Christian virtues as humility, which Hume, something of a fellow spirit, called "the monkish virtue") and further flattened by identification with what Nietzsche called "the herd." The key to the Will to Power, I would suggest, is a strong sense of self, a passionate but disciplined self, a self that follows its powerful "instincts" but has "overcome itself" sufficiently to "give style to one's character," to "become who you are."[47]

What is notoriously absent from this description are such philosophical virtues as rationality and reflection. Nietzsche is certainly much more keen on the unreflective "naturalness" of virtuous behavior than are most moral philosophers (including Aristotle, although Aristotle clearly insisted that being brought up to act correctly precedes ethical reasoning). But he also insisted on a place for reason, and (as in Aristotle) it is more a matter of reason embedded in action than reason as reflective rationality. For instance,

TEMPERANCE: SOPHROSYNE

> *Victory over strength.* Still one lies on one's knees before strength—according
> to the ancient habit of slaves—and yet, when the degree of *worthiness of*
> *being honored* is to be determined, only *the degree of reason in strength* [*der*
> *Grad der Vernunft in der Kraft*] is decisive; one must measure how far strength
> has been overcome by something higher and now serves that as its tool and
> means! (Nietzsche, *Daybreak*, ¶ 548)

The emphasis that Nietzsche notoriously places on "strength" (*Kraft*), particularly in book I of *On the Genealogy of Morals*, must be weighed against many
such qualifications. Simply to equate power with strength (as Nietzsche himself too often suggests, notably in the *Antichrist* quotation above) is to make
Nietzsche out to be something of a barbarian or a moral Darwinian, which
he surely was not. The *übermensch*, if we were to take that cartoonish image
seriously in Nietzsche, might best be interpreted as the projection of Nietzsche's virtue ethics, the embodiment of his ideals.[48] To picture the *übermensch*
as Conan the Barbarian is surely to do Nietzsche no justice; when he speaks
(much more frequently) of "higher types," it is most often the great poet
Goethe whom he has explicitly in mind.[49]

What are the Nietzschean virtues? Perhaps the first and most obvious thing
to say is that many of them are "pagan" virtues, and (as in Hume) designed
to contrast with the Christian or "monkish" virtues that Nietzsche heard re-
iterated as "bourgeois" virtues in Germany. Thus a primary list of Nietzschean
virtues would resemble that of Aristotelian virtues: courage, generosity, honesty, trustworthiness, temperance (*sophrosyne*), justice, pride, friendliness, and
wittiness. But this list of Greek or "pagan" virtues is certainly not Aristotle's,
and it is not Aristotle's gentleman/aristocrat that Nietzsche had in mind. He
considered the philosophies of all three great classic Greek philosophers—
Socrates, Plato, and Aristotle—utterly "decadent." He saw Aristotle's ethics,
in particular, as a sort of wishful thinking about the Athens that may once
have been but certainly was no more. The Greece that captured Nietzsche's
imagination was pre-Socratic Greece, the quasi-mythical Greece of Sophocles,
the warrior Greece of Homer. Nietzsche's understanding of these "pagan"
virtues must therefore be pressed back into time, to a different age, to a
different spirit. Moreover, Nietzsche's take on these virtues is very different
from Aristotle's, beginning, perhaps, with his rejection of the "criterion of
the mean" and the Athenian insistence on "moderation." This in turn requires
a new understanding of what it is to have a virtue, and well-groomed gentlemanly behavior plays at most a very small role.

That small role, perhaps, might be occupied by Nietzsche's own insistence
on "courtesy" as one of the cardinal virtues. Nietzsche certainly has nothing
against the virtues of congeniality and friendship, and insofar as he was concerned with the social virtues (not his primary interest), he was anything but
the "boot in the face" hard-liner that he sometimes portrays himself to be.

(The most obvious instance of this self-portrayal is in his many published objections to pity [*Mitleid*—also translated as "compassion" and "sympathy"], but this, I think, is an argument with a very different aim.) The more dramatic difference with Aristotle, however, and our way into the theme of the passionate life, might be found in an analysis of the first two of the above-named virtues, courage and generosity.

Courage, in Aristotle, is overcoming fear. Or, alternatively, it is having just the right amount of fear: not too much (which would be cowardice), not too little (which would be recklessness). The psychological dynamics are unclear in Aristotle (for instance, what it is to overcome an emotion), but what is clear is that some degree of fear is necessary to courage. Now, consider the following picture, illustrated by an example that is analogous to Aristotle's use of Hector's courage in the Iliad.[50] Achilles, enraged by the death of his friend Patroclus, crashes onto the battlefield outside of Troy with vengeance ("justice") on his mind. There is no fear. There is no room for fear in the midst of all that well-directed fury. To call Achilles "courageous" in such a state would seem to us rather an understatement, if not absurd.

Our own understanding of courage is here in line with Aristotle's. Courage is measured by the amount of resistance, that is, fear, it has to overcome. But suppose we view the matter as Nietzsche (and Homer) did, as if fear and courage are not complementary but opposed, and it is Achilles who is courageous and not the poor soldier with the shaking knees who "forces himself" to stand his ground. (The word "brave" once carried with it this Nietzschean meaning, except insofar as it has also been infected with the Aristotelean understanding of "courage.") Courage, in other words, is not overcoming emotion (namely, fear). It is constituted by overwhelming and yet skillfully directed "gung-ho" emotion, which incorporates rather than excludes one's sense of honor, which because of its keen focus might even be interpreted as calm. It is the power, efficiency, and effectiveness of the passion, not this only apparent calm, that is its virtue.

A similar analysis of generosity (which in *Zarathustra* is called "the gift-giving virtue") is possible. It is not mere giving, nor the habit of giving. Consider generosity in the context of one current charity demand that insists, "Give 'til it hurts!" One can imagine the donor, struggling against the pain of his or her own miserliness, weighing the burden of conscience against that bottle of Chateau le Boeuf on sale at the wine store down the street. Finally, generosity overcomes resistance, and the virtue is admirably displayed. But notice, first of all, that the more one has to struggle to give, the less virtuous one is. Aristotle insists that, with all virtues, their performance is actually pleasurable, not painful; this itself is a test of one's virtuousness. Suppose, however, that one's generosity consisted of what one might call one's "overflowing" nature. This is the way, I hear, that Mick Jagger behaves on tour. Having more money than he (or anyone) could know how to spend, Jagger rather joyfully allows it to flow freely, somewhat indiscriminately, to recipients and causes both deserving and frivolous. This joyful abandon one might argue, is true generosity, not the struggle against personal deprivation but an overflowing that can come only with a sense of fullness.

So, too, the other virtues emerge as "overflow" of a great-souled spirit, of one who has an abundance. To object that the virtues are not this, but rather the sense of duty in contrast to self-interest and personal need, is to fall back into what Nietzsche would consider a pathetic model of the virtues, the model that emerges in Kant and in Christianity, where the poor (not the rich) in spirit become the focus. Aristotle, writing for the aristocracy, would have fallen somewhere in between. But what constitutes a Nietzschean virtue is first of all a kind of passionate fullness, a sense of oneself on top of the world. One need not get hung up on money, prestige, and power to adopt such an ethic. Nietzsche himself, impoverished, passed over by his intellectual peers, and poor in health, might serve as just such an example. Indeed, even temperance (the most tempting counterexample to this account) represents a kind of fullness, a sense of buoyant self-discipline. Consider Nietzsche's many *Californische* comments on diet, good health, and creative well-being.

The centrality of "overflowing" and abundance is the key to this new ethics. Nietzsche uses such terms and images all through his works. But let us, then, briefly flesh out the picture that these terms suggest. For Nietzsche, the good life consists not of humility ("satisfaction" in the minimalist sense, having all that you need) but of exuberance, passion, eros, or what Nietzsche often, in the philosophical style of the century, calls "life." With ample resources, possibly all of them spiritual, one can develop "style" (discipline, not fashion) and "depth," which, as in the American phrase "having soul," means complex, conflicted, agonistic, "Dionysian." If Nietzsche has a metaphysics (and if it were not utterly misleading to call it "Will to Power"), it would be a very modern metaphysics, a metaphyics of energy rather than matter (or "immatter," for that matter). It would be a dynamic metaphysics (hardly the same as what is usually called "process philosophy"), a metaphysics worthy of Heraclitus. When Nietzsche insisted "I am dynamite," in his last book, *Ecce Homo*, he wasn't simply displaying the signs of incipient insanity or being "ironic," nor was he immodestly announcing the potential effects of his philosophy. He was summarizing and personalizing that philosophy in a single, appropriate metaphor.

On the Virtue of the Virtues

Since things that are found in the soul are of three kinds—passions, faculties, states of character—virtue must be one of these . . . [But] neither the virtues nor the vices are passions, because we are not called good or bad on the ground of our passions, and . . . we are neither praised nor blamed for our passions. Again, we feel anger and fear without choice, but the virtues are modes of choice or involve choice. For these reasons also they are not faculties, for we are neither called good or bad, or praised or blamed, for the simple capacity of feeling the passions. . . . If, then, the virtues are neither passions nor faculties, all that remains is that they should be states of character.

Aristotle, Nicomachean Ethics

The virtue of Aristotle's ethics and his focus on the virtues is the relative richness, the thickness, of his account, the way his ethics incorporates the passions of life into the essence of the good life and does not attempt to reduce the complexity of life to a "thin" matter of principle or reasoned argument or to the "greatest good for the greatest number." But what is a virtue? If a virtue were no more than a personal instantiation of an abstract principle— the disposition to do one's duty or to act for the greatest good for the greatest number—then ethics would once again become thin and logical, impersonal and unemotional.[51] What I have tried to suggest is that virtue ethics can be conceived in a very different way, such that this attempt at reduction is quite inappropriate.

But there is a strong tendency, even in Aristotle, to think of the passions in an overly spontaneous, even "stimulus-response," way, as if emotions, unlike virtues, were simply reactions to the particularities of a situation. Indeed, they may appear to be so. The virtues, according to Aristotle, are highly contextual. Indeed, the very identity of the virtues as virtues depends on the context. The meaning of courage differs in a soldier, a statesman, and an AIDS patient. A virtue in one context may well be a vice in another, such as generosity (Aristotle's "liberality") with regard to a needy person as opposed to a spoiled child. In his definition of a virtue,[52] Aristotle emphasizes virtues as "states of character," but elsewhere in the same book he stresses the importance of "perception" and the particularities of the situation. But most passions (and emotions) are not random bursts of enthusiasm or ire, as Aristotle well knew. Emotions are more or less systematic in that together they form a person's "temperament." And when an unusual emotion "bursts" forth (again, falling in love, or finding oneself wholly absorbed in affection for a new baby), such emotions are not to be construed as a literal "burst" but as a dramatic new constellation that, if it is to be believed at all, reconstitutes and redefines the life of the individual.

The insistence that a virtue is a state of character rather than a passion fails even for the first and foremost virtue on Aristotle's list—courage. In Achilles' environment, to be sure, courage was a daily requirement. Today, situations demanding or inviting physical courage—especially Aristotle's paradigm of courage on the battlefield—are in rather short supply. Courage, accordingly, appears as a "burst" or sudden appearance of unexpected heroism or integrity rather than anything like a persistent and long-evident state of character. But would we therefore deny its status as a virtue? Nor does the fact that such courage can be foolish undermine its status as a virtue. Bravely responding to an armed street mugger or a teenage gang is generally regarded (at best) as foolhardiness rather than bravery, but it nevertheless betrays something virtuous, and that something is not construed just as a "burst" but as the emergence of something "deep inside," long hidden, even as a different self.

Love can indeed be foolish, and it is often (indeed, paradigmatically) "out of character." To be frustrated in love may be ennobling at best, humiliating or tragic at its worst, but to be unwilling or unable to love is to mark oneself as a possibly inferior human being. Despite the insistence of many philosophers on morals as a matter of reason and the virtues as distinct from the passions, the emotions nevertheless retain an essential place in our moral world.

2

THE POLITICS OF EMOTION

Destroying the passions and cravings, merely as a preventive measure against their stupidity and unpleasant consequences of this stupidity—today this strikes us as merely another acute form of stupidity.

Nietzsche, *Twilight of the Idols*

Philosophers have often contrasted "reason" and "the passions," typically championing the former against the latter and defending philosophy itself as the love of reason. By implication, at least, philosophy tends to display contempt for the passions. "Appeal to the emotions" gets listed in almost every introductory logic text and ethics book as an "informal" fallacy, something to avoid, not at all costs, perhaps, but at least in term papers. Philosophy gets redefined as the formulation and criticism of argument, the exclusive domain of reason. "Heated" argument, though not uncommon, is considered inappropriate. Dispassionate analysis is encouraged; passionate advocacy is not. Philosophy may still be dutifully described as the "love" of wisdom, but this love is hardly the lusty enthusiasm with which Socrates, if not Plato, approached the subject. The ideal, then as now, is a kind of calm, a contemplative detachment, if not, as in postmodern cynicism, full-fledged *apatheia*. The passionate life hardly gets a hearing.

Even when we find one of the great philosophers defending the passions against the excessive claims of reason, the result is less than edifying and the implications smack of skepticism. David Hume, most notably, insisted that "reason is and ought to be the slave of the passions," dismissing out of hand a long tradition of ethics conceived as the business of reason. But in doing so, he at least implied, and certainly set the stage for others to argue, that morals were beyond the grasp of reason and in some essential sense were unarguable. In juxtaposing reason and the passions, Hume in fact fit in with a long line of philosophers who also set them off against one another and separated emotion from rationality. Hume only reversed the opposition. Descartes and his compatriot Malebranche had, analyzed emotions in terms of physiological "animal spirits," distinctively inferior parts of the psyche—if, indeed, parts of the psyche at all. (Hume employs the same term.) Leibniz thought of emotions as "confused perceptions," and Kant dismissed what he called "pathological love" (love as an emotion) from the love more properly commanded by the Scriptures and practical reason. Kant may also have said that "nothing great is ever accomplished without enthusiasm" (a comment usually attributed to Hegel), but it is clear that enthusiasm as such deserves little place in his grand "critique" of the higher human faculties.

This is the most vulgar of the several senses in which we might talk of "the politics of emotion." Throughout much of the history of philosophy, the emotions have been treated as the *lumpen proletariat* of the soul, playing little role in the productive economy but nevertheless to be feared as a cost and a danger, to be contained as effectively as possible. The politics of emotion denies them legitimacy and significance and thus justifies their suppression and neglect. Let's begin by considering this "political" campaign, waged in the name of "thinness" in philosophy.

The Emotions Demeaned

> The moralists' mania demands not the control but the extirpation of the passions. Their conclusion is ever: only the emasculated man is the good man.
>
> Nietzsche, *Antichrist*

The "moralists' mania" continues in the current philosophical literature. Let me mention two illustrative examples, one a recent address by one of our most distinguished and intellectually open-minded moral philosophers, the other an essay by a well-known philosopher of mind.

In his presidential address to the American Philosophical Association (Pacific Division) Joel Feinberg asked, "What relevance, if any, do appeals to sentiment have for issues in practical ethics?"[1] He began with the usual answer: "The abrupt way with the question is to respond 'none; sentiment is one thing and argument is another, and nothing fogs the mind as thoroughly as emotion'" (p. 19). Feinberg rejected this "abrupt" answer, but his conclusion is far less than an enthusiastic endorsement of emotion; he acknowledged that feelings may be "relevant" or at least not irrelevant to ethics, and he concluded that he "finds no unmanageable conflict between effective humanitarianism and the maintenance, under flexible control, of the essential human sentiments." He added, as if this was not already sufficiently cautious, "I hope that conclusion is not too optimistic" (p. 42)

Feinberg's careful analysis of the place of sentiment in ethics deserves an extended and careful reply, but I only want to call attention to the extreme caution and defensiveness he felt compelled to adopt in presenting his "optimistic" thesis—that sentiment may not be wholly irrelevant to ethical considerations. One notes the extreme effort just to clear a bit of room for emotion, as if, for example, a pregnant woman's feelings about her body and her baby and her "morals" and reputation and her feelings for the father and her career were but personal anecdotes and distractions in the abortion debate, while the philosophers' abstract arguments about the status and rights of the fetus and a woman's (abstract) right to control her own body were the only legitimate concern. Whatever the pros and cons of such an ethics, the emphasis remains wholly on principles and the arguments supporting them, and the emotions contribute nothing worthy to our moral considerations.[2]

The second piece worth mentioning is Jerome Shaffer's "An Assessment of Emotion," published in 1983.[3] Shaffer begins with an example of "undergoing an emotion": "I am driving around a curve and see a log across the road. I take it that bodily harm is likely and I don't want that. I turn pale, my heart beats faster, I feel my stomach tighten. I slam on the brakes."[4] Not surprisingly, Shaffer uses this and similar examples of emotion to conclude that emotions are not very pleasant or valuable experiences and, accordingly, are "neither necessary nor in general desirable for the main concerns of life."[5]

A moment's reflection should establish that this case of unwelcome surprise is not anything like a paradigm of emotion. Indeed, one might object that surprise is not an emotion, despite its physiological similarity to certain emotions. And in any case not all emotions can be characterized, much less defined, by this "turning pale, heart beats faster, stomach tightens," and so on. Consider the very different analysis that would accompany taking as our lead example, say, experiencing a powerful sense of satisfaction that justice has been done, or the possibly decades-long experience of being passionately in love. (Shaffer's analysis of love as an emotion in the same essay reduces love to "butterflies in the stomach" and other such "waves, currents, surges or suffusions," concluding that love, too, is an emotion of little value. This is hardly the passion that moved Tristan and Isolde.) Furthermore, we can readily agree that coming across a log in the road is an undesirable experience without concluding that the fear itself is an undesirable experience.[6] Indeed, in safer surroundings, millions of people have been known to stand in line in order to pay up to ten dollars each to have the wits pleasantly scared out of them by a wide assortment of natural and unnatural phenomena, including twisters, man-eating sharks, giant gorillas, Jurassic clones, various Martians and other E.T.s, flying logs, flowing lava, and psychotic killers.

Shaffer's "assessment" of emotion is, in fact, a political hatchet job, but the glib way he pursues his argument is an indication of emotions' lowly political status. Imagine a philosopher publishing, in a similarly professional journal, an assessment of logic in which the paradigm case was a grotesque instance of sophistry, then concluding that logic played no very important or desirable role in our lives. But the prejudice against emotion in philosophy is so strong that an unfair or frivolous attack does not even provoke a defense, and a defense of emotion, no matter how dispassionate and responsible, tends to invoke the charge of soft-headed sentimentality.

I do not think that it is overstating the case to say that modern American philosophy in general has shown a profound distrust as well as a lack of interest in the role of emotions in philosophy. (This despite the passionate interest of our two most famous philosophers, James and Dewey.) Philosophers, according to the current program, should try to be nothing but rational, not impassioned or—even worse—sentimental. Philosophers should evaluate arguments but not get "caught up" in one position or another. (One of my colleagues tells his students, who are writing about very emotional issues, that he "doesn't care in the least what they believe, but only about the soundness of their arguments.") Indeed, one begins to suspect that the criterion for respectability in current philosophical discourse is the absence of any emotional reaction. Philosophical theses must be argued, calmly and, wherever possible, formally, thus neutralizing the seductive effects of rhetoric and avoiding appeal to the emotions. Not surprisingly, philosophers like Kierkegaard or Nietzsche, who celebrate passion over reason, are simply dismissed as "not really philosophers." The familiar politics of exclusion marginalizes the emotions and then marginalizes emotional philosophers.

Insofar as emotions do appear in philosophy, it has been understood that their place is tangential; their analysis, a side issue. Exemplary theories of emotion, in Descartes and Hume, for example, are typically ignored. Descartes's treatise *On the Passions of the Soul*, which contains, among other things, his most sustained meditations on the intricate relations between mind and body, is typically shunted aside in favor of his more seductive *Meditations* and his far more methodological *Rules for the Direction of the Mind*. Students are routinely asked to read Books I and III of Hume's great *Treatise of Human Nature*, but the middle book, on the passions, is omitted. So, too, students reading Spinoza are typically brought up short after book II of the *Ethics*, leaving out what Spinoza himself certainly took to be the heart of the project, three brilliant books on the emotions.[7] The occasional course titled "The Philosophy of Emotions" is treated as exotic marginalia, sort of like "New Age Philosophy 302" or "The Philosophy of Love and Sex," that is, philosophy for the soft-minded and the easily titillated.

But even when emotions do become a focal concern, the approach is too often too much like the now mandatory philosophical approach to all prob-

Good point.

lems—formal, objectifying, argumentative, dispassionate—in other words, wholly unlike the subject matter itself and even in opposition to it. In major books in the field, the rich topic of emotions is reduced to thin, logical analysis of the nature of "intentionality," of the various forms of "cognition," of the proper understanding of psychological categories. I do not object to such studies and find some of them fascinating, but, with all due respect, the emotion gets lost. But if epistemology has as one of its aims the enhancement of our knowledge, then it would seem that the "knowledge value" of our emotions ought to be an essential avenue of exploration.[8] Instead, many studies of emotion seem to aim at dismissing or defusing our emotions as no more than mere "feelings." Indeed, one could argue that the overwhelming emphasis on epistemology over emotion in modern philosophy betrays an uncritical and probably false assumption about the nature of both philosophy and human nature, that we are first of all *knowing* beings and only secondarily or pathologically *feeling* creatures as well. Politically, that certainly aids those who know and can reason well, but it degrades and demeans those for whom sensitivity and passion are primary virtues. (The traditional image of women as "more sensitive, less rational" is certainly not politically irrelevant to this charge.)

What Is an Emotion? (Toward a Political View)

Ethical philosophers intuit the deontological canons of morality by consulting the emotive centers of their own hypothalmic-limbic systems.

E. O. Wilson, *Sociobiology*

"What is an emotion?" The question was asked in precisely that form by William James, as the title of an essay he wrote for the journal *Mind* over one hundred years ago.[9] Philosophers have been concerned and often worried about the nature of emotion since the beginnings of Western philosophy. Socrates and the pre-Socratics raised deep and by no means consistent questions about the place of emotions in the ideal human life. Although the discipline has grown up as the pursuit of reason (largely because of Socrates and his student Plato), the emotions have always lurked in the background as a threat to reason, as a danger to philosophy and philosophers. Perhaps that is why one of the most enduring metaphors of reason and emotion has been the metaphor of master and slave, with the wisdom of reason firmly in control and the dangerous impulses of emotion safely suppressed, channelled, or, ideally, in harmony with reason.

emotion: Not Just Mere Phenomenon

The master-slave metaphor displays two features that still determine much of the philosophical view of emotion today. First and foremost, there is the inferior role of emotion, the idea that emotion is more primitive, less intelligent, more bestial, less dependable, more dangerous, and thus to be controlled by reason (an argument that Aristotle and other enlightened Athenians used to justify the political institution of human slavery as well). Second, and more profoundly, there is the reason-emotion distinction itself, as if we were dealing with two different natural kinds, two conflicting and antagonistic aspects of the soul. Even those philosophers who sought to integrate them and reduce one to the other (typically reducing emotion to an inferior genus of reason, a "confused perception" or "distorted judgment"), maintained the distinction and continued to insist on the superiority of reason. It was thus a mark of his considerable iconoclasm that Hume declared reason to be the slave of the passions, but even Hume, despite an ingenious analysis of the structure of emotions, fell back on the old models and metaphors.

The question "What is an emotion?"—let us say right away—is not just a theoretical query, not just an attempt to achieve adequate understanding or an explanation of emotion. The question is primarily practical, in the sense that we have to live with and through our emotions. In short, we live our emotions. I mean this in the same sense that a person has to live in and through a marriage, and it is not enough to understand "marriage: the institution, its history, laws regarding, curious facts about, unusual examples of . . ." "What is marriage?" in this perspective is an existential, not a sociological, inquiry. Nor is it just the particularity of *this* marriage or, indeed, that it is *one's own* marriage that is in question. This is why the question matters to us, and why mere generalities (e.g., divorce and reconciliation statistics) will not do us much practical good. But between general knowledge and the particular circumstances of our lives is the interdependence of theory and practice. If one understands a marriage as a personal, passionate commitment, then the marriage itself will be constituted largely by that understanding. If the same marriage is conceived as an unfortunate act of fate, or a social or family obligation, it will certainly be a very different marriage.

So, too, with emotion. If one understands emotions as largely involuntary physiological responses—on the model, for instance, of the much-studied "startle response"—then one will experience and act toward his or her emotions as if they are intrusions, misfortunes, small bouts of illness or curious bodily jerks and winces.[10] On the other hand, if emotion is understood as political or strategic social behavior, then not only one's "view" of emotion but also one's emotional behavior and feelings will be much influenced by that understanding. I am arguing, then, that an emotion is first of all an ongoing practice in which one is actively and interpersonally engaged. It is not a mere phenomenon, "something that appears." It is not merely personal but also interpersonal, socially constructed, and learned. Having an emotion, whether one suffers through it or uses it for all that it's worth, is first of all a kind of social and political practice, one of the definitive practices involved in living a decent and passionate life with other people.

This is not to say that there is no place for theory. On the contrary, I want to combat the damaging opposition between theory and practice just as surely as I want to combat the insidious antagonism between reason and the passions, and as part of the same campaign. All too often, we are handed a phony picture of theoretical life as the dispassionate life of pure inquiry, when acquaintance with any serious scientist or scholar leaves no doubt about the essential passion of their quest, however it is described.[11] Whether practices are theory-driven or theories are practice-driven, it is a mistake to try to separate the two. How we think about our emotions will have a lot to do with how we live them, which includes how we rationalize them and use them in our dealings with ourselves and other people, and how we use them as reasons or as excuses for our own bad behavior.[12]

With this in mind, I want to argue three negative theses that are central to the conception of emotion that I employ throughout this book. The first, and by far most important, is that an emotion *is not a feeling.* The second is that an emotion is not or at least *cannot be reduced to, a physiological occurrence,* however much we may learn about human neurobiology and related subjects. The third is that an emotion *cannot be understood in terms of mere individual behavior,* where the "mere" is not intended to deny that emotion is expressed in behavior or that emotions are in some sense individually experienced, but rather to deny that there can be an adequate understanding of emotion, one's own emotion or others', in theory or in practice, without some consideration of social context, culture, social and interpersonal relationships, and the "meaning" of the behavior in these terms. This, too, is what I have in mind in using the phrase "the politics of emotion."

An emotion is often said to be a feeling, in a quite innocent sense, the same sense that encompasses all sorts of awareness, including, notably, the long-term feelings of love and affection. But the sense that I want to deny is not at all innocent, although it has the virtue, as Nietzsche wrote, "of being refutable." Its most famous advocate is William James, who defended the view that an emotion is a set of sensations (caused by a specifiable physiological disturbance, which in turn is caused by a disturbing perception). At the beginning of the twentieth century, James's view was challenged by W. B. Cannon (author of *The Wisdom of the Body)* and by fellow pragmatist John Dewey, who pointed out that our repertoire of emotions is far more complex and sophisticated than our relatively impoverished repertoire of sensations.[13] The difference between shame and embarrassment, to take a familiar example, cannot be understood simply in terms of sensations or their physiological causes. The difference must be understood in terms of felt responsibility, the social situation and the culture in which the social mishap occurs. The expression "felt responsibility" should be noted, for it is not a "feeling" in the Jamesian sense, but rather a quite complicated, learned way of seeing or understanding or interpreting a bit of (one's own) social behavior in a particular situation. Elsewhere, I have called such "ways of seeing" *judgments* and have argued that emotions are constituted by such judgments.[14]

One might say that an emotion is a feeling to make the very reasonable claim that if a person has an emotion, he or she must in some sense feel it, that is, be aware of it. Needless to say, a host of phenomenological problems come crowding in on us at this point. What do we mean by "aware"? Does this eliminate the possibility of unconscious emotions? Does it eliminate the possibility—or, rather, the obvious fact—that sometimes we are demonstrably wrong about what we claim to feel, that is, what emotion we have? Such considerations undermine the traditional Cartesian temptation to say that we are able to be *immediately* aware of our own mental processes, including emotions, since the very notion of the unconscious, as defended by Freud and as evidenced in such familiar emotional ploys as denial, suggests an inability to come to terms with, to "get in touch with," one's own emotional responses. Nevertheless, it is difficult to deny that there is something to the Cartesian claim, some inescapable requirement that if something is to count as an emotion (as opposed to a mere bodily twitch or robotic behavior), the subject's awareness is an essential condition. This is very different, however, from saying that an emotion is a feeling in the sense advocated by William James.

The view that emotions can be reduced to physiological occurrences is only rarely (and usually metaphorically) advanced as a commonsense argument. To be sure, we have long employed physiological, mechanical, and "hydraulic" imagery to capture the mechanics as well as the feel of emotions.[15] And today, computer metaphors are extremely popular for talking about emotional states ("input/output," "overload," "interface," and the like). But the serious impetus toward a physiological, and more specifically a neurological, model of human emotion comes from the realm of medical practice and scientific theory. A full century ago, two doctors were telling their colleagues that psychology had to take account of the newly developed science of neurology. William James wrote, "The psychologist is forced to be something of a nerve physiologist." Freud, about the same time, identified what he called "the psychic apparatus" with the brain.[16] Today, we readily understand such efforts. Psychiatry has made enormous advances in the past few decades by "reducing" various forms of mental illness to neurobiological malfunctions. Because a great many of these disturbances are emotional in character, it is highly tempting to presume that the emotions in general are simply neurobiological functions. With advances in neurology, this thesis looks ever more promising as new "centers" and syndromes are identified in the brain.

But, of course, this is not all that there is to the picture. One *can* look just at the nervous and endocrine systems in an attempt to understand emotions, but there will always be a very real question whether the processes thereby revealed actually *are* the emotion or, rather, provide the underlying substratum of emotion.[17] This is no semantic quibble. If what we want to understand are such emotions as love, anger, jealousy, and sadness, it is by no means obvious that any understanding of the brain, detached from all considerations of the person and his or her circumstances and culture, will do the job. This is not to challenge the importance of brain and medical research, but only to say that any attempt to equate the various emotions with brain states and processes is at this stage no more than a promissory note, of little help in deciding, for instance, whether to pursue one's anger against a malevolent colleague or fan the first flames of a newfound love. What is indefensible, however, is the use of physiological models to primitivize, reduce, and dismiss emotions from the realm of interesting, full-blooded human phenomena. My reason for rejecting both the feeling and the physiological models of emotion is not that I think either is not worth investigating, but that both are so often used as an excuse to ignore or neglect the significance of emotions in human life—except, perhaps, as disruptive psychiatric disturbances, significant only because they interfere with the good life.

To say that an emotion cannot be understood in terms of mere individual behavior is to condense a number of theses into a very short phrase. Again, the view I want to reject has an innocent and perfectly reasonable interpretation, namely, that individuals "have" emotions and, in an obvious sense, we individuate and identify particular emotions in part by specifying who (what individual) has them. If everyone in the room is delighted to see Alphonse, it makes sense to say that what this means is that every individual in the room has his or her own emotion of delight. Moreover, we do have the well-verified sense that one can have an emotion in the absence of any any external cause or stimulus (although the complete absence of cause or stimulus may be hard to prove). Thus, although emotions are often evoked or provoked by causes external to the subject, we might well want to insist that, whatever those causes—or even in the absence of them—a person's emotion ultimately comes down to what he or she feels, where "feels," again, is not to be limited to sensations but encompasses the whole range of thoughts, perceptions, interpretations, evaluations, appraisals, and so on. But something goes very wrong when this commonsensical view is elevated to the status of an ontological theory and we isolate the subject from the world. It is the context and the social environment that make most emotions intelligible. It is the context and the social environment that render an emotion (more or less) appropriate.[18] But it is also the context and social environment that make the having of most human emotions possible. My aim here is to block one more source of dismissive attitudes toward emotions, namely, the "Cartesian" idea that an emotion is simply an "internal" occurrence.

Martini

To talk about emotions and what emotions really are is to talk about the "meaning" of emotion. And that meaning includes not only the social context, the culture, and the social and interpersonal relationships in which a person "has" the emotion and in which he or she expresses and acts it out, but also the theories and practices through which a person comes to understand what he or she is feeling and doing. Theories are the stuff of philosophy, and psychology and the other social sciences form latter-day branches of the already solid trunk of philosophical viewpoints and prejudices. But it is through these theoretical prejudices that we not only view but also live our emotions, and so theories of emotion, like the emotions themselves, are ultimately political and deeply relevant to our sense of power in the world.

Two Paradigms of Emotion:
Jamesian Arousal and Aristotle's Politics

> Our natural way of thinking about these standard emotions is that the mental perception of some fact excites the mental affection called the emotion, and that this latter state of mind gives rise to the bodily expression. My thesis on the contrary is that *the bodily changes follow directly the* PERCEPTION *of the exciting fact, and that our feeling of the same changes as they occur* IS *the emotion.*
>
> William James, "What Is an Emotion?"

conspicuity

> Let anger be defined as a distressed desire for conspicuous vengeance in return for a conspicuous and unjustifiable contempt/slight of one's person or friends.
>
> Aristotle, *Rhetoric*

William James offered us several different answers to his question What is an emotion?, but the one that every student of emotions knows is summarized in his heavily italicized statement, "*our feeling of [bodily changes] as they occur* IS *the emotion.*"[19] Ever since (and long before, of course), the idea that the core of emotion is some sort of physiological "arousal" has governed a good deal of psychological and, until recently, philosophical theorizing about emotion. An emotion, in short, is a physiological disturbance, caused by some untoward or disturbing perception (thought or memory), which is *felt* in some more or less distinctive way. Thus the focus on emotion is aimed at the individual organism, its physiology, and its feelings. Today it is the neurophysiology of emotion that is attracting a good deal of attention, but the basic model of emotion as "arousal" remains the same.

But that the same question about the nature of emotion was broached by Aristotle, some twenty-three hundred years before James. Aristotle mentioned feelings, physical agitation, and arousal only in passing when he defined anger, as a paradigm of emotion, as "a distressed desire for conspicuous vengeance in return for a conspicuous and unjustifiable contempt/slight of one's person or friends."[20] What should strike us first and foremost about this characterization of emotion is the fact that it seems to have much more to say about ethics, politics, and social relationships than it does about anything that most psychologists would recognize as "emotion." The key terms—"vengeance," "contempt," "person or friends," as well as the twice-repeated "conspicuous"—suggest that the nature of anger is essentially entangled in questions of perceived status, questions of offense and appropriate retaliation, and interpersonal relationships. Indeed, Aristotle goes on to insist that only fools don't get angry, and while overly angry people may be "unbearable," the absence of anger (aimed at the appropriate offenses) is a vice rather than a virtue. It is a "contempt/slight" that causes the anger (perhaps an instance of "scorn, spite, or insolence"), but because of this, it is right, even obligatory to get angry (on the right occasion, for the right reasons, to the appropriate degree). Anger, and other emotions, are political in nature in that they have a great deal to do with relationships between people living together in states.

Between them, James and Aristotle establish two paradigms for thinking about emotion. On the one hand, an emotion is a relatively primitive mental state or process, some combination of physiology and feeling. Like most "mental" phenomena, an emotion is a feature of the individual organism, something "inner," or if "inner experience" is to be eschewed as too "unscientific" (James often denied "the existence of consciousness"), then something literally inside the skull, that is, in the brain. In psychology, because of methodological suspicion of private experience and because the science of neurology is largely unknown territory, the study of emotions is tentatively reduced to or focused on the superficialities of behavior—facial expressions, short-term behavioral sequences, or the not always so credible self-reports of nineteen-year-old psychology students. On the other hand, there is what I call the "political" approach to emotions. It takes as the framework for describing emotions neither the mind nor the body but the social situation, in all of its elaborate ethical and interpersonal complexity.

Beyond the Cartesian Tradition

Theoretical myopia prevents theorists from seeing that their models
still presuppose that somewhere, conveniently hidden in the obscure
"center" of the mind/brain, there is a Cartesian Theater, a place where
"it all comes together" and consciousness happens.

Daniel Dennett, *Consciousness Explained*

primitive, inchoate

Part of what I find so appealing about the "political" approach to emotions is the way it escapes or bypasses what is now generally called the "Cartesian" tradition in mind-body research. That tradition, well summarized in the recent debates involving Dan Dennett, John Searle, David Chalmers, and many others, focuses on the "question of consciousness" and slips back and forth between dualism and reductive materialism.[21] Aristotle, of course, was burdened with no such concerns, enjoying the twin benefits of his innocence of Cartesian dualism (and any such notion as "consciousness") and the reductive obsessions of modern science. The emotions, in particular, play an awkward—some would say unintelligible—role in the Cartesian picture, as an unwieldy causal complex of physiological processes, on the one hand, and personal experiences (or "feelings") on the other. Descartes, who was as sophisticated as anyone in the physiology of his day, spent considerable time (in his *Passions of the Soul*) worrying about how the "animal spirits" in the blood effect the appropriate changes in the soul.[22]

On the "mental" side of the causal relation, however, Descartes's language changes abruptly. Hatred, for example, "ultimately arises from the perception of an object's potential harmfulness and involves a desire to avoid it."[23] Although he may have been fascinated by the physiology, Descartes (like Aristotle) was ultimately interested in a value-oriented, wisdom-minded analysis of emotion: how emotions fit into and define a good life. Nevertheless, the tradition that bears his Latinate name has tended to give scant attention to the political dimension of emotion, and excessive attention to the emotions as feelings or "affects." There is some awestruck and occasionally apocalyptic admiration for the possibilities of neurological research, but Cartesian dualism has pretty much delimited a phenomenon defined on the one side by a neurology that is still largely unknown, and on the other side by a set of experiences—variously described as rich and meaningful or as primitive and inchoate—that each person allegedly has as his or her own private domain.

My own work, which is usually labeled (not by me) a "cognitive" account of emotions, has tended to remain within the same Cartesian tradition.[24] You may take this as a confession. My largely phenomenological approach emphasizes the role of "judgment" in emotions, following (among others) Aristotle, the ancient Stoics, and Sartre. To be sure, I have often emphasized the interpersonal and ethical nature of those judgments—as in judgments of affinity, intimacy, and responsibility—but insofar as I have continued to treat emotions as personal experiences, I have found that I tended to neglect several important dimensions of emotion. I have come to especially appreciate this since the late 1980s in my interdisciplinary work with social scientists and psychobiologists. Neurology and the connection between brain processes and emotion are still beyond my ken, but I have paid inadequate attention to more readily accessible aspects of emotion, such as the role of facial expressions and cultural "display rules" in emotion, despite their prominence in psychol-

Affinity, intimacy, resp.

ogy and anthropology.[25] Indeed, to this day, philosophers in general seem not yet to have discovered the significance of the face in emotion theory, despite the fact that this has all but ruled the work of the psychologists across the hall for more than twenty years (not to mention that it is as obvious as one's own face in the mirror). The reason, of course, is Cartesianism. The face is but superficial body. It is, at best, expression. But that, supposedly, tells us very little about that of which it is an expression, namely, the emotion. And the emotion, on the Cartesian account, is necessarily something "inner," not in the face or the expression but in the private experience of the subject.

Here we return to James, who had his own confusion about how to identify an emotion. Like Hume before him, James nominally identified the emotion as such as a sensation (or a set of sensations, an "impression") that he distinguished from its causes and its expressions. As a physician, James was naturally struck by the importance of the bodily responses, and he was keenly aware of the complex relations between an emotion and its bodily expressions, so much so that he famously urged that the latter were the cause of the former and suggested, anticipating today's Hallmark greeting cards, that putting on a happy face will indeed result in feeling happy. Nevertheless, the official Jamesian doctrine, which resembled the doctrines of so many philosophers before him, was that the emotion IS the feeling, the distinctive set of sensations. An adequate integration of the "felt" and the physical aspects of emotion evaded him.

The Cartesian view of emotions has taken many different forms. Many philosophers and psychologists have thought that the definitive feature of those sensations that make up emotions is the fact that they are either pleasurable or painful. Hume, for instance, distinguished love and hate, pride and humility in this way. Spinoza sometimes made similar suggestions, and his best twentieth-century incarnation, in the person of the Dutch psychologist Nico Frijda, has argued the same.[26] But Spinoza, following the Stoics, more prominently suggested that the emotions are not so much feelings as "judgments" or "thoughts" about the world and oneself. I locate myself in this "cognitive" tradition. Still others, leaning toward behavioral (but not behaviorist) analysis, insisted that emotions were protoactions, intentions, action tendencies.[27] Outright behaviorists suggested, with varying degrees of implausibility, that emotions are *nothing but* behavior and dispositions to behave in certain ways, thus remaining Cartesians but simply denying "the ghost in the machine." More often than not, however, they hung onto some vestige of the mental, as in Ryle's infamous "twinges and itches" and Wittgenstein's "wheel that plays no part in the mechanism."[28] Others suggested that emotions are complexes of beliefs and desires—the rather simpleminded model of "folk psychology" that now reigns supreme in some cognitive science circles. What all of these views have in common is their shared acceptance (or, in the case of behaviorism, a defiant rejection) of an emotion as an "inner" psychological state. The differences between these views are significant, of course, and I have spent much of my career defending some of them over the others. But I now see the challenge in a very different way, one that takes the "emotions as judgments" view and relocates it in non-Cartesian space.

One of the philosophers who best pursued a nondualistic alternative understanding of emotion was James's pragmatist colleague, John Dewey. Dewey insisted on a holistic, all-embracing view of emotion. Two others are Martin Heidegger, whose obscurity on other matters did not seem to cloud his view of "moods" (*Stimmung*, which, in his treatment, clearly includes many emotions), and Jean-Paul Sartre, who despite his seemingly Cartesian ontology defended a view of emotions (and consciousness in general) as thoroughly political.[29] Other such views can be found scattered through the history of philosophy and psychology (before those fields were wrenched apart by university administrators and mutually jealous colleagues). But the prototype of the political approach still seems to me to be Aristotle. What all of these views have in common is a perspective on emotions as primarily situated in human relationships and inextricable from ethics.[30] The problem, as I now see it, is to retain the personal and experiential (phenomenological) grasp of emotions but situate the emotions in an essentially interpersonal and social context, treating them not only as relevant to and the result of, but also as constituted in relations with other people.[31]

The Purpose(s) of Emotions

> We can no longer live in so urgent and difficult a world. However, we must act. So we try to change the world, as if by magic.
>
> Jean-Paul Sartre, *The Emotions*

One of the more exciting theses about emotion to (re)emerge in the twentieth century is the insistence that emotions are purposive. They have what Jean-Paul Sartre called "finalité."[32] That is to say, they are not only functional and occasionally advantageous, and they are not just the fortuitous residue of fickle evolution; they are also *in themselves*, strategic and political. To put it differently and somewhat controversially, emotions do not just "happen" to us, as the whole language of "passion" and "being struck by" seems to suggest. They are, with some contentious stretching of the term, activities that we "do," stratagems that work for us, both individually and collectively. Or, to put it yet another way, there is a sense in which the emotions can be said to be rational (or irrational) despite the fact that "rationality" is often restricted to those contexts involving articulate thought and calculation. To be sure, emotions may involve considerable articulation, thought, and calculation. (Vengeance born of anger is exemplary here.) Rationality is thus employed in an "instrumental" way as well, as the choice of means employed to reach some emotional end. Insofar as emotions are purposive, they themselves have ends. It is not just a matter of their happening (and the problem of how to get rid of or enjoy them). There are also questions about what will *satisfy* them. As strategies, emotions seek their own satisfaction: in anger, through vengeance; in hatred, through vanquishing; in certain kinds of love, through "possessing." This is not to say that all emotions can be satisfied or have conditions of satisfaction. Grief, for example, is an emotion with no such conditions, except, *per impossible*, the resurrection of the lost loved one. Nevertheless, even such emotions may have a purpose or purposes, for example, to help mend a suddenly broken life, not only for the individual but also for the group.

No doubt much of this can be explained via both biological and cultural evolution, but that is not the critical point. Of course, one can readily surmise, the energizing supplied by both anger and fear prepares an organism for extraordinary bursts of aggression or retreat, as the case may be. Such an account of emotions requires nothing whatever by way of self-awareness or voluntariness. In evolutionary theory, an individual or a species need not "figure out" its adaptive advantages. It simply lucks into them. It turns out that frogs and butterflies that resemble poisonous members of their classes have a competitive advantage. They are not so often eaten. It turns out that certain male birds with more tail plummage are more likely to attract a mate, and thus have a reproductive advantage. So, too, it will turn out that creatures with a certain temperament, who react emotionally and express certain emotions in appropriate situations, may have a competitive or reproductive advantage. A dog that growls and attacks may be better suited to survive in certain environments. Dogs that run, hide, or cuddle may have competitive or reproductive advantages in other environments. (Dog breeders thus supplement nature with marketing considerations.) I take it that none of this, as such, is all that controversial.

But most of what passes for evolutionary explanations of emotion in both psychology and philosophy these days is no more enlightening than Molière's famous explanation of a sleeping potion in terms of its soporific powers. To show that something serves a purpose or a function says no more and no less about the evolutionary process than the crudest creationist or contingency theories. Evolution is the new magic wand, which with a wave changes something inexplicable into something only seemingly explained. As Nietzsche noted, we prefer bad explanations to no explanation at all.

But evolutionary theory is only background and does not play the central role in what I am arguing here. Emotions, according to the evolutionary hypothesis, turn out to be strategic or functional because they happen to contribute to "fitness," with all of the ambiguities and objections that term has inspired in the past century or so. A person (or creature) who has an emotion, according to the evolutionary line, does not have it because he, she, or it has a purpose (or because anyone, including "nature," has a purpose), but because it has proved to be useful and alternative strategies have proved to be fatal. In such cases, the emotional responses themselves may be (what used to be called) "instinctual," or, in current computer-based jargon, "hardwired." An overly simple example (because it isn't really an emotion) would be the startle reaction. Much more complicated are various forms of maternal affection and protectiveness, territorial jealousy, fear at the sight of certain shapes or in the presence of certain smells. But what I am arguing is that however biologically based our emotions may be, whether hardwired or not—indeed, whether voluntary or not—our understanding of emotion gains a great deal when we shift from thinking about emotions and emotional responses as mere products to thinking of them as strategies, ways of dealing with other people, and ways of dealing with ourselves.

The idea that emotions are purposive and functional can be found occasionally in ancient and medieval philosophy, and some of the world's great philosophers and religions have endorsed love and compassion in particular as divine strategies. But the thesis emerges with particular power not only in evolutionary accounts of emotions and their development but also in the theories of the pragmatist John Dewey (who had his own qualms about Darwinism) and, more recently and more radically, in the writings of Sartre. Sartre tells us that emotions are "magical transformations of the world," by which he means that emotions are intentional and strategic ways of coping with "difficult" situations. We "choose" them, and we choose them for a purpose.

This Sartrean view of the strategic nature of emotions no doubt strains the credulity of most contemporary emotion theorists, although similar if more modest evolutionary-functionalist theses have been argued by many psychological investigators. Perhaps I can blunt some doubts by noting that there is nothing in this voluntaristic thesis that requires emotional strategies to be recognized, articulated, or even articulable as such. In other words, they do not have to be conscious, in the usual sense of that term, and the "choices" we make need not be explicit, deliberative choices. Nevertheless, an emotion may be a strategy, a way of coping, and in particular, a way of coping with other people. Especially when that way of coping involves power, I believe that we are justified in calling it the politics of emotion. But, as we have indicated this phrase admits of quite a few very different interpretations, beginning with the vulgar campaign against emotional richness in the name of rationalistic "thinness" we considered at the beginning of this chapter.

The politics of emotion also refers to the fact that emotions are not just "inner." They reach out to the world. Essential to the Deweyan-Sartrean view is the idea that emotions are intentional; they are directed toward objects (real or imaginary) in the world. They therefore involve concepts and cognition, including recognition. Of course, they also involve neurology and physiology, and there may be an instinctual or biological basis for intentional states. (William James certainly suggests that this is so. Contemporary writers take this to be something of a starting point for their inquiries.[33]) But what this notion of "intentionality" tends to do is to break down the Cartesian barrier between experience and the world, between the "inner" and the "outer." Of course, the objects of emotion are not always real. (They may be merely imagined, or remembered, or, in extreme cases, hallucinated.) In which case we might continue to talk metaphorically about the whole process as if it were "inside" the subject. But in the more usual case, in which Harry loves Sally, in which Fred hates spinach, in which Woody is jealous of Alan, the intentionality of emotion is directed at something real and in the world. There is an enormous philosophical literature about how to deal with these issues, whether the case of the "nonexistent object" is to be given priority or treated as some sort of odd exception. But these intrigues need not slow us down here. The point is that an emotion is not merely a "feeling," as, say, pain is a feeling. It is also an outlook, an attitude, a reaching out to the world.

As such a reaching out, emotion has aims and values (not just "appraisals," as some of the prominent psychological literature would suggest—appraisal is much too "observational"). We perceive things, people, and events, and have emotions directed toward them that embody attitudes of approval and disapproval, desire and repulsion, and goals of much more intricate sorts. Whatever else they may be, emotions are intimately and not merely contingently tied to behavior. (Which is why they were, for so many years, coupled as a poor cousin to "motivation" in psychology textbooks. No one knew where else to put them.) Strict behaviorists would simply say that an emotion IS the behavior, but here the conceptual tie is too tight, even with the usual qualifications.[34] Others (Nico Frijda, for instance) would more judiciously insist only that an emotion is a set of action tendencies.[35] But it is in the conceptual connection to behavior—which is to say, clumsily, that the emotion and its expression are one thing and not two—that the "politics" of emotion becomes particularly prominent.

If emotion were simply an impersonal judgment, or an "appraisal" and strictly "inner," like a spectator sitting passively, far from the field of play, the idea of emotional strategies and politics would make at most minimal sense. But emotions are tied to action, whether it is in the "cool" and protracted strategies of revenge that sometimes flow from anger or in the spontaneous and momentary expression of delight or surprise on someone's face. It is the controlled, unexpressed, hidden emotion that requires special explanation, however, not the connection between emotions and their expression. When an employee gets angry with her boss, or when a mature, respectful child gets angry with a teacher or a parent, it is not the absence of expression that is notable but the restraint, the distortion of expression that is almost always evident to those who know what to look for. Nevertheless, there are many emotions for which their expressions are of no significance, not because the expressions are controlled but because they occur in a situation in which there is no one to notice or be affected by them. We often have emotions when we are all alone. Accordingly, it is important to note that there is an "internal" politics of emotions, so long as we do not take this in a Cartesian way. A subject may adopt an emotional strategy quite independently of any bit of behavior or expression of emotion, in the absence of any other person or creature who might be influenced, affected, or even amused. Nevertheless, the emotion and not just its expression takes place in a public, not some mysterious Cartesian space. The emotion is "in the world," not in the mind, the psyche, or the soul.

The Politics of Emotion

A mood assails us. It comes neither from outside nor from "inside," but arises out of Being-in-the-world, as a way of such being.

Heidegger, *Being and Time*

The "politics" of emotion might be divided into four (interrelated) levels. There is, first of all, a general thesis about the ontology—or better, the conceptual geography—of emotions: what they are, "where" they are to be located, and the terms in which they should be discussed. The traditional political position of the emotions, as I have complained, is as disenfranchised, the lumpen proletariat of the soul. (Ignore them unless they get rowdy.) Second, there is the most obvious sense in which emotions are political, that is, they are about power, persuasion, manipulation, intimidation. Anger is the most familiar example here, but love, jealousy, shame, resentment, envy, sadness, and even despair deserve recognition as well. Here we can see the sometimes subtle ways in which emotions rule. Third, there is what we might call the internal politics of emotion, the ways in which we position and (one might even say) manipulate ourselves in relation to the world, quite apart from the effects of our emotions or their expression on other people. When I first started seeing the importance of emotional strategies, given my (unacknowledged) Cartesian stance, it was such internal politics that initially intrigued me.[36] Again, getting angry is a paradigm example. One gets angry to "save face," not only in other people's eyes (the overtly public politics of anger) but in one's own eyes as well. Finally, the politics of emotion extends to the "meta" realm of emotion: "labelling," emotion recognition, emotion reportage, emotion description, and theorizing about emotion. It should not be thought that this "level" of emotional politics is easily separated or, sometimes, even distinguished from the other levels of politics in emotion and emotional expression, however. The four political realms often overlap and influence one another.

The Ontology of Emotion

Ontology refers us to the basic nature of things, their place in the universe and how they relate to other things. The ontology of psychology or of psychological phenomena has long been trapped in the Cartesian picture, which, crudely, means that "mental" states, processes, or acts have had to be treated *either* as odd manifestations or misleading descriptions of material states, processes, and behavior (Watson and Skinner in psychology, Gilbert Ryle in philosophy) *or* as extremely odd nonmaterial entities, what Ryle famously mocked as "the ghost in the machine." But Descartes himself was keenly aware that the emotions, in particular, straddled this ontological abyss composed, he said, of both kinds of "substances" (material and immaterial), agitations of the animal spirits (material) on the one hand, and defined by beliefs and desires (immaterial "thoughts") on the other. Behaviorism, whatever its absurdities, had the good sense to reject this implausible dichotomy and point out, with various levels of sophistication, that almost everything we know, and just about everything we want to say, about emotion depends on behavior (including verbal behavior, notably first-person reports). What was left over, of course, was that nagging "first-person case," the subjective "feel" of emotions, but a variety of deft and sometimes daft strokes whittled away at this residue.

Without denying subjectivity, it could nevertheless be argued that much of what philosophers had formerly described as "inner" could just as plausibly be redescribed as "outer," for example, in the expressions of the face, in tendencies to particular actions or action types (aggression, possession, caring for, withdrawing), in the verbal descriptions and evaluations employed to express the emotion. Sadness, for example, can be understood only minimally in terms of the "twinges" and sense of "deflation" that characterized the distinctive "feeling" of sadness. The bulk of this basic emotion can be better understood through an analysis of appraisals and evaluations of loss. So, too, the difference between embarrassment and shame can be understood not so much in terms of any differences in feeling or sensation (are there any?), but rather in terms of the differences in attribution of these emotions in decidedly distinctive contexts.[37] Describing an emotion as shame implies some sense of blame, whereas describing it as embarrassment implies no such accusation. In the wake of Wittgenstein, Ryle, and their psychological counterparts, the mysterious "mental" elements came to play a minimal role in the discussion of emotion.

Phenomenology, conceived not as "the realm of consciousness" but as the world experienced (from one perspective or another), is the natural medium for emotion description. Any description of the body, the brain, the circumstances of behavior, is bound to be incomplete or missing the point (the point of view, that is). Any description of merely "inner" sensation is bound to be pathetic. One can misdescribe the phenomenology as "the peculiarity of the first-person case"—and raise the puzzle of how we recognize our own emotions and what they "feel like," as opposed to how we recognize and understand other people's emotions. But the question of "where" emotions are to be located—in the material or the strange immaterial world—no longer serves any purpose. Emotions are, in every important sense, "out there," about the world. Or, rather, there is no "out there" because there is no contrasting "in here," unless, perhaps, one wishes to speak rather peculiarly indeed about processes "in" the brain. This is not what is commonly called "materialism," which disappears along with the odd view—held only by philosophers, neurologists, and a few social scientists—that emotions are "all in the brain." Nor is it in any way to deny the "existence of consciousness," whatever that odd phrase is supposed to mean. It is just to say that emotions are vital experiences had by conscious social creatures (even if the very limited role of the social is a constant awareness of predators and the occasional awareness of an available mate). Emotions involve any number of interrelated aspects of such creatures' sensibilities, social relationships, self-awareness, shared and individual outlooks on the world, their physiology, their various expressions in speech and behavior. Such complex creatures should not be split into a simplistic ontology of bodies and minds.

Emotions, Power, and Persuasion

The most obvious sense in which emotions are political is that we use our emotions to move other people, or other creatures. Our dogs respond rather quickly to a shout or a scowl, even if it is disciplinary and feigned rather than genuine emotion. This, of course, raises a crucial point about the politics of emotion; it is the convincing expression of emotion, rather than what one might call the emotion itself, that is doing the work. But in our account of the conceptual geography of emotions, I tried to cast some doubt on the distinction between emotion and expression, and to argue that a "convincing" display of emotion either presupposes or—as William James suggested—tends to create the very emotion being displayed. Could one gain the same ends by pretending, by acting *as if* he or she has the emotion in question without, in fact, having it at all? In theory, perhaps, and easily with gullible or hypersensitive targets. But I think that the practical answer is that few of us are such accomplished actors that we can bring off such a performance, so that actually having the emotion seems necessary. If this is so, then it seems to follow that one might have the emotion in order to bring about the desired results.

Whether or not this is so (and certainly the range of cases is far richer than James's simple formula would suggest), it is clear that emotions are not just, and not usually, self-contained, but are more or less continuous with their expression. The lines between authenticity, self-deception, and bad faith get enormously complicated here, but I want to remark, rather baldly for now, on just one piece of this intricately human puzzle. (More in chapter 8.) That is, to have an emotion for a purpose does not entail "not really having" the emotion. That thesis, of course, would undermine everything else I've said here. Nico Frijda puts the thesis rather innocently but, I think, correctly when he says that "emotions—their kind, their intensity, their manifestations—are not only determined by significant eliciting events, but, in addition, are influenced to an important extent by the anticipated desirable effects they exert upon others."[38] Emotions, in other words, are strategies, and there is little reason to doubt that our emotional expressions evolved, in part, because of their effectiveness in communicating our emotions to others.

Sometimes our emotions and emotional displays involve solicitude, a cry for help, an expression of need. Expressions of submissiveness, shrieks of terror, a baby's cries of distress, are all directed (which is not to say consciously) to getting the attention and directing the actions of others. Because they work so well, they can be learned, cultivated, practiced, and thus employed in an intentional (which is not to say "feigned") way. A young female soon learns to win favors by being submissive, which involves feeling submissive, and so she learns to feel submissive. A clever young monkey learns to scatter the troop, at least once, and get the food for himself, by overreacting to a sign of merely modest danger. Babies, children, and even adults learn to cry to win the sympathies of others. Again, they are not "faking it," but just being particularly alert about finding things to cry about. (A young woman on *Seinfeld* bursts into genuine tears when her hotdog slips out of its bun, but later shows no sign of sadness when her grandmother dies. She may be despicable, but she is not, I think, a fraud.)

Many emotions are about power, persuasion, manipulation, and intimidation. We use anger, for example, not only to pump up the energy and boldness needed for a confrontation but also to intimidate the opposition. One of the more unpleasant members of my academic department had the habit of highlighting every meeting in which there was a controversial issue by standing up (he was quite tall), leaning menacingly over the conference table, and shouting quite threateningly at whomever was opposing his position. Since most of the controversial issues discussed were quite trivial, the opposition virtually always gave in, and the bully had his way. Tellingly, these cheap victories rarely had any correlation to the merits of the case, and, more telling still, there was no reason whatever to suppose that his angry displays would ever lead to actual violence. (In fact, the fellow would back away from any real fight.) But, for most of us, our fear of and aversion to anger is so profound that the mere display of anger leads us to react *as if* there were a real threat of harm behind it, even if we know it isn't so. Nor did we ever conclude that these anger displays were feigned or phony. He was just an angry man, who had long learned the lesson that getting angry gets results.

So, too, of the seductive emotions. How many of us have been taken in by appeals that we knew at the time to be insincere, misleading or disasters-in-waiting? Advertising and salemanship depend on such vulnerabilities. Our responses to emotions, as well as the emotions and expressions themselves, are also inbred, habituated, cultivated, and, possibly sometimes, hardwired. It is evident from such experiences that emotions have a political element, that their existence is not a neutral social or psychological fact but a political force, moving us and influencing our actions in any number of ways.

When we turn to the many aspects of the display and expression of emotion, the power of such strategies is obvious. Paul Ekman and Carroll Izard have maintained for years that the facial expressions they have classified have an evolutionary basis, and by this they mean not only that they happened to appear in evolutionary history but also that they served some social and therefore reproductive, advantage. But what is true in the evolutionary story must surely be true in the more ordinary social story. Bad-tempered people tend to get their way by being intimidating. (They could possibly get their way by just pretending to be angry, but, the necessary thespian talents aside, actually getting angry seems to give a double advantage for the reasons suggested above.) To determine to what extent other emotions offer a reproductive or social advantage would involve an emotion-by-emotion analysis. A case can surely be made for love, generally considered. Shame and guilt suggest an advantage for the group, but perhaps not directly for the individual. Grief and sadness invite speculation. (There is certainly manipulative grief, and tears by way of a plea.) Pity and gratitude are fascinating to explore, as Nietzsche has done polemically and at some length.[39] What all such analyses would be looking for would be the ways in which expression and display (whether deliberate or not) provide a strategic advantage with or over other people.

The Internal Politics of Emotion

The internal politics of emotion are the ways in which we position and (one might even say) manipulate ourselves in relation to the world, quite apart from the effects of our emotions or expressions on other people. When Nico Frijda writes that in emotion, politics is "displaying or even experiencing a given emotion because of its desired effects in power," there is an important ambiguity embodied in that word "experiencing." What we experience certainly influences or even determines our attitudes and our behavior, which in turn influence, move, or coerce other people. But we sometimes see a truncated version of the process in which the emotion is unexpressed or undetected, and is intended to remain so. Indeed, it is in privacy that the emotion gets to work its "magic."

Anger, for instance, is a hostile emotion in which one adopts a particular stance in the world, if only in one's own perspective. The nature of that perspective has a powerful effect on how one views the world, whether or not the anger gets expressed or results in action, even (especially) if the subject goes off by him- or herself and avoids all possible detection or prompting to action. It is in the privacy of one's own emotions that thoughts and judgments can go uncorrected and unchallenged by others. (One still has to quiet the voice of conscience, but anger is a noisy emotion that tends to drown out that soft, nagging soliloquy.) Anger requires a judgmental stance, one that resembles a courtroom scenario—a scenario succinctly captured by Lewis Carroll in *Alice in Wonderland* (in "the Mouse's Tale"): "I'll be judge, I'll be jury, Said cunning old fury." The strategic advantage should be obvious. Emerging from a situation in which one has been hurt, offended or humiliated, one positions oneself as nevertheless superior, even as righteous. It is a powerful psychological position. It is emotional politics at its most profound and subtle, whether or not it is effective in the social world.

Nietzsche developed one example at length in his *Genealogy of Morals*. He suggested that resentment, by its very nature, is an emotion that evades direct expression and confrontation, preferring to alter the world as perceived to suit its own particular vulnerabilities and weaknesses. Thus one might talk about these "internal politics" as the "strategic rearrangement of one's own attitudes," or what Sartre more poetically called "magical transformations of the world." This internal politics of emotion fits in very well with what I have often referred to as the judgmental role of emotion, following certain Stoics, who argued a similar thesis two thousand years ago. For the Stoics, the question was not how our emotional behavior affects the world (negatively or negligibly, most of them argued), but rather how our emotional judgments affected our own outlook on the world, and consequently our chances for happiness.

A somewhat more development-minded and social version of the same idea has been nicely characterized by Ronald de Sousa in his *Rationality of Emotion*, where he introduces the notion of a "paradigm scenario" in which one learns not only the "appropriateness" of certain emotions and emotional behaviors but also their power and significance.[40] What one learns is not only the effect of one's emotional responses on others (their approval or disapproval and responses in return) but also the way an emotion makes one "feel." De Sousa mentions the innate smiling of babies as a good early-in-life example. The smile is at first innate, but at between six weeks and three months, the baby begins to use the smile to get a response.[41] The "feeling" in question is by no means to be confused with the sensations caused by the concurrent physiological or muscular changes or that inchoate sense of "affect" alluded to by authors who lack the facility to pin down the "felt" emotion.[42] It involves, rather, the whole complex phenomenology of the situation in question. One could (and de Sousa encourages this) provide an evolutionary background story for such scenarios. But for my purposes here, it is important to insist that these scenarios are not, and need not be, once they have been established, public or socially situated. No doubt they originally must be public and socially situated. But once one has "internalized" the paradigm of an emotion, one can, as it were, play it back privately, rehearse and instantiate a strategy as if it were public, and, in so doing, achieve a sort of competitive advantage, even if only in one's own eyes.

The Politics of Emotion Language and Theory

Thus far, I have been talking about the politics of emotion strictly in terms of the strategies of emotion. But this is only part of the story. We do not just have emotions. We know that we have them. We label them, talk about them, devise theories about them, and, not incidentally, some of us make a good living off those theories. Here is a second level of competitive advantage, if you will, not in the emotions themselves but in the metalevel at which it is talk about the emotions that comes into play. Because we so easily think of language as something over and above the emotions, a facility or faculty quite separate from the "having" of an emotion, we do not tend to take emotion talk as part of the same set of phenomena. But the truth is, our language, our concepts, and our ideas about emotions are intimately linked with, pervade, and define the emotions themselves. (This is not for a moment to deny that animals and preverbal infants have emotions. It is only to deny that adult humans, who do have such a language, are capable of clearly separating their emotions from their talk about them.)

There are several dimensions of this "meta" reflection on emotions. The simplest has to do with the nature of emotions' names, that is, what we *call* them, or what psychologists refer to as "labeling." Whether a person labels her hostile feelings "hatred," "anger," or "resentment," for example, makes quite a difference in how she will express, evaluate, and talk about her emotion, and consequently, how she "feels." More complicated is the way we talk about and sometimes mythologize emotions. Love in America offers an apt illustration. It is a highly mythologized, one might say "hypercognated," emotion, so much so that cynics have often suggested that "love" is *only* a word, a confusion of fantasies, not a genuine emotion.[43] Finally, and most sophisticated of all, is the way we, as philosophers and psychologists, conceptualize and theorize about emotions. For twenty-five years, the target of my arguments has been the still strong tendency to "primitivize" emotions—by way of denying, I suggest, our responsibility for them. It is, I admit, something of a stretch to say that we "choose" our emotions. But as a self-fulfilling prophecy, as a way of taking control and becoming increasingly aware of the emotional choices we do have, I hold that it is an invaluable piece of existentialist wisdom. One alternative view, that emotions are physiological disruptions and psychic "forces" beyond our control, is also a self-fulfilling prophecy, an invitation to think of ourselves as victims and make excuses for our own behavior. Thus the politics of emotions becomes part and parcel of the politics of personal responsibility and the self-cultivation of the virtues.

Does it matter whether we call it "anger" or "ire" or *riri* or "childishness"— or even "fury" or "outrage" or "moral indignation"? (What are the differences here?) Jean Briggs has told us that in Utku the naming of what we call anger as "childishness" serves to demean the emotion even as it is identified.[44] Similarly, Robert Levi has shown us how in Tahitian, *riri* demonizes the emotion even before it is described. Anger is depicted as a kind of devil possession. "Ire" (directly from the Latin) has a nobility about it that anger doesn't have.[45] "Fury" suggests violence, "outrage" indicates an over-the-top sense of violation, and "moral indignation" suggests righteousness. (Mere "irritation" or "pissed off" is dismissive, by contrast.) "Rage," I suggest, refers to something much more (or much less) than anger, a totalizing neurological response that is, comparatively, out of control and for the most part involuntary. There is more in a name, dear Juliet, than that which arbitrarily names that which smells so sweet. And when one supplies a name to his or her own emotion (as Schachter and Singer have shown), it is the emotion itself, and not merely its name, that alters.

The politics of emotion language is by no means limited to the naming of emotion. Consider, for example, the general dismissal of emotion implied in such terms as "sentimentality" and "getting emotional." Once upon a time, it used to be that "sentimentality" suggested the superior sensibility of aristocrats. No more. Today, it tends to refer to bad art, cheap morals, and a distinctive defect of character. "Emotional" and "sentimental" are employed as put-downs, for example, in the long-standing (and still not extinct) dismissal of women and "effeminate" men from positions of responsibility.[46]

Finally, there is the politics of our theories. The treatments of emotion by Joel Feinberg and Jerome Shaffer cited toward the beginning of this chapter are apt examples of the ways in which emotions are diminished and dismissed through unsympathetic perspectives and demeaning descriptions. Such views are also contained in what are misleadingly called "folk-psychological" theories.[47] A good deal of commonsense theory (and the language of emotions) implies what I have called "the hydraulic theory." This is the dismissive view that emotions are "nothing but" physiological "pressure," as depicted, for example, by Freud in his "boiler system" model of the "psychic apparatus," in the early decades of his career. My objection here is not only theoretical but also existential or ethical. The politics of the hydraulic model (and a good deal of folk psychology) is a politics of irresponsibility: "Our emotions are an 'it' and not part of the 'I'." So, too, those ancient theories that make out love and anger to be a breed of madness rather than strategies. Here is where Sartre and I come charging in with an "existential" theory: No, the emotions do not "take over" or "sweep us away." I have argued that they are strategies, and we *choose* them.[48] Personal responsibility is an important piece of the emotions story, and any theory that does not face up to this is itself political (or should we say politically irresponsible?).

There is one further form of politics regarding emotion that ought to be mentioned, and that is the academic politics of departments and professional prestige. We redefine emotions to suit our methods. Philosophers, not surprisingly, tend to view emotions through the frame of conceptual analysis or as "cognitive science," when they talk about emotions at all, favoring the familiar resources of logic and linguistic analyses wherever available. Neurologists tend to view emotions as first of all neurological. Behavioral psychologists naturally tend to view emotions by way of their expression in behavior, and so on. There is nothing wrong with this, but we all too easily let our politics get in the way of joint efforts and mutual understanding. Philosophers are particularly skilled at dismissing as conceptual confusion or nonsense the most devoted efforts of the social scientists, without applying anything resembling a principle of charity.[49] How much more constructive to seek out what social scientists might be saying that philosophers have systematically ignored or overlooked. In retaliation, predictably, social scientists lampoon "armchair philosophers" without bothering to see what they might learn from conceptual and phenomenological analyses.

Emotions have a multiplicity of dimensions and aspects, and consequently, offer a multiplicity of lines of investigation. We should stop imitating those proverbial blind Persians, each dogmatic about his own particular part of the elephant. If we are aware of the politics that pervade and surround not only emotion but also our treatments of emotion, we can work together and answer some of the hardest questions, namely, how these different approaches fit together. There may be no single objective standpoint. Indeed, there may be no "objective" viewpoint at all where such "subjective" phenomena are concerned. The ultimate "truth" about human emotion may be that we never get outside ourselves or outside of our emotional perspectives, and so there will always be political interests and power relationships both in emotion and in the study of emotions. But the fact that emotions are political may be precisely the reason why our emotional life is or can be so rich and why the emotions remain of such enduring interest to us, even in philosophy.

The Politics of Emotion and Rationality

As if every passion didn't contain its quantum of reason!
Nietzsche, *Will to Power*

It was Socrates, the great champion of reason, who took as his motto the slogan at Delphi, "Know thyself" and the rather extreme injunction "The unexamined life isn't worth living." Part of that knowledge, surely, is our understanding and appreciation of our emotions, which are, after all, much of what does make life worth living. Emotions are a matter, to use a contentious phrase at this juncture, of immanent rationality. To talk about emotions in terms of politics is to argue that the emotions, quite unlike mere feelings and more primitive responses, are purposive, strategic, intelligent—in other words, *rational*. But we will still underestimate the power and importance of emotions if we think of them merely in this means–end, "instrumental" way, as means of getting what we want in the world. To be sure, the emotions are means, but they are often the ends as well. Love is not just a means but an "end in itself." Sadness and grief need not be means to anything, but they nevertheless play an essential role in our lives. Anger may be a means, but it also represents a certain stance in life, a way of being; and the rationality of anger may well come down to the appropriateness or "fit" of that emotional stance in a well-ordered or rational life. What that might mean is a question to which we now must turn.

3

RATIONALITY AND
ITS VICISSITUDES

When some feature of things weighs with people in their
deliberations, we can say that they see it as a reason for or
against a course of action. But which side of the question explains
the other? Does the weight come first and explain what is meant
by seeing something as a reason? On that side lie philosophers
like Hume and St. Augustine, who wrote that "in the pull of the
will and of love appears the worth of everything to be sought or
avoided, to be thought of greater or less value." On the other side
lie philosophers owing allegiance to Plato, Aristotle, and
sometimes Kant. They hold that our passionate natures come
entirely under the control of truth and reason. Apollo rules
Dionysus. The trouble with this sunny picture is that Apollo's
control is unintelligible. . . . Why should we care about anything
. . . ? On Augustine's side there is no difficulty: we talk of reasons
to reflect the fact that we already care.

Simon Blackburn

The word *philosophy* means love of wisdom, but what
philosophers really love is reasoning.

Robert Nozick, The Nature of Rationality

The heart has its reasons, which reason does not know.

Pascal, Pensées

Having said so much about emotion, what about rationality? Is
the defense of emotion and the passionate life a rejection of
rationality, or an addendum, perhaps a complement or even an enhancement

of rationality? But to think in terms of reason *and* the emotions leaves the old dichotomy in place, and though it certainly matters whether one insists that reason should be the slave of the passions or the other way around, the underlying problem, as I see it, is a false and damaging opposition between reason and emotion, as if they occupy two distinct realms of human existence and issue from two separate faculties of the human mind. The passionate life is not living irrationally, without reasons or against reason. Indeed, not only do our emotions provide us with reasons but, as I have suggested, the passionate life is itself a rational way to live. Coming at this the other way around, rationality is not independent of the passions, nor is it merely the logical structure around which the emotions take their proper place. Rationality, in philosophy at least, threatens to become the "thinnest" concept of them all, "thought thinking itself" (as Aristotle declared, in a moment of cosmic myopia). All too often, rationality tends to become pure logic, mere "reasoning," devoid or at least independent of sensitivity, curiosity, and experience.[1]

Note that in the dichotomy "reason and the emotions," reason is singular. Reason, along with reasoning and rationality, suggests a single faculty, exemplified by thinking correctly, by following the proven path to the truth or, at least, to the best argued account or justification. The emotions, by contrast, are plural. We are assured that there are any number of ways of being irrational. But reason, I argue, is no such monolith, and it is only at our peril that we so divorce rationality from our emotional lives and relegate emotions to the realm of the irrational. According to the legacy left to us by Hume ("Reason is and ought to be the slave of the passions, and can never pretend to any other office than to serve and obey them"[2]), rationality is to be construed as a means only, as purely "instrumental." Ultimate ends are neither rational nor irrational. But to take the ultimate goals of life out of the realm of rationality—to put them beyond criticism, evaluation and appraisal—is absurd, as Hume himself clearly recognizes when he comments, " 'Tis not contrary to reason to prefer the destruction of the whole world to the scratching of my finger."[3] Though they are surely also instrumental, the emotions are constitutive of ends—indeed, ultimate ends, the things we *really* care about.

William James speaks of two primary passions in philosophy, "our passion for distinguishing" and "the passion for simplicity." Together, these opposing passions form a "dialectic" that escapes the model of rationality as linear "reasoning" and suggests that rationality is something more complex and interesting than mere "reasoning."[4] It involves the heart as well as the mind (two organs that the Chinese wisely refuse to distinguish [*hsin*]). If philosophy itself is not only driven but also constituted by such passions, then the idea of philosophy as rationality at war with the emotions is surely wrong. To put it another way: It is not as if emotions are to be judged in the almighty court of reason. Reason itself is subject to judgment, and not just—as in Kant and a number of other philosophers—in its own court of law. Indeed, perhaps the question should be, How does rationality satisfy our passions, in particular, our passion for life?[5]

What is rationality? The word suggests nothing of thinness. Quite the contrary, it suggests complexity, organization, even elegance. Rationality, at its core, suggests something rich and textured about our experience. Reasoning, accordingly, is not limited to our ability to criticize and argue or even to "figure things out" but rather includes the perspicacity and vision to see complexity as order, to find meaning in disorder and confusion, to distinguish as well as to simplify. (Chuang Tzu on Confucius: "from the point of view of their sameness, . . . the ten thousand things are one."[6]) Mere criticism and the techniques of argument, without perspicacity, caring and vision, are not only empty. Outside of philosophy, they tend to be blind, threatening us with social catastrophe by promoting cynicism.[7]

"Rationality" is an honorific, an endorsement, a word of praise. To say that something is rational is to give it high marks indeed—in philosophy, the highest marks (given the current timidity about asserting that any philosophical claim is "true"). To say of human beings that they are "rational" is not just a piece of descriptive anthropology. It is also a bit of self-congratulation. To say of a person's behavior or of an idea that it is rational is to say that there is something very right about it, something orderly, fit, appropriate, praiseworthy. Nevertheless, "rationality" remains one of those essentially contested concepts that we can neither give up nor ultimately agree on. In philosophy, reason and rationality may earn high praise, but it is by no means obvious what it is that is being praised—or, sometimes, whether it ought to be.

To limit or focus the notion of rationality to reasoning in philosophy, to merely "instrumental" rationality, is to thin it down to nothing and to deprive it of a rich theological, philosophical, and scientific history.[8] Rationality, whether by way of reflection or of insight, has long had an important relation to God, to the ultimate truth, to the way the world really is. For Plato, rational insight was akin to erotic ecstasy, an insight into the perfect Forms. Rationality—as the demand for insight, and understanding—has always been the subject of philosophy, not just its method or a means or its primary "faculty." And rationality has always been intimately attached to the Good, to values, not just to validity and cleverness. To reduce rationality to reasoning, and reasoning to logic and argument, is to deprive philosophy not only of its passion but also of its substance. To think of the free will problem, for example, as only a number of opposing theses and arguments is to miss the very human pathos and the anxiety that give rise to that problem. So, too, there are many philosophers today who without shame or embarrassment discuss such emotion-charged contemporary problems as abortion and euthanasia as mainly matters of competing arguments. To be sure, this may be preferable to the violence that sometimes punctuates such debates, but surely it leaves out the heart of the matter. Philosophers today all too often praise logic and argument to the exclusion of everything else. This compulsive focus on the thinnest aspect of philosophy has chased good students, the public, and academic colleagues away in droves, and it has led some (perhaps foolishly) to ally themselves with those au courant philosophers who seem to reject rationality altogether.[9]

Rationality in Perspective

> I cannot see the true face of Mount Lu because I am standing on top of it.
>
> Chinese popular saying (*chengyu*)

In India, at a conference on Mount Abu in 1991, a local philosopher is presenting. Slow windup, a few casual words of praise, an expression of modesty, a tweak of humor, a thesis, then another one, a reference to a Hindu myth, another expression of modesty. He shifts from thesis to thesis, building as he goes, speeding up his delivery. I wonder, eager philosophy student that I still am, where he is going and what, really, is the thesis, as he, Nagarjuna-like, offers us theses and countertheses, a few quick arguments, a tentative conclusion that seems like "none of the above." The theses come faster and more furiously, though no theme as such has been stated. Rather, the theme is the stream (of dialogue, although only one voice is actually heard). The speaker has lost track of (or never bothered attending to) the time. He is already twenty-five minutes over his preassigned "slot." The speed increases to a controlled frenzy. Then, in a burst of cosmic chutzpah, it comes to an end. Thinking about it afterward, I realize that I have just enjoyed a philosophical raga.

The contrast provided by the next speaker, a well-known American philosopher, could not have been more pronounced. In the first paragraph, he presented a problem, proposed a thesis, mentioned two famous (Western) philosophers who had written contrary views on the subject, and announced the method and the argument he would pursue. And, indeed, he did just that, in four brief, equally apportioned sections, the first devoted to a study of the problem, the second dedicated to examining (and arguing against) the opposing views of his predecessors, the third the presentation of his own thesis and its argument, and the last (and briefest) mentioning a few loose ends and suggesting a few modest implications. I considered the idea that I had just listened to a classical sonata: utterly predictable, perfect in form, and lasting precisely fifty minutes, the time alloted. But then I thought, No, this wasn't music. It was only form.

The analogy of philosophy and music is not far-fetched; it has been utilized many times before, all the way back to the Indic Vedas and, of course, by Nietzsche. Confucius, and the Greeks, particularly Pythagoras, thought music and philosophy inseparable. The Australian Aborigines thought, and think, that the order of the world was created and is maintained through song. But as a way of illuminating rationality, the comparison of philosophy to music has certain additional benefits. Different musics have at their basis different senses of order, different rationalities, so to speak. My Western colleagues shared my confusion about the direction and nature of the Indian raga, and the Indians, not surprisingly, found the Western talks stiff, static, uncreative, and not very interesting. (A famous Indian musician, Pandit Nikhil Banerjee, was taken to a Mistoslav Rostrapovich concert, his first exposure to Western music. He sat in silence, aghast. Afterward, he complained, "He played out of tune the whole time, he never developed any themes, and it sounded as if someone else had written the music for him."[10])

In India, a culture with a two-thousand-year history of logic and careful linguistic analysis, one of the central concepts of philosophy is *rasa*, a term that refers to the emotional tone that pervades a work of art.[11] Everyone— musician and listeners alike—is an active participant. Order (*rta*) is defined by a complex emotional (and technical) progression, the goal of which is to "gradually become free of limitations, selfless," and see the world from a nonobjective (but not thereby subjective) point of view.[12] Lewis Rowell comments: "To equate *rasa* with mood is to reduce the concept to a cliche."[13] It is worth noting that Aristotle, in his classic aesthetic work (*Poetics*), highlighted drama, and (with Plato) downplayed the importance of music. By contrast, Bharata's *Natyasatra*, the primary aesthetic text of India, celebrates music above all. Aristotle, not surprisingly, emphasizes the logic of the play, the plot. Bharata, by contrast, focuses in on *bhava*—affect, emotion, mental state.[14] The "logic" is to be found in the shared emotion, encapsulated (like the leitmotif in Western Romantic music) in the themes that play against one another until they fuse in ecstasy.

What counts as rationality depends on what is expected in the way of an account, a "reckoning." Philosophers who talk too glibly about rationality neglect the possibility of different kinds of accounts, different styles of reckoning. They may emphasize rigor at the cost of creativity and passion, neither of which is known for its neatness. Or they may ignore development and "flow" in favor of eternal (static) soundness, truth, and validity. Looking further east, we might say that too many philosophers ignore *Tao* in favor of *Logos*, insist on one kind of order while abandoning another, perhaps a more "natural" one. As we know from visiting one another's desks and offices, one person's order is another's chaos.[15] One people's rationality is to another lack of imagination, even a refusal to see what is right in front of their eyes. It is one thing to define an extremely "thin" nonnormative conception of rationality, such as the ability to manipulate symbols or the choice of the most efficient means to an end or the inference to the best explanation. It is something quite different to specify what a well-ordered life or, in a different vein, a rich and all-embracing understanding of nature, should be.

The rationality of science and the scientific method is the starting point for most contemporary discussions of rationality, whether science is taken as the paradigm or, the recent intellectual fad, as the target of criticism. But the idea that rationality admits of perspectives raises serious questions. Is there such a thing as "the unity of science," not just in terms of the reduction of one scientific theory to another but also in terms of the method(s) of scientific research and the nature of the questions themselves? Or, to touch a raw nerve, does it make sense to say that, from a religious perspective, creationism might be more rational than evolutionary theory? (I am not talking about "creation science," which seems to me a fatal strategic error.) If one admits that evolution has the whole weight of science behind it, does it follow that to accept the account in Genesis is irrational? If we define rationality in terms of the scientific method, in terms of evidence and constrained inference and so on, what are we then to say about the rationality *of* science—simply (and unconvincingly) that it is rational *by definition?* Is religion then, as some of the Enlightenment philosophers insisted, inherently irrational, mere superstition? What about aesthetic visions of nature, which may offer something different than the elegance of scientific theories and an appreciation of the wonders of science?[16] I was having coffee with a poet friend of mine, and he coined a few brilliant phrases about the lonesome flower that was straining for attention at our table. Old biologist that I was, I thought, clumsily, "turgor, tropism." Which of us was being more insightful, more rational?

To what extent does the context determine the standards of rationality, and to what extent do the demands of rationality overflow and trump contextual considerations? Are science and the scientific method unlimited in their reach, or are they just one more set of social practices with no special claim to truth, as some recent "science theorists" have argued? Is an exciting myth less rational than a dry, statistical study? On what grounds? And those grounds better not be simply the fact that the myth is exciting and the study is dry, and therefore rational. Is a life full of risk and adventure less rational than a life of minimal risk (Nietzsche's blinking couch potato, the "last man")? One common definition of rationality (as risk aversion, maximizing security, "minimax") begs the question. Rationality can act as a set of blinders, as rationalization, as well as a clarifying lens on the world.

Some Reasons for Being Suspicious
(of Reason)

> I can stand brute force, but brute reason is quite unreasonable. There
> is something unfair about its use. It is hitting below the intellect.
>
> Oscar Wilde, *Portrait of Dorian Gray*

As an existentialist of sorts, I have always been suspicious of philosophical
talk about reason. "Reason" is one of those glowing words in philosophy that
are endowed with theological overtones and interpretations. Some philosophers
insist that God Himself is "Reason" (thus short-circuiting any question about
whether believing in Him is rational). Many others modestly describe reason
as "Godlike." Reason is often presented as if it were the ultimate arbiter, the
supreme court of all human endeavors, the definitive method for resolving all
disputes and disagreements, in and out of philosophy. Defenders of reason
sometimes assure us (more often simply presume) that to every dilemma there
is a right answer, to every paradox there is a solution, to every (sensible)
question there is an answer, for every mystery and miracle a rational explanation. The reigning premise of the seventeenth and eighteenth centuries (the
Enlightenment) was that everything could be explained, "the principle of
sufficient reason."[17] The universe is rational, because "God wouldn't do anything without a reason." Human behavior and human society, because we
are rational animals, can also be put in order, by human hands and human
thinking, according to the same God-given reason and its natural laws.

With such mighty claims and high expectations, with such promises and
a vision of transcendental unity in all things, it is no wonder that our modern
age—the age of two world wars, nuclear weapons, and now the "New World
Order"—is rife with disappointment, frustration and anger, all manifesting
itself in "a rage against reason," in Richard Bernstein's apt alliterative phrase.
And, indeed, the promises of reason nowadays all too often resemble political
campaign promises. Too often, it is apparent that the emphasis on reason is
really just rhetoric, an attempt to persuade the opposition of the superiority
of one's position simply by calling it "rational," by submitting an argument
that cannot be refuted and is thereby mistaken for a proof. (One of the more
curious but enduring sophistical rhetorical devices in philosophy is the insistence that someone's failure to refute an argument for an outrageous position
is thereby an argument in favor of the position.)

There is a thesis afoot to the effect that rationality is a male, Caucasian,
capitalist plot against women, people of color, and third world cultures. So
stated, this is surely a misunderstanding of rationality. But I can readily sympathize with those who suspect that what is called "reason" and then employed against their sensibilities, customs, and beliefs is nothing more than

those schoolboy debating tricks that were mastered at Oxbridge and other elite universities, and became part of the armament of colonial rule. To put down the righteous anger provoked by exploitation or oppression in the name of being "reasonable" is just too obviously a power ploy. To dismiss the inarticulate indignation of the uneducated and deprived because their case is not rationally (that is, properly) stated is, to put it minimally, to beg the question at hand. Too often, rationality is invoked to do no more than defend one's own interests; we have all met Kantians who can find a rational (even "categorical") principle to defend just about anything, even grubby self-interest.

And then, of course, there is that use of "rational" whose function is that of a damper, a wet blanket, to put down compassion as well as the hotter passions in favor of cold, dispassionate reason. The cause of those who really care is dismissed with extreme prejudice, while the policies of those who can claim "rationality"—often in a particularly narrow, economic sense, favorable primarily to themselves—are favored. And how often the rational point of view turns out to be the uninterested (as opposed to the disinterested) point of view, the viewpoint of someone who is uninvolved, disengaged, even uncaring. Indeed, for every accusation of "irrationality," I would suggest that some explanatory elaboration be required, for example, "uneducated," "clumsy," "inattentive," "inefficient," "self-defeating," "not in accordance with procedures," "not conducive to the best outcome," "overly caring," "unjust," "unfair," or, sometimes, "overly fair and against our interests." In philosophy, I suspect, the elaboration will usually turn out to be not so much "invalid," "unsound," or "incoherent" as something more along the lines of "heartfelt," "overly emotional," "too personally involved," or "embarrassing to me." I have often noted, in philosophical discussion, the put-down, "not philosophical," that is "not sufficiently aloof and detached," or, what might be understood pathologically, "not sufficiently anal compulsive," that is, "not playing the philosophical game." "Rationality" thus becomes an honorific whose elaboration may show it for what it is, cold professionalism, callousness, or insensitivity—or perhaps neurosis—in disguise.

Needless to say, philosophers (or most of them) are in favor of rationality. Even those who attack it (Kierkegaard, Nietzsche, and Heidegger, for example) typically do so on recognizably rational grounds, employing argument, analogy, and counterexample, not to mention the fact that they employ thought and language, and, for the most part, do so grammatically and logically. But one should not give too much weight to this only apparent self-contradiction. Philosophers often exercise great ingenuity to establish what they in fact all began by acknowledging: that rationality is that virtue best exemplified by philosophers. Ideally, rationality might dispense with the philosopher altogether and become pure thought thinking itself, but short of this divine purity, the Anglo-American philosopher, merely finite as he or she may be, becomes the very measure of reason. All other putatively rational creatures, from the squid to the dolphin and the ape, from "primitive" and "developing" societies to the most sophisticated cultures of the East, not to mention the French, the Italians, and the Finns, are more or less rational insofar as they are or are not capable of doing what philosophers in the (narrowly defined) Western tradition do so well—articulating abstract concepts, distinguishing *modus ponens* and *modus tollens*, gathering evidence and mustering arguments, rooting out and criticizing presuppositions (including, of course, their own), reflecting on the meaningfulness of what they say, and disputing with those who raise objections against them.

The concept of rationality, however, admits of no simple interpretation. Technical meanings have proliferated, and ever more stringent criteria have been applied to guarantee that, in the last analysis, no one could possibly qualify as a rational agent unless he or she had pursued at the minimum a baccalaureate, if not a Ph.D. in philosophy. ("What will philosophers do when they teach an ape to speak?" Cambridge philosopher G. E. M. Anscombe was once asked. "They'll up the ante," she replied. And, indeed, they have.) It is often said or at least implied that rationality demands not only the use of a complex self-referential language and the usual demands for consistency and coherence, but also a self-critical metatheory.[18] Nor is this a strictly Western inflation of the currency of reason. In a detailed analysis of the Vedic concept of *pramana*, J. N. Mohanty, one of the world's foremost Sanskrit scholars, has argued that rationality not only must be conceived in terms of a philosophical view but also requires a "theory of evidence, rational justification, and critical appraisal . . . and also a theory of these theoretical practices."[19] To insist that the rational life requires such thoroughgoing theoretical articulation ("the examined life") would render most of us immobile.[20]

Philosophers ever since Socrates (who may or may not have had such a "theory" himself) have made philosophical reflection the hallmark of rationality, even a condition for a life "worth living." Needless to say, this eliminates from candidacy a great many cultures in which self-reflection and self-criticism have not been encouraged or developed, myth and metaphor remain far more interesting than vulgar and unimaginative literal description, the theory of knowledge is not an interesting or an intelligible set of concerns, and "justification" may be a matter of authority or tradition and not of intellectual autonomy. Nor would such a notion of rationality apply to virtually any species of "higher" animal, no matter how intelligent.[21] Nevertheless, watching our dogs, Lou and Fritz, discover yet a new way of breaking out of their fenced-in yard or a new ploy for getting us to open the Dog Treat jar, we have no hesitation to attribute some sort of rationality to them, just as we have no hesitation withholding it when they do something surprisingly stupid (Fritz runs through the twenty-inch doorway with a thirty-six inch-stick in his mouth, not for the first time. Lou scratches at a sore until she has to be carted to the vet, yet again.) The question What does it mean to be "rational"? admits of many answers, depending on exactly what is being asked and what is at stake. If it is only the chauvinist celebration of our peculiarly self-destructive species, I think we would be right to postpone the party.[22]

Once we have given up the self-reflective overlay superimposed on the good life by such philosophers as Aristotle and Socrates, who insisted absurdly that "the unexamined life is not worth living," and the equally chauvinistic and angst-ridden emphasis on "purifying" reflection and "absolute freedom" imposed on us by Jean-Paul Sartre, it becomes quite evident that a rational (and possibly happy) life may be readily available to those who do not display any predilection or talent for philosophy or reflection whatever. Indeed, on the other side of the coin, we should remember that Dostoevsky, Kierkegaard, Camus, and Miguel de Unamuno, as well as a number of iconoclastic ancient Greek and Asian philosophers, insisted that rationality *means* anxiety and suffering. Nietzsche remarked (in his *Gay Science*) that reflective consciousness becomes philosophically interesting only when we realize how dispensable it is, and much of Nietzsche's philosophy is an apologia for the more "instinctual" and the less reflective aspects of creative life.[23]

Philosophers sometimes insist that rationality is essentially bound up with reflection, with thinking, with "second-order" evaluations (preferences regarding our various desires, acceptance concerning our beliefs).[24] But it is the behavior itself that is rational or irrational, not the evaluation of it. (This in turn may be rational or irrational, of course, but let's not leap to the meta-level, to discussions about methods and standards and optimum strategies.) Rationality does not need to be reflective, although reflective beings such as ourselves are obviously more complicated in certain interesting ways. The paradigm of scientific rationality is a faulty foundation from which to gain a general understanding of rationality. So, too, is "the examined life." An excessive emphasis on language or thought or deliberation or principles may be demanding too much of rationality. Or too little, for I do not see this overemphasis on reasoning and articulate rationality as a matter of neglect. I see it as a device for restricting the philosophical discussion—and perhaps the concept of the good life, too—to just those skills and personality traits typically possessed by professional philosophers.

From Sums to Selfishness: Reason as an Essentially Contested Concept

> The madman is not the man who has lost his reason. The madman is the man who has lost everything except his reason.
>
> G. K. Chesterton, *Orthodoxy*

Rationality is one of those "essentially contested concepts" of philosophy (like "freedom," "truth," and "justice") that play a polemical as well as a normative role in our conversations. While the word may have neutral meanings, as the mere exercise or application of certain skills, "rationality" remains an honorific, referring to a virtue. But that virtue is variously described. Bertrand Russell once wryly suggested that rationality is "our ability to do sums." Many philosophers have indeed treated the capacity for abstract thought as the epitome of rationality. In its practical applications, however, the role of abstract reason is by no means so clear, not because of the casuist's problem of fitting principle to particular but because the principles themselves often seem superfluous. Understanding a practice, knowing how to proceed, often renders irrelevant the abstract descriptive knowledge of the process, the *knowing that* that philosophers, in general, prize so highly.[25] Masters at their craft are often inarticulate, or inadequately articulate, in attempting to explain just what it is they do. Their apprentices, who would probably not learn much from the master's description—even if he or she could provide one—learn by doing, by imitating, by experimenting with the process themselves. Even mathematics, the "doing of sums," is learned mainly by doing, by imitating—through practice, not theory. The theory of what one is doing when one does even the simplest arithmetical calculations remains the most difficult and essentially technical aspect of philosophy, the philosophy of mathematics (the one in which Russell established his brilliance[26]). Wittgenstein (one of Russell's students) later went on to argue that theory can be worse than irrelevant to mathematics, insofar as "knowing how to go on" is something one can know only from within the practice. Rationality as "theory," Wittgenstein deeply believed, was a limitation, perhaps even an obstacle, and not the royal road to wisdom and happiness.

I have no qualms about accepting our ability to do mathematics, no matter how modest, as proof of our rationality in one obvious sense. But math isn't life, as our students repeatedly tell us; and living a rational life, as some of our most brilliant math heroes have demonstrated, is not necessarily enhanced by doing mathematics. In general, a calculating life is not the most rational, both because it overextends the proper role of calculation and because of what it leaves out. (Russell's own peculiar lovelife, a source of tremendous indignation for Wittgenstein, speaks volumes on the subject.) Rationality in living cannot be reduced to a formula or an algorithm, and one of the many possibilities is that the life of reason is by its very nature not rational, that thinking disrupts the natural rhythm of life.[27]

Most philosophers, of course, ape Socrates and insist that a life without reflection, if not "not worth living," nevertheless lacks an essential dimension. But is rationality necessary for the good life, or is it just one of several possibilities? Is living well the same thing as living coherently, with reasons for what one does? Or would it make sense to live "according to nature," perhaps without coherence and without bothering with reasons? If with reasons, which reasons? What kind of reasons? Could the rational life—the best life—be a life ruled by instinct, by compassion, by affection, without reflection or rationalization? Such a life may not be what most of us recognize to be a distinctively human life, but that, perhaps, just suggests the depth of our seduction by the wiles of rationality. More plausibly, we can certainly ask to what extent the hyperrationality of the philosophical life, the reflective life, is mandatory (as Socrates suggests), and to what extent it is, as Nietzsche notes, dispensable.

To what extent is rational action measured by the amount of deliberation that precedes the action, and to what extent is acting rationally simply determined by the nature of the action itself?[28] Consider (again) this familiar example: One person is generous. Generosity just flows from him, unthinkingly, as water flows from a fountain. He has no "theory" of generosity. He has never thought about why he gives, nor does he think much about to whom he gives. He has no principle "Be generous," although he is generous. Compare him with the Man of Practical Reason, who insists that every potential act of generosity is a matter for deliberation and, ultimately, a matter of principle. There are so many questions to be asked: Who is this? Why does he need it? Can I afford it? What will be the consequences? How will he spend it? What about all of the others in need? Would he do the same for me if I were in his position? What sort of precedent will this set? Will my act encourage or discourage others? Will my act of generosity encourage the government to cut more social welfare programs? Is this an example of treating the other person as mere means (to show off my generosity) rather than as an end? And so on, to the heights of ethical theory. In the end, the Man of Practical Reason also gives. But is he generous? Or has this virtuous act been so plastered over with doubts, analysis, questions, and principles that it has lost the spontaneity necessary if it is to count as generosity. Perhaps the Man of Practical Reason still deserves credit, for having a good policy. But it seems to me plausible that his goodness has been compromised, not enhanced, by rational deliberation. Without being a bit the behaviorist, I would say that the rationality of generosity lies in the behavior, not in the mental exercise that precedes the action.

Contra much of philosophical ethics, rationality in the moral life is not, for the most part, deliberative reasoning but its very opposite: spontaneous, "natural" action. This is the enduring appeal not only of virtue ethics with its concrete questions of character and context but also, I think, of some forms of utilitarianism (notably Mill's) and other forms of consequentialism in ethics, despite the fact that they also involve overly abstract principles (e.g., the principle of utility).[29] Necessarily, these forms of ethics make reference to concrete situations, to the actual people involved in a decision or a course of action, to such questions as "What would actually happen?" "Who was actually harmed?" "Who, exactly, is this person?" To be sure, utilitarianism can manifest itself in an irrational compulsiveness (by way of the quantitative calculus introduced by Jeremy Bentham, for example, and worries about "preference," "commensurability," and "satisfaction"[30]) but, as such, utilitarianism is the banal humanistic reminder that people (and not only people) count more than abstract principles, however "rational."[31]

Unlike "deontological" theory, Millian utilitarianism and virtue ethics dispense, for the most part, with ethical general principles (and, according to some practitioners, dispense with ethical theory as well). Ethics is necessarily thick, not thin, not a matter of rational principle but of concrete considerations. Reason still enters in, all over the place, of course. The utilitarian has to figure out which is the best course of action for all concerned; the person of virtuous character acts "with reason." But this does not necessarily mean deliberation, reflection, and reasoning, and even in Aristotle it is far from clear that rational behavior is necessarily reflective behavior.[32] What rational action clearly requires is that sense of measure or *phronesis* which Aristotle took to be the key to ethics, but seeing a situation with understanding and compassion, and "judgment" and judging, are not the same as reasoning.

Many philosophers, misunderstanding Kant, have argued that rationality in ethics means absolute impersonality, the purified ability to formulate and follow abstract moral principles rather than, say, personal inclinations, conscience, or the "promptings of the heart."[33] Rationality, so conceived, is sometimes described as the ability to imagine oneself as "no one in particular," viewing the world or the situation "from nowhere."[34] But since, to say the obvious, we always view our world from somewhere, meaning not only from a perspective but also with a lifetime of experience, emotions, and values, there is no such rationality, no possibility of such Godlike objectivity, strictly understood. Nor does this impossible God's-eye perspective make sense even as an aspiration, an ideal.[35] In the face of such extreme and impossible demands, the rejection of "reason," in the sense presupposed by such theories, is a natural and tempting alternative.

There is one conception of rationality, however, that is the very opposite of impossible idealism and deserves special mention, if only for the purpose of heaping abuse. In opposition to such selfless views of rationality, there has been a cynical appropriation of the honorific "rationality" to refer, often straightforwardly, though sometimes subtly, to self-interest—not quite to say "selfishness"—as such. According to this now widespread notion (allegedly derived from the philosophy of Thomas Hobbes), rationality is simply the ability to get what you want in a competitive, noncooperative situation, a context in which what is rational (maximizing one's own interests) may be quite at odds with what is optimal or best for everyone. Philosophers who hold such a thesis take great pains to demonstrate that reason demands maximizing one's desires, but within constraints that *ideally* might be optimal for all.[36] This "realist" (in fact cynical) version of rationality, sometimes called "enlightened egoism," has the virtue of riding on a motivational theory that, these days, usually goes unchallenged. What is motivating is self-interest. Rationality, accordingly, is the pursuit of self-interest—in an "enlightened" way, of course. The right to pursue happiness is now translated as "Everyone has the right to pursue what they want, whatever they want, and no one has the right to deny them this (except insofar as it interferes with the equally valid pursuits of others)." Instrumental rationality has never been quite so vulgarly conceived.

Politically, this theory sometimes asserts itself as a particularly virulent form of libertarianism, embellished with a concept of "inalienable rights." In philosophy (even more enthusiastically in economics and the social sciences), it gives rise to "game theory" (also "rational choice theory"), innocent-sounding disciplines coupled with a cornucopia of mathematical techniques and paradoxes that hide a hideous vision of life. To be sure, game theorists cover this vision with all sorts of disclaimers (for instance, there is no specification of *whose* goals or preferences are to be satisfied), but the unavoidable suggestion of the theory is that rationality is selfishness and selfishness is rationality, a bleak view that, luckily, most game theorists do not pursue into their everyday social lives.[37]

This use of "rationality" as smart selfishness is diametrically at odds with the older sense of the term, common to Kant and the utilitarians, in which to think "rationally" in ethics is precisely *not* to think in terms of one's own interests. It is also opposed to that sense of rationality which takes the ultimate good to be not the good of the individual but the good of the whole, the community, the larger society, humanity. The good of the individual is by no means excluded in this larger pursuit—indeed, the good of the individual is both the result and the measure of the larger public good. But the fact that "rationality" can refer to such different ends—the strategic interests of a selfish (even if "enlightened") individual, the public good, and the principle that says "Do not make an exception or special case of yourself"—suggests that the nature of rationality is by no means settled but remains a matter of considerable dispute.[38]

The Rationality of Emotions and the Emotional Grounding of Rationality

> The misunderstanding of passion and reason, as if the latter existed as an entity by itself, and not rather as a state of the relations between different passions and desires . . .
>
> Nietzsche, *Will to Power*

Among the many meanings that have been suggested for the concepts of reason and rationality, none has been more destructive than the attempt to systematically oppose reason to emotion, to think of rationality as reasonableness, which in turn is flatly opposed to "being emotional." To be rational is to be dispassionate, "cool," unmoved by emotion. By way of contrast, I argue that the opposition between rationality and emotion needs to be reconsidered, and the priority of dispassionate (or passionless) reason deeply questioned.

With this in mind, let me suggest that we would not go so wrong in thinking of rationality in terms of having the right emotions, caring about the right sorts of things. The "right sorts of things" would be other people (and animals), to start with, truth, freedom and justice, by extension. Too much of the history and too many conceptions of rationality have cut off caring from the more cold-blooded concepts, rules, reasons, norms, principles, symbols, and arguments that make up the basic vocabulary of philosophical rationality. But what if we started to think about rationality not as the philosopher's or the social scientist's special subject matter, but as a matter of cultivated, engaged sensitivity? What would our philosophy look like as the study, but more important as the practice, of rationality in *that* sense?

If we were to view rationality, first of all, as caring about the right things, it becomes obvious that we are no longer talking "instrumentally," except perhaps trivially (in order to live a good life, in order to be virtuous). Caring about the right things, one could argue, is an essential precondition of living a good life, not a mere means. Being virtuous *is* caring about the right things. Rationality, as Aristotle argued, is first of all a matter of ends, not merely of means. Happiness and well-being are constituted, not just helped along, by the right emotions, by caring about the right things. The very notion of "the right things" opens up all sorts of questions and dangers, but it is the caring part of the equation that should draw our primary attention. That points directly to the emotions, and although how one determines what things are "right" may well be shot through with personal, cultural, and moral conflicts, at least we are now clearly in the realm of ethics and not in the no-man's land of "rational choice" and game theory, where preferences eclipse values and questions of strategy trump moral intuitions. Rationality once again becomes the quest for the good, and the good in turn can be understood in terms of our most important passions. Rationality is no longer the thin set of procedures, mere "reasoning," presented to us by many philosophers.

One cannot talk about the rationality of emotions without first getting clear about which of many conceptions of rationality is being appealed to. The more abstract the conception of rationality, the less appropriate (and consequently less rational) the emotions will appear. Insofar as rationality is exemplified by mathematics, we would not expect the emotions to score very well by that measure. With a sufficiently earthy and practical conception of reason and a sufficiently rich conception of emotion, however, the complementarity and the interdependency of reason and emotions—"the rationality of emotions"—is easy to justify. Emotions, we can say without much argument, provide reasons for action. What is perhaps not so obvious is that they provide reasons for belief, or at least reasons for looking for evidence of one kind rather than another, or reasons for accepting a conclusion rather than struggling to refute it. Whether emotions provide good reasons for action or belief or the right kinds of reasons for rational behavior is a lot more of a challenge, but here we should insist that no a priori, across-the-board answer will do. Some emotions are justified or at least appropriate, and others are not, depending on the context and the culture as well as the specific circumstances. Some philosophers would argue that emotions are never the right kind of reason for rational action, although they might be considered more or less desirable motivational aids. (Kant is sometimes interpreted this way.) The eleventh-century logician Saint Anselm took the passion of faith as the right motivation for reason, and thus (as Kant did) rendered faith itself rational and rationality faithful.

Some of the plausibility attached to the view that emotions are never rational (that is, they are nonrational, not irrational) stems from the archaic view that they are bestial and primitive (we share them with the animals) or the modern, sophisticated view that they are of physiological, especially neurological, origin. On the first, even if we were to agree that (most) animals are not rational insofar as they do not evidently think in any systematic way, it does not follow that they are not rational in any number of other ways: their ability to choose means most conducive to a desired end, their acting for reasons (even if they cannot explain them), their following rules (for example, the rather complex rules of the pack), their ability to recognize and to a limited extent understand symbols, and, of course, their ability to recognize and to choose the right ends (for themselves or their group or their offspring) and care about the right things (for them, which is not always a matter of self-interest). Insofar as we and they share these varieties of rationality as well as (some of) our emotional repertoire, the much-vaunted superiority of our species in matters of abstract rationality are of no particular relevance. As for the modern, sophisticated view, perhaps it is enough to say that our most sophisticated rational faculties and activities, as well as the most mundane, undeniably have their origins in the brain. One might allow a moment for the argument that mere hormonal disturbances surely do not count as rational, but (a) no hormonal disturbance by itself is sufficient to count as an emotion and (b) again, the physiological origins of an emotion may have no bearing on its rationality. *Au contraire*, sometimes a good rush of adrenaline allows us to be our most rational, cutting through the intellectual sludge that can accumulate after too much abstract philosophizing.

Consistency presents us with special problems, since it is clear both that emotions are sometimes capable of a vicious consistency—in obsession and intractability, for instance—and that our emotions are often "mixed": love and hate, most dramatically, but also grief and gratitude, joy and sadness, anger and shame, loathing and pity. The rational status of obsession and intractability seems to me to be dependent on the specific emotion. Being obsessed with love requited or justice denied seems rational indeed; being obsessed with revenge is rarely so. The intractability of love, I have argued, might well be seen as one of its virtues, but not, usually, the intractability of anger or jealousy. On "mixed" or ambivalent emotions, on the other hand, the argument seems similarly particular to the case. If one emotion is rational and a contrary emotion is rational, the logic of emotion would seem to say that the two emotions together are rational. Of course, much more would have to be said about what it means to have contrary emotions "together" (do they sit side by side? Do they alternate like an AC electric current? Do they occupy different perspectives and wait to be noticed in turn? Do they intermingle like two different colors of paint, to form a vibrant purple or a muddy brown?).

One might make a philosopher's point and insist that two emotions together cannot incorporate a *logical* inconsistency, a dreaded "P & not-P," but emotional inconsistency is rarely so unsubtle. To be both joyful and envious that my friend has just won an award I desired, for example, will include feeling both glad and sad, but one might say either that these emotions have two different objects ("My friend won the award and he's happy" and "He won the award, I didn't") or, if one insists that there is only one object ("He won the award, lucky guy, and I didn't"), one might say that there are nonetheless two different reasons for the different emotions.[39] The conflicting emotions may include such thoughts as "I deserved that award, not she" and "She deserved that award more than me" in fairly rapid succession, but one might argue that this is not so much logical inconsistency as it is uncertainty: alternatively entertaining, not resolutely asserting, the two propositions at once. But however one finesses the apparent logical inconsistency, the plain fact seems to be that we have such mixed emotions a good deal of the time, and it is far more rational to have both emotions together than either one alone (or neither).

I have already insisted (and elsewhere argued) that emotions necessarily involve "cognition"—concepts, perception, judgments, beliefs, inferences, perspectives—but the sense in which or the extent to which this involves symbolic interaction, language, and articulation is a sensitive matter in any discussion of the ways in which emotions are or are not rational. Throughout this chapter, precisely for this reason, I have tried to batter away at the philosopher's pretension that rationality always requires articulation and argumentation. Our emotions are often "felt" much more clearly than they can be articulated, but this does not mean that they cannot be rational. They are rational insofar as they "fit," if they are appropriate, if someone else could articulate reasons to support them even if the subject cannot do so him- or her- or itself (in the case of an animal or an infant, for instance). An emotion is rational if it is suited to relevant norms, whether or not the norms or the suitability or the relevance can be reflected on or explicated. (Here, I want to be very careful about what is read into Gibbard's crucial phrase "acceptance of norms."[40]) But to think that an emotion—or all emotions—is/are irrational (or nonrational) because it/they need not be (whether or not it they can be) articulated seems to me just—irrational. It is the emotion itself, not just its articulation, that can be rational (or irrational), that fits, is appropriate, relevant, or life-enhancing (or not).

If rationality entails being able to stand up to critical evaluation and deliberation, then only some emotions come off as rational. But surely there are a great many such emotions, although we are not often called upon to defend them. The question is only whether we could defend them if we had to (including to ourselves, of course). If rationality demands actually standing up to critical evaluation and deliberation, then we might complain that this is far too Socratic a requirement, too adamant that our emotions not only can be but also must be subjected to scrutiny and justification. We do not have to justify ourselves or our feelings, at least not all of the time. But surely the opposite view, that our feelings need not and cannot be justified, is also wrong. ("I'm just telling you how I feel.") We often defend our emotions. ("I have a right to be angry because . . . ," "I'm sad because . . . ," "How do I love you? Let me count the reasons.") The mistake is thinking that an emotion is rational only when it has in fact been defended; it is sufficient that it *could be* defended. If the rationality of emotion is said to require employing critical evaluation and deliberation as part of (and not just concerning) the emotion, again, the demand is excessive. But it is not obvious that emotions are incapable of including such activity. Granted, emotions are typically unreflective and nondeliberative. They do not necessarily include their own critical evaluations. Some seem to be devoid of any such critical ability—"blind" rage, "blind" faith, "blind" love, "blind" jealousy, for example—but note that "blindness" marks off an unusual and probably pathological emotional condition, not the standard case. Other emotions, even though they may involve elaborate criticism, evaluation, and deliberation, fail to stand up to some larger scrutiny—for instance, resentment, hatred and the urge for revenge—even though backed by powerful reasons or rationalization. But what should be obvious even from this short discussion is that even the critical concerns of rationality and the aims and objects of emotions are intimately linked, and that far from being the "opposite" of emotion, critical rationality may be part and parcel of the life of emotions. The passionate life is not a life devoid of critical acumen.

Rationality as autonomy presents a special challenge in the realm of emotions. Insofar as autonomy means "free from the influence of emotions," of course, there is very little to be said. But insofar as the notion refers to a certain independence of mind, a certain "ownness" to one's feelings, thoughts, and actions, it is often said, and with some truth, that a person is never more him- or herself than in a passion, in the particular circumstances about which he or she cares most. Reason and reasoning, by their very nature, involve rules and procedures not one's own. (Kant could talk about reason's "dictates" while defending autonomy.) But passions, even if similar and even if shared, are very much one's own. (Thousands of people can share grief, for example, but each nevertheless has it as his or her own.) More challenging still is the question of whether emotions are autonomous in the sense of being, in some sense, voluntary acts rather than sufferings. I have argued elsewhere that they should be so considered, but that would take us far afield for now.[41] Perhaps it is enough to note that our thoughts and beliefs are not obviously acts of will either, but nevertheless we hold ourselves responsible for informing, maintaining, and sometimes changing them. (Nietzsche: "A thought comes when 'it' will, not when I will."[42]) We take them to be very much our own. If rationality means autonomy it is by no means obvious that the emotions are not in many ways rational and exemplary, not enemies, of that feature so praised by philosophers.

Insofar as ("instrumental") rationality is restricted to means and not ends, tools and capacities and not ultimate goals or truths, there is no single argument to the effect that emotions are rational or not. Ronald de Sousa suggests that "appropriateness" is the "truth" of emotions—what makes them rational. I think this is an enormous insight.[43] It bypasses a great many annoying traditional problems that begin with an overly rigid distinction between judgments of value and judgments of fact. It also locates emotions in their proper context—not as abstract propositions ("judgments" misconstrued) but as essentially situational, defined by their "fit." Here the purposiveness of emotions becomes critical, and to say that emotions are rational is to say that they serve purposes, often well but sometimes poorly. But to talk about the rationality of emotions is not to say only this. They are instruments, if you like, in the same sense that other practiced, intelligent responses are instruments: means of coping with the world, ways of reacting and responding to the world, modes of interacting and (in the deepest sense) being-with other people. But it is often the case that our means become ends, and we sometimes confuse the one for the other. Emotions can serve as instruments of rationality (and of irrationality too, of course), but they also frame that rationality within which (and toward which) they function.

Here, as elsewhere, it is essential that we do not think of the emotions as too "thin," as if they were atomistic flotsam in the stream of experience. An emotion is not so much an element or item "in" experience as it is the ordering of experience. Love, quite the contrary of interfering with rational order in our lives, puts our priorities right. Anger, even when it is clearly inappropriate or irrational, does not so much intrude as it reorders our priorities. Emotional experience is not an odd, "unextended" phenomenon in our heads, so to speak; it is the ordering structure of our being-in-the-world. This "ordering structure" is nothing less than rationality, and to speak of emotions is already to speak of our reasons for living. Emotions are not just means or instruments. They provide the ends, the well-earned sense of flourishing that Aristotle talked about as *eudaimonia*, with all of its rich component passions of pride, affection, and friendship—in short, the meanings of life. What more could rationality demand?

An adequate discussion of the rationality of emotions cannot remain on the level of emotions (and rationality) in general, however. It requires a case-by-case typology, a detailed analysis of the conditions for rational (warranted) anger, and jealousy, and love, and grief. Every emotion involves what Robert Gordon calls its own conceptual "structure" of judgments that can be well-wrought or foolish, warranted or unwarranted, correct or incorrect.[44] Anger involves judgments of blame; jealousy includes judgments about a potential threat of loss. Love involves evaluative judgments, typically overblown, but so does hatred. Grief involves recognition of a loss; vengeance—often maligned in philosophy—already involves a small-scale theory of justice, an "eye for an eye," or what Kant much less violently but more ambiguously called "equality." In all of these examples, one can readily recognize what can go wrong, what might be "dis-ordered" or inappropriate in the emotion, and consequently what is required for it to go right, for it to be "in order," for it to be appropriate and functional in the situation.

In anger, for instance, one can be confused about the facts. He or she is still angry, but wrongfully so. And if one has leapt to conclusions or has not examined the readily available evidence, he or she is foolishly so. One can be right about the facts but wrong about the harm done or the blameworthiness of the person with whom one is angry. (The "intensity" of anger, I want to suggest, has much more to do with the harshness of such evaluations than with the physiological accompaniments of the emotion.) One can be right about the facts and justified about the warrant for anger, yet go wrong in its expression, misdirecting it (a common problem with vengeance) or overdoing it. As in any strategy, the irrationality of an emotion may be a fault in performance or timing rather than a mistake in the emotion as such. And, of course, the fault may lie in the aim or purpose of the emotion, in excessive demand, or in a confusion of goals, as in greed leading to insatiability, or in petty and malicious purpose violating one's sense of integrity whether or not it also violates social norms and justice.

Similar analyses are available for love and grief and every other emotion, even the seemingly simplest of them. Fear, for example, is not just a rush of adrenaline but also the recognition of a danger, and one can be wrong about the danger, its imminence or its gravity. At its extremes fear can be "paralyzing," but it is at least an open question whether such immobility is always detrimental. It may well have served an evolutionary purpose, for instance, *not* running from predators with the consequence of avoiding their notice. We might distinguish fear from panic, first on the grounds that only the latter, not the former, is generically irrational and, second, because panic, unlike fear, is almost wholly a physiological reaction, not an intelligent or strategic one. In general, we might say that fear can be irrational in that it is composed of and subject to the judgments of rationality, the correctness of our estimations of danger, the appropriateness of our means of escape or response. But if it can be irrational by getting these wrong, it follows that it can be rational when it gets them right. So, too, the sense of compassion, the desire for revenge, the sting of injustice, and the generalized sense of justice. To say that these can go wrong and be irrational is also to say that, properly exercised, they can be rational as well.

What is perhaps even more provocative in this "cognitive" analysis of emotion and a caring conception of reason is the implication that the concepts and judgments that are constitutive of our emotions are constitutive of the criteria for rationality as well. Indeed, one might think of rationality as emotional prudence, that is, prudence in the broad virtuous sense, *prudentia*, not the game-theoretical sense of long-term self-interest. Thus what I want to advocate is not just the rationality of the emotions but also what one might call the emotional grounding of rationality.

I want to reject the now-prevalent idea that rational criteria are simply the presuppositions of emotion, for example, the idea that fear presupposes the belief that one is in danger but that belief is not itself part of the emotion. Cognition is an essential aspect of emotion, defining its structure and its object. I also want to reject the idea that rational criteria lie only in the external standards by which emotions and their appropriateness may be judged. That would leave standing the idea of a rational framework within which the emotions may be appropriate or inappropriate, warranted or unwarranted, wise or foolish. I want to suggest rather, that emotions constitute the framework (or frameworks) of rationality itself. Of course, a single emotion does not do this. It fits (or does not fit) into the framework. But together our emotions dictate the context, the character, the culture in which some values take priority, serve as ultimate ends, provide the criteria for rationality and reasonable behavior. Our sense of justice, for example, as well as the grand theories that are constructed as expressions of that sense of justice, is not a single emotion but a systematic totality of emotions, appropriate to our culture and our character, that determines not only particular emotions (for example, hope or resentment) but also the standards and expectations according to which those emotions are provoked.

This presupposes a holistic conception in which the whole field of one's experience (or one's culture) is defined and framed by his or her engagements and attachments, in which truly "dispassionate" judgment is more often pathological than rational, and detachment more likely signals alienation than objectivity.[45] Martin Heidegger's punsical conception of mood (*Stimmung*) as our mode of "being tuned" (*Bestimmen*) to the world is instructive here, both because of its welcome shift in emphasis from detached knowing to holistic personal caring (*Sorge*) and because he emphasizes moods—which are general, diffuse, and devoid of any determinate object—rather than emotion as such.[46] But what is important about both moods and emotions is the fact that they thoroughly permeate our experience and are not, as several honorable ancient views would have it, interruptions, intrusions, or brief bouts of madness that get in the way of the otherwise calm and cool transparency of rational objectivity. We do not have a framework of rationality within which we measure our various emotions as more or less appropriate, more or less rational. The conceptual frameworks that philosophers refer to are themselves the product of our emotions and what we really care about. What is rational is what fits best into our emotional world.

We should be very careful about dismissing the emotions as merely "subjective" or "irrational" for their admittedly biased and sometimes distorted vision of the world. There are wise and foolish emotions, emotions that fit in well with the rest of our lives and enhance them, and emotions that "drag us down with their stupidity" (Nietzsche). But virtually all of the emotions play a role in constituting the structure of our lives and what then comes to be recognized as the structure of our rationality. Even those emotions which have typically been dubbed "negative," for instance, the seven "deadly sins," fit into this picture in an important way. They reflect, sometimes in exaggerated form, our needs and values, our ultimate concerns. What is the alternative—not caring at all? In opposition to lust, should we champion libidinal indifference? As opposed to greed, should we instead champion sloth? But sloth itself is an odd sin, betraying as it does just that sort of indifference that some of the ancients cited as the ultimate wisdom (but that Aquinas quite properly thought was not conducive to attentive worship and faith.) Hume chastized humility as the "monkish virtue," although what he had in mind, no doubt, was a particular mincing and often hypocritical version of that virtue. Pride, by contrast, comes off as concern for the self, "care of the soul," perhaps an essential ingredient for integrity. (One might object that there is false pride, but there is also false humility.) One might rightly reject pride and all emotions when they are inappropriate or overly grandiose. But it does not follow that pride or emotions in general are biased, except in the unobjectionable sense that they care about the self and the world.

Should we admire a life devoid of affections and offenses, a life without commitments or attachments, the supposedly "rational" approach to a life without the possibility of loss suggested by various ascetics and religious thinkers?[47]) Such "eviscerated" lives are the targets of Nietzsche's renowned attack on asceticism in the third essay on the *Genealogy of Morals*, where he claims that ascetics (like everyone) seek power and self-assertion but obtain it, as it were, backward, by stealth and self-denial.[48] But Nietzsche's attack is not on self-denial as such. It is on the very idea of a life lacking passion. Caring about the right things often requires self-denial, and sometimes the denial of emotions. Caring about congeniality requires modulating one's sense of anger and indignation. Caring about creativity means that one must control some impulses to make room for others. But this is a matter not of eviscerating the passions but of cultivating and disciplining them. For Nietzsche as for Aristotle, we are responsible for cultivating our own talents and our virtues. We "naturally" care for our family and friends, then, perhaps, for our compatriots and neighbors. But we can also cultivate our affections to include the broader culture and the environment, ultimately the world. This is what defines rationality: not logic, but the scope of our concerns. It is not reason (as opposed to emotion) that allows us to extend our reach, but the expansive scope of the emotions themselves. What one cares about is defined by one's conception of the world, but one's conception of the world is itself defined by the scope and objects of one's emotional cares and concerns.[49] Cultivation, or "civilization," is the internalization of the larger concepts of history, humanity, and religion, conceptions of morality and ethics that go beyond personal and provincial self-interests. But this is not to say that the emotional nature of these concerns is replaced by something more abstract and impersonal; the emotions themselves become more expansive.[50]

Rationality is not the grand structure of human experience, and emotions are not just "reactions." Rationality is the product not only of thought but also of caring, and although they undoubtedly have an evolutionary history that precedes the arrival of the human species by hundreds of millions of years, the emotions evolved not only along with but also inseparably from the evolution of reason and rationality. Emotions and rationality together make us capable of an awareness of a larger human and global context in which all of our fates are engaged and our mutual interests are involved. There is nothing particularly human about emotion as such (a dog can be as rightfully angry or sad as a person), but there are distinctively human emotions. Indeed, some of the peculiarly human emotions—notably love of distant neighbors, moral indignation, a keen sense of justice, religious passion, and scientific curiosity—are precisely those that are typically designated as proof of our species' rationality.

4

JUSTICE, SYMPATHY, VENGEANCE

For this command which I am enjoining upon you today is not
too difficult for you; neither is it far off. It is not in heaven, that
you should say, "who will go up for us to heaven and bring it
down to make us hear it, so we may do it?" ... No, the word is
very near you in your life and in your heart in order that you
may do it.

Deuteronomy 30:11–12, 14

Justice herself, fam'd for fair dealing,
By blindness had not lost her feeling.
Bernard de Mandeville, The Grumbling Hive

What is justice? Socrates asked that question twenty-five centuries ago, and ever since it has been one of the leading questions of Western philosophy. But from Plato to John Rawls, philosophical discussions of justice have tended to be "thin," aiming at broad,
all-encompassing theories and principles, or focussing on such abstract and
supposedly universal conceptions as "rights." Referring to the relatively
context-rich and historical musings of John Locke on justice, Rawls proudly
announces his own project as raising the discussion to "a higher order of
abstraction." He methodically removes all personal affections and attachments, and all of the benefits and burdens of fate, that Aristotle presumed to
be the preconditions of our outlook on life. Behind the "veil of ignorance,"
we denude ourselves, take away our personal preferences and prejudices, our
individual advantages and liabilities, our distinctive virtues and vices alike.

From this depersonalized and dispassionate perspective, the principles of justice are supposed to emerge.

So, too, Plato had appealed to nous, a special way of "seeing." Its eidetic objects, including justice, are so "thin" that they defy description and to us hoi polloi seem to have no content whatever. From Plato to Rawls, philosophical discussions of justice have so emphasized the supremacy of reason that there has been little room for an adequate appreciation for the role of feelings. Plato does insist on "harmony" between passions and reason, but he sufficiently warns us against the emotions that the musical metaphor is not entirely convincing.[1] Rawls devotes a late section or two to "the moral sentiments" and defends their ineliminability from human life,[2] but by "sentiment" he seems to mean no more than certain dispositions to act on rational principles. Many authors, of course, have dismissed the sentiments as mere "sentimentality" and insisted that the emotions only confuse and distort the rational deliberations of justice. Kant famously degrades the various "inclinations" as at best secondary to morality, sarcastically dismisses "melting compassion" or "tender sympathy," and vigorously rejects any role for vengeance in his retributive account of justice.[3] Harking back to a neglected tradition in ethics, however, I want to argue that there can be no adequate understanding of justice without an appreciation and understanding of the role of the emotions. This includes not only those benign "moral sentiments" such as sympathy, care, and compassion and other "fellow feelings," but also the nastier emotions of envy, jealousy, resentment, and, especially, vengeance.[4]

Justice, according to many philosophers, is a matter of rational principles, and if those principles or their consequences should turn out to be "callous"— as Nozick declares in his preface to *Anarchy, State and Utopia*—so much the worse for our feelings.[5] I do not suggest that we dismiss reason from considerations of justice, of course, but much of what is called "reason" in political philosophy is rather callousness, mere cleverness, insensitivity, distrust of our own (or others') sensibilities, and pigheadedness. The impersonality and detachment with which we philosophers so often identify and on which we so pride ourselves may, in the instance of social philosophy in particular, be misplaced. What is essential to justice, I want to argue, is our supposedly unphilosophical sense of compassion and various other passions, too long swept under the carpet laid down by Kant and so many other sarcastic critics of "melting compassion" and the "inclinations." And perhaps even more controversial, I want to argue that "negative" emotions such as indignation and vengeance are part and parcel of our human nature and equally essential to justice, not just untoward interruptions in our otherwise rational deliberations.

It is often said that social views ruled by passions are dangerous. Of course, we can all think of prominent examples that would make such caution necessary. But I would like to suggest, in reply, that the ideal of a rational, all-encompassing theory of justice is also dangerous. On the one side, it too easily encourages passivity, even as it provokes, intellectual controversy and debate. It too often discourages constructive action. Grand theories too readily leave us detached from and uninvolved in the world, absorbed in the defense of our views, as if the implementation of justice were then up to others, God, or the government, or perhaps it is in the hands of fate or history. Justice, construed as theory, is not a personal virtue to be cultivated and exercised. But on the other side, theories invite dogmatism, tyranny, insensitivity, and callousness. When we are so focussed on the big picture and its principles, we too easily lose sight of and sympathy for the exceptions, the particular cases that all too often fail to conform to our theories. In such cases, we rightly conclude that it is abstract rationality, when it comes into conflict with our intuitions of what's right, that has gone wrong.[6]

One problem with our loftier philosophical conceptions of justice is that they seem to descend upon us from nowhere, "out of thin air." Philosophers' insistence that we "ground" claims about rights and justice are revealing in this regard. Nevertheless, we ignore the very down-to-earth and human emotional foundations of justice and neglect those passions that make justice both necessary and possible. Justice is not, first of all, a set of principles or policies; it is, first of all, a set of personal feelings, a way of participating in the world. Without the cultivation of those feelings—and some of them are by no means attractive—the principles of justice are nothing but words, and the policies that would make us just, however justified, tend to be both overambitious and irrelevant. By injecting emotion back into discussions of justice, perhaps we can get philosophers first of all to care (and not feel embarrassed about caring). Better indignation and even vengefulness than contemplative detachment and indifference.

Justice and Vengeance:
The Missing Paradigm

If, then, anyone tells us that it is just to give everyone his due, and he means by this that from the just man harm is due to his enemies and benefit due to his friends—the man who says that is not wise, for it is not true.

Socrates to Polymarchus, *The Republic*,

Justice [in Plato's *Republic*] has emerged in its true colors as a property, not primarily of actions or political institutions, but of *psyches*.

C. D. C. Reeves, *Philosopher Kings*

Our sense of justice is a more or less particular, more or less personal, partially emotional response to a situation or circumstances, no matter how then generalized or abstracted, no matter the distance or the global dimensions of our conclusions. Our thoughts about justice are typically—if not necessarily—prompted by perceptions of *injustice*, often in the face of disagreement, deprivation, or disharmony. Of course, the contexts in which justice is discussed and debated are various, and may even be incommensurable. For instance, the spheres of retributive and distributive justice are often segregated, albeit with some embarrassment and equivocation over terms. Within the sphere of distributive justice, the perennial disagreements between those who defend egalitarian, libertarian, need-based, and various entitlement and merit-based conceptions of justice constitute a discipline of their own. It has been well argued, however, that these different theoretical conceptions are in fact based on historical, contextual, and cultural as well as ideological differences.[7]

The delineation of spheres of justice may well be much more fine-grained than that, and these spheres, too, may be incommensurable.[8] I do not intend to argue that thesis here, although I am obviously sympathetic to it.[9] What I do want to argue, particularly with reference to retributive justice, is that justice begins with and consists in an emotional reaction to a more or less particular state of affairs, within a cultural tradition and with a substantial, concrete history. (By "substantial, concrete history" I mean to imply something more than the "thin" and conscientiously limited history of entitlements suggested by Robert Nozick, in particular, in his argument against the "ahistorical" Rawlsian position.) Even the God's-eye view of fairness so often championed by philosophers might best be considered an example of a particular reaction within a particular cultural and historical context. One of the problems with that so-called God's-eye view is that it tends to be an exceptionally thin view, one that masks all reference to cultural or local customs, traditions, and expectations.[10] That, no doubt, is why philosophers are so drawn to it.[11]

In order to underscore that point, I want to suggest something that will at first sound outrageous: Not only can vengeance be defended as a significant ingredient in justice (retributive justice most plausibly), but there is also a sense in which justice in general might better be construed on the model of vengeance. Justice has two roots, I want to suggest, first the retributive desire to "undo" a hurtful slight or offense, second the more difficult promptings of gratitude, the recognition that one has advantages to which one is not entitled. That, in turn, prompts compassion, not just the "natural" sentiment proclaimed by some philosophers but a highly sophisticated, cultivated, and reflective passion. Retribution and gratitude are both responses that involve questions of merit, blame in the first, a debt in the second, but the asymmetry between retribution and gratitude is also worth noting: vengeance seeks to get even by inflicting harm, gratitude need not seek to give a reward (giving "thanks" should not be so construed) and need not make any pretense of getting even. It is this sense of gratitude that is readily (but not necessarily) conducive to a keener sense of compassion, an awareness (because one perceives oneself as not wholly deserving) of the fact that others, no less deserving, are in need. But the point of all this is to insist that justice descends not from the heavens but begins with the concrete facts of life, our personal responses to them according to the conventions and paradigms of our culture. It is not the product of abstract thought but is learned through experience within our families and neighborhoods and no doubt, in our earliest moral and religious instruction.

Needless to say, I do not want to pursue this thesis too far, but justice has become so overgeneralized and abstracted, and vengeance has become so routinely dismissed as barbaric and irrelevant to justice, that I believe such an argument, even somewhat tongue-in-cheek, can be revealing. The idea is this: Our sense of justice typically begins with a personal, impassioned reaction to a slight or hurt, a more or less particular, historical state of affairs within the context of a culture and its various narratives. (It is this notion of "thick" narrative, the myths and legends of heroes and villains, for example, as well as the more or less factual narrative of a community and its history and the detailed circumstances surrounding this particular case of alleged injustice that I want to juxtapose against both Nozick's "thin" histories and Rawl's "ahistorical" position.) We then generalize, we develop our own personal narratives, we learn to empathize with similar slights and harms to others, and perhaps we also learn to theorize and raise the discussion to "a higher order of abstraction." (How could we—generalizing, rational, principled, articulate, argumentative beings—avoid doing so?) It is nevertheless a mistake to jettison that personal, impassioned reaction as if it were nothing more than a trigger, a coincidental inclination, a primitive drive or a mere motive looking for a justification. So, too, the promptings of gratitude and compassion get generalized into views about needs and the perceptions (and rationalizations about) human inequalities, which finally get projected into a grand notion of equality, one that has always had far more appeal in theory than in actual practice.

This view of justice as personal, passionate, and situated in a society with established paradigms of violation, harms and slights, of honor and offenses against honor, can be found in Plato and in Aristotle. Before Plato, of course, "justice" (variations on *diké*) had this ineliminably personal and vindictive aspect, and in the *Iliad*, for example, it is typically introduced as a matter of personal (or tribal) honor.[12] In the complex weave of duties and morals in Homer's two immortal epics, justice appears again and again in the straightforward guise of personal retribution, coupled with appropriate rewards and demands for tribute. In Plato, the terms of justice change a great deal, not least in the central Socratic teaching that one should not under any circumstances do harm to others. But for Plato as for Aristotle, justice remains a personal virtue, whether or not it is also (in Plato, not in Aristotle) an abstract ideal. It does not eliminate the passions but employs them. And if vengeance as such is condemned (or, in Aristotle, subordinated to righteous anger), the particularist vision of justice as "giving each his due" nevertheless remains, however embellished and ontologically disguised by Socrates and then Plato.

In *The Republic*, however, the older, more Homeric conception of justice has its day, if only briefly. In book I, Cephalus's son Polymarchus tries to defend the notion that justice is "giving each his due." Admittedly, he does not do a very good job of it, and Socrates undermines the argument at every turn and humiliates him. In one of its several versions the purported definition becomes "Be good to your friends and do harm to your enemies," which Socrates dispatches with his usual wit and dialectical skill. This invites the infamous but philosophically underrated bullying tactics of Thrasymachus, who fights against the philosophical effort to understand justice as an ideal detached from the rough-and-tumble of human relationships.[13] Socrates dispatches him with humor and irony. Socrates also argues, against Cephalus, that one does not return arms to a madman, even if it is his due. But it seems to me that the upshot of Socrates' arguments against all three of them— Polymarchus, Thrasymachus, and Cephalus—is that judgments about justice are essentially contextual. They depend upon the particular situation and one's relationships vis-à-vis the other parties involved. If Socrates' counterexamples show the proposed "definitions" of justice to be inadequate, perhaps that is because there is no such context-free general rule about justice that is not either incomplete or vacuous. Justice is always defined within some context or other.[14]

And yet, generously reinterpreted, I think that Polymarchus has a good case against Socrates. "Be good to your friends and do harm to your enemies" is an unfortunate but nevertheless insightful way of underscoring the importance of particular attachments and relationships in justice, as well as the feelings of reciprocity that motivate us. What is only implied are the larger issues according to which we choose and maintain our friendship and whether the friends are "true." I also suspect that friends and enemies are not nearly so opposite as the dialogue makes them appear. More generally, Polymarchus's insistence on the significance of personal context and "honor" is opposed to Socrates' more idealized and abstract insistence on decontextualized and nonpolitical virtue. Socrates attacks the very idea of punishment as a "return of evil for evil." Polymarchus wisely recognizes the necessity of doing or at least threatening harm to those who have done you wrong. Socrates argues against the appeal to emotion in ethics. Polymarchus rightly insists that personal feelings are not only important motives but also important grounds for ethical action. It would be stretching the intelligibility of the dialogue to suggest that Polymarchus has in mind the thesis that justice combines retribution and gratitude, but in spite of the brilliant dialectical maneuvering of Socrates, a case can be made for his young stooge–interlocutor. Personal feelings and context are essential to ethics, although the "personal" here can be stretched to include such sentiments as camaraderie and loyalty and compassion and social (suprapersonal) views about retributive punishment. The point is not to leave the laurels with Socrates alone, but to see, as in other dialogues, another side of the story.[15]

Socrates, it seems, had two very different lessons to teach us. The first, exemplified in his character as well as his discussions, is the importance of justice—admittedly in a broader sense than our use of the term—as a personal virtue, a way of responding to the world and other people. So conceived, justice is highly personal and always situated in a particular social context. Indeed, the political vision of *The Republic* can be viewed as an attempt to schematize just that social context (which in many ways resembles Plato's own) which will most effectively manifest and cultivate that virtue in each and every citizen. The second lesson has to do with the more philosophical vision of a singular ideal Form of justice, which today translates into the search for an all-embracing philosophical theory. (It is not at all clear that Plato ever came up with one.) The two lessons are not obviously compatible, but in any case, they certainly urge us in two very different directions. There is no question in which direction Anglo-American philosophy has gone. Justice, we are reminded again and again and again, is a matter of abstract, dispassionate, impersonal, rational principles derived from some radically depersonalized account of society.[16]

Just as vengeance always consists of a personal, impassioned reaction to a more or less particular state of affairs, so a sense of justice in general consists at least in part of a culturally scripted reaction to a historically rich narrative and a more or less particular state of affairs—the punishment of a criminal, the rectification of wrongs suffered by a group after centuries of slavery or oppression, the establishment of a new nation still smarting from the abuses of a foreign king, the distribution of goods in circumstances of scarcity, the availability of services in times of need, the distribution of awards or bonuses in times of plenty. I admit that vengeance is a misleading and overly restrictive paradigm for justice insofar as it emphasizes only a particularly desert-minded conception of retributive justice and virtually ignores distributive and compensatory justice (for instance, the matter of needs) except insofar as these involve punishments and rewards. But I want to suggest that the emphasis has been too lopsided in precisely the other direction. Indeed, philosophers who write at great length about distributive justice often keep surprisingly silent on matters of retribution. Observing recent policy in the United States and around the world, one would have to be ideologically blind to claim that retributive concepts play no part in the distribution of the world's unequally distributed goods. But whether the increasing gap between the world's rich and poor is taken to be a matter for shame, embarrassment, pride, resentment, moral indignation, fear, or defensiveness, it is out of such feelings that the sweeping claims and theories about justice, rights, desert, exploitation, and fairness arise.

Justice versus Vengeance: An Untenable Opposition

> As for Duhring's proposition that the home of justice is to be sought in the sphere of the reactive feelings, one is obliged for truth's sake to counter it with a blunt antithesis: the *last* sphere to be conquered by the spirit of justice is the sphere of the reactive feelings!
>
> Nietzsche, *Genealogy of Morals*

Vengeance is usually contrasted with justice, even opposed to it. ("I don't want vengeance; I want justice" is the obligatory retributive demand.[17]) Vengeance is said to be an Evil, a return of "Evil for Evil," and from Socrates in the *Crito* to contemporary debates about capital punishment, this formulation gets used simply to banish any further mention of vengeance from the discussion of justice.[18] The perverse suggestion that vengeance should be seriously considered as a paradigm of justice turns the usual considerations of justice on their head. For example, vengeance is personal, not impersonal.[19] Vengeance is passionate, not dispassionate. Vengeance is retributive, that is, it consists of an appropriate response to a particular situation. It is not an abstract theory about equality or entitlements, and may appear to be ad hoc given the details of the particular situation and the various characters and their history involved. But justice, by its very nature, implies legitimacy and justification. Can vengeance ever be justified? Isn't the subjectivity of vengeance more than sufficient reason to rule it out of the court of justice? What rationality is there in the personal, passionate, retributive desire to get even for a possibly unique offense that may have no precedents and allow no room for proof or argument?

"Getting even" refers to an idea of balance that underlies virtually all theories of justice. Vengeance requires measured reciprocity. It presupposes one's personal involvement, notions of loss, desert, and personal debt, not the aloof and merely judgmental attitude of an observer, a judge, a jury, the Law, or one or another philosophical game theorist. Vengeance may be more or less established, respectable, and even institutionalized in some cultures and societies, but it is only rarely elevated to full legal status. Indeed, it might be argued that vengeance, even if justified and rational, is by its very nature extralegal. Vengeance can often be found as an established and obligatory social practice, even where outlawed. But even where it is legal and legitimate, it almost always remains in the hands of the individual, the family, or the local community. It tends not to be considered the responsibility or even the concern of the law or of the larger society.[20] Indeed, whether or not vengeance is socially sanctioned, and however it may be structured or restricted, the underlying motivation of vengeance may not be socially created. Individuals in "the state of nature," like most "higher" animals, will retaliate in case of attack, typically in measured reactions. Vengeance as a social practice will be cultivated according to certain cultural norms and concepts, including notions of self, a set of notions about what counts as an offense (although some of these, such as theft, rape, and murder, may have a prima facie claim to universality), a set of standards of "fit," "balance," or "getting even" that distinguish revenge from further wrongdoing. And yet, vengeance and its satisfaction, whether acknowledged or denied, continue to be essential ingredients in the criminal law and provide a standard for what we consider to be just and fair.

I would not want to leave the matter here, of course. Vengeance is often irrational, in the straightforward sense that it oversteps its bounds, mismeasures its response, misidentifies its targets and its aims. Personal judgment must be improved and to a degree supplanted by intersubjective standards and agreements and social controls. Violence must be minimized and contained. And the all-too-natural tendency to escalation and "vendetta" obviously needs correction. All of this requires, yes, theories of justice and abstract generalizations and rules of various kinds, but what I want to do is to assure that we do not lose sight of the original motives and intuitions that drive and then guide our more civilized views of punishment in particular and justice in general. Wherever justice is at issue, the lingering shadow of vengeance is not far behind.

The particularist focus of vengeance also applies in the realm of distributive justice. I have already mentioned what I take to be an important link between gratitude and compassion. The impetus behind general schemes of distributive justice, I would argue, is to be found in such situated and concrete emotions such as evoke sympathy, compassion, guilt, shame, embarrassment and pity, even when those emotions are evoked by the plight of people at a distance, large groups or even humanity as a whole. It is worth noting that we are most often "moved" not by horrifying statistics but rather, for example, by a photograph of a single, suffering child. The statistics become horrific when we try, if we can, to multiply that singular compassion logarithmically. So, too, our sense of distributive as well as retributive justice is moved by such straightforwardly "reactive" emotions as envy, possessiveness, resentment and revenge, even when directed against faceless institutions (such as the abstract construal of "Big Government"), political buzz-words ("the re-distribution of wealth") or, like Camus's Sisyphus, toward the personified universe as a whole.[21]

The familiar claim of *entitlement*, for instance, though it presents itself as a matter of abstract rights, often betrays itself in terms of very personal and particular feelings. In some cases, these may be backed up by well-established conventions (property rights being the most obvious example). More often, they are quasi objective appeals to personal merit, for example, "I am x (someone who works hard/is a member of the team/is the best performer here/is a citizen of this realm) and so I deserve z." More often than we like to admit in our theories of justice, the argument is more of the form, "I have (or have had) x for such time that I am entitled to x." The fact that there are many such feelings and the fact that they do not in themselves determine any particular scheme or blueprint for society as a whole explains why there are and will continue to be conflicts so long as we talk about entitlements (and how could we not do so?). Consequently, there will emerge very different, incommensurable, competing conceptions of justice.[22] What counts as a fair distribution will have much to do with the particularities of the case, the place, the people, their history, culture and the concrete circumstances.

I want to suggest that all of these emotions can be seen to resemble vengeance at least in their concrete, personal, *reactive* nature. They may involve one's own suffering or oppression, the suffering or oppression of others, the memory or vivid image of suffering or oppression, one's own suffering in response to the suffering or oppression of others, or the desire that others suffer because of one's own suffering or oppression. Or they may be reactions to one's good fortune. Such emotions may result from the embarrassing or grateful recognition of one's own, unearned advantages. One may share in another's rightful sense of resentment or search for revenge, though one may not have been wronged in any way oneself. One may be only defending what one considers his or her own, against encroachment, against appropriation, against theft. It is the same shared sense of reciprocity in revenge that also dictates a general sense of desert and reward and of favors to be returned. It has often been suggested that no pattern of distribution is in itself unjust. It is only when it is compared with some ideal scheme or personal expectations that it can be said to be so. That is why, and not for lack of a "social compact," Hobbes was right in insisting that there is no justice in the state of nature.

I am *not* suggesting—let me be clumsily clear—that favoritism or vindictiveness (say, in a politician, a bureaucrat, or the chairman of my department) is in any way justifiable or tolerable. Such socially-defined positions make impersonality and neutrality an essential virtue and render excessive expressions of compassion, affection, or contempt a vice. And, to be sure, it is possible to be compassionate or vengeful and oblivious to justice. It is not always a bad thing to be coldly just and dispassionately fair. But what I want to argue is that this is not all that there is to justice, and our supposedly unphilosophical sense of caring, compassion, and various "negative" passions are just as important to an adequate sense of justice as dispassionate fairness.

The emotions are the stuff of which our conceptions of justice are constructed and in which they remain anchored. Without emotion, without caring, a theory of justice is just another numbers game.

The Kindly Side of Justice: Sympathy and the Moral Sentiments

> How selfish soever man may be supposed, there are evidently some principles in his nature, which interest him in the fortune of others, and render their happiness necessary to him, though he derives nothing from it except the pleasure of seeing it. Of this kind is pity or compassion, the emotion which we feel for the misery of others. . . . The greatest ruffian, the most hardened violator of the laws of society, is not altogether without it.
>
> Adam Smith *Theory of the Moral Sentiments*

My aim in defending vengeance as a paradigm of justice is to reestablish the role of the emotions in shaping and motivating our sense of justice. But with that in mind it would be misleading, if not perverse, to focus only on the retributive side of justice and ignore the benign sentiments that help shape and motivate our sense of distributive justice. Needs, as well as deserts, need to be addressed by justice. All too often, distributive justice is debated solely in terms of patterns of fair distribution or, alternatively, as constrained by general claims to entitlement. What is wrong with both of these philosophical positions is that they approach the subject of justice from the "outside," so to speak, imagining possible states of affairs instead of confronting the actual state of the world around us. But our sense of justice is not prompted by the abstract sense of "equality." It is, rather, provoked by the direct perception of inequality, by the recognition of needs—our own or others', by the fact that others suffer while we do not or, alternatively, by the fact that we suffer while others do not. In the latter case, we are moved by envy and resentment (more on that later), but in the former case, we are or should be moved by compassion.

Compassion is often contrasted with justice, much as vengeance is contrasted with retributive justice. Compassion is personal; justice is said to be impersonal. Compassion is directed at isolated individuals (even if there are millions of them). Justice is said to be concerned with the bigger picture, with the overall scheme of distribution (or punishment). Compassion is merely an emotion, a "sentiment," while justice is said to demand the judgments of reason. But it is just these contrasts, between the personal and the impersonal, between the particular and the universal, between the emotions and reason, that I want to challenge. Compassion, I want to argue, is an essential ingredient in our sense of justice.

As vengeance is a hostile reaction toward someone who is personally responsible for a wrong or an offense, so compassion is a benign reaction to the suffering of others, regardless of the existence of a wrong or an offense. The recipient of compassion need not be a person of one's actual acquaintance, but compassion is felt personally and directed at a person. Compassion is often taken to be a disposition—indeed, even the generalized disposition to feel whatever another person is feeling. What is right about this is that it underscores its role as a personal reaction, but what is wrong with this dispositional view is that it underplays compassion's special character. Compassion is first of all a form of caring, even if at a distance, even if intermingled with fear and loathing (as in pity).

It has been suggested that what is missing from the standard analyses and theories of justice is an adequate sense of care and compassion.[23] This is, I believe, true and important. Even so pivotal figure as John Rawls, whose liberal credentials and sense of compassion are not in question, finds it necessary to dress his sentiments in formal costume, and most of the literature that has followed him has shown far more enthusiasm for his form than for his feelings. Perhaps that is why so much of social philosophy today resembles a debate in game theory rather than an expression of concern for human suffering, even if "the needy" and "the least advantaged" often appear as abstracted players.

Unfortunately, this important point has been politicized and polemicized as a difference between "male and female" and "masculine and feminine" approaches to ethics. Nell Noddings, for example, uses the division between "masculine" and "feminine" ethics as something of Iron Curtain, or as a "great chasm" in the war between the sexes.[24] ("Men of principle have been wrecking the world; caring women could save it."[25]) Instead of insisting that *any* adequate sense of justice presupposes care and compassion, some recent authors have opposed the (supposedly male) concept of justice to (female) caring and compassion. But this seeming duality is no Kierkegaardian "either/or," impersonal justice *or* personal concern. Care (like eros) is neither exclusively a woman's nor a mother's emotion, and it is not an emotion that by itself can save the world. The kindly sentiments cannot by themselves explain the enormous range or the profound depth of the passions that constitute our sense of justice, and sentiment alone cannot solve the large policy issues that inevitably are part of any discussion of justice. Nevertheless, any sense of justice whatever begins with caring—about ourselves, our reputations, and our belongings; about those whom we love and live with, feel akin to, or responsible for; about the way the world is and the fate of the sentient creatures on it. Why else would any of this matter to us—the distribution of goods in the world, fair and equal treatment, just rewards and the felt need to punish, even questions of life and death? Justice begins with and presupposes our emotional engagement in the world.

The Kantian turn in philosophy is often blamed for the exile of the kindly sentiments and the "inclinations" in general from moral philosophy.[26] But in the wake of this Kantian tradition, it is always worth remembering how closely Kant (Rawls, too) claims to follow on the heels of his hero, Rousseau, one of the great defenders of the natural inclinations.[27] Before Kant, and about the same time as Rousseau, the "moral sentiment theorists" emerged in Scotland (and elsewhere). The leading and best-known proponents of moral sentiment theory were David Hume and Adam Smith. They defended the centrality of the "natural" sentiment of sympathy in morals, distinguishing between sympathy and justice, which Hume, in particular, declared not to be "natural" at all.[28] Some years later, Schopenhauer, turning against his mentor Kant, defended a similar view.[29] Moral sentiment theory began with the insight that the basis of morality and justice is to be found in our natural disposition to have certain other-directed emotions.

Both Hume and Smith emerged as early champions of the importance of "utility" as well as defenders of what is now called "virtue ethics." But it is clear that the right things don't usually get done for the wrong reasons, and justice is only rarely and ironically the result of malicious intentions. But surely among the "right reasons" are the sympathetic emotions. Contrary to much of the Kantian tradition, to be moral and to be just does not mean, first of all, that one must act on principle. A good reason for helping another person in need is "I feel sorry for him." Indeed, one is hard put to think of any other reason that is so impervious to argument (which is not to say that it is indefeasible). And yet, reading through the philosophy of the past two centuries, the ordinary reader would be shocked to find that "I feel sorry for him" as a moral reason is all but ignored, when not simply dismissed, as a basis for morality or justice. Such sentiments are said to be capricious, naive, undependable, unpredictable, and, in any case, beside the point. But I would argue that without such feelings, some sense of deprivation and pity, the calculations of just distribution are empty, souless, if not mindless, exercises in equity.

There is considerable confusion about the meaning of "sympathy," both in the writings of the moral sentiment theorists and in everyday conversation. In common parlance, sympathy means "feeling sorry for" someone, while for many philosophers (notably Hume) it is conflated with benevolence. (Smith tries to keep these distinct.) "Feeling sorry for" can be a sign of caring, but surely a minimal one, as we can feel sorry for strangers and even our enemies. Benevolence has much in common with the more activist concept of "caring for," but it has much greater scope than sympathy as such. We can feel benevolence in the abstract without any particular object, and benevolence toward those whose feelings are utterly malicious or indifferent to us (e.g., in being merciful to a condemned and still hateful wrongdoer, perhaps as an expression of our own largesse but out of benevolence nevertheless.) We often use "sympathy" or the verb "sympathize" to register agreement or approval, although none of these qualifies as an adequate philosophical conception or a correct dictionary definition of the term.

Technically, sympathy (literally, "feeling with," like "com/passion") is the sharing of feeling or, as a disposition, the ability to share the feelings of others. Or, if one wants to insist that the emotions can be individuated only by virtue of the persons who have them and thus cannot be shared, one might say that sympathy is an "agreement of feelings," in the sense of "having the same [type of] emotion."[30] One need not "agree with," in the sense of "approve of," the feeling in question, of course, any more than one must always enjoy, like, or approve of one's own emotions. The feelings may agree but we need not; sharing a feeling is one thing, and accepting or approving of the feeling is something quite different. (In B movies, we might well share the offended hero's sense of revenge even while berating ourselves for doing that.)

Adam Smith uses the term in this technical way, as "agreement of emotion." Thus there is a serious ambiguity between sympathy as a specific sentiment and sympathy as a disposition to share sentiments (whatever sentiments) with others. Sympathy in the latter sense is not actually a sentiment at all, but rather a vehicle for understanding other people's sentiments, "fellow-feeling with any passion whatever."[31] One can sympathize with any number of feelings in another person, not only the kindly and social moral sentiments but such unsocial sentiments as envy and hatred as well. Sympathy is not an actual sharing of sentiments (in the sense of "having the same feeling"), but rather an act of imagination by which one can appreciate the feelings of another person by "putting oneself in his place," "a principle which interests him in the fortunes of others."[32] This provides Smith with a way of accounting for how it can be that people are not essentially selfish or self-interested, but are social creatures who can act on behalf of others whose feelings they do not (and logically cannot) actually share.

Hume's earlier theory of sympathy and justice, which greatly influenced Smith, is somewhat different, and to make matters more difficult, it is clear that he changed his mind between the writing of his early masterpiece, *A Treatise of Human Nature*, and his later *Inquiry Concerning the Principles of Morals*. In the early work, Hume treats sympathy rather casually, commenting that it is usually a weak emotion compared with most of the motives of self-interest. In the later work, Hume defends sympathy as a universal sentiment that is sufficiently powerful to overcome self-interest in a great many cases. In the *Inquiry*, Hume takes sympathy to be a form of benevolence, a feeling for one's fellow citizens, and a concern for their well-being. But for Hume, as for Smith, sympathy is too often countered and overwhelmed by selfishness, and for this reason, a sense of justice is also required. But whereas Smith takes the sense of justice to be a somewhat natural revulsion at harming one's fellows, Hume takes justice to be an "artificial" virtue that is constructed by reason for our mutual well-being. It is an advantageous conventional "scheme" rather than a natural sentiment. Thus for Hume sympathy is a genuine moral sentiment and justice is not. Even so, Hume admitted that justice was so beneficial that it became inseparably associated with the moral sentiments, for what could be more basic to these sentiments than our sense of the general good for everyone, "a feeling for the happiness of mankind and a resentment of their misery"? He writes:

> No virtue is more esteemed than justice, and no vice more detested than injustice; nor are there any qualities, which go farther to the fixing of character, either as amiable or odious. Now justice is a moral virtue, merely because it has that tendency to the good of mankind; and, indeed, is nothing but an artificial invention to that purpose.[33]
>
> The whole scheme, however, of law and justice is advantageous to the society; and 'twas with a view to this advantage, that men, by their voluntary conventions, establish'd it. . . . Once established, it is *naturally* attended with a strong sentiment of morals.[34]

Hume does not go so far as to say that justice itself is a matter of sentiment, but he insists that the moral sentiments in general, and sympathy for others in particular, are so essential to morals that there can be no ethics without them. Both Hume and Smith are dead-set against the Hobbesian view that people are motivated only by their own selfish interests, and advocate the importance of distinctive, natural "social passions." Indeed, the core of their argument is, in Smith's terms, that "Nature, when she formed man for society, endowed him with an original desire to please, and an original aversion to offend his brethren."[35] Moreover, "Nature endowed him not only with a desire for being approved of, but with a desire of being what ought to be approved of, or of being what he himself approves of in other men."[36] It is not just sympathy but a whole complex of mutually aware and reciprocal passions that tie us together. Thus it does not take too much tinkering with Scottish moral sentiment theory to incorporate justice along with sympathy under its auspices and take the whole as a welcome alternative to both the "man is essentially selfish" thesis and the overly thin "morality is rationality" view of Kant and most current justice theorists.

The problem with sympathy is that it always seems to suggest more than it actually provides. It is one thing to say that one is upset and has kindly feelings towards a fellow creature in pain, that one in some sense "shares" the suffering. But feeling sorry is not the same as wanting to help, and while benevolence typically leads to beneficence and helping behavior, "feeling sorry for" usually just stops at pity. One may be kindly or generous "out of pity," but though pity may motivate, it readily remains a feeling unto itself—one of the reasons why Nietzsche so relentlessly attacked it. Pity includes within its structure an unmistakable sense of "looking down" at its object and, even on a more benign account than Nietzsche's, cannot be conceived of as an unalloyed kindly sentiment, which sympathy is so often said to be. Moreover, insofar as sympathy involves actually sharing feelings, it is clear that the suffering one shares with the sufferer is, for the most part, pretty limp stuff and not nearly adequate to motivate ethical behavior. I may in fact feel slightly ill because you have just broken your leg in three places, but it would be absurd to compare my feelings with yours, much less to say that I am "sharing" your suffering. Of course, if the suffering is genuinely shared—for example, if it is *our* grandfather who died—it would be perfectly plausible to say that we share the appropriate feelings. But this would not be a matter of "sympathy," for the idea behind moral sentiment theory is that I can and do feel for you on the basis of your suffering and not my own.

Sympathy and justice, together with a sense of benevolence, provide Smith with a portrait of human nature far more flattering than the Hobbesian picture of human life as "a war of all against all" and "nasty, brutish and short." But the tendency to split the passions into a set of "selfish" sentiments and an "other-regarding" set, such as sympathy and compassion, raises deep questions about how such internal warfare can produce a coherent individual life, much less a coherent and harmonious society. The mistake, which Hume and Smith seemed to pick up from Shaftesbury and Hutcheson,[37] was to polarize the passions and characterize a few of these as "moral" or "social" and others as "selfish" or "asocial," when in fact almost all passions and sentiments of any complexity at all pour across these artificial boundaries like clouds across state lines. Sympathy, in particular, is no simple sentiment and does indeed involve competitive and "self-interested" components as well as pure altruism and concern for the other. Accordingly, we should expect considerable strain in these theories, as Hume goes on to defend the British propertied classes and as Smith goes on to defend what has since been dubbed the "magic" of free market capitalism. But the central and undeniable truth of moral sentiment theory, I believe, is that we are essentially and "naturally" social creatures with fellow feeling, care, and compassion for others, not concerned only with our own interests and ambitions in life. We are not mysteriously moved by the impersonal promptings of practical reason.[38]

The Nasty Side of Justice:
In Defense of Resentment

Revenge, the excess of resentment, appears to be the most detestable of all the passions.

Adam Smith, *Theory of the Moral Sentiments*

> The slaves' revolt in morals begins with this, that ressentiment itself
> becomes creative and gives birth to values.
>
> Friedrich Nietzsche, *On the Genealogy of Morals*

My argument is that justice is a passion or a set of passions to be cultivated and not an abstract set of principles to be formulated and imposed upon society. Justice begins not with Socratic insights but with the promptings of some basic emotions, foremost among them such "negative" emotions as envy, jealousy, and resentment, a keen sense of having been personally cheated or neglected, and the desire to "get even."[39] This is not the usual list of "moral sentiments," to be sure. In Smith, in Hume, and across the Channel in Rousseau, we hear a great deal about those supposedly basic feelings of fellow feeling, compassion, and sympathy. Of course these are essential, but the problem is that they are only a small piece—albeit an absolutely essential piece—of the picture. It may be worth noting, with some sense of irony, that sympathy and the other undeniably positive passions are often not just neglected but actually denied, for example, by cynics who would not dream of denying the existence of the antipathetic passions—envy and resentment in particular.

Both conceptual analysis and empirical research show that the emotions of justice essentially come in a "package." Just as one cannot feel love without the potential for grief, and one cannot feel pride without the capacity for shame, one cannot have or develop a passion for suprapersonal justice without a primary sense of personal injustice.[40] The emotions of justice must be particular as well as general, and when we speak of a "sense of justice," it cannot be just a universal sensibility, a Platonic love of the good, that we have in mind.[41] The sense of justice includes not just the noble or sympathetic emotions but also the often nasty, even hateful, antipathetic emotions, sometimes generalized from personal maxims to universal political principles.

The usual set of altruistic, or what Rescher calls "vicarious," passions is too limited to account for justice. The "negative" or antipathetic emotions are as essential as the sympathetic passions to our sense of justice. Envy and jealousy have as much to do with the origins and development of justice as do pity and compassion. At the very beginning of our historical sense of justice (antedating our own rather ethnocentric notion of "distributive justice" by several millennia) is the sense of justice as outrage, resentment, and revenge. It is too easily assumed that a fully developed sense of justice, because it is such a noble sense, must be derived only from equally noble (though perhaps more primitive) emotions. I think that this is wrong. Our sense of justice emerges as a generalization and a rationalization (not in the bad Freudian sense but in the good Hegelian sense) of a personal sense of *in*justice.

Our sense of injustice isn't a general sense of outrage—that comes later and involves a number of grand generalizations. We have already suggested that our sense of injustice—and thereby justice, too—begins with a personal slight, a perceived inequity. But perhaps the "negative" emotions are not that negative after all. It has been argued, for instance, that envy is itself an important emotion, an engine of capitalism and the consumer society that encourages us to want more and be more competitive.[42] Nietzsche argued at length that resentment is the main ingredient in much of what we call morality, and Dostoesvsky (or one of his most famous characters) maintained that spite is the very essence of the free and autonomous self. The argument that I want to suggest, if not pursue, here is that our sense of justice cannot ignore, and to some extent even develops out of, these rather vile emotions. This is not to deny that justice requires and presupposes compassion, respect, and a sense of duty as well, but justice also involves the often despised and dismissed emotion of vengeance, which may, in fact, be (both historically and psychologically) the seed from which the entire plant of justice has grown.

Vengeance and resentment are kindred emotions (as Adam Smith makes quite clear). Both have close ties to our sense of justice. Both are paradigms of negative emotion, as Nietzsche argued at length.[43] Our sense of justice is not just concerned with what happens to us. It is also and more importantly concerned with what is done to us. A sense of responsibility—our own and others'—is utterly essential to our sense of injustice. To be sure, there are cultures in which ascriptions of responsibility are by no means so central, and there are some aspects of distributive justice (e.g., the distribution of health care) in which considerations of responsibility are marginal.[44] But in general, injustice is not just getting the short end; it also requires that someone be to blame. Anger, indignation, outrage, vengeance are all emotions that ascribe responsibility (in the form of blame), but then so do gratitude, admiration, and emotions of "debt"—ascriptions of praise instead of blame— and all evaluations of "desert" and "merit." Our sense of justice (but not every people's sense of justice) places a premium on personal responsibility. (This includes emotions of self-ascribed responsibility: shame, guilt, embarrassment, remorse, regret, and humiliation; pride, self-love, sense of honor.)

How we feel about justice obviously depends in part on how we see ourselves and our roles in the world. John Rawls may try to derive the liberal principles of justice from a selfless situation of rational deliberation, but I think that conservative critics are closer to the mark when they argue (ad hominem) that liberalism is first of all a keen sense of personal guilt about one's own privileged place in the world. (But don't they share that sense of guilt, and why do liberals so often feel compelled to deny it?) We first of all feel uncomfortable about our comparative wealth, health, and opportunities; then we try to devise principles to give this discomfort some structure, to rationalize our privileges or at least allow us to live with them, to correct the inequities in some systematic way that is not wholly self-destructive at the same time. A big part of justice, in other words, is being able to blame (as well as praise) oneself, to have the humility to relinquish one's privileges and entitlements and admit one's good fortune, to admit one's responsibility for justice and not just delegate it to some "system" or social structure in which one is at most a contingent party or perhaps just an observer. The keenest sense of injustice, perhaps, is not outrage at being slighted but rather distress at finding that we ourselves are the beneficiaries of injustice to another. It is there, perhaps, that our often childish sense of injustice turns into a mature sense of justice, not because we have learned to generalize our personal notions of "rights" and "desert" into an abstract theory, but rather because we learn to see ourselves in others' places and realize that we are never mere observers of injustice but almost always participants as well.

At least in the Nietzschean context, we are so accustomed to thinking of resentment in its seething, vicious, nastiest embodiment that we may fail to see that the same emotion invites a very different sort of interpretation.[45] Resentment is an extremely philosophical emotion. It is aware of the larger view. It has keen eyesight (the more Aristotelean analogue of Nietzsche's sense of smell). It is quite conscious not only of how things are but also of how they might be and, most important, how they ought to be. True, resentment always has a personal touch; one is always to some extent resentful *for oneself*, but resentment has not only the capacity but also the tendency to open itself up to more general considerations. It is therefore a harsh and unfair analysis that insists that the camaraderie of the resentful is only of the misery-loves-company variety. It can also be mutually supportive and actively political. Resentment lies at the heart of democracy—Nietzsche was right about that—but it is not "life-stultifying" and it is not necessarily weakness or "herd" mentality.

What Nietzsche ignores—in part because of his biological determinism— is the legitimacy of the felt need to change the world. The sentiment of resentment may often be a legitimate sense of oppression. It is not the voice of mediocrity or incompetence, but the passion of justice denied. This is not to deny that resentment can be nasty and vindictive. But to insist that resentment is nothing but mediocrity undermining excellence has only limited application. Resentment provides the dialectic of the modern world, perhaps the basic dialectic of all human competitive relations, as Hegel suggested (hardly argued) in the "master–slave" section of the *Phenomenology*.[46] One of the most common mistakes in discussions of emotion is the assumption that emotions (misconceived as "feelings") are to be ascribed only to individuals, not groups. But resentment, in particular, is an emotion that is often shared by whole communities or cultures. Even when it is contained within a single individual, resentment tends to generalize and encompass the oppression of a larger community, however ill-defined.[47]

On this more positive view, resentment is not just a selfish emotion, though it always has its self-interested element. Resentment often appeals to compassion when it insists on projecting its own sense of misfortune onto others and objecting on their behalf. This is much more conceptually elevated than "herd mentality," which is unthinking, unreflective, imitative rather than compassionate. At the same time, we should be cautious about concluding that compassion alone yields anything like a true sense of community.[48] But awareness of one's own suffering makes one prone to recognize suffering in others, and this in turn encourages (but does not guarantee) the recognition that other people are worse off than ourselves. (It may also lead to schadenfreude, of course, delight in the fact that other people are worse off than ourselves.) One may feel resentful just for oneself and for some slight offense or failure of recognition—indeed, we usually consider this to be petty, selfish, and meanspirited. But—and this is the crucial point—it is not the resentment per se that we so criticize, but its pettiness, selfishness, and mean-spiritedness.

Vengeance as Justice: The Rationality of Revenge

> There is no denying the aesthetic satisfaction, the sense of poetic justice, that pleasures us when evil-doers get the comeuppance they deserve. The impulse to punish is primarily an impulse to even the score. . . . That satisfaction is heightened when it becomes possible to measure out punishment in exact proportion to the size and shape of the wrong that has been done . . . *mida k'neged mida*—measure for measure, *lex talionis*.
>
> Arthur Lelyveld *Punishment: For and Against*

> Merciful God, do not have mercy on those who had no mercy.
> Elie Wiesel, on the fiftieth anniversary of the liberation of Auschwitz

Finally, on the rationality of revenge. Vengeance is the original passion for justice. The word "justice" in the Old Testament virtually always refers to revenge. In Kant and Hegel, the word *Gerechtigkeit* certainly includes a strong implication of retribution, and throughout most of history the concept of justice has been far more concerned with the punishment of crimes and the balancing of wrongs than with the fair distribution of goods and services. "Getting even" is and has always been one of the most basic metaphors of our moral vocabulary, and the frightening emotion of righteous anger has been the emotional basis for justice just as much as benign compassion. "Don't get mad, get even"—apart from whether it is prudent counsel—is conceptually confused. Getting even is just an effective way of being mad, and getting mad already includes the desire to get even. The pleasure, the aesthetic satisfaction referred to by Arthur Lelyveld in this section's epigraph, reveals the depth of that passion. The need for "proportion" in vengeance already suggests the modicum of intelligence involved in this supposedly most irrational and uncontrollable emotion.

This is not to say, of course, that the motive of revenge as such is always legitimate or the action of revenge always justified. Sometimes vengeance is wholly called for, even obligatory, and revenge is both legitimate and justified. Sometimes it is not, notably when one is mistaken about the offender or the offense. But to seek vengeance for a grievous wrong, to revenge oneself against evil—that seems to lie at the very foundation of our sense of justice, indeed, of our very sense of ourselves, our dignity, and our sense of right and wrong. Even sentimentalist Smith wrotes, "The violation of justice is injury . . . it is, therefore, the proper object of resentment, and of punishment, which is the natural consequence of resentment."[49] We are not mere observers of the moral life, and the desire for vengeance could be argued to be nothing less than an integral aspect of our ability to recognize and resist evil.

Vengeance is often assumed to be "out of control," but it contains—or can be cultivated to contain—a sense of its own limits, a recognition of the need for balance. Thus the Old Testament instructs us that revenge should be *limited to* "eye for eye, tooth for tooth, hand for hand, foot for foot, burning for burning, wound for wound, stripe for stripe" (the *lex talionis*).[50] It was such "equality" that Kant took to be an absolute rational principle in his *Philosophy of Law*, and, in more modern, jovial guise, there is Gilbert and Sullivan's *Mikado*: "an object all sublime/make the punishment fit the crime." The New Testament demands even more restraint: abstention from revenge oneself and patience to entrust it to God. Both the Old and New Testaments (more the latter than the former) also encourage "forgiveness," but there can be no forgiveness if there is not first the desire (and the warrant) for revenge.[51]

Vengeance is often allied with such emotions of offense as anger and resentment, but it is something more in its core commitment to action. One can be angry or resentful and not feel the necessity to "get even." Even when anger and resentment are tied to punishment, it is not necessary that one gets to carry out the punishment oneself.[52] But this is essential to revenge. In that classic spaghetti western, *Once upon a Time in the West*, the avenger (Charles Bronson) saves the life of the villain (wickedly played by Henry Fonda) just in order to be able to kill him personally at the climax of the movie. This is essential to vengeance (which is why, in the Bible and in Mickey Spillane's immortal words, "vengeance is mine"). What is crucial to vengeance, in other words, is one's own essential part in the process of justice. This is just what makes it anathema to the modern legal system, of course, for the system wants to retain justice, and in particular punishment, for itself. It is also what makes it such an important if perverse paradigm for us here.

Vengeance is personal, not impersonal; passionate, not dispassionate; engaged, not merely philosophical.

Not all passions are explosive, however. It is a serious mistake to assume that all passions are, by their very nature, episodic, momentary phenomena characterized by a rush of feeling and the usual physiological accompaniments. Many emotions are durable, ongoing psychological attitudes—"simmering," perhaps, but by no means episodic. Resentment is an obvious example. So is love. But because love endures and may not manifest itself in a sensational bodily commotion for months or years, I have heard philosophers deny that love is even an emotion. (It is, perhaps, a "disposition" to have an emotion.) But this is absurd. Our sense of justice, to get back to the subject at hand, is also such an enduring passion, what Hume called a "calm" passion, though it may well explode in particular episodes, typically prompted by the perception of injustice. Vengeance, too, is an enduring passion, so much so that it may seem no longer to be a passion at all. As the Sicilians say, "Revenge is a dish better served cold." The drama of delay seems to be essential to revenge. Retaliation is immediate, but vengeance takes its time. Indeed, vengeance can become a raison d'être, as evidenced by so many movies and classic tales of revenge, from the Dumas classic *Count of Monte Cristo* to Fay Weldon's camp *Confessions of a She-Devil*. Vengeance has its reasons (though, to be sure, these can be mistaken, irrelevant, out of proportion or otherwise bad). In cultures where vengeance is an established social practice and a matter of obligation, it may even become a paradigm of rationality and a matter of family honor.[53]

Vengeance is the need to "get even," put the world back in balance, and these simple phrases already embody a whole philosophy of justice, even if (as yet) unarticulated and unjustified. Philosophers have been much too quick to attribute this sense of "balance" or "retribution" to reason, but I would want to argue that it is a function of emotion as well. Kant, of course, immediately opts for the former, dismissing the latter suggestion virtually altogether. Vengeance, he suggests, is purely subjective, wholly irrational, undependable, and unjustifiable. It is wholly without measure or reason, devoid of any sense of balance or justice. In defense of retributivism, Robert Gerstein writes: "Vengefulness is an emotional response to injuries done to us by others: we feel a desire to injure those who have injured us. Retributivism is not the idea that it is good to have and satisfy this emotion. It is rather the view that there are good arguments for including the kernel of rationality to be found in the passion for vengeance as a part of any just system of laws."[54] It is this kernel of rationality, in just that sense of measure or balance, that Kant (and so many other philosophers) deny to vengeance and attribute to reason alone. But where would our reasoning about punishment begin if not with our emotional sense of the need for retaliation and retribution? (I should stress here that retaliation and mere compensation, which may sometimes "undo" the damage, do not as such count as punishment.)

Perhaps nowhere is the denial of what is most human about us (that is, our passions) more evident than in the various debates and concerns that surround the problems of punishment in criminal justice. The ongoing dispute between the "utilitarians" (who believe in a "deterrence" theory of punishment) and the "retributivists" (who believe that punishment is necessary in order to satisfy the demands of justice as such) not only neglects but also explicitly dismisses any mention of that passion which alone would seem to give some fuel to the notion of punishment, namely, the emotion of vengeance. This is not to say that punishment should serve *only* as revenge, but it is to say that punishment is in part the satisfaction of the need for vengeance and makes no sense without this. Susan Jacoby has argued that our denial of the desire for vengeance is analogous to the Victorian denial of sexual desire, and we are paying a similar psychological price for it.[55] But as with our hunger for sex, we do not succeed very well in suppressing our thirst for revenge.

How did our passion for retribution—our need for vengeance—come about? I think that evolutionary speculations can go a long way in answering this question. Earlier in this chapter, I stressed the accounts of the moral sentiment theorists as an important insight into "human nature," but I hope that I was sufficiently careful not to give the impression that we are naturally "nice" in any ridiculous sense. Evolutionary theory has shown, conclusively I think, that there is demonstrable advantage for groups and species—if not always for individuals—in the evolution of cooperation. But cooperation has two sides, the willingness to cooperate, first of all, and then the resentment and punishment of those who do not cooperate. (This includes the expectation that one will be punished if one does not cooperate.) One cannot easily imagine the evolution of cooperation without the evolution of punishment.

Robert Axelrod's now classic model of the evolution of cooperation as "tit-for-tat" explains both the evolution of cooperation and the evolution of punishment.[56] In a repetitive "prisoner's dilemma" type of situation, or in any ongoing situation in which one person frequently has the ability to cheat the other(s), an optimum strategy for discouraging such cheating is to respond, dependably, with retribution. A creature endowed only with compassion who would "understand" and forgive the motives of cheats and trespassers, and not punish them, would be just as much of an evolutionary failure as a creature who did nothing but watch out for his or her own advantage and cheated every time. Swift and dependable retaliation is thus in the nature of social animals as well as the lesson of game theory. Vengeance is not the antagonist to rationality but its natural manifestation.

Perhaps the point was overstated in the majority opinion in the U.S. Supreme Court decision in *Gregg* v *Georgia* (1976):

> The instinct for retribution is part of the nature of man, and channeling that instinct in the administration of criminal justice serves an important purpose in promoting the stability of a society governed by law. When people begin to believe that organized society is unwilling or unable to impose upon criminal offenders the punishment they "deserve," then there are sown the seeds of anarchy—of self-help, vigilante justice, and lynch law.

Here the emotion of vengeance is taken seriously and not merely sacrificed to the dispassionate authority of the law. We are creatures who have the natural urge to punish as well as natural sympathy and a sense of social solidarity. Retributive justice is not a purely rational matter—but neither is it thereby "irrational." Most of the arguments that have been advanced against vengeance could, with only slight modifications, be applied to the standard notions of retributive justice as well—which is not surprising if vengeance and retributive justice are in the end related. But in the end, it is perhaps not just a question of whether revenge is rational or not, but whether it is—at the bottom of our hearts as well as off the top of our heads—an undeniable aspect of the way we react to the world, not just as instinct but as a ineliminable part of our worldview and our moral sense of ourselves.

Vengeance, as opposed to justice, is often said to be "blind," although it is worth reminding ourselves which of the two is depicted in established mythology as blindfolded. The truth is that vengeance, as a sense of justice, has or should have a reasonably clear picture of its ends and means. But every violation dictates (however vaguely) its "poetic" if not "natural" end.[57] We are keenly aware of the point at which vengeance is excessive or fails to be satisfied.[58] Like every emotion, vengeance admits of excessive, crude, and genuinely stupid manifestations as well as refined, even exquisite, expressions. Cultivated vengeance can be subtle and even sublime. (Although, to be sure, this is far more often the case in literature than it is real life.) Crude vengeance is usually ugly and self-defeating, but that is often because it is never clear about what it is doing. The problem with vengeance, accordingly, is that it tends to be narrow-minded and overly focused on past transgressions. It loses sight of the larger picture and future consequences. As the Chinese say, "If you seek vengeance, dig two graves." When revenge escalates (the logic of vendetta), the harm may well exceed even the most spiteful satisfaction. Accordingly, limitation of revenge through institutionalization is necessary. But it does not follow that vengeance itself is illegitimate or without measure or of no importance in considerations of punishment.

It is here that mercy and forgiveness enter into the picture. They are an essential aspect of that larger picture that vengeance too easily obscures. Against the tradition that would distinguish mercy and justice (vengeance) and play them off against one another, I want to say that they are part of the same holistic package. They are contasted because of an overly narrow conception of justice (justice as following the law, unbending rules) instead of looking at the overall pattern of emotional and social relationships. One shows mercy because the crime does not really deserve the prescribed punishment, or one shows mercy because, even though the punishment fits the crime, it does not fit the criminal. He or she has virtues that speak louder than the crime. Of course, one might show mercy in order to demonstrate one's virtues, one's power, one's kindness, even one's whimsicality and unpredictability. Or, as part of that larger picture, mercy and forgiveness may be an expression of religious conviction, faith in the importance of something much greater than oneself and the crime at hand. But mercy is not opposed to vengeance. It is, in that larger picture, an attempt to see farther and aim at a much larger sense of satisfaction than vengeance alone could ever provide.

It is worth noting that mercy and forgiveness are often contrasted with justice, as in the Old Testament, where mercy undercuts the claims of justice as vengeance and retaliation. And we noted earlier that mercy, as a form of compassion, complements the desire for vengeance. Nietzsche, playing against the biblical tradition, takes mercy to be the hallmark of true justice, available only to godlike beings (his *Übermenschen*), and links the desire for vengeance with resentment, the emotion of the weak. The New Testament, of course, makes much more of the virtue of forgiveness, although critics and commentators have often been perplexed about what sort of act or emotion this is supposed to be. "Turning the other cheek" seems to provide a kind of paradigm, but in many instances, the availability of a second cheek is not all that obvious. Consider, too, the common pairing of "forgiving" and "forgetting." Why does one need both? I would suggest that forgiving means giving up one's plans or hopes for vengeance, but forgetting is something quite different. Forgetting alludes to a kind of satisfaction. Anthropologist Steven Feld has described to me the practice of "buying off anger" in New Guinea and other cultures. A victim of an offense or his or her family demands compensation, and although it is clearly not a payment in kind, it can provide "satisfaction" and avoid an escalation of violence.[59] Such material finagling may strike us as inappropriate, but the analogy of the "debt," as Nietzsche so insightfully pointed out, lies at the heart of our very notion of guilt. We are willing to hand over our grievances to the law for compensation and retribution, but only so long as we believe that the debt is to be paid. (It is not hard to see our out-of-control system of liability law and tort action as our own version of this practice.) Any system of legal principles that does not take such emotions as the urge for vengeance into account, that does not motivate itself on their behalf, is not—whatever else it may be—a system of justice.

I have not tried to defend vengeance as such, but my claim is that vengeance deserves a central place in any theory of justice and, whatever else we are to say about punishment, the desire for revenge must enter into our deliberations. The notion of satisfaction is particularly important. Gerstein insists that "retributivism is not the idea that it is good to . . . satisfy this emotion," but it seems to me that it is precisely this good, when the emotion is justified, that justifies retribution. We speak of "satisfying one's thirst for vengeance" and, somewhat less metaphorically, we recognize that a given punishment does or does not satisfy the demand for retribution. The ten-month sentence handed down to a rapist does not satisfy the perfectly understandable demand for revenge on the part of the person who was violated. The five-year sentence handed down to a murderer does not satisfy the family of the victim. And the life sentence inflicted on a college student for marijuana possession offends us too. Without such satisfaction (corrected, of course, for personal misperceptions and excessive expectations), justice is not done.

How Justice Satisfies

Justice fulfilled is justice that satisfies our (justifiable) emotions. It is not the fulfillment of some abstract scheme (how much blood has been spilled in those fantasies!) but the case by case resolution of concrete human dilemmas, including the quite natural and justifiable desire to get even. To overemphasize the negative emotions at the expense of such emotions as sympathy and compassion, however, would be to defend a truly perverse concept of justice. What I have tried to suggest is that an adequate account of justice would pay attention to both the "positive" and "negative" emotions, with the added complication that this simpleminded polarity, too, will disintegrate as we probe the social role and function of the various emotions. What I reject is the idea that some dispassionate mode of calculation, whether based on utility or quasi-legal entitlement or some less than empirical notion of "fairness," is the basis of our sense of justice. This is not to dismiss the relevance or the importance of such ideas, but when they lose touch with the feelings that provoke them or fail to recognize those feelings for what they are, the theory of justice suffers accordingly. In a society where abstract individualism and an obsession with contracts threatens to replace interpersonal dynamics and any sense of community, impersonality and a pathological form of "dispassionate rationality" tend to spread far beyond their proper sphere and threaten to become vices instead of virtues. My argument, accordingly, is that justice depends not so much on large scale schemes for redistribution or abstract arguments about the necessity of punishment as on a more primary sense of community and human relationships. Justice is to be found neither in the heavens nor in our contractual attempts to get beyond the State of Nature. The danger is that, like country singers looking for love, we are looking for justice in all the wrong places.

5

THE TRAGIC SENSE OF LIFE

My formula for greatness in a human being is *amor fati*: that one wants nothing to be different, not forward, not backward, not in all eternity. Not merely to bear what is necessary, still less conceal it . . . but *love* it.

Friedrich Nietzsche, Ecce Homo

For the first time, I laid my heart open to the benign indifference of the universe.

Meursault, in Camus's The Stranger

It is comparatively easy for philosophers to talk about justice, keeping the subject at arm's length, abstracting and reducing it to a theory and debating without resolution rights versus needs versus merit versus equality. Other topics are not so easy to talk about. The hardest of these, I think, is the awful fact of human suffering. Can the joy of philosophy stand up to the reality of tragedy?

Here, one suspects, the philosophical quest for formality and "thinness" has an ulterior motive. Human suffering, by its very nature, is never "thin."[1] The phrase "being philosophical" is commonly used to refer to an ability to cope with misfortune through thought, but philosophy, in its professional incarnation, has proved to be notoriously unwilling to grapple with the hard and sensitive questions surrounding tragedy. To be sure, there has been a burgeoning philosophical literature about the Holocaust, the most modern, most horrible example of massive tragedy and evil, although it has been kept safely out of the mainstream journals. But as an example of evil, the Holocaust tends to provoke blame and species self-scrutiny rather than, say, that blameless, awesome silence that follows a natural disaster (an earthquake, a tornado, the sudden onslaught of an epidemic). Why do horrible things happen to good people? How should we think about tragedy? How should we cope with disease and debilitating accidents? What can we philosophers say, beyond the usual platitudes and condolences, to someone who has lost a loved one, or an arm, or the ability to see? How should we ourselves live, and what should we think, when one or another of the ultimately inevitable tragedies happens to us?[2] We have all met or read about those rare sages who have suffered the most profound misfortunes and retained a sense of acceptance, graciousness, and even humor about their lives. Can philosophy help us to do the same?

We might want to distinguish between tragedy and misfortune (or tragedies), recognizing the latter as an unavoidable aspect of life but reserving the former for cases with exceptional nobility, as in "the tragedy of Oedipus" or "the tragedy of King Lear." But here our egalitarianism kicks in, and we rebel against this aristocratic (and theatrical) tradition. The suffering and misfortune of a princess or a Princeton graduate, we insist, is no more (and no less) significant than the suffering and misfortune of a pauper or a street bum. Given the recent outpouring of grief surrounding several much-publicized celebrity deaths, we might note that it is not entirely obvious that we as a people really believe that all suffering is equal in significance. Nevertheless, the philosophical point can be made in an egalitarian way. What counts as suffering—what makes someone suffer—may well vary enormously from case to case, from individual to individual. But suffering as such is a part of every life, and, as tragedy, it is not just suffering. As tragedy, I will argue, it has meaning. What gives meaning to suffering is what it is philosophy's job to investigate.

Miguel de Unamuno wrote his classic *The Tragic Sense of Life* just before World War I.[3] Today, unfortunately, the book and its subject have dropped out of the "canon." Virtually no serious philosophy student ever reads *The Tragic Sense* or has much sympathy for its tragic sensibility. The poignant questions about death, suffering, and undeserved misfortune that Unamuno addresses, so central to virtually all of the world's religions, have been virtually exorcised from philosophy. Unamuno's vision was ultimately religious, but in the despairing tones of Dostoevsky, not the "glad tidings for the melancholy" melody of Kierkegaard. The brute fact of human life is that there is suffering that has no resolution and evil that has no redemption.[4] So says our reason.

As an early existentialist, Unamuno held a kind of "irrationalist" line, arguing against any scientific or "objective" solution to the philosophical problems of suffering and evil. Reason, he argued, can only lead us to skepticism. It leaves life devoid of meaning. Like Pascal, along with Kierkegaard (his two philosophical heroes), Unamuno insisted that reason has to be combatted by faith. But faith, although it is the alternative to reason and despair, never emerges from the shadow of reason, so it, too, cannot escape from skepticism. In that sense, we are incapable of being nonrational.

In his tentative answer to this dilemma, Unamuno follows Kierkegaard, attempting a "leap of faith," a version of Kierkegaard's "subjective truth," beyond reason, beyond objectivity. But unlike Kierkegaard, Unamuno finds that wholehearted, passionate commitment is always compromised by our rationality. We cannot ignore or deny the facts of unresolved suffering and unredeemed evil, and we cannot ultimately see beyond them. Unamuno sometimes insists that facing up to this "hopelessness" is itself the meaning of human life. (Later, Camus would insist that the meaning of life was facing up to "the Absurd.") What gives life meaning is a form of rebellion, rebellion against reason, an insistence on believing passionately what we cannot believe rationally. The meaning of life is to be found in passion—romantic passion, religious passion, passion for work and for play, passionate commitments in the face of what reason "knows" to be meaningless. Philosophy, because it is on the side of reason, is by contrast a kind of resignation coupled with playful distraction and self-deception.[5]

The view that I want to defend here echoes Unamuno's vision, but without the morbid associations and the mock-heroic stance often associated with it.[6] As an existentialist, Unamuno holds a strong line on personal responsibility and the importance of personal commitment. Whether or not life has a meaning—whatever that is taken to mean—we make meaning by way of our commitments. It is in the context of those made meanings that suffering and evil can be moved from the center stage of human existence to wait in the wings (from which they will inevitably appear, without direction and oblivious to the plot of the play). Reason can indeed prove to be the enemy of such commitments and meanings, especially through cynicism—the wholesale dismissal of all such efforts—and through those forms of philosophy that reduce the tragedies of life to logical puzzles devoid of personal meaning. Such rational devices accommodate tragedy, but at a terrible price.

From what I have already said in this book, it should be obvious that I think that Unamuno, like many of the existentialists, grossly inflates the opposition between rationality and "the heart," and, consequently, between reason and faith in matters of ultimate meaning. But I think that he is right to say that we find meaning primarily in our grandest passions, and that we make meaning through our passionate commitments. Love certainly has this stature in our lives. So do our sense of community, our passion for justice, our commitments to our work, whose real importance to us should be not what it reaps (a salary, substantial royalties, recognition, and fame) but the engagement itself, the exercise of skills and talents, the social role, the commitment, the responsibilities.[7]

But here, too, tragedy and suffering make their entrance. If the meanings of life are the meanings we make, we recognize a fatal contingency to our passions and our projects. There is nothing necessary about them. Indeed, there is nothing necessary about us. As Camus and Unamuno both argue, our commitments are ultimately limited, there is no ultimate answer to the "Why?" question, and it all ends in death ("the brotherhood of man," according to both authors). Here Unamuno finds himself torn between paroxysms of despair and cosmic chutzpah. We demand either immortality or identity with God. ("Either all or nothing!")[8] In his more reasonable pronouncements, Unamuno simply encourages religion—in his own case, a return to the Catholic Church. But tragedy, whatever we do and however we "leap," is real and undeniable. Camus, like Unamuno, turns this obvious fact into a heroic stance. He calls it "keeping the Absurd alive" and "rebellion." Sisyphus shakes his fist "with scorn and defiance" at the gods who condemned him, and thus simultaneously affirms and transcends his absurd situation.

There is something both beautiful and pathetic in this quasi-rational, emphatically existential attitude. Shaking that puny fist at God or the gods is so poignantly human, so pointless, and at the same time meaningful. Of course, such behavior makes no conceivable difference to anything, except in our own attitudes. Our rational, more reasonable philosophical minds want to resist such absurd postures and simply insist that life is indeed meaningful, if only because the overreaching philosophical question (about the meaning of life) is itself meaningless. Life is meaningful, in other words, by default, by not taking the question seriously. But what is beautiful and revealing about Unamuno and Camus (and Sartre, too) is precisely their refusal either to dismiss the question or to despair at the answer. They provoke an irresolvable tension, not between reason and passion but between our passionate commitments and our awareness that, nevertheless, our lives are ultimately not in our hands.

What I find admirable in the existentialists is their resolute insistence that the messiest questions are not to be swept under the philosophical rug or scrutinized only with philosophical tweezers. Suffering and death are real. The ultimate frustration of our projects is inevitable. Love entails not only the possibility but, certain romantic illusions aside, also the inevitability of loss. We try to hold together our love of life and our dread of what is to come in an uncomfortable philosophical consciousness. Unamuno is right. Our passion can never escape or eclipse our reason. (Indeed, there is no passion without rationality.) Camus is right. There is no viable alternative to this "absurd" confrontation between our rational, demanding minds and the "indifferent" universe (however that distinction between mind and universe is to be made). There is no denying suffering. Neither is there need to dwell on it, but if philosophy is not to be unbearably light or "thin," it has to try to come to terms with the inevitable. Suffering has meaning, in short, because life has meaning. Tragedy, on the face of it, seems to undermine that meaning. How, then, can tragedy be meaningful?

First, without going quite so far as Unamuno does, let's clear away a certain philosophical presumption. In real life, both justice and rationality have their limits. In the abstract, we may insist that virtue deserves its reward, vice its punishment, and arrogance its comeuppance; but in actuality we know that life is not fair, that misfortunes befall the innocent and the virtuous, that children are killed in natural disasters, that people die "before their time" and sometimes on the very brink of an elusive success, that villains often flourish and sometimes get away with murder. To be sure, we may feel a slightly guilty satisfaction when evildoing actually gets its due, and selfless delight when goodness is miraculously rewarded, but we do not pretend that it is always thus or that the world is just after all. Only in philosophy and theology do we dare to argue—or simply presume—that there is an explanation, a rational account, of all that happens, or to hide behind the demand that there *should* be such a rational accounting. In life, we know, bad things just happen. And then our cherished rationality shows one of its more embarrassing aspects: our ability and readiness to *rationalize*. As Nietzsche said, a universe that is explained even with bad reasons is better than no explanation at all.

"What can one say?" is a proper response to extreme misfortune, in the sense that, held up against the enormity of much human tragedy, words and ideas seem to make little difference. But, in another sense, something must be said, if only by way of condolences and sympathy, which already imply at least the effort to understand and make sense of misfortune. Here is where philosophy can actually do some good. Taoism, for instance, is brilliant in this regard. It teaches us to see everything that happens as necessary for everything else to be as it is, and thus to see everything as significant in a holistic perspective. (The view of the cynic and the pessimist, by contrast, is that the larger perspective shows everything to be *insignificant*.[9]) It is hard to believe that anyone could embrace Chuang-tzu and turn away unaffected.[10] But if philosophy can help, it can also hide the problem of tragedy. Rationality so easily turns to rationalization. We say, against all reason and feeling, "It's all for the best," or we dismiss a horrible tragedy with the empty theological assurance "It's God's will." "From rationality to rationalization" is a crude way of marking the difference between those responses that I believe are appropriate, sensitive, and philosophically warranted, and those that are inappropriate, insensitive, and philosophically suspect. If we are going to try to get a grip on tragedy, let's begin with an example of the philosophically suspect.

Instead of Tragedy:
Blame and Entitlement

"Shit Happens" is one of the more popular T-shirt and bumper-sticker slogans among the high school and junior college crowd. Apart from the vulgarity, it is shocking because it is so obviously, undeniably, unavoidably true. Nevertheless, this global insight collapses when the shit actually happens. Tragedy gets denied—even by those who have (regarding themselves) a very weak or even negligible notion of personal responsibility—by looking for someone to blame. Tragedy does not just "happen," in other words. It is brought about, it is the product of agency, and someone, or something, must be held accountable.

The denial of tragedy begins in a seemingly innocent philosophical thesis: *Whatever happens, happens for a reason.* And harking back to Aristotle, that notion of "reason" (or "cause") is ultimately to be understood in terms of intentions, purposes, teleology. Most immediately, we look for someone—someone responsible or, as the case may be, irresponsible: the driver, the manufacturer, the doctor or the hospital, the parents. Or, a bit less directly, we blame the institution, the constitution, the country, the culture. We personify nature, thus creating "someone" who can be held responsible. (The Chinese still refer to earthquakes as "the anger of the earth." Second-rate evolutionists still talk about natural selection as if it is a purposive process.) And, of course, we personify machines—kicking our cars, cursing our computers. In desperation, we blame "the system." But if no one more tangible comes forward as a plausible candidate, there is always God.

Natural disasters are revealingly referred to as "acts of God." People who would never think of thanking and giving credit to God for their accomplishments seem to have no hesitation to blame Him for their misfortunes. "It's God's Will" is an all-purpose summary of a philosophy and an attitude that refuse to accept tragedy and insist on rationalization instead. But even without such divine appeal, we look for the good, the reason, in everything. Here, we might say, it is reason that is irrational. We edit our narratives to suit our sense of the way things ought to be. And where we cannot find a purpose, we invent our own. Losses are a "learning experience." A death in the family "teaches us all a lesson," and death after a long illness is "really a blessing."

In the history of philosophy, this has often been called "the Principle of Sufficient Reason."[11] It dates back to ancient times but hit its heyday, oddly enough, in modern times, in particular with the "rationalist" philosophers of Europe, notably Spinoza and Leibniz, and the Romantic pessimist Arthur Schopenhauer. There is a version of the principle operative in science, of course ("Everything that happens has an explanation"), but in Spinoza and Leibniz it is more of a theological principle, an all-purpose account of God's various manifestations. For Leibniz, it is a straightforward principle concerning God's various choices. For Spinoza, it is rather an attempt (as in Taoism) to account for the "necessity" of all that happens, but the upshot is pretty much the same. Everything that happens, happens for a reason, and the ultimate reason is God. Schopenhauer is in many ways a more interesting case. He is a straightforward teleologist, with the twin twist that he believes neither in God nor in the ultimate purposefulness of the universe. Schopenhauer's thesis is ultimately much like the one that I want to pursue here (but

I dispense with the pessimism). The appeal to the Principle of Sufficient Reason, says Schopenhauer, is ultimately illusory and frustrating, increasing rather than decreasing the amount of suffering in the world. Nevertheless, it may be that we cannot get it out of our minds.

The Principle of Sufficient Reason covers enormous territory, from the philosophical defense of scientific inquiry to those nineteenth-century theodicies that try to illuminate God's plan in human history. But it has a more mundane, less sophisticated, prephilosophical function, by way of rationalization. Conspiracy theorists, for example, working on the darker side of reasoning, will always insist on a culprit: some secretive cabal, communism, the Defense Department, the Mafia, international bankers, the Jews, the Arabs, international capitalism, the patriarchy, the CIA, or the contemporary favorite, visitors from outer space. There is no such thing as "circumstantial," on this view. (Or in philosophical terms, *post hoc, ergo propter hoc.*) The blame may fall on whoever is a ready target for suspicion or criticism and may just have a motive, if not the wherewithal, to carry it off. One might say that conspiracy theorists are people with overactive imaginations but limited philosophical sensibilities. Everything that happens—they, too, believe—happens for a reason. It just happens to be a malevolent reason, something to inspire not our gratitude or our worship but our fear, loathing, and hatred. Nevertheless, the logic is the same.

The logic is that bad things never *just* happen. We are loath to recognize tragedy, the fact that life is tragic and no one and nothing need be "responsible." So *someone* must have done it to us. In its most vulgar expression, the Principle of Sufficient Reason is the view that "someone has to pay for this!" This is not just a philosophical misunderstanding, of course. Culturally, the popular and legal ideology of American society seems devoted to the idea that there are no "accidents," that someone is always to blame. When lawyers refer to "acts of God," this might be mistaken for a throwaway phrase or casual piety, but on reflection it betrays a denial of liability, the flip-side of that particularly opportunistic version of the assumption that nothing happens without a reason, without a purpose, and therefore without an agent who is responsible. If the person who is the most immediate cause has an excuse or has to be let off the hook, there are always more distant parties who can be made accountable: the agency, the institution, the manufacturer, the licensing bureau.

Indeed, according to "strict liability," blame and responsibility may even part company. One may be held liable even in the absence of guilt of any kind. The default position is that there can be no literal accidents, that is, events without a cause, an agent, and a purpose, without someone to blame. The practical dimension of this position in America involves, by some estimates, $300 billion a year.[12] It is the continuing tort-liability crisis, which is, in a philosophical nutshell, our insistence on blaming others for our misfortunes, sometimes quite apart from any reasonable notion of "fault," and claiming compensation ("justice") in return. What gets lost, in addition to billions of dollars and millions of hours of court time and anxiety, is any sense of the tragic life. "Somebody is going to pay for this!"

The tort-liability problem discloses another ugly aspect of the denial of tragedy, one firmly tied to the insistence on blame—blaming others, that is. It is the phenomenon of *entitlement*. There is an irony here, not to mention some sort of radical inconsistency. We readily blame others for our misfortunes, but we just as readily deny responsibility ourselves, both for our own misfortunes and for those we wreak on others, directly or indirectly. When we suffer, our sufferings are not our fault, and so we deserve compensation. The underlying understanding is that we are entitled to a good life, a happy, healthy, comfortable life. (Even the Declaration of Independence claims only that we are entitled to the "*pursuit* of happiness.") If we fail to find that happiness, then someone must be to blame. In the case of an accident or (these days) even an illness, there must be someone or some organization that can be shown to have deprived us of the good life we deserve, and he, she, or it owes us. Even parents are now the targets of such "wrongful life" suits. Note the logic of such demands, and the key terms "desert," "entitlement," and "debt." This may be the language of justice, but it is not the language of tragedy. In the big picture, none of us is "entitled" to anything, much less happiness. That is not to say, what is very different, that happiness is not worth having and promoting, but it is to say that the language of justice loses its place in the larger questions of tragedy.

And yet, the idea of "compensation" dies hard with us, even in—especially in—the horrible circumstances of tragedy. A person crippled in an automobile accident naturally sues the other driver, even if it was, literally, an "accident." (No one was drunk, reckless, or unusually inattentive.) As a bit of social engineering—a device for making sure that the seriously incapacitated have some means of financial support—the goal is unassailable even if the mechanism is inefficient. But that is not what is going on here. The idea that one might be just plain unlucky does not sit well with us. Although we would rather be unlucky than responsible for our own misfortunes, we would much rather blame someone else and feel entitled to get even. And if they, too, were just unlucky? Well, then they can damn well pay for it. And if "they" is a corporation or professional who has been lucky enough to make a profit on the product or practice involved, so much the better. The claims and expectations of victims have been a topic in Western philosophy at least since the Biblical prophets, if not before. But nowhere have these been both universalized and institutionaliazed as in America, where, in Plato's parlance, every citizen deserves his or her due, or at least his or her day in court.

On the other hand, the realization that life is not fair can also be a rationalization, a shrug of the shoulders that eliminates thought as well as blame and responsibility. When President Jimmy Carter said that, it provoked deep resentment, not only because it was his job to see to it that life, at least in these United States, would become fair, but also because what he said was so obviously true. He had also trampled on one of our most heartfelt hopes: that in America, at least, life *is* fair. (Ronald Reagan swept the next election, assuring us that, by way of "trickle-down economics," "morning in America" would once again bring fairness.) Carter's verbal faux pas is fair warning. The idea that the good will prosper (or that those who do prosper must therefore be good) and that the bad will fall (or, if fallen, they must have done something wrong) is not to be challenged. The Hollywood happy endings on which Reagan was nurtured have produced a required plot outline that is not confined to the movies but expected, as a matter of entitlement, in real life.

So let me say the obvious: Some things are within our control, and this is the proper sphere of justice. We live with others in a society such that people can be held responsible for what they do. Within that social context, we are right to be offended, angered, resentful, and even punitive when they cheat us. But we also live in and are sometimes confronted by an "indifferent" universe. This is a very different context. We say that nature "cheats" us, but we realize that we have now moved to the land of metaphor. Nature doesn't cheat. There is no one to blame. Even the most pious recognize that some acts of God are not acts of God. At worst, they are omissions of God, still blameworthy or theologically perplexing, perhaps, but not direct harms for which reasons are expected or an explanation forthcoming. It is therefore not clear who could be to blame or to what we may be entitled. Which brings us to one of the most celebrated of philosophy's problems.

The Problem of Evil

> When a man does not do what he ought, God the Creator is not at fault.
>
> Saint Augustine, *The City of God*

Sixteen hundred years ago, the philosopher Saint Augustine worried extensively about what has since been codified as "the Problem of Evil." I want to consider that "problem" as itself a problem, reflecting our extravagant expectations and demands of the world and of God. The Problem of Evil turns out to be one more manifestation of our tendency to blame and our unwarranted sense of entitlement.

Since prehistoric times, it has been obvious that bad things happen to good people. And since prehistoric times, this has been a source of concern, of consternation, a conundrum, an excuse for extravagant philosophizing, theologizing, rationalizing. More annoying, perhaps, but no less metaphysically demanding, is the equally obvious fact that good things happen to bad people, that those who cause harm do not always get their due. In response to this troubling pair of facts, many Heavens and Hells have been invented, most (but not all) of them dedicated to the proposition that, in the end, there will be commensuration.

The overwhelming fact that defines the Problem of Evil is the fact of suffering. "Life is suffering," teaches the Buddha, the first of his Noble Truths. But where the Buddhists swear off the cravings and expectations that result in suffering, we insist on satisfying them and, when they are frustrated, we ask "Why?" Suffering requires some other explanation. What makes the problem so intractable in the Judeo-Christian tradition is the omnipresence of an all-knowing, all-powerful God. The problem becomes a paradox: If bad things happen to good people, then it must be because (1) God doesn't know about it—but he is all-knowing, or (2) God cannot do anything about it—but he is all-powerful, or (3) God doesn't care about it—but the premise of the entire argument, the very conception of God, is such that it is his caring—and ultimately, perhaps only his caring—that counts.

In the twentieth century, Camus sums it up in his uncheeriest novel, *The Plague*: "People die, and they are not happy." In his earlier work, he summarized the modern sensibility in "the Absurd," the recognition that life ultimately makes no sense, that there is no justice, that our prayers are not answered, that there is no God to answer them. In *The Myth of Sisyphus*, Camus poignantly, if rather obscurely, wrote, "We have to learn to live *without appeal*." For many years, I did not get what he meant, but now, I think, I do. I no longer think of it as a denial of God, despite Camus's professed atheism. Indeed, he was a sympathetic admirer of Augustine. What he rejected, I believe, was the use of God to deny tragedy, the Absurd. To do so, Camus said, is a form of "philosophical suicide." It is much as Nietzsche intended when he urged us to live without "judgment" (even if Nietzsche so obviously failed to do so himself). Life is absurd, but we nonetheless have to live it and face it together.[13]

There have been many attempts to get around the paradox of an all-powerful, all-knowing, good God who allows evil in His domain. The most prominent of these in Christianity and Islam is the dual promise and threat of Heaven and Hell. Despite earthly appearances, there *will be* compensation, reward, and punishment, justice overflowing both in the eternal bliss of the saved and in the unending suffering of the damned. This conversion of human tragedy into divine justice takes many forms, both crude and refined, from the crude reward–punishment model of the most offensive television preachers to the sophisticated "moral order of the world" views of Rousseau and Kant; I do not want to enter into the theological labyrinth to sort them out. My general attitude, which I am willing to leave undefended here, is that such a belief is perfectly respectable, if undemonstrable. Belief in the afterlife, whether otherworldly Christian or Islamic Heaven or this-worldly reincarnation, ghosts, and joining the ancestors, is one of the sweetest and most easily understandable beliefs that people have, and even the most empiricist-minded philosophers ought to respect that.

But not all versions of this belief are sweet. Their use as cudgels for thrashing nonbelievers or as excuses to send mere boys to meaningless deaths as "martyrs," for instance, is unspeakable. Less offensive but still problematic is their use as balm for the distraught. Saying to a bereaved parent, who has suitable religious beliefs, "It's God's will" should evoke only sympathy, not philosophical disputation. But what serves as balm does not succeed as a cure, and beyond its role as therapy and from the point of view of *this* life, eternal bliss is no compensation for a life cut short by tragedy. It is not the belief in the afterlife that gets called into question but (as Kant and many other believers have insisted) the appropriateness of any such notion of compensation. God does not play tit-for-tat (nor dice) with His universe.

Among the numerous more and less ingenious attempts to answer or get around the Problem of Evil, one way is by tinkering with and weakening the conception of God. It is suggested, for instance, that faith only requires one to believe that God is very powerful, not that He is all-powerful, or that it is sufficient that God has vastly superior knowledge rather than, what may be logically impossible, total knowledge. At the very sophisticated end of the scale, there are the predictably "thin" logical attempts to resolve the problem, notably without fleshing out the concept of "evil" that is the tangible core of the issue.[14] On the other hand, with only a modicum of philosophical or theological sophistry, ordinary people are easily persuaded to buy the explanation that we cannot expect to know God's "mysterious ways." Thus the fact that He allows suffering and death in human life need not contradict the idea that he cares, and comparisons with ordinary human sentiments and expectations are beside the point. It has been famously suggested that this Creation of his is "the best of all possible worlds" and there is no more evil and suffering than necessary—in some sense that we cannot possibly comprehend. It has been suggested that God is, in effect, "too busy" to look after all of the ills of the world, and then there is the "deep green" response that we are deceiving ourselves if we think that it is us whom God cares about exclusively, whether that "us" refers to a single "chosen people" or to humanity as a whole.[15]

I have a good deal of sympathy for some of those views, particularly the ecological Gaia view, which reaches its most sublime expression in Taoism. But the slip from ecological respect and responsibility to the dismissal of humans as "insignificant" too readily leads to a rabid antihumanism in which the interests and needs of mere humans can simply be discounted, or can be viewed as counting no more than the interests and needs of mosquitoes.

Whether or not such views account for the existence of human suffering in the world (by saying, in effect, it doesn't really matter), they are also views that share all of the potential for viciousness of the Inquisition and Damnation crowd. The problem of evil cannot be solved by denying the significance of evil and human suffering.

Contrary to the way it is usually framed, I want to suggest that the Problem of Evil has little to do with belief in the existence of God or in an afterlife. Camus was an atheist, and yet it was the Problem of Evil, the presence of human suffering, that violated his innate sense of justice and fairness, that evoked his dramatic conception of "the Absurd." Nietzsche was also an atheist ("by instinct," he tells us in *Ecce Homo*), but it is neither God nor Heaven as such that draws his heaviest fire. It is rather the cheap and petty use of theology to deny or rationalize suffering rather than face up to it and, like the ancient Greeks he adored, make something of it—if not something beautiful, then at least something meaningful. To challenge the Problem of Evil, we do not need to call into question either the nature and existence of God or the belief in an afterlife. To challenge the Problem of Evil, we must, rather, remind ourselves of the contingency of our good fortune and how unreasonable we are to deny the inevitability of misfortune and the finitude of our lives. As Bernard Williams writes, "There is a problem of evil only for those who expect the world to be good."[16] We thus call into question those abuses of God and the idea of an afterlife that block our deepest emotional responses by assuring us, against all evidence, that our suffering is well worthwhile.

Blaming the Victim:
The "Free Will" Solution

Human reason needs only to will more strongly than fate, and she *is* fate

Thomas Mann

The most powerful responses to the Problem of Evil, even within theology, have come to focus not on the nature of God and His ways or on our own insignificance but, to the contrary, on our own very significant role in the creation of evil and suffering in the world. Disaster happens because *we* are evil, or selfish, or irresponsible. A catastrophe, accordingly, may well be a punishment, not a mere accident. It may be an "act of God" in the most literal, punitive sense of the term. According to Augustine, it is our own "free will" that is the cause and the explanation of evil; God is not to blame. The theological and philosophical tangles that follow, such as whether God is nevertheless responsible for letting us do the wrong He necessarily knew we would do, need not concern us here. Such debates only point once again to our tendency to blame God, even if indirectly, rather than face up to suffering "without appeal."

What makes the assignment of blame so attractive these days is the fact that comparatively few of our disasters and tragedies are natural catastrophes or acts of God. When a statistician wants to indicate how rarely a certain event occurs, he or she compares it with "being hit by lightning" or "dying of a bee sting." Natural disasters are increasingly rare, compared with our own human-made disasters. These are clearly or at least arguably the result of our own doing, our own tinkering with nature, our own manufacturing of and experimentation with dangerous machinery and complex biological processes, our love of speed and the internal combustion engine, our love of comfort and convenience despite the terrible though not immediately obvious costs. Earthquakes and hurricanes still occur, but buildings are made to withstand them. When people die in a storm, the blame is usually put on the developers, the builders, even the residents themselves. Most people today who are killed in avalanches, rock slides and blizzards are not innocent, unsuspecting victims, but daredevils, adventurers, sportsmen who have gone out seeking the thrill of danger. One might hesitate to call the resulting tragedies kin to the Problem of Evil, but nevertheless, Augustine's "free will" solution to the traditional problem surely applies in a convincing way today.

The conception of suffering as punishment is not limited, of course, to man-made disasters. In 1755, the philosophers of the European Enlightenment struggled with a particularly gruesome and paradoxical act of God: an earthquake in Lisbon, Portugal, that killed thousands of worshipers, many of them women and children, in their churches on a Sunday morning. This calamitous loss of innocent lives was a particularly poignant reminder of the difficulty of the Problem of Evil, and no amount of self-blame seemed sufficient to explain, much less justify, this terrible natural disaster. The "free will" account of evil seems to leave out an essential distinction that only those obsessed with human depravity would ignore. There are evils that are indeed our own doing, that we bring about directly or indirectly. But there are also evils that do not seem attributable, no matter how remotely, to our acts or intentions. It seems, without question, that they cannot be construed as punishments. Nevertheless, our metaphysics and our social practices continue to do just that. "Blaming the victim" is not just an element of perversity in our current legal system and our culture. It is a long-standing and still popular metaphysical and theological doctrine.

Much of Hebrew history and "Jewish guilt" is based on the doctrine that misfortunes are one's own fault. Suffering, accordingly, is punishment. It therefore has a meaning. The theme is familiar: Better to blame oneself than to acknowledge that suffering may be meaningless. The troublesome fact that God's punishments seem to be visited not only on the guilty but on the innocent as well must then be explained by the idea—common to many cultures, including the tribes of the Old Testament—that justice is done not just to the individual but also to the family, the tribe, the whole society. Whole cities are destroyed by God, although simple demographics would suggest that among the inhabitants of both Sodom and Gomorrah were innocent infants and children who had not yet indulged in the sins of their elders. The idea that only the individual is punished for misdeeds is still an oddity in the world, no matter how precious a principle it may be to us. The brutal fact of the matter is that even in our society, innocents often pay for their parents' or their neighbors' or their political leaders' crimes.[17]

But even the Old Testament is by no means secure with this radical answer to the Problem of Evil. Consider the most troubling tale of unwarranted suffering in the Judeo-Christian tradition, the problem—the "test"—of Job. Job's God is not so much mysterious as malicious. In any case, He is clearly unjust by any reasonable standard, human or divine. Job was entirely innocent. Indeed, that innocence is the premise of the story, without which there would be no problem, no dilemma, no test of faith. To cause a good man to suffer to prove a point or test his patience is not, in any civilized sense, an act of justice. It doesn't matter that all is restored to him at the end of the story. Compensation is not all there is to justice. The pain of losing one's family is not compensated by the joy of finding them whole again, much less by the substitution of a new family. The suffering of protracted illness and infirmity is not, and cannot be, compensated by being made well again. But what really raises the problem of evil is not so much the question of God's will or the adequacy of compensation but Job's own reaction to his suffering. Millions of pages have been written on the "patience" of Job, and how (or whether) he passed the test of faith. But even a casual look at Job's story shows a character who was anything but patient or undoubting. Job was indignant. He was resentful. He did not accept his suffering and did not think of it as justice.[18] He knew that he was blameless, and we know it, too.

One clearly unsatisfactory solution to the Problem of Evil is unjust blame. Unjustly blaming the victim does nothing to save the doctrine of an all-powerful, just God. But it is different, perhaps, when we blame ourselves. This is, presumably, what Augustine had in mind: that we take responsibility for our own flaws and failures. It is undeniable that we ourselves cause a good deal of human suffering, if only by our extravagant lifestyles and expectations. In our misfortunes, we can discern a much-deserved "comeuppance" or delayed retaliation for suffering inflicted on others. The South Asian notion of karma, whatever further metaphysical baggage it may be called upon to carry, is first of all the recognition that what we suffer in life is in part the "residue" of our previous actions.[19] Indeed, such rough justice provides the theme of some of the best-loved stories in every society. We also recognize rough justice in the suffering of whole societies, notably in the aftermath of war. Sartre summarized this harsh vision of extended responsibility without compromise when, at the height of World War II and during the Nazi occupation of Paris, he declared, "We all get the war we deserve." One does not need the notion of original sin to understand this idea. It is enough to believe in the Principle of Sufficient Reason, here understood as the belief that whatever happens is in some sense one's own responsibility.

An excessive—and awful—example of our tendency to blame ourselves is the way in which we often regard illness. Instead of viewing disease and bodily malfunction as something natural and, for all of us, inevitable, we tend to tie illness to blame. At least, we do this with respect to other people's illness. When they get sick, we blame them for not taking better care of themselves. Or we blame them for their attitude, their lifestyle, their diet. This is especially true with the most terrifying of all diseases, cancer. In her most personal and perhaps most profound book, *Illness as Metaphor*, Susan Sontag rightly complains about our medieval tendency to interpret all illness as a sign, a punishment, a payback. We refuse to believe, except in our own case, that people just get sick. In one's own case, of course, it is other people who are to blame. It is the environment, the polluted air, the excess minerals in the drinking water, the factory in the town, the lax government controls, the doctor's careless diagnosis, the inefficacy of the prescriptions, the stress of one's job, family tensions, and so on. But one does not just "get sick." Here, too, there are no accidents. There is always someone to blame, if only the victim.

Granted, most human tragedies now have a human cause, or a whole history of human causes. At every stage of this human causal chain, there will be those acts that have "intent," in the word of the law, that are undertaken with full awareness and purposiveness and, when things go wrong, are therefore blameworthy. Punishment is appropriate. But there are also accidents, which is to say that there are disasters and damages that are without intent, even if human beings brought them about. Some consequences and side effects cannot be foretold. All uses and abuses of products cannot be reasonably predicted. Sometimes one sees that an intended action or product will have a second, unintended consequence, but often the risks of that "double effect" cannot be readily calculated. Some tragedies are the result of shortsightedness, sloppiness, or other forms of "negligence," but others are not. They occur despite all reasonable precautions, care, and good intentions. We know that a vaccine that will prevent a horrible disease in millions will predictably have some terrible effect on a very few, but we cannot detect who these few will be beforehand. Such calamities are tragic in the classical sense; there is no "sufficient reason," no rational and just explanation for them, and no one is to blame. Why can we not just leave the matter there?

I certainly do not mean to belittle victims whose tragic misfortunes leave them grasping for metaphysical straws, nor do I want to limit the liability of those who truly are blameworthy for the misfortunes of others. Rather, my suspicion is that the appeal to "God's will" and the "Problem of Evil" is all too often a way of not facing up to suffering, particularly the suffering of others. The insistence on blame may be a form of inverse cynicism, a demand for satisfaction where there can be no satisfaction. To many people, it may be clear that God will assure that justice will triumph in the end. But it is not at all clear what this means in the context of tragedy, what compensation might mean, what standard of justice would be intelligible. In the meantime, many of these same believers will do their bit in His behalf, collecting not only compensatory but also punitive damages, enjoying their day in court, and turning the bad things that happen into an illusion of taking charge of their world in His name.

Oedipus Redux:
The Death of Tragedy

Why should a man fear since chance is all in all like him, and he can clearly foreknow nothing? Best to live lightly, as one can, unthinkingly.
                                                    Jocasta, in *Oedipus Rex*

Whatever happened to tragedy? This was the question Nietzsche asked of his own German culture—the culture of Wagner, Goethe, and Schopenhauer—over against the brilliance of the ancient Greeks.[20] It was not that people suffered significantly less. Nietzsche saw firsthand the suffering that war and illness inflicted on people. But what he saw was the beginning of the depersonalization of war, the medical institutionalization of illness, the increasing pettiness of the rationalizations with which his age faced its fate. Nietzsche's question was how and why the modern age had lost the concept of the tragic, the experience of tragedy, that profound sense of loss that engages our sense of meaning and awe rather than our often petty propensity to blame.

Nietzsche accused his fellow Germans of having lost any sense of profundity, and with it the concept of tragedy. He noted that they would rather wallow in the romantic melodrama of the time than face up to the sufferings (and also the joys) of life. In America today, romantic melodrama is not extinct, but it has been eclipsed by an illusion much more powerful: the happy ending. No scene is more familiar to English-speaking TV audiences than the courtroom drama with the surprise twist and happy ending, or the western film where the good guy rides into the sunset (or flies back home to his or her galaxy). To be sure, there is always the made-for-television melodrama, the fatal illness or child-abuse movie of the week. But our apparent fascination with the courageous response of others to the events and diseases that we ourselves fear points not to the tragic sense but away from it. Not surprisingly, most such melodramas also tend to have a villain, someone to blame, and even if the courageous victim succumbs (as promised) in the end, the villain gets his or her comeuppance as compensation. The happy ending, like the romantic melodrama, is the very antithesis of tragedy. It is often said (for example, in Plato's *Symposium*) that the opposite of tragedy is comedy. It is not. The opposite of tragedy is kitsch.[21]

The fact that the question of tragedy does not get asked today, even in academic circles, is itself a symptom of our times. It is as if we have outlived tragedy, as if the notion of tragedy may have been quaintly appropriate in the days of Sophocles or Shakespeare but it is no longer an appropriate way of talking about the human condition. We readily admit, of course, that there are "tragedies," that is, awful things that happen—a young child killed in a bicycling accident, two teenagers killed when their car is hit by a drunken driver, a young woman at the pinnacle of her career who is struck down by cancer, an Afghan city levelled by an earthquake with thousands killed—but the notion of tragedy has nevertheless been eclipsed. Tragedy remains *other*, something that happens to others, leaving ample room for unsubstantiated explanation and rationalization. Aristotle, by contrast, was adamant about the fact that tragedy moves us precisely because we emotionally identify with the tragic hero. Furthermore, tragedies regarding others at a distance can be easily treated as if they are devoid of meaning, just bad luck, and not really tragedies at all. Simple neglect—distancing oneself—is a powerful philosophical tool.

But this tool can be used in many ways, not all of them simple. Consider Aristotle's treatment of Sophocles' account of Oedipus. The tragedy itself is well enough known. It was prophesied at his birth that Oedipus would commit the worst crime imaginable, murdering his father and then marrying his mother, now a Freudian scenario that still subverts the sanctity of "family values." His parents, no fools, decided to get rid of the baby, and in a society that permitted infanticide on demand, this was not hard to do. They gave young Oedipus to a servant, who gave him to a shepherd, who instead of leaving him out on the mountain to die, put him up for adoption. His new parents, it turns out, were also a king and queen. (Oedipus was an unusually lucky orphan.) But he heard of the original prophecy and dutifully left his "parents" and took off for Thebes. On the road, he killed a man (guess who?) and, after a series of adventures (including a game show with a Sphinx), arrived in Thebes, married the recently widowed queen, and became the king of Thebes. This is when Sophocles' play *Oedipus Rex* begins.

Thebes is under a curse. The wisest prophets are sent around to discover the reason (for then, as now, nothing happens without a reason). The wisest of them, Thesias, quickly ascertains the truth, but for obvious reasons is reticent about telling the king. Indeed, his sage advice, and the advice of almost everyone else in the court, is to not pursue the matter. But Oedipus, concerned about the well-being of Thebes and taking this on himself (more than he knows), pursues the cause of the curse until he finally comes to realize that it is he himself and his unforgivable (if unknowing) behavior. The entire body of the play, then, is Oedipus's painfully protracted realization that it is he who "polluted" Thebes. The audience, of course, knows this when they enter the theater, raising the question, then, is why the play is so "cathartic," so affective.

The Greeks evidently felt pity. Americans often experience discomfort. The Greeks recognized, as Aristotle summed it up in his great book *Poetics*, that the tragedy of Oedipus was in fact the tragedy of all or any of us. Oedipus was the "particular who represented the universal," the king who could be Anyman. Commentators ever since, however, have tried to isolate Oedipus and his tragedy and to explain why, indeed, it could not be applicable to all or any of us. He was obtuse. He was stubborn. He was irresponsible. Never mind that we, too, often tend to be irresponsible, obtuse, and stubborn. And, of course, he was a king, a king in a world that still believed in curses, prophecies, and fate. We live in no such world and, by way of a gigantic leap of wishful logic, we do not live in a tragic world either.

Despite his general claim, however, Aristotle, too, adopts a distancing strategy to make the tragedy more palatable. In his *Poetics*, Aristotle advanced a theory of tragedy that is being taught to literate schoolchildren at this very moment, the theory of the "tragic flaw." According to the "tragic flaw" (*hamartia*) theory, Oedipus—and every other tragic hero—has some critical vice, or at least something much less than a virtue, that marks his fate and makes more or less inevitable the tragedy that ensues. The "more or less" is in fact extremely important here, for it was an open question for Aristotle, as it is for us, to what extent tragedy (and fate more generally) was truly inevitable, and to what extent it was amenable to human control and willful intervention. But more immediately the question is whether or not the tragedy itself can be traced to the flaw, or whether, indeed, there must be such a flaw.

Oedipus is presented, to be sure, as something less than a perfect human being. But what those imperfections actually are, is very much in the eyes of the audience. He certainly seems haughty to us, but after all, he was a king in ancient Greece, when tyrants were a drachma a dozen. He was indeed stubborn, but couldn't this stubbornness to get to the truth, this obstinacy when the well-being of his city was at stake, be viewed as a great virtue, an essential virtue in a good leader, rather than a vice or even a weakness? Pursuing the truth to the bitter end, isn't that what we elsewhere praise as courage? Socrates has been held up by a hundred generations of truth seekers for his courageous acceptance of death rather than betray his dear philosophy. Why do we, and why would Aristotle (Socrates' grandstudent, via Plato), consider Oedipus's obstinacy a "flaw"? Because in Oedipus's case, unlike Socrates', the flaw led to unmitigated disaster. Socrates became a martyr and then a perennial hero. Oedipus became, in the words of Sophocles' play, "one to pity for all mankind." We do not mind heroes, or martyrs, for that matter, so long as they remain a safe distance from us; but the victims of tragedy are not martyrs, even if they once were called "heroes," and their tragedy must be explained, that is, explained away. The idea that they suffered because of a flaw in their own character appeals to us mightily. It means that they deserved what they got, even if the punishment, on reflection, was excessive indeed.[22]

There are other ways of dealing with Oedipus, as there are many ways of dealing with the Problem of Evil, and few of them have not been tried. For example, there is the ancient idea—no longer so familiar to modern audiences—that one's fate is inherited. A curse, initially deserved, might be passed down to sons and daughters. Oedipus himself was cursed because of the misdeeds of his father Laius, and Antigone was cursed as the daughter of Oedipus, though she committed no misdeed herself. Indeed, the case of Antigone was so poignant, and so much the obvious exception to Aristotle's generalized analysis, that she (and Sophocles' play, *Antigone*) became the paradigm of a flatly competing theory of tragedy, developed most famously by Hegel in the early nineteenth century. On Hegel's theory, the victim of tragedy is not necessarily flawed at all, but rather is caught in the middle of crushing, contradictory forces. Antigone, caught between the ancient and "divine" obligation of burying her dead brother and the absolute commandment of her king not to do so, could not escape her fate, but she nevertheless did what she (and we) considered to be right, sealing her doom. Thus Hegel sought to undo Aristotle's classical "blame the victim" approach to tragedy.

The distancing mechanism remains, however, in the very notion of a "fate" inflicted on tragic characters. Antigone's doom was already sealed by fate and her father, and Oedipus in turn was doomed by his father, Laius, who was guilty of a serious version of what we today would call child abuse. Thus the sins of the fathers were visited upon the children, and tragedy could be explained, if not in terms of individual guilt and responsibility, then in terms of fate and a peculiar family history. We, by contrast, do not believe in fate, and in any case, we ourselves are not so cursed and fated. Again, the object of the exercise is to except ourselves. Or, rather, we would like to believe that Oedipus and Antigone are the exceptions, not we.

Fate, McFate, and the Invisible Hand

> This, to use an American term in which discovery, retribution, torture, death, eternity appear in the shape of a singularly repulsive nutshell, was *it*.
>
> Vladimir Nabokov, *Lolita*

The metaphysical choice we are offered all too often comes down to this: One believes in God (actually, a very particular conception of God) or one is stuck with blind chance. But there is another option, once a vital ingredient in virtually all philosophy and religion, and that is the notion of fate. Fate is often dismissed as primitive, the residue of terrified people facing the natural calamities of the world in complete scientific ignorance, converting the inexplicable into something that they do understand, their own personalities. Thus the world is controlled by anthropomorphic spirits, and misfortunes are caused by the malicious whims and jealousies of the gods and goddesses. Catastrophes such as earthquakes and typhoons are brought about by angry divinities. For us scientifically sophisticated moderns, this quaint picture can comfortably be dismissed as so much superstition and nonsense. But the notion of fate need not be so simpleminded.

Ancient philosophers were obsessed with the idea that our lives are not under our control.[23] To be sure, we make our daily decisions and seemingly "choose" to go this way or that, but in the larger vision of things, those choices are, in one way or another, already determined. The nature of the determining power has always been the subject of lively dispute, ranging from anthropomorphic "fates" to sophisticated philosophical theories of determinism to New Age kitsch—aptly labeled by Vladimir Nabokov "McFate," the banal idea that everything that happens "was meant to happen that way." During medieval times, of course, the determining power was God. What the Judeo-Christian God added to the notion of fate was a clear conception of caring. Accordingly, faith and fidelity counted for something, and if one could not actually influence the way God would do things, at least one could have some confidence in His goodness.

Today, by contrast, the idea of an unseen hand that guides or controls our actions is compromised both by our pervasive belief in scientific determinism and by our compulsive sense of personal responsibility and, with it, the demand for control. This antinomy seems not to bother us, except, of course, for philosophers.[24] But taken together, scientific determinism and personal responsibility eliminate any room for fate, the former by its exclusive emphasis on antecedent natural causation, the latter by refusing to countenance any agency other than ourselves. Add to this the more upscale contemporary view of science in terms of unpredictability, chaos, and quantum theory, and the antediluvian antiscientistic belief in a caretaker God who prefers miracles to natural laws, and you have a real intellectual mess. The one thing that remains, the one solid fact that protrudes through all of the paradoxes and high-level contradictions, is the recognition that our lives are not ultimately under our own control. Shit happens, indeed, and it only sometimes happens to us by way of our own design or responsibilities.

The concept of fate has a perfectly natural, intelligible home. "Character is fate," wrote the Ephesian philosopher Heraclitus, a few decades after Confucius had developed a similar idea in China. Nowhere is this more evident than in the slightly traumatic and amusing experience of attending one's high school reunion. What is so shocking is how little one's classmates have changed after ten, twenty, even thirty years. Some of them will have fallen prey to serious illness or personal trauma, but the majority remain amazingly the same. The metaphor that comes to mind, trite but profoundly philosophical, is that of a sprout growing into a tree. The basic shape, kind, and character, are already established. The rest is all contingency and details. One of one's classmates was, one remembers, "destined to be president." Of course, not everyone so "destined" in the thousands of high schools in the United States can in fact become president, but most of the time that chosen classmate will be president of something, in some leadership position. One of one's classmates was, one remembers, destined for prison. And the odds are indeed that he (less likely she) will not show up, bound up in another long-term engagement.

Character as fate strikes a middle position between determinism and chance. Indeed, the notion of character is employed by a few great philosophers (David Hume, John Stuart Mill) as an answer to the free will–determinism puzzle. (An act is free if it flows from one's character, but character is both determined by antecedent circumstances and it determines future acts, which, in turn, determine character.) Character can be cultivated, to be sure, but the range of choices, while theoretically unrestricted, is far more restricted in practice than we like to think. Trying to break a simple habit—a small speech defect, a rude spontaneous gesture, an awkward walk, not to mention smoking—can be excruciatingly difficult. Trying to change one's personality, from shyness to socialite, from cowardice to courage, may require a wholesale life change, which, in retrospect, also gets recognized as an essential part of one's character (as resoluteness, as determination). The fact that character is cultivated over a long period of time prevents us from interpreting who we are as simply a matter of chance, although many coincidences and contingencies go into the formation of character. A remarkable number of characteristics seem to be "in born"—or, at least, present from birth. But one cannot say of one's character, in quite the same way that one can say of one's time of birth or national origin, that it "simply happened that way," that it was "out of one's hands." To do so ("I am a coward, and I can't do anything about it") is a paradigm of what Sartre called "bad faith" (*mauvaise foi*).[25] But, at the same time, one cannot view one's character as simply a matter of one's own choices. (To do so would be, in effect, to deny the notion of character.) Insofar as a person's future follows from his or her character, we can accept as perfectly intelligible one prominent notion of fate.

In *Slaughterhouse Five*, Kurt Vonnegut has his Trafalmadorians reveal to us (by way of his hero, Billy Pilgrim) that they had inventoried hundreds of civilizations on as many planets, and only on Earth did they find creatures who believed in "free will."[26] But even the most libertarian among us find ourselves believing in hands other than our own controlling our destinies. In romance, we find the idea of fate irresistible. Indeed, it seems built into our romantic conception of love. ("We were meant for each other."[27]) In economics, we find it hard to get away from Adam Smith's famous metaphor, from *Wealth of Nations*, of the "invisible hand" that assures prosperity despite the narrow, self-interested focus of an entrepreneurial society.[28] In biology, all but the most fervent and ruthlessly consistent evolutionists tend to adopt a vision of progress, of purposiveness, for example, when they explain the "function" of this or that feature for the survival of a species.[29] We have choices, true, and we may take responsibility for them. But we also sense some larger destiny, some sense in which we cannot escape our fate. We are swept along by global forces, the world economy, international politics, the dynamic ecology of our planet, and by more easily identifiable local forces (department and university politics, the threat of crime and violence, the pervasiveness of popular culture, the personalities of our neighbors). Hegel's portrait of the zeitgeist and his view of the relative unimportance of the individual captures this humbling picture so well, as does Tolstoy in *War and Peace* a few decades later. Our lives and fortunes are to a large extent the products not only of our own character but also of the more embracing character of the culture and times we live in. Whatever one thinks of the celebrated free will issue, it is undeniable that we are hostages of fate in this more modest sense. We are not the sole authors of our lives, and, without denying the role of chance—or just plain luck (good or bad)—our futures are for the most part set out before us. Whatever our libertarian and existentialist pretenses, we grow into them rather than make them for ourselves.

But not all conceptions of fate are limited to character and culture. Soldiers and cinema cowboys sometimes talk of "a bullet with my name on it." It is a way of appealing to fate, in morbidly concrete terms. Either an event will happen or it will not. In physics, in evolutionary biology, in economics, we may talk freely about chance, but when it comes down to our lives, chance is all but impossible to swallow. We can envision the future. We can envision the possibilities—some of them, anyway. And it is therefore hard to believe that one of them will not happen, indeed, that in some sense it has not already happened. (In *Slaughterhouse Five*, Vonnegut has his enlightened Billy, speaking of his own death, say, "That moment has always happened. It always will happen.") Aristotle took this common insight and turned it into a logical paradox. ("If it is true that there will be a sea battle tomorrow, then it must *already* be true that there will be a sea battle tomorrow.") We are less precise, but no less puzzled. If an event is fated, then it will happen. Turning perplexity into paradox is a now prevalent way of evading difficult questions, the "thinning" of an ancient and vital philosophial question to the point where it no longer has anything to do with us. But what motivates Aristotle's paradox is fascination not just with tense logic but also with the inexplicable sense of inevitability that he inherited from his tragedy-minded Greek predecessors.

Fate refers to this necessity, the idea that some event or state of affairs must happen, no matter what.[30] Fate is not just the nebulous view that "something will happen," as in anticipation, dread, and anxiety. It is the more precise view that some specific event or outcome will, indeed must, take place. Fate, in the classical sense, remains uncommitted on the means, the path that this fated future must take. In more philosophical terms, fate is not committed one way or the other to "determinism," the idea that every event is brought about, "determined," by a set of antecedent conditions and causes. Nor is fate necessarily wedded to preexisting purposes.[31] Oedipus heard the prophecy that he would kill his father and marry his mother, and he immediately left town. That was his decision. But his fate was such that he did, nevertheless, kill his father and marry his mother. Fate trumps chance as well as choice. What is fated does not just "happen" to come about. Fate necessarily involves an explanation, murky and obscure on details, perhaps ("it must have been fate"), but to explain an event by reference to fate is to exclude the possibility of mere chance as well as to deny individual control.

In its strongest versions, what is fated is said to be inevitable. "It is written," says the Koran, and nothing can happen otherwise. But fate can also be given a more modest and commonsense reading as an eventuality that is not wholly set in stone. For instance, when I get the flu (typically every February), I characteristically fight it, deny it, push myself to the point where I get so sick that my body refuses to get out of bed. As soon as I feel a little bit better, I'm up and at my work, in my classes, with the predictable result. I have often marveled at myself, at my own stupidity and stubbornness, but my obstinacy has, as might be expected, a philosophical structure. If I am going to get better anyway, then staying in bed is a waste of time. On the other hand, if I am going to get worse, I might as well work in the meantime. A modest deterministic reminder would show me that what I do "in the meantime" will itself be a determinant of the outcome, but I am a fatalist, not a determinist (at least in this context). Either I will or I will not get better, and so it does not much matter what I do in the meantime. This is not to say that I know whether I will get better or not; fatalism does not imply knowledge in this sense. It only requires the sense that what will be, will be (*que será, será*), and that what will be is somehow already settled.

The notion of fate is charming, not because it takes away our sense of responsibility but because it makes the future seem so settled. It is as if one's grandchildren are already waiting, as if one has already earned that Ph.D. when one is now but a fledgling graduate student, as if the fate of the world is already settled. Fate is the larger narrative in which a present choice or an event that might otherwise seem meaningless can be seen to have profound significance from the point of view of the future. Fate is, by its very nature, a retrospective phenomenon. It refers to the future, but it can be acknowledged only by looking back. A couple may say, even on a first, wonderful date, "We were meant for each other." But whether that is true, or perhaps just a bad joke, will be evident only years later. We act in ignorance, but we always act with an eye on the future, in the light of the past, in a narrative that gives meaning to our actions.

Most of us are proud of our accomplishments. Does believing in fate compromise them? Pride urges us to deny fate, to insist that we are in full control. "One is responsible for what one is," wrote Sartre in his early days. And throughout his career he would contend, with only a small qualification, "One is always responsible for what one makes of what is made of one."[32] But even Sartre always gave due credit to circumstances, one's "facticity," "the situation." The past, for example, is always an example of facticity. It is over and done with, it is settled, once and for all. A person did not have a choice about where he or she would be born, or when, or in what circumstances. A Jew did not have a choice, in Germany in 1933, whether or not to have been born a Jew, to have been raised in Germany, and to have to face the rise of the Nazi party. But within that situation, one can and must make choices, including the choice to accept the situation as determining or to reject it, possibly lying about it, denying it, obliterating the facts—but not, of course, actually changing them. Perhaps the question is, Can the same sort of analysis be imagined for the future, the future as settled even if unknown? Practically, existentially, one might insist that it could make no conceivable difference. If one knew the future, then one would not be making choices, just following the plot. And since we do not and cannot know, what is the point of thinking this way? (I ask my students: "I have a fortune-teller friend who is right 95 percent of the time. Would you ask her whom you will marry or when you will die?" Almost all of them say "no" to both opportunities.)

Nevertheless, I find it hard not to believe in fate. I think that when we are not carried away by fits of abstraction or intellectually compelled by the peer pressures of ontological correctness, we appeal to it all the time. We complain, in the face of disease or natural misfortune, "It had to happen." It is a natural approach to every calamity, from business bankruptcy to homelessness: "He had it coming." (The growing volume of commentary on the homeless and their personal "choice" of homelessness is an appalling illustration of this tendency, but such views have always been prevalent, even in the most "enlightened" societies, about the poor.) We expect things to "work out" in a certain way. This may be just a residuum of our more or less secure upbringing, parents who made promises and protected us and served us and made sure that everything came out all right, who soothed us when we were hurt, made excuses for us, consoled us for our failures with ready-made rationalizations. When we suffered from our own mistakes, the ready response was "I told you so," and when we succeeded, that praise was always embellished with "I knew you could do it." The future seemed laid out for us, and to a certain extent assured. We came to expect a rational universe, and we never got over it. This, of course, is the positive spin on Freud's thesis about religion in *The Future of an Illusion*, and it was Albert Camus's view of "the Absurd." We all feel it, at least whenever something bad happens to us. We can't help but ask "Why me?," as if the universe owes us an answer.

Good Luck, Bad Luck, and No Luck at All: A Plea for Gratitude

If it wasn't for bad luck,
I wouldn't have any luck at all.

Traditional blues riff

Luck is the missing ingredient in a good deal of philosophy. Typically, it is lumped with the impersonal notion of "chance." In the infamous free will problem, luck is dismissed along with chance as a nonstarter in any explanation in terms of the causes of human action (if only because it is neither a cause nor an explanation).[33] In the philosophy of science, chance and probabilities, but not luck—which has an ineliminable value component—is the substance of scientific explanation. In ethics, it is ruled out of consideration as efficiently as possible. (Kant gets rid of it in one long sentence at the very beginning of his *Grounding for the Metaphysics of Morals*.[34]) In ordinary life, to be sure, we appeal to luck quite often. We try our luck in the lottery. We thank our "lucky stars" if we win. We often realize that we have averted tragedy or disaster just by luck, especially when driving a car or other fast-moving vehicle where a split second's difference may make *all* the difference. But there is something hollow in our appeal, as if we do not really believe in it, in luck. No matter how lucky we may be, we almost inevitably feel that we deserve what we have received—at least, in the case of good luck. In the case of bad luck, by contrast, we feel exactly the opposite. Here again is that familiar asymmetry we have found throughout our exploration of tragedy. But good or bad, luck is suspect as an ad hoc, throwaway notion, a stand-in for more substantial accounts to come.

Kant rather famously denied that luck plays any role in what he called "moral worth." What was good without qualification, he insisted, was a "good will," which would manifest itself even (especially) in the face of the most awful misfortunes. Aristotle, by contrast, explicitly included good fortune (in its various guises) as essential to the happy life. Well, of course. He was writing for a bunch of well-born aristocrats. But when it came time to deal with tragedy and misfortune, Aristotle, like Plato and Socrates, tried to retreat into a position of philosophical invulnerability. Socrates called it "the good of his soul." Aristotle called it "virtue."[35] For both of them—and for many philosophers ever since—the ultimate escape was into the world of thought, the life of "contemplation." Whatever its other virtues, the ideal of such a life was not just the joy of philosophy. It was—as more explicitly in the later Stoics—an attempt to minimize one's exposure to the cruelties of luck and life.

Readers of books published by Oxford University Press tend to be born into an enviable affluence, with possibilities and potentialities that are clearly unavailable to most of the humans with whom we unequally share the planet. We may give lip service to luck, in rare moments of philosophical reflection, but we act and think as if we are entitled to the gifts that good fortune gave us. A businessman in Dallas was interviewed on television, at the height of the 1980s Texas boom (just before the 1980s Texas bust). He said, "I just thank the good Lord that I came of age when I did and that I was born and live in Dallas, Texas." But it was amply clear from what else he said that he did not see himself as either "lucky" or grateful at all, but as a man who had been responsible and smart, and had worked hard. He deserved his considerable fortune, and, as he made amply clear, he saw no obligation to share it with anyone. So, too, successful athletes ritually thank the Lord for their talents, but they leave no doubt that it is by virtue of their years of practice and their special abilities that they, and they alone, are responsible for their success (though perhaps with the encouragement of their mothers). This is not hypocrisy, but it is a carefully, very philosophically edited version of life. It is a narrative that focuses on and takes credit for what we can control and ignores what we cannot. We do not see the world or society, for example, as a strictly shared enterprise, in which the talents of one are, properly speaking, the talents of all, in which rewards are to be shared and credit is to be taken lightly. We do not, and perhaps cannot, see that it is mere luck that some of us have talents, abilities, and resources, and others do not.

It is important to distinguish luck from mere chance. Luck is a very human notion, loaded with hopes, fears, and regrets. Chance, by contrast, is an impersonal notion, a matter of mere probabilities. Modern science has reduced the world to matters of chance, "indeterminism" rather than determinism, quantum statistics rather than classical mechanics. Contrary to Einstein, God (if there is one) does "play dice with the universe." In biology, the distinguished Darwinian Stephen Jay Gould at Harvard wages war on every version of evolution that retains any residual notion of aim or purpose—"adaptivism," in short—anything that would lend the already brutal and aimless process of natural selection some hint of meaning or method. The great philosophers tell us that the world is everything that just happens to be the case, and nothing more. It could all be quite different: There is no reason that the world is one way rather than another. "The remarkable thing," Wittgenstein tells us, "is not that the universe is as it is, but that it is at all." Wittgenstein had a larger spiritual picture in mind (though one that never seems to enter into his philosophy), but his blunt statements are easily interpreted as very modern assertions of pure chance.[36]

I would not quibble with quantum physics or the best evolutionary theories. The problem is that we cannot look at our lives that way. To see what happens to us as mere chance, without explanation, is unthinkable. We are, for better or worse, rationalizing animals. But when we are thinking about our lives, our modern scientific attitude simply disintegrates. The idea that subatomic particles fly off without cause is a "fact" that we happily accept, taken on the authority of physicists who, after all, know what they are talking about. The idea that distant galaxies explode more or less spontaneously is not a problem, although we might airily imagine that one or more planets of one or more stars of one of those distant galaxies might have contained creatures and civilizations not unlike our own. Even the idea that life has evolved on Earth as a matter of mere chance strikes most people without a religious stake in the matter as utterly implausible. Indeed, even those who would give up this "teleology" and admit that human existence, like all existence, is strictly happenstance and contingent, nevertheless hold onto the idea that we are somehow not here for nothing. What would it mean to believe that it is all, we are all, just chance? Note how easily our minds move from the idea of chance to the notion of meaninglessness, from the idea that life and the particular events in life cannot be explained to the idea that they amount to nothing. Indeed, some of the most influential philosophies of our time have combined these two thoughts into a single argument, although their ultimate conclusions and consequences vary considerably. If chance is the rule of the universe, then where are we to find values, meaning, and an adequate way of thinking about our own lives?[37]

To see our lives in terms of luck, by contrast, is to see our lives as meaningful, even if inexplicable. Here it is also important to clearly distinguish luck from fate. The two are often conflated, even though they have what would seem to be diametrically opposite meanings. Luck refers to an event that admits of no further explanation: the fall of a coin, heads or tails; the random pick of a number or a card; a random radio quiz program call. There may or may not be such an explanation in theory. (A detailed microanalysis of the surface and weight distribution of the coin, the precise torque of the "flip," the distance to and nature of the surface, all told might provide a full account and an accurate prediction of the coin toss. Coins, unlike quanta, do obey deterministic laws.) But for all practical purposes, the possibility of an explanation is excluded. It is chance that the coin lands this way or that. It is luck (good or bad) that one bet on that particular outcome. Within the scope of the reference to luck, no further explanation is called for (whether or not one is available).[38]

Fate, on the other hand, provides an explanation, even if a vacuous one. ("It is fate that has brought us together.") To say that the coin came up heads (our bet) because of fate is very different from saying simply that the fall of the coin was a matter of chance that came out in accordance with our preference. It is to say that in some sense, it was "meant" to come out that way, it "had" to come out that way (the very opposite of the probability measure in chance and the uncertainty involved in luck). It is to say that there is some weighty reason why it came out that way, which might have to do with merit ("I deserved to win"), or perhaps with more subtle forces in the universe ("That's a hopeful sign"). Fate is necessarily part of a larger, more all-encompassing narrative, and although its explanatory value may be slight to nil, its ability to convey meaning is extraordinary. People who believe that "nothing happens by chance" must lead incredibly rich (if overburdened) lives. But if fate enriches, luck, or too much emphasis on luck, tends to diminish life, not only in the case of the pathetic gambler whose sole ambition in life is to "win the jackpot" but also in the more philosophical case of those scientific types who insist on seeing everything as a matter of chance and therefore find the search for meaning a naive and silly notion.[39]

Sometimes luck and fate provide two alternative interpretations of a single event. For example, two people meet by chance on a train, they talk, have coffee, later meet for dinner, fall in love. To say that it was luck is to say that it was a good thing but there was no reason for it. It just happened. To say that it was luck is to say that there is no explanation. On the other hand, one can view a seemingly chance meeting as fate. Filmmaker Claude Lelouch made a movie (*And Now My Love*, 1975) in which he shows three generations of two families, virtually at opposite ends of the world, and how their lives slowly converge until—in the last scene of the movie—their two grandchildren "happen" to meet on a plane. The romance of the story is that what seems utterly coincidental, indeed utterly insignificant otherwise, is made to appear predestined. This is a narrative of fate, not luck.

Fate depends on such narratives. But the truth, of course, is that we act in ignorance, at least to a certain degree. We are usually unaware of the larger story in which our acts play some possibly significant role. Thomas Pynchon's great novel, *Gravity's Rainbow*, casts its main character in a pivotal role in World War II—a role of which he is and remains entirely ignorant. What seems like luck to us, in our limited vision, may well turn out, in the larger story, to be fate. But in either case this larger picture is (for the most part) out of our control. Whether something happens by luck or is fated to happen, it is not up to us. And that is why we tend to reject both notions. We minimize luck and dismiss fate, for if luck leaves us without full credit for our actions, fate goes on to deprive us of even more. We like to plan and think of ourselves as planning our future. What good are plans if what is to happen is planned for us already?

But the reintroduction of luck and fate into philosophy brings with it at least one very important consequence, and that is a renewed sense of gratitude. Luck, fate, and chance suggest intriguingly different views of the world. To see one's good fortune in terms of sheer chance is to wave away any sense of obligation to be grateful or thankful for it. To see one's good fortune in terms of luck, by contrast, is, or should be, to be appreciative. To see one's good fortune in terms of fate, however, is to see one's whole life in a much grander context. "Appreciative" perhaps is not the right word here. There may or may not be sufficient personification of fate to warrant gratitude or thankfulness. (The predetermined nature of fate may make such attitudes a bit odd in any case. One need not be thankful for that which is going to happen anyway. One is thankful for that which might not have happened but did, or for that which did not happen but might have.) Gratitude, I want to suggest, is perhaps the best answer to the tragedies of life. It is odd and unfortunate that we take the blessings of life for granted—or insist that we deserve them—but then take special offense at the bad things in life, as if we could not possibly deserve those. The proper recognition of tragedy and the tragic sense of life is not shaking one's fist at the gods or the universe "in scorn and defiance," but rather, as Kierkegaard writes in a religious context, "going down on one's knees" and giving thanks. Whether or not there is a God or gods to be thanked, however, seems to me not to be the main issue. It is the importance and the significance of being thankful, to whomever or whatever, for life itself.

Instead of gratitude, our culture and its philosophers tend to substitute game theoretical calculations of prudence and mutual advantage, abstract conceptions of equality and equal opportunity, minimally historical claims to entitlement, and, at its most vulgar, rationalizations for callousness: "Why can't he pull himself out of the gutter as I did (or could have)?" Instead of gratitude, we get abstract constructions of the original position and make-believe social contracts. Even at the most basic ontological level, it seems, it is far preferable to see ourselves as independent and self-determining rather than as dependent on others and appropriately grateful for our advantageous role in life.[40]

In a study some years ago, Boston psychologist Shula Sommers found that American men, in particular, found gratitude to be the most discomforting and humiliating emotion, worse than fear. It is not hard to understand why. Gratitude recognizes the fact that we are not, in fact, the authors of our own destiny, that we owe our good fortune to others and, in particular, to luck. If one were to think in terms of the abstract possibility of being any one or another of the many human beings on Earth at the moment, the odds are that one would be born impoverished, raised malnourished and ignorant, and find oneself living in the middle of a famine, a civil war, under a harsh dictatorship, without real hope or possibilities. That we were not so condemned to a miserable life and an early death is surely, whatever our virtues, a matter of luck. But though we may acknowledge this in the abstract, it seems almost impossible to live with, much less base our lives on, this profoundly disturbing realization. What would we owe, and to whom, if all of our successes and even our health and our talents had to be credited to luck? Here is where Fate—and God—come in to lend a helping hand. But, then, how could we tolerate misfortune in others if we knew, really knew, that "there but for the grace ... go I"? On the other hand, how different would our understanding of our own misfortunes be if we knew, really knew, that it is "just the way it turned out," or had to turn out, or was ordained by God to turn out, and that all in all, in any case, we really have been extremely ... lucky?

The Meaning of Tragedy

All are architects of fare, working in these walls of time.
Henry Wadsworth Longfellow, "Builders"

Discussions of suffering and the tragic sense of life have been hampered by one of those extremely popular but unfortunate dichotomies that the simpleminded use to discuss philosophy, namely, the categories of optimism and pessimism. An optimist is one who looks on "the bright side of things."[41] (One thinks of the song that ends the 1979 Monty Python movie *Life of Brian*.) In other words, the glass is half full. A pessimist, on the other hand, is one who sees life, if not as inherently meaningless, as nevertheless more of a curse than a blessing, for whom the glass is half empty. F. H. Bradley, the English Hegelian, defined the optimist (tongue-in-cheek) as "one who believes that this is the best possible world, and everything in it is a necessary evil." He defines a pessimist, by contrast, as one who thinks that "everything is bad, but it is good to know the worst." Such wisecracks are just about what the dichotomy deserves, insofar as it falsely forces us to choose between two "perspectives" that are neither distinct nor, in any substantial sense, perspectives.

In the nineteenth century, Arthur Schopenhauer emerged as a brilliant, self-appointed pessimist, although he based much of his philosophy on Buddhism, which he knew quite well was not a pessimistic philosophy. In contrast, Schopenhauer's philosophical archenemy, Hegel, is often cited as an optimist. But anyone who knows Hegel's philosophy at all knows what a stretch and a simpleminded gloss that is. So, too, to try to divide philosophical attitudes into "positive" and "negative" almost guarantees, with the one exceptional case of Schopenhauer, that one will misunderstand virtually everything ever written in philosophy. This is philosophical "thinness" at its most simpleminded, its silliest. Nevertheless, the categories refer us, at least, to this hardest of all philosophical problems. How are we to look at life, given that it includes suffering and death? Tragedy is, perhaps, the real source of philosophy. If we couldn't be hurt, harmed, disappointed, or humiliated, what would we have to think about?

It is often suggested, particularly by philosophers, that it is the thinking about it that makes life meaningful. My own view is that this is one more instance of philosophical self-glorification. It is life, not thinking about life, that must be meaningful. But thinking about it is by no means irrelevant, and, as Camus argued, it is in the conjunction of the two—life and reflection—that the meaning we seek is to be found.

A few years ago, the mother of a boy who had lost his two best friends in a tragic accident tried to help her son discern some meaning in it all. She wrote up her agony in a popular news magazine, and concluded, "I don't think that tragedies happen on purpose, but, and I echo his [her son's] words, if people learn to value one another more and to appreciate how precious life is, then perhaps some good can come from something so awful." Wise and modest words. She finished by adding, "In the end, the musings of a 9-year-old boy, struggling to find a reason, are the musings of us all."[42] Those who would give an "answer" to tragedy, or reduce it to two silly perspectives, lack this wisdom.

There is an answer in such thoughts that does justice to life and justice to tragedy together. It does not deny suffering but does not wallow in it either. One might well say "Life is not fair." To that extent, the tragic sense of life is no more than the simple recognition of the obvious. But this is not to say that life is meaningless, nor is it to justify our dwelling on the tragedies of life to the exclusion of its blessings and benefits. Nietzsche quite rightly combined his own keen sense of the tragic life with an uncontained joy (although he is not always convincing), and Unamuno, in his own life, did much the same. We too often opt for victimization or cynicism, the products of our overactive faculty for blame and our extravagant sense of entitlement. Or we take refuge in pessimism. (If we expect the worst, what worse can happen?) But there are better ways to think about life. Gratitude is one of them. A good sense of humor is another. But, all in all, I think the best philosophical response to tragedy is some combination of gratitude and humor, a dash of that mock-heroic Camusian confrontation with the Absurd, and a passionate engagement with the details and the people in our lives. The important thing is not to deny tragedy, but to embrace it as an essential part of the life we love and for which we should be so grateful. Nietzsche said that we should live life as a work of art, and he had in mind what we *make* of it, misfortunes and all. In such a perspective, our suffering has meaning because life has meaning, and more than this we have no right to demand.

6

THINKING DEATH IN THE FACE

Death Fetishism, Morbid Solipsism

When Chuang-Tzu's wife died, Hui Shih came to console him. As for Chuang-Tzu, he was squatting with his knees out, drumming on a pot and singing.

"When you have lived with someone," said Hui Shih, "and brought up children, and grown old together, to refuse to bewail her death would be bad enough, but to drum on a pot and sing— could there be anything more shameful?"

"Not so. When she first died, do you suppose that I was able not to feel the loss? I peered back into her beginnings; there was a time before there was a life. Not only was there no life, there was a time before there was a shape. Not only was there no shape, there was a time before there was energy. Mingled together in the amorphous, something altered, and there was the energy; by alteration in the energy, there was the shape; by alteration in the shape, there was the life. Now once more altered she has gone over to death. This is to be a companion with spring and autumn, summer and winter, in the procession of the four seasons. When someone was about to lie down and sleep in the greatest of mansions, I with my sobbing knew no better than to bewail her. The thought came to me that I was being uncomprehending towards destiny, so I stopped.

Chuang-Tzu

It has been suggested that death is the ultimate philosophical topic, ultimate not just in the trivial sense of "last" (as in "the end of our lives") but also in the sense that death, along with serious suffering, provokes even the most practical person to philosophical reflection. This may sometimes be true, but it is overstated. Martin Heidegger's famous if not always crystal clear thesis that our very existence is that of a Being-Toward-Death has received many respectful nods, as has the much older view of Boethius (480–524), that the "consolation of philosophy" is the transcendence of death.[1] But although philosophers certainly have something to think about in the inevitability of death, I think it is a mistake to exaggerate the importance of this. This does not seem to be a problem, however, insofar as relatively few philosophers these days, outside of the Heideggerian circle, seem to write about death at all.[2] To be sure, the definition of death enters into some recent questions in bioethics, and the undesirability of death functions as a basic premise in ethics, but the nature of death and the undesirability of death are too rarely taken up as topics in their own right. Perhaps that is why, when death does become an issue in philosophy it is typically overplayed. Not only philosophers but also people in general are accused, in various ways, of "denying death." Death is "thinned" to a mere abstraction, and the thinnest of thin treatments is, of course, no treatment at all. But some of this thinness is itself a philosophical doctrine of some prominence, namely, Epicurus's view that death, in short, is "nothing at all."

By contrast, I have heard many people say that death is the ultimate tragedy. This seems to me to be trite and also false. One might well fear (and rightly) that the death of his or her spouse or child would be much more of a tragedy than one's own death (restricting the field to personal tragedies and ignoring the collective horrors of war, mass murders, nuclear accidents, and holocausts). Again, one might hold that it is one's *last* (and in that sense ultimate) tragedy, but even this supposed truism seems to me to be false without trivializing qualification. Aristotle, in a famous passage quoting Solon, argued that "no man should be called happy until after his death."[3] At first glance, this seems like nonsense, both as a statement about happiness and as a statement about death. What sense could it possibly make to speak of a person's happiness after his or her death? And what would it mean to call a dead man happy? But Aristotle's argument, rendered in full, makes good sense. Once we have given up our modern hedonistic sense of "feeling happy" and taken up Aristotle's much more embracing sense of "living and having lived a good life," then we realize that tragedy is by no means limited to the living. Humiliation and scandal that affect a person's "good name," even after death, reflect on that life and the way it was lived. "X must be spinning in his grave" is but one of several poor poetic allusions to this obvious fact, which has nothing whatever to do with any more ambitious belief in immortality, reincarnation, or life after death.[4] One's own death is not the ultimate tragedy. There may be much worse, whether before or after one's death, even from the perspective (vicarious though it may be) of the dead.

It is also said, equally unthinkingly, that death is the ultimate punishment, and this, of course, is the justification typically given for punishing capital crimes, those "heinous" enough to deserve the death penalty. But death is by no means the ultimate punishment, except, again, in that trivial sense that it is the *last* punishment. (In fact, even this is not so. When Israeli soldiers bulldozed the houses of the Palestinian family of a deceased terrorist, this was supposed to be further punishment *of the terrorist*. When awards and honors are posthumously stripped, death is not the last punishment but, one might say, one of a series of humiliations.) There are many things worse than death. Painful, debilitating, terminal illness is worse than death, which is why we will always have rightful demands for the legitimacy of suicide and consensual euthanasia. Torture is often thought to be worse than death. The effect of Elizabethan executions, long, drawn-out affairs in which the victim was castrated, drawn and quartered, sometimes flayed and disfigured, all in the utter humiliation of a public spectacle, was to render death a merciful respite. Prisoners with life sentences sometimes insist that death would be far preferable, and, occasionally, they get their wish. Gary Gilmore in Provo, Utah, demanded the death penalty for his crimes in 1965, initiating the long, bloody carnival of executions that Americans alone, among the "advanced civilized" nations, seems to demand and enjoy.[5] The suicide rate in those same civilized countries, not all of them with Scandinavian winters, attests to the popularity, if not the rationality, of preferring death to any number of social, economic, family, professional, or psychological humiliations and failures. Death is not the worst punishment or the worst thing that can happen to someone. Indeed, there is such a thing as a good death, ideally at the end of a good life, which is what we must keep in mind.[6]

Thinking Death in the Face

> The truth was, that life was meaningless. Every day of life, every step in it, brought me, as it were, nearer the precipice; and I saw clearly that there was nothing but ruin. And to stop it was impossible; to go back was impossible; and it was impossible to shut my eyes so as not to see that there was nothing before me but suffering and actual death, absolute annihilation.
>
> Leo Tolstoy "Confession"

> I'm dying as I lived, beyond my means.
>
> Oscar Wilde

I have only twice looked death in the face (not counting numerous close calls in cars and on motorcycles, too quick to provide a conscious confrontation). As Heidegger says, though obscurely, such experiences bring one face-to-face with oneself, whether or not they provoke, much less assure, any kind of "authenticity." But I often think about death, as I presume Heidegger did, which is not the same thing as facing it. Confronting death is a very emotional experience, to say the least. Thinking about death, by contrast, seems curiously detached, abstracted, out of touch with the phenomenon it ponders. As Descartes so famously noted, one never knows better that one is alive—or finds it more inconceivable that one should not be—than when one is thinking.

Nevertheless, I find it difficult to think about death without becoming facile, even giddy. It all seems so abstract, even when, as happened this week (and, in these times, seemingly more often), a good friend or acquaintance has suddenly died. But is it always so sudden—or is it just that the news is always a shock? Even the word, the dull phonetics of "dead," the hissing lisp of "death," conveys the unreality of it all.[7] And then there is the idea of death, dreadful and incomprehensible at the same time. Without going into the details of my autobiography, I have been avoiding death all of my life, evidently successfully, not always responsibly. I suspect that I am not alone in this. But as a child who was born and raised with a medical death sentence over his head, and as a philosopher who has had ample occasion to reflect on such matters, I have not been able to avoid thinking about death, and consequently the meaning of life. I could never entirely "lose myself" in the hustle and bustle of the everyday world in order to evade the question, although, to be sure, I often do so.

Philosophy has provided me with a means to cope with the issue—if not evade it altogether—in a subtle, perhaps hypocritical way. Most people, it seems, feel uncomfortable talking about death. In philosophy, one can do so quite comfortably, but is that because we "face up," or because we insulate, perhaps inoculate, ourselves from really thinking about it? And needless to say, as the language becomes more abstruse and farther from everyday "chatter," the chances of self-deception on this score become greater, not less. But by talking, thinking, and writing about death, I have at least managed to face up to death as an abstraction, Philosophical ideas, as I keep saying, can actually have some impact on one's feelings and behavior, on one's real life. Both Kierkegaard and Heidegger warned us against confusing the crude syllogism "All mortals are going to die, I am mortal, . . ." with actually facing up to death. But where the abstract thoughts become palpable and passionate, where the mere thoughts become an actual facing up to, that is the hard "meta" question for philosophers. There is no necessary connection between the very sophisticated abstractions afforded those who can spend their time reading Heidegger and Sartre, chuckling their way through Chuang-tzu, or skimming the Tibetan Book of the Dead and truly coming to terms with death. But neither is *not* thinking about death and simply admitting one's incomprehension a more honest way of sharing a seat on the Grim Reaper's subway. When I am being honest with myself, it becomes clear that all of this talk about "one's own death" has nothing to do with me at all. This lends my glibness a scholarly as well as a slightly hysterical air, like a dervish dancing in order not to fall down.

How could one possibly be "clear" on such matters? I read through treatises on death and dying—that is, on *other people's* deaths and dying—and I am astounded by the idea that such matters should be so scientifically debated and cataloged. Not that such work isn't necessary or interesting. It's a morbid job, but somebody has to do it. But I remember when I was in medical school—a long, long time ago—and watched my young colleagues become initiated into the insulating practice of dealing with death by not dealing with it, by making it part of a routine, by casting themselves always in the role of "other," whether hero, helper, or mere spectator. I was also fascinated when I read through some of the best analytic philosophers writing on death, where so much careful and often sensitive thought has been forced through the screen of technical puzzles.[8] There, too, insulation has become a practice. The technique is the familiar one, of turning a brute fact into a paradox, and then focussing all of one's attention on resolving the paradox. A few years ago, I participated in a symposium on evil, and I listened to a very clever analytic philosopher shift the topic from evil to the Socratic paradox ("Can one knowingly do wrong?") that ended up in a long discussion about what it meant to want to eat a banana. (I'm not kidding.) Gone from view were the Holocaust, the horrors of Bosnia, Rwanda, and Burma, the drug cartels. In their place was a technical question about the connection between desires, intentions, and (minimal) actions. So, too, it is possible to discuss death in some depth without even touching on the topic that really concerns us.

Such evasions are accused of "denying death." This, perhaps, is too strong, but they are techniques for not facing up to the issue. My problem is, What is it, really, to face up to death—in other words, *not* to deny death? The truth is that philosophy is a way to play with death, or the idea of death. This is something other than "consolation," and it is certainly something lighter than Heidegger's *Sein-zum-Tode* (Being-unto-Death). Perhaps it is part of the joy of philosophy, this license to play at a safe distance from the weightiest of all human topics. But I do not know how to avoid being facile or hypocritical on this impossible but seemingly simple question: What is death? Or, rather, what is my death to me?

I think that these are two quite distinct questions, one concerning one's (in each case "my") own death and another concerning the death of others. The relation between the two is problematic, to say the least. Concerning other misfortunes in life—pain and poverty, for instance—one can appeal (still problematically) to that often confused notion of "empathy," that is, "putting oneself in the other's place." One can imagine oneself with a similar injury, perhaps comparable with one suffered years ago. One can imagine, perhaps with some difficulty, what it would be like not to be able to afford medicine, decent food, a car, books, a computer. But when the issue is death, it is not at all clear what this could possibly mean, "what would it be like to be dead?"

It is sometimes said that the ideal attitude to maintain regarding one's own death is a somewhat modest (but not necessarily dark) sense of humor, of which "gallows humor" is the most obvious, most morbid, and most extreme example. (The strategy of resentment confuses the picture. To joke about one's death to one's executioner, for example, is to suggest that the punishment is not being taken seriously—in other words, it is that much less of a punishment.) But to adopt a joking attitude toward another person's death—even the death of an old enemy or someone who is evil—seems inappropriate. The asymmetry here is overwhelming, more, perhaps, than in any other philosophical question.[9] I do not want to be callous, but in writing glibly about my own death, I cannot help but seem to be writing glibly about other people's deaths as well. But writing and thinking about someone else's death, even someone very close to you, is a very different matter from writing and thinking about your own. I hope the reader will appreciate this autobiographical quandary, and my refusal to take the usual philosophical way out, which is to reduce the issue to a series of nonperspectival epistemological and metaphysical puzzles that avoid offense only by avoiding the issue.

I do not know how to analyze that which is, in more senses than one, simply *nothing*. Indeed, my thesis here is that death is not nothing, although it is not "something" either. I hope that does not sound too silly, or too profound. I do not know how to be profound, that is, deep (a metaphor that naturally leads us toward the grave). Profundity is all too easily confused with gloom, but the truth is on the surface. From the moment we are born, the end is given, not perhaps as metaphysical necessity but as the essence of the human narrative. What makes us human is the fact that we recognize the inevitability of death not just in general or in others but also in ourselves, even if we repress that recognition and deny that knowledge as best we can. An essay on death is an attempt to say something lively about the most deadly silence of all. And perhaps it is to say something, with all due apologies, about what it is to be human.

The Denial of Death:
A Brief History

The main thing is to start talking about death and dying. In our
society, death is a taboo subject. One of the main things that [we]
want to do is change our culture so that death is not seen as a failure.
Rosalynn Carter, *Newsweek*

Almost thirty years ago, Ernest Becker wrote his classic treatise—as he was dying—*The Denial of Death*. The phrase and the theme quickly became a watchword of the more depressed intelligensia and found its way into several (almost all) Woody Allen films. Becker's thesis, in fact a familiar existential thesis, was that we Americans had so busied and buried ourselves in the everyday world that we had not so much lost as purposively denied the basic facts of life, death in particular. Becker, who succumbed to cancer, busied himself with his book through his final days, almost as if living out his own thesis. But the word hit home, and intelligent, healthy Americans started worrying more and more about whether they should be worrying more about their eventual demise. Incipit Woody Allen. Of course, there were good reasons, not all of them metaphysical or spiritual, why Americans should have been timid about facing death. Jessica Mitford wrote her wonderful and horrifying exposé of the funeral industry *The American Way of Death*, in 1963. The death scam was not confined to America, of course. (A good cynic could no doubt trace it back to the Egyptians.) Evelyn Waugh had satirized the same industry in *The Loved One* in 1948, which was made into a high-grossing movie in 1965 (screenplay by Terry Southern and Christopher Isherwood). By the mid-1960s, with the Vietnam war looming in the background, death had come of age in America. "The denial of death" had become virtually a cliché, but like most oft-spoken denials, it seemed to be contradicted by its very exposition. One of the most popular music groups of the era, The Grateful Dead, was in this, as in so many matters, perfectly tuned to the times.

What began as a lament became a celebration, not of death but of the denial of death. Indeed, all of the talk about the denial of death itself became a convenient way of ignoring death. In place of existential angst and reflection, it became—sociology. And in the wake of the accusations ("Americans won't face up to mortality," "Analytic philosophers are denying death," "Television and movie producers are trivializing death"), questions about the meaning of death just seemed to melt away. There were increasingly heated arguments about the depiction of lethal violence in movies and cartoons, and, as the baby boomers got older, there was more concern about retirement and Social Security. People exercised more, ate healthier, stopped smoking, and started to plan to live to be ninety or a hundred years old. Death, according to contemporary thinking, is thus deferred. Perhaps that is not the same as denial, but it seems to me rather close. But then, just what does it mean to "deny death" anyway?

Elsewhere in the world, and throughout most of history, death has been hard to deny. It was everywhere, unhidden and all too evident to the senses. But ever since the discovery of death (and when and how would that have been?), the denial of death—of death as once and for always—has been an unavoidable temptation. One hundred thousand years ago, the Neanderthals practiced ceremonial rituals for the dead. We have no way of knowing what they believed, but it is not unreasonable to suspect that they were hedging their bets, both appealing to and protecting themselves from the dead. Death was as significant as birth, often more dramatic, and almost always a disruption for the survivors. Children were left without parents, tribes were left without leaders, hunters were left without trackers. Whether the Neanderthals feared their own deaths or just acknowledged and coped with the mortality of others is a question we cannot answer. What must have been absolutely clear was that death was a part of life. It had to be dealt with. Presumably there were no Neanderthal nurses, hospitals, or undertakers to hide or remove that unpleasantness from daily life. Nor were there lawyers to further complicate matters. Death was death. But, even then, maybe not.

"Primitive" people since at least the Cro-Magnon have developed detailed strategies for placating and warding off the spirits of the dead. The dead, in other words, were not wholly dead, even after giving up most of their earthly pleasures and powers. The oldest known epic (at least a century before the Hebrew Bible), the Babylonian tale of Gilgamesh, is largely set in the land of the dead. The Egyptians were exemplary but not unique in their full-scale preparations for the afterlife. They looked forward, not to death, perhaps, but to the life that followed. Death and its details, accordingly, were given enormous, even obsessive, amounts of attention. It was not only life after death that received so much attention, nor was it the nasty business of dying. It was the nature of death itself, the gateway or the transition, that received the pharaoh's share of attention.

On the other hand, the ancient Hindus of the Vedas, and later the Buddhists and the Jains, were concerned that the soul (or *jiva*) would not die but would continue to carry on (in some other body) well into the future. Unlike their colleagues to the west, they were not delighted by this prospect. They viewed life as suffering, as a burden to be relieved by ultimate "liberation" (which was very different from mere death). Death was taken quite seriously, as if something of a mix of cosmic graduation and karmic condemnation. The Greeks, by contrast, assumed only the survival of that pathetic shadow called the "breath" (*psyche*), banished from the body but nevertheless not nothing. The depictions of Hades are by no means enticing, and though the Greeks did not deny death, they certainly did not welcome it. Two millennia later Friedrich Nietzsche would speculate that the great virtue of the Greeks was their fatalistic acceptance of death and suffering as the ground of human existence. And it was this acceptance, he enthusiastically proclaimed (in 1872), that made them and their lives "so beautiful!"

It was Socrates who transformed the soul into a philosophical phenomenon as he fantasized being freed from his body. In Plato's *Apology*, Socrates more or less obliges the jury to give him the death penalty, declaring that he would rather be dead than stop doing philosophy. Socrates' (Plato's) vision of the soul is a matter of much philological debate, but what is amply evident is that he did believe in the immortal soul, and a mighty substantial immortal soul at that. However little personality the thus liberated soul might have, it was clearly capable of thinking. Socrates imagined that, as an unencumbered soul, he could spend eternity thinking nothing but philosophy. In this he broke ranks with most of his predecessors and opened the way to a rich life after life. (He also hinted at some form of reincarnation, which he probably got from Pythagoras, who in turn borrowed it from the Egyptians.) It was only a matter of a few centuries before this aspect of the Platonic philosophy would ignite one of the greatest religious awakenings in the ancient world.

To the east, in Palestine, the Jewish Pharisees believed in an afterlife, although the full significance of this belief was largely unspecified until the Christians came onto the scene. Indeed, one of the most appealing promises of early Christianity was Christ's anticipated "conquest of death." This went far beyond the hopes of any previous peoples. Not only was there life after death, life eternal, but it would be more glorious, more righteous than even the greatest of great empires, and it would be free of suffering. The travel brochures made the promise of Heaven irresistible. Life was but a short sentence, and death was barely even punctuation. Given the pervasiveness of such thinking, one might almost conclude that death would no longer be an issue. It was only a "gateway" to the kingdom of God. Nevertheless, the most passionate of beliefs has to cope with the evidence of the senses, and while the plain fact of death was obvious, the existence of the promised Hereafter was not.

What does it mean to deny death? I asked that question before, but only as a rhetorical tease. But now it is time to attempt some answers. To deny death is, first of all, to refuse to believe that "it" will happen to you. But to think of death as an "it," and to think of yourself as its victim, is but another strategy of denial, another way of putting it at one remove, of abstracting it, of denying responsibility—if not for one's death (which is more often the case than one thinks), then for facing up to one's death. In its most mundane but pervasive strategy, to deny death is to focus on the hurly-burly of the everyday world and not ever look up to the horizon, to one's own mortal limits. I suspect that we all do this. We plan our projects, stretching indefinitely into the future. We believe, every day, that "tomorrow will be another day." We act and feel as if we have all the time in the world. Of death we simply say, "it will come when it comes." (Again, thinking of death as an "it" and yourself as its victim as a strategy of denial.) This comes out in our priorities, putting off the truly important until we "clear the path" and "put out a few fires," take care of the urgencies.[10] But the path is never clear, and the fires keep burning, and someday there is no tomorrow.

The most effective denial of death simply insists that death is not really death, that life goes on in some more or less self-identical medium. This might be the survival of the soul pure and simple. It might be the survival of one's mind, one's memories, one's sense of self. It might be the reincarnation of the soul into another creature, perhaps another person. It might be something much grander, unification with the Godhead or joining the divine Inner Circle. I watched the Reverend Billy Graham's son on television recently, and he was asked by his interviewer what he would feel when his father died. He carefully explained that he would feel terribly sad when his dad retired from the ministry, but he would feel nothing but joy when he "departed," knowing that he would then be far happier than he had ever been before. That, surely, is the denial of death plain and simple. And what, you might ask, could possibly be wrong with that?

I do not doubt the appeal of such beliefs, nor do I have any convincing arguments against them. Indeed, I worry a bit about those who take it as their mission to debunk them. Paul Edwards, for example, who is best known for his editing of the *Encyclopedia of Philosophy*, has spent much of his career refuting first the Heideggerian view of death and, more recently, the idea of reincarnation.[11] Who reads these books? Certainly not the believers. Nor, most likely, the nonbelievers. As an existentialist, I rather agree with at least some of Heidegger's insights, and as an old biologist and animal lover, I am rather fond of the idea of reincarnation, whatever its plausibility. Nevertheless, I want to suggest that belief in an afterlife of any kind might well be considered a form of denial of death. There may be full acceptance of the death of the body, but in some important sense the person is said to survive. Personally, I doubt it—or, let me just say, I do not believe it, although my personal belief, I would be the first to insist, is of no importance or interest to anyone but me. Indeed, it may well be my loss. But my own belief is that this just defers the question, which is, whether or not there is an afterlife, "What is death, and how should I think about it?" What happens after death is another matter; in my case almost anything would be a rather remarkable surprise. But "What happens after death?" is not a substitute for, "What is death and how should I think about it?" To think that it is, is just another form of denial.

From the Denial of Death to Death Fetishism

> Nothing, nothing had the least importance . . . From the dark horizon of my future a sort of slow persistent breeze had been blowing toward me, all my life long. . . . What difference could they make to me, the deaths of others, or a mother's love, or his God, or the way a man chooses to live, the fate he chooses, since one and the same fate was bound to "choose" not only me but thousands of millions of privileged people. . . . All would be condemned to die one day.
>
> —Albert Camus (*The Stranger*)

Death has often been considered a trial, a test, a definitive event in a life that often flirted with fatalities. In Homeric ethics, notably, the mode of a man's death was considered a definitive mark of his character. To die bravely in battle was virtuous. To die young of the flu or pneumonia was—not to be too unkind—pathetic. (Alexander the Great and Lord Byron are cases in point.) To die of old age was commendable, but only if one had the full background of battle scars and near misses. In classical cowboy ethics, to jump thirty centuries, it was considered essential "to die with your boots on." Death was a ritual, and if it meant that you lost the fight, it also signified that you put up a good one. (Being shot in the back not only meant cowardice on the part of your assassin. It also deprived you of your chance for an honorable death.) Dueling rituals of the American South and contemporary urban gang-fighting maintain similar codes of honor, loyalty, and death, where death is not only a part of life but also its ultimate test. Death is an evil and also inevitable, but *how* one dies means everything.[12] The biology of death is of little importance.

In much of the Christian tradition, the aim is to die with a clear conscience, whether by reason of right behavior or by way of well-timed repentance. Throughout the Middle Ages, warrior ethics joined the ethics of salvation in an uneasy collaboration, as Christianity and Islam joined in battle in the Holy Land. To kill and be killed for God, but to die with absolution, was as much of the chivalric ideal as the languor of love and the oath of undying loyalty. Death remained a highlight of a person's life, because of the significance of the manner of exit as well as the promise of another life to come.

A woman's death, through much of the same history, was thought to be a simpler thing, preferably quiet and uncomplaining, or tragically in childbirth. Just as women were denied the right and the capacity to a full life, so they were denied the right and the capacity to a full death. Only rarely was a woman's death an exceptional act of honor, heroism, or patriotism (Joan of Arc, for example). One of the dubious achievements of the women's equality movement is that women are inching closer to combat positions in the modern military, while their street-fighting sisters in urban gangs are now accumulating rap sheets as lengthy as those of their male comrades. From such evidence, one might conclude that at least some young people have lost their fear of death and do not in any sense deny death. Perhaps this is a phenomenon to be explained by socioeconomic disadvantage, as a class phenomenon, but the evidence points elsewhere. I would suggest that a new love affair with death transcends class and signifies something more.

In recent philosophy (and in a great deal of avante-garde poetry, theater and lifestyle pretensions, for example, in the "death warmed over" fashions of Calvin Klein), death has become the ultimate experience. One thinks immediately of the French: Foucault, depicted so vividly by Jim Miller in his recent biography; Artaud, so celebrated by Susan Sontag in some of her more intoxicated writings of the 1970s; Rimbaud and his exalted status among

French poets, mainly because of his deliciously early death.[13] One thinks of Heidegger and his always to be carefully qualified notion of "Being-unto-Death." For Heidegger himself, of course, this was emphatically *not* to be thought of as an "experience"—indeed, Heidegger had not much to say, except sarcastically, about "experience" in general.[14] But as Heidegger has been read, first by the French and now by the Americans and some Australasians, "Being-unto-Death" has certainly become the focal point for a certain kind of experience, an "authentic experience," perhaps also a certain kind of mood, not just in the rather abstract Heideggerian sense of that term but also as a palpable affect, a feeling of nihilistic depression mixed with an exhilarating sense of freedom. (That false sense of freedom—and the sense of irresponsibility that tends to go with it—is the proper target of Sartre's put-down of such nihilistic philosophy.)

Strictly speaking, the idea of death as the ultimate experience may be nonsense. Death isn't an experience. As Epicurus assured us two millennia ago, it is "nothing." But now *nothing*, too, has been elevated into a life-defining experience, and the process of dying, the moment of dying, the keen awareness of one's dying, the recklessness with which one lives in anticipation of dying, all of this has come to be regarded as a kind of heroic sensibility. Of course, all too often the most dramatic characters exit prematurely in a drug-induced haze, like the artist Basquiat or Kurt Cobain, the lead singer of the rock group Nirvana a few years ago. A great deal of emphasis has been put on the notion of *choice* in dying, inspired in part, perhaps, by the dehumanizing medical and hospital practices of the past few decades. More profoundly, this newfound emphasis on choice in dying may be a dramatic realization of the Heideggerian emphasis on making one's death "one's own." This, I think, is the more philosophically significant explanation of the explosion of youth violence around the world. In a world without jobs, in which relationships are problematic, in which big-screen heroes come to life by continuously challenging death, facing death and, often, dying becomes not so much escape as mode of self-expression. Stunt pilots crash alone in the mountains on drunken or foolish runs and come to be seen as heroes, not fools. Criminals who throw their lives away in a hopeless shoot-out are lionized. (Consider the undeniably charming characters in *Breathless* and *Butch Cassidy and the Sundance Kid*.) To be sure, there are many sociological and psychological dimensions to such phenomena, but we should not underestimate the power of the philosophical rage for free will, for dying on one's own terms, even (if necessary) by one's own hand.

Making death one's own and savoring (or believing that one will savor) the experience has become a powerful existential motive. Alasdair MacIntyre bemoans the fact that his contemporaries generally express the opinion that they would prefer to die instantly, without warning and not suffer the slow, lingering death that allowed people in earlier times to reflect and ruminate on their lives and on their sins, to put together the story and meaning of their existence.[15] This topic has become part of popular discourse. In the wake of the explosion of TWA flight 800 out of New York (in July 1996), the conversations were revealing. On the one hand, the passengers were said to be victims. (It is a degradation of the language and not an expression of sympathy to insist, as politicians often do, that they were "heroes.") But, on the other hand, there were many anguished, quasi-empathic discussions about what it would mean to be such a victim. What was often commented on, given the suddenness of the explosion, was the awful fact that (for the victims) not only was there no choice but there was no time. No time to savor or anticipate the experience. No time for anything more than shock and fear. No time, in other words, to make the death one's own.

Then the news was released that some of the passengers (those toward the back of coach) continued to fly through the air, presumably in full consciousness, for another ten to twelve seconds. That inspired horror of exactly the opposite kind. Some people insisted that it is better to go "all at once" ("not knowing what hit you"). Others declared it far preferable to have those precious seconds—to come to an understanding, to collect one's soul, so to speak, and to live, if not savor, the experience. In this detached, petty squabble on the heels of a horrible tragedy, one can see the whole history, indeed the very nature, of the human preoccupation with death. How should we think about death? What does it mean to "prepare" for death? Would it be better not to think of it at all, even when it is immediately upon us? Is it possible to make one's death "one's own"?

The glorification of the death experience is what I call *death fetishism*. It is an extreme but perverted version of the heroic warrior mentality in which death is the critical moment in life. But the hero and the warrior do not think of death as an "experience." For death fetishists, on the other hand, it is the ultimate (and not just the last) experience. It is a familiar ingredient in some of the more dangerous, even lethal, sexual practices of the S&M crowd. It certainly followed (though it may not have been the cause of) the deaths of Basquiat and Cobain. It threads its way through the later works of Michel Foucault, and, if one accepts James Miller's telling of that tale, it provided the motivating force behind Foucault's last works and years. Death fetishism utterly rejects the Epicurean view that death is nothing and insists, with considerable enthusiasm, that it is quite a *something*, something essential, something to be celebrated, something even to be loved. It is, its proponents are only too eager to argue, the very opposite of the denial of death. It is the refusal to trivialize death or to explain it away with an appeal to continuing existence of any kind. Death fetishism epitomizes the heroic facing up to (and impatience about) the "necessary possibility" that we are all going to die.

Unlike the heroes who face death but hope to avoid it in battle, the death fetishist flirts with death on his or her own terms. Indeed, the verb "flirt" seems perfectly proper to the phenomenon, both because death fetishism is undeniably an erotic if not also a sexual phenomenon, and because one is never quite certain of one's intention to go through with it. Death fetishism is, whatever else it is, a distilled example of what Heidegger suggested when he wrote of "making death one's own," and of human existence as "Being-unto-Death." No doubt the celebration of death was not Heidegger's view. He was a man who lived (like Nietzsche) quite free from the temptations of physical danger. However dramatic his writing, the risks and fatalism he pronounced were not allowed to interfere with his own rather domestic sensibilities. (Unlike Nietzsche, he lived quite healthily well into his eighties.) But Heidegger is, I think, the patriarch of death fetishism in philosophy. Most of the history of philosophy, perhaps, tried to deny death its proper place in human life, whether by touting the likelihood of the afterlife or by ignoring the subject altogether. But it was Heidegger, most prominently, who embraced death and gave it its due. Then the post-Heideggerian French—Bataille, Artaud, Foucault—turned it into a fetish.

A fetish, in many religions, is a sacred object, perhaps one endowed with magical powers. Since Freud, the word also describes an erotic and arousing object, although one could argue that the distinction between the religious and the erotic is itself the product of Judeo-Christian mischief, and Freud one of its latter-day seducees. But mainly, in secular and quite sexless terms, a fetish is any object of excessive attention and devotion. Thus Marx quite rightly pointed out the fetishism for money and commodities in present-day capitalism, and pop-culture historians talk with considerable nostalgia about that all-American fetish, the automobile (at least before the 1980s, when most of the cars became not only Japanese or German but also so loaded with computer gadgetry that intimacy under the hood was no longer possible for most amateur enthusiasts). In America, then—and now in the rest of the world—the automobile is not just useful and sometimes necessary, not to mention a sign of status. It also represents the concretization of one's powers, one's personality, one's very self. And yet, it is just a piece of machinery. Death fetishism similarly converts death, one moment in the machinery of life, into the meaning of life, the ultimate test of life, even the point of life. At the very end of *The Stranger*, Camus's character Meursault declares, "There was only one class of men, the privileged class. All alike would be condemned to die one day." Meursault goes on to note that nothing else, none of a person's choices, none of his or her actions or concerns made any difference before that "dark horizon" from whence "a "slow, persistent breeze had been blowing toward me, all my life long."

In his *Myth of Sisyphus*, Camus similarly notes, in his own voice this time, that "by the mere activity of consciousness I transform into a rule of life what was an invitation to death." Refusing to commit suicide, according to the young Camus, is what gives meaning to life. And if Camus's philosophy is throughout a kind of celebration of life, one cannot help but notice that it is always also a fascination with death, as he more or less admits in his most autobiographical works.[16] The "passion for life" he so celebrates is often indistinguishable from an obsession with death. One cannot ultimately ignore or deny death, but just as one can try to ignore it, deny it, belittle it, or render it Hollywood, so one can make too much of death. Death is not the focal point of our existence. We are not "Being-unto-Death," despite the inevitable fact that we are going to die.[17]

Death is one fact of life among many (birth, the appetites, excretion, and, according common folk wisdom, taxes.[18]). We can accept that fact without thereby viewing everything else in its shadow. Too often, in Camus, in Foucault and Artaud, in Heidegger, too much is made of death. Death fetishism deserves recognition as a rebellious opposition to the denial of death, but I think that we need to be more critical about the very idea of "denial of death." Much of what falls under that accusation seems to me no more than a healthy appreciation of life. Death fetishism, by contrast, comes off not as the acceptance but as the celebration of death. Death, according to the death fetishist, is exciting, something to savor. For the death fetishist, death is not "nothing," nor is it a gateway to the afterlife. No doubt, beneath the bravado of death fetishism, there is terror and irresponsibility. But there are also some serious questions that might serve an important role in getting us to see just what is significant and what is not about death.

The Bald Scenario:
"Death Is Nothing"

Become accustomed to the belief that death is nothing to us. For all good and evil consists in sensation, but death is deprivation of sensation. And therefore a right understanding that death is nothing to us makes the mortality of life enjoyable, not because it adds to it an infinite span of time, but because it takes away the craving for immortality. For there is nothing terrible in life for the man who has truly comprehended that there is nothing terrible in not living.

Epicurus, *Letter to Menoeceus*

Admittedly, we know no greater game of chance than the game of life and death. Here every decision is faced with supreme suspense, concern, fear. In our eyes, it is all or nothing. On the other hand Nature, ever honest and open, does not lie. It speaks very differently on the theme, much as Krishna does in the Bhagavad Gita. Its testimony is that nothing at all rides on the life or death of the individual.

Arthur Schopenhauer, *World as Will and Idea*

Most people do not think much about death—their own death, that is. The well-to-do may engage in a prudential modicum of estate-planning and almost everyone is now encouraged to draw up a will.[19] But such planning says much less about the anticipation of death than it does about the average citizen's attitudes toward lawyers and the government. It is merely an ideological refusal to give up one's hard-earned money. Indeed, "estate-planning" can even be the vehicle for denying death, by putting it at a distance and absorbing oneself in the business matters of the world. My own father—an old-fashioned attorney who still thought that being a lawyer was a gentlemanly way of helping people with their lives—dutifully loaded himself down with life insurance and other protections for the family, should anything ever happen to him. When, inevitably, something did, my mother found that he had neglected to mention where most of these policies could be found. Actually thinking about death, as opposed to responsible estate-planning, was something that he dared not do.

The refusal to think about death—that is, one's own death—is what Heidegger, following Kierkegaard, was on about. And, undoubtedly, there is an important sociological as well as existential point to this. The sociology is distinctively European–American and modern. Death rituals are generally tucked away, and only rarely the subject of elaborate thought or planning. The existential point is that the denial of death is, in some hard-to-pin-down way, a denial of life as well. But this is a charge that has not been substantiated, however often it has been made. And it runs into one of the most classic of the classical bits of wisdom on the subject, the idea that "death is nothing." And therefore, it follows, there is nothing to fear—and nothing to deny. It is time to look at this philosophy head-on.

Whole schools of philosophy have been dedicated to the pair of propositions that death is nothing and death therefore is nothing to fear. In this context, the most famous name is Epicurus (341–270 B.C.E.), followed by his Roman successor, Lucretius (98–55 B.C.E.). Thousands of miles to the east, Chuang-tzu (369–286 B.C.E.) and other Taoists also insisted that death was "nothing," a view defended later by many Buddhists and in modern times by Schopenhauer. For the Epicureans, death was nothing in a rather straightforward way: "Accustom yourself to the belief that death is of no concern to us, since all good and evil lie in sensation and sensation ends in death. While we exist death is not present and when death is present we no longer exist."[20] One might note the negative twist to Epicurus's philosophy, ignored by those who treat him as a hedonist and who use "*epicure*" to refer to those who know only how to enjoy themselves. Epicurus did not focus on pleasure but rather on the awfulness of pain. Indeed, "pleasure," for him as for many philosophers, principly means the absence of pain.

Lucretius, like Epicurus a follower of Democritus, suggested that the human soul was nothing more than an arrangement of atoms, which on death dispersed, leaving nothing. Chuang-tzu endorsed a similar image, even though Taoism is a holistic as opposed to an atomistic philosophy. Like the Western philosophers, the Taoists placed enormous emphasis on the idea that human beings are part of nature. Our individuality is something of an illusion, and one of the ideals in life is to regard both life and death with equanimity and serenity. Chuang-tzu leaves us with a series of beautiful images, for example, depicting the death of an individual as a drop of water joining all of the other drops of water in a stream. Thus death is nothing, and nothing to be afraid of.

The thesis that death is nothing is not, one could argue, a form of denial of death. It accepts death, and it accepts death *as* death, not as a gateway to an afterlife. The Epicureans and the Taoists did not deny that death is inevitable (although some later Taoists toyed with the idea of personal immortality[21]). It was just that death did not matter, and in some sense it was unreal. The dispersal of atoms, or the merging of what was never really disconnected in the first place—why should such matters matter? But the serious charge is that the view that death is nothing feeds on or mistakenly leads to the idea that life is nothing, or nothing significant, or even that life is a burden, something to be relieved. This comes across in the four Noble Truths of Buddhism and sometimes seems to be lurking in Taoism as well. It is central to the notion of "liberation" in all three of the great South Asian religions (Hinduism, Jainism, and Buddhism), and, of course, it plays a central role in Schopenhauer's pessimism.

The idea that life is pain is particularly poignant in the Judeo-Christian–Islamic tradition. In both Judaism and Christianity, there is the continuing urge to transcend suffering and "conquer" death. In Christianity, death is not even death (a very different way of saying that "death is nothing"). But isn't this also a way of deprecating life? To view life as essentially pain and suffering, and death as relief from pain and suffering, may soften our fear of death, but at considerable cost to our appreciation of life. Several versions of Christianity are pretty straightforward about this. In them, the Christian soul is not part of nature and this world ("in the world but not of it" in the New Testament formulation). It is one's "eternal life" that counts, not mere earthly life. This, Nietzsche charges, is the "nay-saying" of "otherworldly" thinkers, beginning with Socrates, who hated life and dreamed of other, better worlds instead. The Epicurean and the Taoist, by contrast, do not promise any such Otherworld, but they, too, seem to remove the sting of death by making too little of life. If death is nothing, just the dispersal of atoms or the substance of our bodies or our souls rejoining that nature from which they have never really been separated, is life then anything special, or is it nothing more than atoms and souls conjoined?

I think that the Epicurean and the Taoist can be cleared of such charges. What we must understand is the context in which the idea that death is nothing was introduced. The idea that death is nothing should be seen as a reaction to the idea that death is something to be taken seriously, something to worry about. Epicurus taught and wrote against the worry and ceremony surrounding death in the context of religious fanaticism. The Roman Stoics preached a similar lesson in the midst of a carnival of crackpot religions. Pushing the significance of death to the extremes—and by no means did nascent Christianity go the farthest in this direction—popular attitudes toward death naturally inspired an opposite if not equal reaction. Epicurus's comment, "Death is nothing," is the bumper sticker of that reaction.

In place of increasing panic about the nature of the afterlife and the punitive nature of the gods, Epicurus's saying strikes us a sign of sanity. But it is taken out of context. The longer phrase is significant—"death is nothing *to us*"—leaving open the possibility that death nevertheless might be of considerable importance for the survivors or for society more generally. The larger passage makes clear Epicurus's deflationary intention. In fact, Epicurus did not so much take aim against death (or the concern with death) as against the gods and worry about the gods. He simply insisted that there were no gods, as well as no afterlife in which gods could act on us. There was, in this context, "nothing" to worry about. One can only imagine, against the terrifying religious backdrop of the times, that what Betty Sue Flowers calls "the Bald Scenario" must have been a tremendous relief.[22]

Even more important, I think, is Epicurus's emphasis on the social significance of death. This is a point I want to come back to in some detail, and it is not to be confused with the obvious observation that death affects the survivors as well as the deceased. Although his name and the word derived from it (Epicurean) have become synonymous with hedonism, Epicurus carefully distinguished (as would John Stuart Mill two millennia later) between "qualities" of pleasures, insisting that honor (or what we would call "integrity") was of the greatest importance. Quite contrary to the thrill-of-death fetishists of his own time, Epicurus recommended *ataraxia*, or peace of mind. Not worrying about death was one aspect of not worrying in general, but *ataraxia* could not and should not be purchased through oblivion or irresponsibility. Living a good, virtuous life was the ticket, a life in which the very highest values were friendship and community. Unlike the popular caricature of him, Epicurus was not a pleasure-seeking solipsist, but neither did he accept the idea that life is all pain. His insistence that death is nothing "for us" is the assurance that there is no pain or suffering that comes with death, that there are no tortures waiting for the newly liberated soul, that there is no experience—either good or bad—for us to anticipate or worry about. But this is not to say that life is also nothing. Life is or should be filled with virtue and friendship and with these, the best pleasures. But when it ends, it just—ends.

When we think of death, we often think of what we will miss. Dead, one might miss the party, but that is no longer a concern. Nor should your friends worry—not that they don't care or miss you—but you aren't "missing" anything, since you are nowhere, nor are you liable to any harm, since you are nothing. If the Epicureans did not indulge themselves in the often fatuous thinking that the dead are, after all, much better off and happier than we are, they could at least in good conscience feel tranquil about the fact that the dead were no worse off or unhappy. As, someday, they would be themselves.

The Thin Reaper:
Death as Paradox

> Death has always been—rightly or wrongly is what we cannot yet determine—considered as the final boundary of human life. As such it was natural that a philosophy which was primarily concerned to make precise the human position in relation to the non-human which surrounded it would first consider death as a door opening upon the nothingness of human-reality, and that this nothingness would be the absolute cessation of being or else existence in non-human form. Thus there has been a realistic conception of death such that death appeared as an immediate contact with the non-human. Thus death escaped man at the same time that it rounded him off.
>
> Jean-Paul Sartre, *Being and Nothingness*

The Epicurean antidote has been a source of considerable wisdom and peace of mind throughout Western philosophy and religion. David Hume, for example, in many ways an Epicurean, adopted this philosophical strategy.[23] On his deathbed, he repeated an argument borrowed from Epicurus's Roman disciple, Lucretius. Boswell reports the conversation thus: "I asked him if the thought of Annihilation never gave him any uneasiness. He said not the least; no more than the thought that he had not been, as Lucretius observes."[24]

So stated, Hume's reflection has two parts. The first is that "death is nothing." The second is a "symmetry" argument, which asserts that the "nothing" that follows my death is no different from the "nothing" that preceded my birth. I find this dreadfully problematic. Tom Nagel argues, rightly I think, that death is not "simply the mirror image of the prior abyss."[25] He writes, "The time after [a person's] death is time of which his death deprives him. It is time in which, had he not died then, he would be alive."[26] He continues:

> But we cannot say that the time prior to a man's birth is time in which he would have lived had he been born not then but earlier. For aside from the

brief margin permitted by premature labor, he *could* not have been born earlier: anyone born substantially earlier than he was would have been someone else. Therefore the time prior to his birth is not time in which his subsequent birth prevents him from living. His birth, when it occurs, does not entail the loss to him of any life whatever.[27]

One might well probe into the notion of "deprived" in this context. In what sense are the dead "deprived" of time? Deprivation implies a loss, perhaps even a cheat, a betrayal, an injustice. But in what sense does one "have" or "deserve" the time that is then lost? Purveyors of death (Hollywood and the military, for example) are fond of saying "It's time," or "It's your/my/his/her time." In which case, there is no loss because nothing was to be expected. This is callous, of course, but one finds similar conceptions in many religions, often collected under the easily misunderstood notion of "fate." Fate, one might say, is allotted time. To die is simply to have used up one's time, no matter how "cut short" it may seem in the light of one's projects, one's expectations, one's hopes, one's health. From this perspective, one might say that a person's death is indeed like his or her birth, in that both before and after, he or she is "out of" time. One does not exist, and the difference between "not yet" and "anymore" turns out to be no difference at all. But this cannot be an adequate defense of Hume's argument.

What bothers me about this way of thinking is not only its potential callousness but also the fact that, as in so many such arguments in philosophy, the perspective seriously confuses the first-and third-person cases. In a sneaky philosophical sense, *for me* there is (at the moments referred to) no difference between the void that preceded my birth and the void that will follow my death. But that is only because there is *nothing* for me, no sense to "for me," neither sameness nor difference. As "void," there is no difference, there could be no difference. (A hole in a piece of cheese is different from the hole in the ozone layer, but the difference is the difference between cheese and the ozone layer, not between voids.[28]) So, *for me*, there is no difference, but *who* is describing this void, and from what perspective? It surely cannot be *me*. In the world of other people, however, there is at least one critical difference: After my death, as opposed to before my birth, some people will miss me. (Lonely people in the unfortunate position of having no one to miss them revealingly complain, "It's as if I never was born.") Indeed, during my life, I can anticipate being missed. But before my birth and after my death, there is no one in a position to describe the similarity between the prior abyss and the posterior abyss. On the other hand, if I am doing the describing from the present— that is, while I am alive—the difference between the emptiness before my birth and the emptiness that I anticipate after my death is an enormous difference indeed. The former is simply a past without me, and (except under the most extraordinary circumstances) a past in which I and my specific roles are of no concrete significance.[29] The latter is filled with my hopes, fears, and expectations, both up until the moment I die and after my death as well.

Among the concerns in my life one might include my projects, ambitions, social status, threats of injury and disease, the manner or mode of my death. Among the concerns for my future—those hopes, fears, and expectations pointing after my death—one would include how I am to be remembered, the fate of my children, what will be done with my property, whether my books will still be read, whether my body will be properly respected, or abused, or used for science, or recycled for some unseemly purpose. But all of these future-oriented concerns essentially involve me, and could not be described except in terms of who I am and who I have been and what I have made of myself and the nature of my living existence. That is not true of the past, except, again, by way of some very creative hyperteleological storytelling.[30] I can imagine having been born years or even centuries before I actually was born, but leaving aside the question of whether I would then be a different person (as Nagel argues), it seems clear that what I am doing is transporting myself as a whole—my entire life, character, history—into an imaginary past. I am not missing or anticipating missing the time before I was born.

The opposite sort of argument, similar to Epicurus, might be called the "phenomenological" argument. It is impossible to imagine one's not being from the first-person point of view. One can all too easily imagine not being, of course, but there is always that nagging perspectival question: From where is one imagining his or her own nonbeing? Thus Freud imagines himself at his own funeral, a ghostly presence but there nonetheless. So, too, Sartre's characters in *No Exit* watch and comment on the behavior of their friends at and after their funerals. Jimmy Stewart's character in *It's a Wonderful Life* gets to see what his world would have been without him, but he nevertheless gets to be there, see it, walk through it, drive a car, and even connect with his old friends and neighbors (who do not remember him) and his wife (who, of course, is an old maid without him).[31] In other words, it is Jimmy Stewart playing himself, not as no one, even if he is a stranger to his friends. But, as an argument against the void, the phenomenology is phony. There is no perspective for us to occupy when we are dead.

What is worrisome about this whole line of argument, from the ancients to the New York and Parisian moderns, is that it really evades the poignancy, if not the point, of the question "What is my death to me, and why should I fear it?" One can appreciate the contexts in which Epicurus and Chuang-tzu tried to neutralize the hysteria that surrounded death in their cultures, but in the contemporary context of death denial and death fetishism, I think a very different dialectic is in order. What happens, particularly in contemporary Anglo-American attempts to argue that "death is nothing," is that the natural perplexity and confusion surrounding the fear of death are supposedly resolved by "clarifying the question." Indeed, many philosophers I know would say that the whole business of philosophy is to clarify confusions of just this sort. But some questions cannot and should not be clarified, and this is one of them. What we see here is a philosopher's trick: First, eliminate everything that isn't death as such, for example, the pain and suffering of dying, all questions about how one dies, where and with whom; eliminate all consideration of future potentialities (since, once dead, supposedly the person no longer has any such potentialities); remove the fear of death and any hopes for an afterlife (no matter how conceived). Bingo!—there's nothing left. Death is nothing. One would like to say that this misses the point, but a "point" is precisely what there is not. The fear of death is, rather, a web of concerns and confusions, not only about the possibility of an afterlife but also about the life that is brought to an end in death. To dismiss these as merely "nothing" is to dismiss our concerns about life as well. Thus we back away from Epicurus.

Fearing Death:
What's to Be Afraid Of?

Death thus horrifies and disgusts not just because it smells bad, but because it is *not* [italics mine] an end to the process of living. . . . The having lived and the living unite to make up the organic world of generative rot, rank smelling and upsetting to the touch. The gooey mud, the scummy pond are life soup, fecundity itself: slimy, slippery, wiggling teeming animal life.

William Miller, *An Anatomy of Disgust*

Why should we fear death? If we take the reductionist route, insisting on "death itself" and nothing more, we will end up with such a thin concept of death that, by necessity, it will come to nothing. Let's look instead at the equivocation and confusion the question engenders. Looking at death as an event, as a moment, as merely "the end," belies the place of death in a life. We do not think of our death that way, nor can we, except, perhaps as philosophers. Death is bound up with dying and being dead, which in turn are comprehensible only in terms of life and the living of it. It is our concept of ourselves as persons—as students, professors, lovers, husbands, wives, friends, parents, children, grandparents, citizens, authors, authorities, athletes, gourmets, property owners—that informs our concept of death. Camus and all of the others are just plain wrong when they suggest that death is the same for all of us. Like Tolstoy's unhappy families, we all have our different stories, and it is in terms of those individual stories that death must be understood.

First, of course, there is the fact of death as ending the aspirations, plans, and hopes that make up a life, whether these are grand and global, like Alexander's ambition to conquer the world, or modest and limited to the living room sofa, like wanting to see who wins Superbowl XXXIV or the triathlon at the Sydney Olympics in the year 2000. To understand death is to understand each and every death as the frustration of such desires, particular to the person, the family, the community, and the culture. Death, in that sense, is always untimely. It always, even at the age of ninety-nine, cuts life "short." The fact that death is sometimes "timely"—just following the achievement of some lifelong ambition, some great celebration or milestone—is a special case, a case in which the most basic desire may *not* be frustrated.

But usually, such a vision is a falsification of the always multiple aspirations and pleasures that invigorate most people. Such comfort usually comes from the mouths of the survivors, only occasionally from the person dying. ("Now, finally, I can die happy.") To be sure, such occasions are inspiring and well worth remembering, if only as a reminder that lives can be more or less completed as well as ended, and that death does not have to be the ruination of life. A good death, almost (but not quite) by definition, comes at the end of a good life. Also memorable, however, are all of those people—most of us—who do not "die at the right time." Friedrich Nietzsche, who famously insisted on this, is perhaps the most poignant example of someone who did *not* die at the right time. This most dynamic philosopher and man of letters lingered for more than a decade in a state that only occasionally made him more exciting than a vegetable, thus darkening a life of brilliant polemics under a lasting shadow of insanity and pathos.

The idea of death as putting an end to life's plans and projects should not be interpreted as simply self-interested, as referring only to *my* projects. Many of my plans and projects essentially involve other people, not just their connection with me or their opinions of me or their affections for me, but also their own plans and projects and, in general, well-being. Thus, however unphilosophical this might seem, one central concern in the fear of death is what will happen to them. Now, to be sure, such protectiveness may be self-aggrandizing. One may not be as necessary as one thinks, and there is a too plausible chain of thought that goes from "My family will starve without me" to the somewhat reassuring "Someone else will take care of them" to the deflating realization "Someone else will take my place" to the awful "They will eventually forget about me." And, of course, this is so. One does tend to become a mere memory, and after a generation or two, not even that. It is probably a good thing for most of us that we are not around to see that this is so. (We would all be like that Jimmy Stewart character, screaming "Don't you know me?!") This is a probable disappointment looming in the afterlife that all of those tales of "eternal bliss" and "heavenly delights" typically fail to mention. Sartre had it right. His unforgettable characters in limbo "live" to rue the day they can overhear the posthumous gossip about them. But, then, as a matter of psychological truth as well as poetic license, Sartre soon rendered it impossible for them to do so.

Perhaps the most human of our fears about death are our worries about other people. Our primary and most easily justified concerns about death involve our roles in families, in communities, in organizations, in projects, in groups, in causes where other people have come to depend on us. We also worry about the adequacy of our lives, how our story will be told when the narrative is completely out of our hands. (How many dull autobiographies have been written in the attempt to prevent this loss? And how many muck-raking biographies seem to have the purpose of removing the subject's last vestiges of control?) If such thoughts are not adequately "philosophical," because they ignore the logic of nothingness and the solipsism that the "death is nothing" scenario tends to presuppose, then so much the worse for philosophy.

But philosophy is not just logic, and the self is not just that solipsistic atom portrayed by some philosophers and embodied by the occasional sociopath. The philosophical question about death is not just about the logic of nothing, but also about the self and the end of the self in all of its trappings and details. Being human—not just being philosophical—involves having some complex set of beliefs, expectations, hopes, worries, and fears about death: death as death, death as disappearance, death as absence, death as the frustration of ideals and desires. What is not so clear is whether human beings are the only creatures who know about or worry about death. It is often argued that elephants have some such understanding, and other "higher" mammals, too.[32] It is probably true that all human beings, whatever and no matter how fervid their beliefs, share some apprehension about death or, at least, some apprehension about dying.

Heidegger's notion of *Dasein* as "Being-unto-Death" thus taps into an essential aspect of our existential makeup. One never knows, until it is time, whether one's being will go quietly into that "good night" or "rage" against it. One never knows, in the heat of battle or the pain and fever of disease, whether he or she will die a noble or a pathetic death. This uncertainty—not knowing how it will be, how we will be, and what we will do or suffer—is surely an enormous part of our concern about death, perhaps inordinately so.[33] I suspect that much of the seemingly metaphysical fear of death is really a much more personal fear of dying—not the suffering part of it, which I think is often overrated—but the personal character part of it, the nobility of it, so celebrated in other cultures, in Homer, in Mishima, even in Dickens. In America, with our insistence on "happy endings," the question of a heroic death tends to become moot. Except, of course, for the death fetishists and the warriors.

The fear of death also has to do with the question "What happens after death?," not in terms of those difficult questions about the afterlife but rather the far more tangible question of the fate of the body. Hector did not die badly, but being dragged behind Achilles' chariot was utterly humiliating.[34] Indeed, there is probably no culture on Earth that has not thought long and deeply about the proper disposal of the body after death. And it is certainly worth asking (an empirical question) how much of the fear of death is fear of neither death nor dying but the vain fear of how one's face and body will look once one is no longer alive. I think that this question, of death and vanity, is too often overlooked in the overly metaphysical and religious discussions about the significance of death. For Hector, the horror of death was neither an experience nor, presumably, was his dying, which (we read) was quick and probably painless. It was the humiliation of death that was the horror, the fact that he lost the fight and the even more humiliating fact that his body was denied a proper burial.[35] Indeed, one suspects that the apparatus of burial and cremation (the two primary forms of disposal) has as much to do with hiding the fact of death as it does with hygienic safeguards. In (newer) westerns and in gangster movies (as in real life) there is a special fear of being shot in the face. The pain is negligible, but the threat to one's vanity is overwhelming. (One of the favorite forms of male suicide is a pistol or shotgun barrel in the mouth, blowing out brains but leaving the face untouched.)

The fact of death does not include just the "bald" fact that someone has died. It also includes the disgusting embellishing details of death, details that are quickly glossed over in most discussions of the resurrection of the body. Thus William Miller, writing about death and disgust in the Middle Ages, suggests that death was horrible not because it was an event that ended consciousness, but because it was part of oozing, disgusting, uncontrollable biological process. "Death thus horrifies and disgusts not just because it smells bad, but because it is *not* [italics mine] an end to the process of living."[36] And for good measure, Miller leaves us with a few lines from Spenser's *Faerie Queene*: "Huge heaps of mudd he leaves, wherein there breed/ten thousand kindes of creatures . . . such ugly monstrous shapes elsewhere may no man reed."[37]

This is disgusting, but I think it is also essential. In (most) movies, where the dead simply fall down or disappear, death itself is not to be feared, only the end of one's role and possibly the cancellation of one's contract. The awful truth is that when we die, we do not just disappear, but rather lie around for some period of time, a source of disgust and horror to those around us. We all say, of course, that we would rather die surrounded by friends and family. But behind this wish is usually another, more often unspoken, that we should die in a decent manner, preferably well-dressed, makeup unsmeared, face undistorted by pain or unbroken by violence, still pink and flushed and untainted by anything quite so offensive as blood. A moment's reflection may make us rethink this scenario, and understand why some people, like elephants, go off by themselves to die.

What happens to the body, as well as what happens to the soul, is of considerable fascination and importance to us. It is not surprising that some religions (for instance, Orthodox Judaism) and many individuals balk at the idea of "using" the dead body for any purpose whatever, whether it is for the education of future physicians (it is hard not to think of one's *self* lying there on the dissecting slab) or the saving of another's life with a still healthy heart or liver. Our sense of bodily selfhood may end with death, but while we are alive it is projected forward after death. It may be vanity, but it is hardly foolish (although it may be selfish, at least in the medical case). It is a form of vanity that cannot be simply ignored or denied. Talk as we like, filled with bravado, about "dust to dust" and the victory of the worms, the humiliating circumstances that surround being dead offer good reason indeed for being concerned about death, and are not to be dismissed as of no importance *to us*. We do not become nothing in death, but rather quite something, an object of revulsion and disgust. And when we anticipate this, quite naturally, we have good reason to be concerned.

The future of the soul, the ethereal self, is but one of many questions about death, and the only one that tends to be metaphysically detached from the concerns of life itself. But this, too, is an illusion. Socrates envisioned his death as an uninterrupted continuation of the one thing he loved to do most in life.[38] The Islamic Heaven is more explicitly depicted than the Christian Heaven, as a "Garden of Delights" containing all of the pleasures most treasured in life. But of course one never knows, however strong one's faith, what will happen afterward, to the soul, to the spirit, to one's mind, to one's memories. There can be no more than metaphysical speculation, devoid of evidence or testimony, despite dubious commentary from those few who claim to have already "been there." But the future of the self or soul can be much more than this, even if, from the grand theological perspective, somewhat less.

Early in this chapter, I quoted Aristotle, quoting Solon: "Call no man happy until after he is dead." A person's desires may end with death, but the satisfaction of those desires does not. A couple wish nothing but the best for their children and their grandchildren. When they die, the wishing ends but the wish remains, and may be satisfied or thwarted only years later. A poet wants his poetry appreciated, but dies when he is still unknown and unrecognized. Years later, perhaps even centuries later, he is "discovered" and his wish is fulfilled. There are many meanings of "afterlife" and "immortality," not all of them so separated from life. Socrates points to Homer's "children" (the *Iliad* and the *Odyssey*) in the *Symposium*, as well as to all children everywhere, as the meaning of immortality. Next to that concrete sense of life's continuation and meaning, Socrates' esoteric and rather Egyptian view of the immortality of the soul pales by comparison.

Even if one does believe in an afterlife, the question of death—and with it the question of life—will not go away. The promise of an afterlife should not be used to eclipse the worldly questions of ethics and attachment, to minimize the importance of relationships and trivialize obligations (even if it also makes ethical behavior and success in relationships a criterion for a desirable place in the afterlife). Even in the most eschatological thinking, the Socratic question of "how to live" occupies central stage, and the question of how to think about death becomes a challenge to think about life. Thus Spinoza, a devoutly religious man, tells us, "A free man, that is to say, a man who lives according to the dictates of reason alone, is not led by the fear of death, but directly desires the good; that is to say, desires to act, to live, and to preserve his being in accordance with the principle of seeking his own profit. He thinks, therefore, of nothing less than of death, and his wisdom is a meditation upon life."[39] Whether Jewish or Christian or Muslim or Hindu, questions of the afterlife are ethically if not ontologically secondary to questions of life. To live for death is a denial of life, which is much more serious than the denial of death.

Beyond Morbid Solipsism:
The Social Dimension of Death

When you cease to make a contribution, you die.

Eleanor Roosevelt

The fear of death easily presents itself as a metaphysical or logical perplexity, as a dread of the unknown, as a confrontation with nothingness. The truth, I think, is much less flattering. We worry about the pain of dying, or the pain that precedes dying. We vainly worry about the disposition of our bodies after death. We worry about the people we care for, but then we also worry that they will be fine without our care, indeed, that they will not even remember us without our constant, even if kindly, reminders. The idea that death is nothing, too, may not be so much a matter of metaphysics as an awkward sense of absence. Put in the least flattering way, we might say that my death is a bad thing because it deprives the universe of me. I picture the world without me, like Sartre's characters in *No Exit*. I see them talk about me, laugh about me, pity me. I watch someone date and marry my wife, raise my children, refute my books. Or worse, I see that they ignore me. Death may be nothing, but it is a nothing that hurts.

All of this is not grand metaphysics or "fundamental ontology," but petty selfishness wrapped up in enigma. It is what I call *morbid solipsism*, an image of death solely in terms of the self. What I have been arguing toward, and what I believe has been neglected in philosophy, is the social dimension of death. To appreciate the importance of this, it is not necessary to abandon the first-person posture that is basic to the philosophical question, nor is it in any way to compromise our robust sense of individual life and the personal concern about death. But it is to say that we are first and foremost, phenomenologically and ontologically as well as biologically, social animals. One's own death is always, except in the most lonely of cases, a disruption (one hopes not too minor) of a network of relationships. And even in those lonely cases, one's death is, in one's own thinking, a disruption of past or possible relationships or, at the outer reaches of pathos, a lament that one is, quite unnaturally, dying all alone.

What Heidegger marks off as the "uniqueness" of Being-unto-Death seems to me to be a version of morbid solipsism, a denial of the obvious in favor of an obscure and mock-heroic philosophical theory. And Sartre, too, as much as I agree with him, seems to me to be falling into the same solipsistic trap, talking of "my projects" and juxtaposing "my mortality" with that of "the *Other.*" But Sartre is also keenly aware of the fact that when I think of my death, I cannot help but think of what others will see in me, how others will see me, how others will think of and remember me. When I imagine myself at my own funeral, à la Freud, it is the eyes of others I am imagining, not my own, whether or not "my perspective" is, logically and irreducibly, mine and mine alone. When I imagine my body on a slab, or bloodied in the street, or frozen from terminal pain, it is others I imagine thus seeing me, not I. When I worry about how I will die, it is for others that I am concerned. Of course, I also worry about my reputation, but here, more dramatically than anywhere else, the social nature of the self is in evidence. After all, what difference could it make to me, in that attentuated posthumous philosophical sense, whether I exited as the hero, the coward, or the clown?[40]

Most societies, of course, would consider this obvious. Their mourning rituals take it for granted. But in our advanced decadent philosophies, such thinking is all but ignored, or explicitly denied. How many philosophers have looked at grief and mourning as aspects of death, rather than as mere cultural artifacts that properly belong to the anthropologists? How many philosophers have taken nothing less than the whole narrative of a life as the essential "moment" in death (apart from morbid Silenus, for whom all of life was dying)? In cartoon wisdom, it has long been a cliché that, as one is dying, the whole of one's life flashes before one's (inner) eyes.[41] In place of the "death is nothing" argument, philosophers should argue that it is the richness of life that provokes the pathos surrounding death. And the richness of our lives is not so much due to the phenomenology of experience as to the very particular phenomenology of *social* experience.[42] I want to live because of other people. I want to live because I love. I want to live because I am steeped in my projects, virtually all of which are social projects, as Sartre above all would be the first to appreciate, no matter how solipsistic their practice (writing, for example). I want to live because others need me, and because I care for and about others. I am part of their world as they are part of mine.

In thinking about death, it becomes clear to me that what I really care about is the people I leave behind. This is, in part, because of my interests, my pride, my vanity. My concern is not just altruism. It also self-interest, love, ambition, shame, and the fear of loss of control (the real horror of *No Exit*). Death is what individuates us only insofar as it targets the vulnerability of intimate and significant relationships. In itself, death is nothing and dying is nothing worth celebrating. If dying is a test, a challenge, an occasion for bravery, it is so only in the category of "Being-for/with-Others," not "Being-for-Itself" or "Being-unto-Death." Death is not nothing, but it surely can be made into something, a noble death, a death not just "one's own" but with others in mind and for the sake of others. According to Heidegger, this may be an "inauthentic" death, but it is death such as the Homeric heroes would have contemplated. That is the way our philosophies should once again take us—out of solipsism, away from death fetishism, away from morbid solipsism, away from nothingness, and back into the richness of our lives.

7

RECOVERING PERSONAL IDENTITY

The Chinese philosopher awakened with a start, for he had been
dreaming that he was a butterfly. And for the rest of his days,
he did not know whether he was a Chinese philosopher who had
dreamed that he was a butterfly, or a butterfly who was now
dreaming that he was a Chinese philosopher.

Chuang-tzu

Personal identity is one of those problems rightly said to be universal and perennial in philosophy. In its "thick" manifestations,
of course, personal identity raises very different sorts of questions in different
cultures. "Who are you?" in China most likely means "Who is your family?"
"Who are you?" in the United States most likely means "What do you do (for
a living)?" Indeed, it raises very different sorts of questions for different individuals, depending on their lot in life, their temperament, their talents, and
their possibilities. "Who am I?" asked by a Stanislavsky-trained actor implies
a very different concern from "Who am I?" asked by a student selecting a
major or "Who am I?" asked by a frustrated mother and housewife who has
never had the opportunity to test her talents in the marketplace. But, on
narrower reading, it seems that every human being has *some* conception of
him or herself, and that conception can be called into question.

Nevertheless, in many of its currently most argued versions, the so-called
problem of personal identity is actually quite localized and only a couple of
hundred years old, a provincial upstart in the Hellenic–Judeo-Christian philosophical tradition. The problem is easily if misleadingly summarized: "Who
am I?" The most obvious answer, of course, is "It depends who's asking." But

this seemingly simple quest for reference and identification suggests a number of distinct and quite different questions with different presuppositions and, accordingly, very different cultural and conceptual responses.

Taken at face value, the question "Who am I?" would seem to be a request for a name—appropriate, perhaps, after an accident or a long, drugged sleep. The name in turn implies a history and a place in a social nexus. In moments of moral crisis, the same question can be a cry of despair or deep existential confusion. "Who am I?" means "What am I now to do?" My history and my social place and position have been called into question. What concerns me is not what I have been but what I should be. It is the narrative of my life (and perhaps others' too) that has been brought up for renewal, to be reconsidered, perhaps considerably revised. Such existential crises evoke the angst much celebrated by Kierkegaard, Heidegger, Sartre, and all of those millions of Eriksonian adolescents. On the other hand, the problem of personal identity might be taken more generally to mean "What is it to be a human being?" The answer to this question is built into virtually every language, if not every philosophical tradition, oral and mythological as well as scientistic and epistemological. In most cultural contexts, not excluding Europe and North America, to be a human being means to be a person much like us, where "much like us" (and "person") refers in one instance to Aristotle's fellow male Athenian aristocrats, in another to Clifford Geertz's Javanese, in another to George Bush's faithful Republicans, and in still another to the Chinese. In every case, a history, a developed way of being, a shared narrative, is implied. The definition excludes as well as includes. So used, the term "human being" is not a biological category. It is a clumsy and often oppressive political weapon.

Taken back to the level of the individual, the problem of personal identity might be "What is it to be a self?" That question readily invites an ontological or phenomenological response, a discourse on the transcendental unity of consciousness or Cartesian introspection, but it should also suggest the urgency of a cross-cultural and comparative quest. Insofar as the self—and one's concept of self—is socially constructed as a (more or less) culturally specific narrative, there is every reason (and now volumes of research) to suggest that different peoples have different self-conceptions. So asked, the question is thus incomplete. It should rather be formulated, "What is it to be a self in Chinese society?" "What is it to be a self in Yoruba society?" "What is it to be a self in Kaluli society?" "What is it to be a self in bourgeois Parisian society?" "What is it to be a self in Utku society?" But, again, the question "What is it to be a self in Chinese/Yoruba/Kaluli/French/bourgeois/Utku society?" should not be assumed to be merely descriptive anthropology. It slips easily into the question "What is it to be a person?"—an explicitly ethical notion. The debates over abortion and animal rights, for example, often turn on whether fetuses and some vertebrates (at least) are persons. The question of personhood accordingly commands considerable attention in cultures that have suffered a severe dislocation, for example, by way of colonialism, or are just breaking out of traditional feudal or other hierarchical caste systems. There the problem of personal identity becomes nothing less than the philosophical quest for legitimacy and dignity.

Back in the academy, however, the problem of personal identity has become primarily an ontological puzzle—"What is it to remain 'the same' person over time?"—and secondarily the more particular empirical inquiry "What is it to be this particular human being who I am?" The first of these is sometimes distinguished as the problem of self-identity (as opposed to the secondary question of personal identity), although the answer to the one question obviously serves as part of an answer to the other as well. The ontological puzzle, like most of the puzzles that have defined Anglo-American philosophy in the last half of the twentieth century, invites ingenious moves and countermoves, and has proved to be remarkably intractable. Because it has turned out to be so difficult, it is therefore considered a serious philosophical question and is much in vogue today. It is often coupled with the more general problem of identity, "What is it for anything to be 'the same' over time?" And to test the limits of both our ordinary concept of identity and our extraordinary philosophical imaginations, the problem gets defined in terms of the darnedest transformations, far stranger than any Hindu or Greek or even Kafka ever dreamed of in their wildest tales of metamorphoses and miscegenation between humans and beasts, gods and humans.

John Locke began this tradition, wondering offhandedly what one would say if one man's memories were transposed to another person's mind. In the past few decades, Bernard Williams, among others, has enriched the example to extravagant dimensions. Mind and brain transplants have become extremely popular with philosophers. A generic example: A's brain, and consequently A's memory, personality, and sense of personal identity, are put in B's body while B's brain, and consequently B's memory, personality, and sense of personal identity, are put in A's body. Such mind and body swaps are sometimes accompanied with tantalizing questions, for example, What would you say if confronted with an extremely painful operation, to be performed on your body without anesthetic, but while it is "occupied" by someone else?[1] One can envision how imaginative such discussions can become, and some of the best and brightest philosophers in the Anglo-American tradition have leapt into the ring.[2] By the 1980s, the idea that A's brain, and consequently A's memory, personality, and sense of personal identity, might be fully functioning in B's body had become a philosophical (and science fiction) commonplace. Who, then, is who? Philosophers were both disappointed and impressed when it was pointed out that our ordinary conception of a person is not really equipped to deal with such circumstances.[3]

In the explosion of multicultural concerns and the tumult over self-identity that defines the beginning of the twenty-first century, however, one would think that such effete intellectual puzzles would give way to those problems of self- and personal identity that provide such fertile ground for cross-cultural and comparative philosophical investigation and understanding. Instead, there has continued to be an almost obsessive exclusion of any but the (presumably universal) ontological version of the problem from the mainstream philosophy journals, despite the fact that, according to one of the best and the brightest, it has become "desiccated."[4] Philosophical problems don't die, of course, and they are rarely resolved. But they do get ever more "thin," logical, and tedious. The technical wizardry currently employed in solving the problem of self-identity is evidence not of progress but of advanced conceptual osteoporosis. But given the fact that the question of personal identity continues to be a subject that fascinates nonphilosophers and would also seem to provide the philosophical key to a worldwide philosophical interchange, we might well retrace our steps and ask how that question has become so uninteresting, a mere puzzle, a professional brainteaser (if that is an appropriate expression in this context).[5]

What is it that nonphilosophers find so exciting? What, after all, is the question? How has the debate gotten so restricted? Indeed, even in France—only a few dozen miles removed from some Anglo-American academies—the concept of a singular self that is taken for granted in the current debates has been fragmented and buried along with "the author" and what Derrida has famously dubbed "the ontotheological illusion of presence." What are to we to make of the notion of a multiplicity of selves, which has now moved from the annals of psychiatry into mainstream personality theory?[6] What are to we to make of the notion of "no-self," so central to several forms of Buddhism? Indeed, what should we make of the thesis that in some societies, the self and personal identity have little or nothing to do with introspection and memories, but everything to do with one's place in the family, the group, the community? Why should this inward-looking Cartesian paradigm of selfhood be taken as essential and presumed to be universal?

Why should we expect that the concept of a person—or the criteria for "the same" person—should be the same for a Buddhist and a Muslim, a Hindu and a Taoist, a monk and a Wall Street banker? What are we to make of the mythological–tribal concept of personhood among the Yoruba?[7] How important is reflection in the conception of self? Is it essential? In Western philosophy, there is the facile fusion of self-reference, self-consciousness, thoughtful self-description, and personal reflection.[8] And, as in so many self-referential matters, provocative if not profound insights are sacrificed to the tantalizing temptations of puzzles and paradox, "brainteasers." Where we had what seemed to be a perennial problem, we now have an intellectual Rubik's Cube, a mere academic puzzle.

The Puzzle's Progress

> Should the soul of a prince, carrying with it the consciousness of the prince's past life, enter and inform the body of a cobbler, as soon as deserted by his own soul, everyone sees he would be the same person with the prince, but who would say it was the same man?
>
> John Locke, *Essay Concerning Human Understanding*

> Consider these possibilities. One is that a single soul, one and the same, has been with this body I call mine since it was born. The other is that one soul was associated with it until five years ago and then another, psychologically similar, inheriting all the old memories and beliefs, took over. A third hypothesis is that every five years a new soul takes over. A fourth is that every five minutes a new soul takes over. The most radical is that there is a constant flow of souls through the body, each psychologically similar to the preceding, as there is a constant flow of water molecules down the Blue.
>
> John Perry, *Dialogue on Personal Identity and Immortality*

The problem of self-identity, in its current incarnation, can be plausibly traced back to suggestions in Descartes and Locke, from whom we get the peculiar notions that one's identity is first of all bound up with "consciousness," or, more precisely, that one is ultimately a "thinking substance" (Descartes), or that one's personal identity is bound up with memory (Locke). The total extent of published discussion in both authors is considerably less than ten pages, but contemporary elaborations of their theses fill department libraries. The current argument is filtered through Hume, who declared somewhat paradoxically that when he looked into himself, there was no self to be found. ("For my part, when I enter most intimately into what I call *myself*, I always stumble on some particular perception or other, of heat or cold, light or shade, love or hatred, pain or pleasure. I never can catch *myself* at any time without a perception, and never can observe any thing but the perception."[9]) Hume further complicated the picture, following Locke, by casting his skeptical eye on the identity through time of even the most mundane objects. The human body, we all know now, rebuilds itself completely with new tissues every few years. Thus the further puzzle: What, besides continuity, renders our bodies "the same" bodies over a lifetime?

After Hume, the notions of self and identity began a long swim in the murky waters of German idealism, where they gained transcendental and eventually absolute status. ("Himself as everything! How can Mrs. Fichte stand it?"[10]) The current crop of philosophers have for the most part avoided those Gothic transformations and confined themselves to the tried-and-true puzzles raised by Descartes, Locke, and Hume. Perhaps this is a mistake. If nothing else, Kant, Fichte, Hegel, and Schopenhauer force us to reexamine the concept of personal identity from a radically new perspective. Suppose the self is indeterminate and personal identity is not necessarily equated with the individual person. The seemingly obvious fact of our individual identity, which Descartes, Locke, Hume, and most contemporary theorists take for granted, is thrown to the wind in German philosophy. And once that becomes open to question, then the notion of personal identity does indeed become interesting.

The notions of the self and personal identity do not give rise to just those puzzles and paradoxes of which G. E. Moore complained, "I find that all of my problems come only from other philosophers." Every American teenager can provide a heartfelt if philosophically ill-informed survey of the problem. Every instance of ethnic strife both at home and abroad raises the issue, and every criminal case more or less depends on it. Indeed, every intimate relationship calls personal identity into question, as do pregnancy, serious accidents and illnesses, the loss of one's job, the death of a loved one or that authentic (*eigentlich*) mood that Heidegger called Being-unto-Death (*Sein-zur-Tod*). Some philosophers might quickly object, "But those are not peculiarly philosophical problems of self-identity," to which there are a number of appropriate replies, foremost among them a shrug of the shoulders. If indeed we are going to put the question of personal identity back into what one current author calls "a broadly naturalistic conception of the world," and consider "the more interesting and specific conceptions that have guided practical life," then these very real contexts are indeed properly (though not peculiarly) philosophical.[11] Looking back to the "peculiarly philosophical" context in which the question(s) of self and personal identity arose, I think that a considerably broadened view of the problem is justified.

Descartes, Locke, and Hume, or at least Descartes and Locke, were not particularly fascinated by philosophical "puzzles," that is, brainteasers of a "peculiarly philosophical" kind. They raised them in passing, but they had bigger quarry in mind. They were concerned with a defense of the very notion of reason (which in its ordinary meaning did not arouse any particular excitement about the distinction between scientific and rationalist philosophies[12]). They were anxious to defend the autonomy of the individual against the authorities. They were, in their different ways, exploring the realm of "subjectivity" and defending the claim that through personal thought and experience could be found genuine knowledge. Descartes and Locke were concerned to prove, yet once again, the existence of God. Locke and Hume intended to provide a comprehensive theory of human nature and establish the universality of man[sic]. Hume, of course, challenged the limits of reason far more vigorously than his two predecessors, but his skepticism can be understood only within the embrace of the Enlightenment project of which he was so much a part. Puzzles about self and personal identity were of interest only within the context of a general philosophy that placed great importance, and perhaps impossible weight, on the notion of individual autonomy. Even Hume seemed quite happy to forget his doubts about the self within a few pages of his paradoxical observation that he could not find one. Kant, who followed, resolved Hume's paradox by splitting the lingering Lockean distinction between personal ("empirical") and self- (now "transcendental") identity.[13] But if we are not to be satisfied with puzzles, that does not mean that we should search for impressive profundities either. However attractive the dark waters of German idealism may on occasion seem, the very real and practical problems of self-identity should not provide an excuse to scuba dive in the obscure.[14]

Instead, I want to outline four different ordinary, but also important, philosophical concerns where philosophical investigation of the self and personal identity is in order. No doubt there are "puzzles" to be found in all of them, which may serve as bait for philosophers who feel uncomfortable very far outside the bounds of narrowly epistemic justification. Whether any of these questions is "peculiarly philosophical" is not my concern, except insofar as I would want to defend the interdisciplinary status and multicultural import of such questions as their virtue rather than their vice.

The first question remains fairly conservative, well within the bounds of philosophical and political orthodoxy, and simply raises to a somewhat more abstract (but not nonempirical) level the "existential" questions that are involved in any "identity crisis," whether in the growing pains of adolescence or the angst of later life crises. To what extent, however, is this much-celebrated angst the product of a uniquely Western view, the painful consequence of an excessive emphasis on individual autonomy and a denial of the importance of cultural and intellectual tradition, combined with neglect—indeed, oblivion—regarding the place of narrative in establishing every life story, that is, everyone's personal identity? And to what extent—as evidenced by the Japanese enthusiasm for existentialist philosophy, for example—is it a question with larger and growing trans-cultural and multi-narrative dimensions?

The second question follows quite naturally from the recently renewed interest in what has come to be called "virtue ethics," which, often using Aristotle (less often Nietzsche) as a guide, emphasizes considerations of "character" rather than moral or utilitarian rules or principles in ethics. Again, it is a question that straightforwardly requires a narrative answer (that is, the story, told both by oneself and others, of who this person is *and has been*. It, too, has clear multicultural implications. Confucius taught a vision of the good life that was thoroughly defined by considerations of good character and the virtues that make up good character. Less obviously, many tribal ethics place character at the center of their moral concerns. (The ancient inhabitants of the island of Maui used to throw the umbilical cords of their newborn infants into the crater of the active volcano Haleakala, in order to ensure the honesty of their children.)

The third question raises more radical issues about individuality and the social construction of the self. In current debates about multiculturalism and the welcome new interest in other cultures and traditions of thought—not just in philosophy but also in literature and the social sciences—the idea of alternative conceptions of selfhood, as "interdependent" rather than "independent," have been much discussed.[15] It is unfortunate that so few of our most prestigious philosophers and philosophy journals have joined in that discussion, rife as it is with conceptual confusions and inflammatory hyperbole.[16]

Finally, I want to focus again on love, which since the *Symposium* has atttracted an enormous philosophical audience but only an occasional philosopher. In particular, I want to raise some questions concerning what Amelie Rorty has called the "permeability" of love, the fact that in love one changes his or her conception of (his or her own) personal identity in response to the features of the beloved. Indeed, love is, I have suggested and will suggest again here, just such a sense of "shared identity" as Aristophanes in his well-known allegory imagined so many years ago.[17]

Personal Identity and the Existential Social Self

> When Gregor Samsa woke up one morning from unsettling dreams, he found himself changed in his bed into a monstrous vermin. . . . What's happened to me he thought. It was no dream.
>
> Franz Kafka, *Metamorphosis*

> Dr. Means continued to read me the riot act. I would have to learn to love my new body, my new sex, my new tail. . . . And I should feel pleased as pisque to have an extra hand.
>
> Justin Leiber, *Beyond Rejection*

What is an "identity crisis"? It is not, to begin with the obvious, the sudden realization that the body one inhabits is not one's own. To be sure, such scenarios, for instance in Kafka's classic *Metamorphosis* or in Justin Leiber's philosophically delectable novel *Beyond Rejection*, raise all sorts of tantalizing questions (particularly when the switch in question is transspecies or transsexual), but these questions are far less concerned with the general idea of identity than with the details of coping. The question "Who is Gregor Samsa?" does not arise in its preeminently philosophical form. Gregor Samsa is the unfortunate narrator of the tale, the horribly transformed family member, the petty functionary who cannot figure out how he can possibly make it to the office today. The question of personal identity and the subdued horror, from start to finish, have to do with the concrete problems of what one might continue to call the "empirical" self, not the "transcendental" narrative frame. How does one turn one's enormous, inflexible body over?[18] How is one to think of oneself with (in?) a giant insect's body? How does one cope with the horrified screams and disgust of one's dear sister? How can one deal with one's increasingly dysfunctional family, knowing that (through no fault of one's own[19]) one is responsible for the dysfunctionality? What is one to do with long-habituated conceptions of oneself as a loyal, hardworking employee, a good provider, an innocuous, perfectly ordinary citizen, when one finds oneself turned into a cockroach?

An identity crisis is, unhelpfully, confusion about who one is. It is not, for the most part, self-contained. Despite its existential focus, it is, for the most part, a social problem. Waking up as a giant insect in a world all his own, Gregor might still have to cope with the problem of getting off his back, but the fact that he has turned into an insect is no longer a source of embarrassment or an obstacle to social success. Indeed, it might never occur to him at all, for where would the concept "insect" come from? An adolescent is at "that awkward age" not so much because his or her body is out of control so much as his or her social position—no longer a child, incompetent as an adult—is intolerable. Camus's Meursault ("the stranger") has great difficulty getting used to being called "criminal," not because of the negative meaning of the term but because he has never understood what it is to be called or classified as anything. He is "strange" in part because he has no sense of self-identity.

An identity crisis is a social crisis. That is why Sartre, after three hundred pages on the dualistic dialectic between Being "in-Itself' and "for-Itself," "facticity" and "transcendence," insists on introducing "Being-for-Others" as a third "primordial" and "not derivative" category of Being.[20] In plain English, what one *is*, is a function not only of the facts about one and what one thinks of oneself, but also of what others think of one and what they make of those facts. Indeed, one can read the third part of *L'Être et le néant* as a systematic undoing of what has been going on in the previous two parts. The facts that constrain personal identity are neither given nor determined by the subject. They are a matter of social construal, dependent on the context as well as the (often malevolent) motives of others. (Thus Garcin, a character in Sartre's play *Huis clos*, try as he may to construe himself as a hero despite his final cowardly performance in front of the firing squad, finds himself ultimately the victim of his two eternal roommates: Estelle, who could not care less about his ex post facto identity crisis, and Inez, who despises him.)

This picture of mutually construed personhood is borrowed from Hegel (from whom some of Sartre's awkward Teutonic terminology is also taken).

In his "master and slave" parable in *The Phenomenology of Spirit*, Hegel suggests (the text is too understated to do more than "suggest") that personhood essentially depends on what he calls "recognition" by another. The suggestion yields two philosophical theses, one very general and one, which Hegel pursues, more particular. The general thesis is that one would not be a self at all without mutual recognition, and this recognition obviously refers to oneself as publicly embodied (as opposed to the Cartesian model of introspective self-identification). The argument is rendered somewhat more complicated by virtue of the fact that Hegel refers to the individuals involved as "self-consciousnesses," indicating that they already have some sense of self-awareness,[21] but the primacy of recognition of persons (human beings) rather than the purely mental self is evident enough, as it would be many years later for P. F. Strawson and Mark Johnston.

It is Hegel's second thesis, however, that he actually follows up in the text and employs as the vehicle for several subsequent twists and turns of the dialectic. This second thesis is that the self and self-consciousness are first of all a matter of status, and status can be obtained, again, only through mutual recognition. In the stripped-down world of the parable, the protopersons engaged in mutual recognition have not much to rely on, since they are presumably without social rank, bank accounts, a wardrobe, good upbringing, philosophical wit, or any of the other pedestrian features by which we compare and measure ourselves. So, Hegel says, they fight, "to the death" if necessary, but of course the death of one would defeat the aim of the other, namely, to be recognized. Hegel then describes the curious inversion that confuses all questions of status and, consequently, compels both master and slave to more philosophical attempts at self-understanding.[22] But the general point is this: Personal self-identity is not just the abstraction "self-consciousness." It is concrete and it is social, even when it perversely rejects both the concrete and the social (as in Hegel's subsequent chapters on hedonism, "The Law of the Heart" and "The Way of the World"). Our identity is never just as a person, a human being, an organism, or a member of a particular animal species; it is as a particular person, a particular social being with particular features, virtues and vices.[23] Anything less is but "the dry articulation of a vague generality" (Mark Johnson) or, as Hegel would say, "an empty universal."

An identity crisis, then, is not just confusion about who one is. It is an inevitable result of our mutually construed personhood. If the identity of the self is always underdetermined, as Sartre argued, and if the determination of that identity always rests in part with the sometimes competitive and often noncooperative recognition of others, as both Hegel and Sartre suggest, then personal identity proves to be a spectacularly dynamic conception. What is more, it turns out to be particularly prone to philosophical manipulation. How we think about ourselves to a large extent determines who we actually are.

Hegel's grand conception of oneself as *Geist*, and Sartre's harsh conception of consciousness as "for-itself" and inescapably responsible for the world, have been powerful incentives for those struggling to gain an adequate conception of self (although the message is more likely engendered by AA or EST than by way of the original texts or a serious philosopher). So, too, one thinks of many serious philosophers, including not only Hegel and Sartre but also Hobbes and Rousseau and Hume (despite his "self" doubts), who have contributed to this literature of personal identity and changed the way we think of ourselves. For all of them, identity is not just a puzzle to be solved. It is our shared and personal human existence that needs conceptual shaping.

Personal Identity and Virtue Ethics

> There are those who are like cheap clocks, . . . they tick and they want the tick-tock to be called virtue.
>
> Nietzsche, *Thus Spoke Zarathustra*

Virtue ethics depends on the intelligibility of the concept "virtue," which in turn, as a "state of character," depends on the adequacy of some special but rarely spelled-out sense of "character." Too often, character is taken to be just a collection of more or less coherent traits, which in turn are analyzed as dispositions to act in certain ways. To be sure, such traits are by no means wooden, mere clockwork reactions that are oblivious to context and more or less "automatic." Indeed, one of the primary traits of character insisted upon by virtue ethicists ever since Aristotle is *good judgment*, which means precisely this sensitivity to the nuances of context. Courage, for example, manifests itself in very different actions when facing a hostile mob, on the one hand, or a malignant tumor, on the other. But the concept of character as a collection of more or less coherent traits is inadequate, particularly given some of the considerations concerning the social determination and the indeterminacy of personal identity. Is a person a collection of more or less coherent traits, or do these traits depend to a considerable extent on the construal of others? (What is charming in one society is repulsive in another. What is witty in the philosophy seminar may be tedious and tiresome in ordinary conversation.) Does a person's character determine his or her behavior—as many defenders of "compatibilism" in discussions of "the free will problem" (including Hume) have suggested—or do we need to make room for the spontaneous gesture, the unexpected "act of will," behavior "out of character" that may become, nevertheless, clearly and perhaps even paradigmatically the hallmark of a person's self-identity?[24]

This is not the place (is there ever a place?) to take on the seemingly interminable problem of free will, but the expression often used by both compatibilists and virtue ethicists, that an act "flows from a person's character," is worth critical scrutiny. To be sure, we usually understand what that metaphor means. A person has been brought up to be generous. He or she frequently has generous thoughts. He or she tends to perform generous actions "spontaneously," without deliberation or hesitation. (Indeed, deliberation, while it may be a philosophical virtue, may be evidence that one may not yet have the virtue in question.) Generosity "flows" from one's character in the sense that one does what one is used to doing, what inclination dictates doing, what seems perfectly "natural" for that person in that situation. No "act of Will" is called for, no conscious "push" or nagging reminder. A person acting "in character" does exactly what we would expect him or her to do. So understood, a person's identity can readily be comprehended as a collection of traits from which predictable actions flow as freely as rain from a darkened sky.

It does not follow, however, that "flowing from" is a causal notion, or the manifestation of an inherent disposition, nor indeed anything other than a metaphor suggesting "meeting (and not disturbing) our expectations." But what of those cases in which the action in question does not "flow" from, but rather flatly contradicts, the person's established character? It will not do simply to deny the possibility of such an action. The problem is to account for what appear to be such actions. But the question here is not one of free will but of personal identity. From that point of view, how do we construe such behavior? The answer is not quickly forthcoming. Sometimes we celebrate it, change our opinion of the person, and, consequently, our praise (or blame) changes him or her as well. Sometimes we dismiss it as an aberration of some curiosity but of no importance to our estimation of character. Most of the time we decide simply to wait and see what follows. Which way we go has much to do with the importance of the action in question, the ordinariness of the circumstances, the power of our prior expectations, the role and status of the agent in our company, and whether we will have to rely on the same person in similar circumstances in the future. So, too, when an act has magnificent or devastating consequences, it is difficult to dismiss it as insignificant (regarding the character of the agent), no matter how hard it is to explain or incorporate into our prior picture of the person. If, on the other hand, we with equal uncertainty find ourselves needing a similarly dramatic response in the future, we may well be reticent about shifting our expectations and our judgment of the hero-of-the-day's character. We will celebrate the response but withhold our praise of his or her virtue.

In extreme situations, for instance the exigencies of combat or life-and-death emergencies, people sometimes perform remarkable feats that could not possibly have been predicted on the basis of their more mundane, day-to-day behavior. Accordingly, such behavior may not be exactly "out of character," even though it goes against what we might well have expected. We have not yet had the opportunity to estimate their character in extreme situations. But this already raises a serious problem about the seemingly monolithic concept of character: Character depends on context. If we can have different and divergent views of a person's character in "ordinary" life and in extreme situations, we should at least suspect that a person's character might vary from the classroom to the bedroom to the office to the frenzy of the streets.[25] And do we want to say that these are merely different "aspects" of character? How does one individuate character, and why should we suppose that it is, as in the orthodox notion of self-identity, distributed one to a customer? But if character is contextual and segregated into different aspects of a person, then haven't we lost much of what we wanted of character and personal identity, too? "He's quite a character on the squash courts." Perhaps. But then it is hard to see how virtue ethics can provide the strong alternative to the option of evaluating a person's actions on the basis of consequences or conformity to rational principles.[26]

What we have been describing, however, is *our* estimation of *another's* character; but personal identity, regardless of our philosophical approach or sympathies, is not primarily an other-regarding question. It is self-regarding, a matter (in part, at least) of self-estimation, a matter to be considered from the first-person, not the second- or third-person, standpoint. This point stands quite independent of the thesis that self-identity is a matter of mutual recognition. But this introduces a predictable twist into the relation of character to personal identity. Character, as usually understood, is a factual matter. Character is a question of what in fact a person will do in such-and-such situations, and presumably there is some fact about him or her—summarized as a "trait"—that explains why he or she will do it. There are the usual problems about the status and nature of dispositions and how they serve as explanations, but they do not present any particular difficulty here. The problem is rather that self-identity is not simply the recognition of one's own character. Indeed, one's self-conception may neglect or even deny the virtues that actually constitute one's character.[27] Courageous people often do not see themselves as courageous (nor do cowards usually see themselves as cowards, rather, perhaps, as champions of "discretion").

This is why, for example, some virtue ethicists insist so strongly on the "spontaneous" and nondeliberative nature of virtuous action, not simply to underscore their insistence that an act must "flow" from a person's character but also to further insist that the virtue in question is a virtue precisely because it is not the product of thought and self-conscious reflection. A person who thinks to himself, as he gives to charity, "I am a generous person" (not to mention "What a generous person I am"), is thereby thought to be less generous. A person who primes herself for action with "I've got to have courage" thereby shows herself to be less than courageous. Of course there are limits to this diminution of virtue, and only someone wholly steeped in what Hume called "the monkish virtues" would insist that such implicit self-praise or self-prompting undermines or erases the virtue in question (which raises special problems, well recorded in the history of Christian psychology, about such self-conscious virtues as humility). But it is a plain fact that generous people often do not recognize their generosity, and courageous people do not acknowledge their behavior as brave. Their sense of their own identity, then, is quite distinct from the attributions of character that are due them from others. But then, how are we to understand their virtues?

One way to put this question is to think (with Aristotle and Hume) about the place of pride and shame in the list of virtues. Pride, in part, is the virtue of recognizing one's own virtues. Hume, following Aristotle, praises pride and condemns humility, accusing the latter of unavoidable hypocrisy. This may be too harsh, but it makes what I believe to be an important, if paradoxical, point about character. It is not enough to act virtuously, Aristotle tells us. One must comprehend one's actions as virtuous. A person trained to act in conformity with the requirements of virtue, as a dog might be trained to mimic human courtesies, would not thereby be virtuous, only well-behaved. But the matter of the relation between the exercise of the virtue and its self-recognition becomes rather delicate, all the more so as the "spontaneous" nature of the virtue is emphasized. At what point does self-consciousness undermine virtue? And yet, the comprehension of oneself as virtuous is part and parcel of personal identity—in fact, for many people the most essential part of their personal identities, more important than competitive status and success. (In Hegel, this is where the competitive nature of the master–slave confrontation turns into *Sittlichkeit*, tragically exemplified in the sisterly virtues of Antigone.[28]) It is the ongoing narrative of "who one is"—confused and sometimes conflicted between the stories one tells about oneself and the stories imposed by "the facts" and by others—that determines personal identity. (Antigone got caught between two stories, two opposed "forms of consciousness".)

A more complicated route to the same conclusion goes by way of Aristotle's somewhat uncomfortable examination of shame.[29] Displaying his discomfort, he calls shame a "quasi virtue." Shame itself is no virtue, of course; rather, it is the proper reaction to a lapse in virtue. But this is just the point. A person who feels no shame, who is "shameless," cannot possibly be virtuous. Virtue is in part the self-consciousness of being virtuous, and the shameful recognition of lapses in virtue—or worse, one's lack of virtue—is an essential ingredient in good character. Shame, however, is a proof of good character only in very small doses. Pervasive shame, if warranted, means that one's character is deeply flawed. Pervasive shame, if unwarranted, is morbid and pathetic. Nevertheless, and in either case, pervasive shame is one of those emotions that do serve to constitute a more or less unified conception of personal identity based on character, albeit an unhappy one. One further problem, of course, is that matters of both shame and pride are particularly prone to the distortion of self-deception (a matter that seemed not to bother the Greeks much but drove Christians like Augustine and Pascal to desperation[30]). What one conceives one's virtues to be and what they can justifiably be shown to be may be notoriously out of harmony, and here we come back to a new set of variations on the complex of "existential" questions we considered before. To what extent can a person's self-identity be based on self-deception? To what extent is a person's character determined by his or her conception of (his or her own) personal identity? To what extent is a person's character not merely a matter of "fact" but rather a matter of social construal, in which the first-person account of one's own identity is but a single, occasionally overpowered voice in the crowd?

Here are two final considerations for the virtue ethics notion of character and its relation to the problem of personal identity. First, it has often been pointed out—particularly by Nietzsche—that the Aristotelian (and Platonic) ideal of the "unity of the virtues" is in fact most implausible. One virtue conflicts with another and, quite the contrary of mutual reinforcement, one aspect of one's character undermines another.[31] But just as character can be split by opposing virtues, so personal identity can be split by identifying with these opposing virtues and features of character. Why would philosophers assume that the self is coherent or "transparent" to itself? Indeed, the devoted practice of philosophy itself would seem to be a prime example of how one set of virtues can wreak havoc with another, more mundane set of virtues. (Philosophers who refuse to recognize the usual social reaction to their continuous skepticism, logic-chopping, and overly critical examination of every casual thesis, and the literal construal of even the most hackneyed idiom may miss this point.) It is not only the phenomenon of self-deception that prompts us to think of the self as far more labyrinthine than the Cartesian *cogito* would suggest.[32] It is also the familiar fact that we recognize in ourselves not just one identity but several, some of them conveniently sorted according to circumstance and social surroundings and others, particularly in a time of crisis, in full-blown confrontation. One does not need to invoke "split brain" phenomena or other extreme psychiatric disorders in order to raise fascinating philosophical questions about the fragmented and partially hidden self.[33]

The other complication to be raised here has to do with, appropriately, final moments. It is a question that has always perplexed me: how a deathbed conversion, for example, or a horrible death can undo the whole history of a person's life and set in stone, as it were, an identity that may not in any sense be deserved. At the risk of becoming tedious, we might use Sartre's Garcin as an example again. His final act of cowardice seems utterly to undermine his lifetime of heroic dedication, as Inez cruelly reminds him. Or, consider the final scene in Goethe's *Faust*, when at the last moment the philosophical protagonist reneges on his pact with Mephistopheles and has his little worm of a soul carried up to Heaven by angels. Villains are saved by a final gesture of contrition, and good souls are condemned to Purgatory because of the accident that they died a few moments too soon, out of reach of a priest or savior. This is not just a question of character, of course. A person with a long and happy life may suffer briefly at the moment of death, through suffocation, strangulation, drowning, a bullet to the chest or abdomen, bleeding to death from an unseen wound, crushed by a heavy vehicle, or mutilated in an accident. But rather than think of a long and happy life ended by a few moments of horror (and sometimes the most horrible experiences in fact involve virtually no pain at all), why do we tend to dwell on those moments of horror as now having somehow defined the person's life? Why should they have anything to do with, much less define, a person's identity?

Now, to be sure, the problem here is not, by its very nature, one of *self*-identity, since the person whose identity it is no longer exists. But it is by no means a leap of "unconstrained imaginative conceit"[34] that we consider such a person, like Sartre's Garcin, to be sitting in some philosophical Hell or Heaven trying to ex post facto get their sense of themselves in order. Or, if this stretches one's eschatological imagination too far, one can always imagine, without theological presuppositions, one's entire life flashing before his or her eyes in one's final moments, not just by way of instant replay but combined with a philosophical narrative and commentary with an epitaph in mind. What, then, do we make of the relation of last moments to personal identity? The idea that our encounter with death defines us is a sobering thought (so sobering, in fact, that Heidegger wove his existential sense of "authenticity" around just such an experience). That our final experience may be extremely unpleasant and even humiliating is obvious enough, but that the moment of dying itself requires some alteration in our very conception of ourselves remains something of a mystery to me. That we should remember the gruesome moments of someone else's death and not be able to get the awful picture out of our minds is clear enough. It took me years to get beyond my memories of my father's frail last years and remember him again as the vital, energetic man that he was. But the fixity of memories is not the test of identity, and it surely has little or nothing to do with character. If a final act culminates a life of virtue (or vice), it is significant only emblematically, because it does act as a summary. Or if a final act is quite out of character, it may be significant for exactly the opposite reason. But its status as "final act" seems to me to be of no special importance at all. The fact that it is so emphasized I attribute to a sales trick of the missionary trade rather than any insight about the nature of virtue.

What warrants the emphasis on character in virtue ethics is indeed a strong sense of the importance of constancy and continuity, as opposed to the merely momentary and accidental. It is quite reasonable, then, to think of character in terms of the self and personal identity. The mistake is thinking that character, self, and personal identity are "essences" of a sort, properties of the person rather than complex and dynamic functions of the (partially true) stories we tell about (and to) ourselves and about (and to) others. What motivates the search for personal identity, is at bottom an ethical quest, not just knowing "Who I am" but the pursuit of the Good as well.

Personal Identity and Multiculturalism

> We construct ethical identities—woman, man, African-American, "white"—in ways that depend crucially on false beliefs about metaphysical identities; something like each one of them could be reconstructed out of other materials. But if we were to live in a society that did not institutionalize those false beliefs, it is unclear that the project of reconstruction would be an attractive one.
> Kwame Anthony Appiah, "But Would That Still Be Me?"

It is now virtually a platitude in the social sciences (and a tiresome piece of political jargon) that the concept of self varies from culture to culture (an enormous weight that is uncritically loaded on the simple word "difference"). In a summary article that has received widespread attention in psychology and anthropology, Hazel Rose Markus and Shinobu Kitayama argued that "divergent construals of self, others and the interdependence of the two" suggest deep implications for the understanding of different cultures, their systems of knowledge, ways of behaving, and the relativity of emotions.[35] The authors limited themselves to a somewhat unspecified discussion of two different modes of self-construal, "Western" and "non-Western," exemplified by American and Asian societies, respectively. They referred to the essential difference between these two construals of self as "independent" and "interdependent." Their discussion was on occasion conceptually confused and their analysis cried out for a sympathetic philosophical commentary, but what they said certainly does throw a dark shadow across the universal pretensions of the "so-called Western view of the individual as an independent, self-contained, autonomous entity who (a) comprises a unique configuration of internal attributes . . . and (b) behaves primarily as a consequence of these internal attributes."[36]

Some of this description is admittedly exaggerated, overgeneralized, and metaphorical, but the assumption that the self of personal identity is and must be individuated according to either the contingent enclosure of the epidermis or, more in the tradition, the peculiar contents of a single "mind" (whether or not this needs to be explained as a transcendental unity), is, and should be, open to question. Hegel defended the notion of the nonindividual self (or "Spirit") on more or less a priori grounds, taking his departure from Kant.[37] The self is, as the French anthropologist Mauss suggested in 1938, a "delicate category," subject to substantial variation.[38] Markus and Kitayama, referring to hundreds of other authors, provide an account based on empirical observation and experiment (for example, comparing ascriptions of attributes and character as opposed to evaluating actions only, and comparing measures of self-esteem in different cultures).[39] A sympathetic philosopher could do wonders with this material.

The very conception of personal identity is now up for grabs. Not only do we have the opportunity (indeed the obligation) to examine "*all* [or at least some of] the more interesting and specific conceptions that have guided practical life,"[40] but we have an opportunity to do it in precisely that arena which some philosophers still refuse to acknowledge, namely, under the auspices of "alternative conceptual schemes."[41]

This is not the place to pursue the rich conceptual geography of alternative construals of the self and the person in any detail, but it seems to me that the "multicultural" question of personal identity is an exceedingly promising topic for philosophy as we enter the new millennium (itself an ethnocentric construal of time, needless to say). The distinction between "independent" and "interdependent" construals of self seems to me simpleminded and only clumsily applicable to the hardly homogeneous societies mentioned by Markus and Kitayama. The United States and Canada are, despite the prevalent themes of certain sorts of movies, not at all so obviously wedded to their own romantic conception of the individual, and the idea that all non-Western, nonindividualistic societies can be understood together under the single rubric "interdependent" flies in the face of so much of the rich anthropological evidence that Markus and Kitayama cite in their discussion. Nevertheless, philosophy coupled with anthropology, conceptual analysis combined with careful and detailed attention to the diversity of what gets said and thought and displayed in behavior around the world, might produce the kind of cross-cultural dialogue and mutual understanding that, as of now, less fanatical multiculturalists just dreamily imagine.

I want to use as an example just one rather specific multicultural confrontation of considerable historical significance, at least to the people involved, and arguably a model for historically troubled, cultural confrontations elsewhere as well. It is the confrontation between the indigenous aboriginal Polynesians, the Maori of New Zealand, who arrived before the end of the first millennium, and the British settlers who arrived during the nineteenth century. The historical account is by no means pleasant, but it is considerably more edifying than many similar tales of arrival, conquest, and "manifest destiny." Indeed, the Maoris and the "Pakeha" achieved such a mutually satisfying living arrangement that for several decades New Zealand could present itself to the world—and entertain as its own self-identity—as the ideal harmonious biracial culture. This illusion was shattered by a series of events in the last two decades of the twentieth century, and what in fact has been a long-standing confrontation over land rights and reparation for past abuses continues in the courts.[42]

What is of particular philosophical interest and relevance in this confrontation is the mutual misunderstanding of two very different sets of conceptions of justice and responsibility, which rest on two very different sets of conceptions of self and personal identity. Maori justice, and the device by which the nineteenth-century settlers "legally" deprived the Maori of their territories, depended on wholly joint identity with (not "ownership" of) their land.[43] So, too, the Maori sense of responsibility was entirely collective, not individual, resulting in considerable disharmony in the essentially "Western" New Zealand criminal courts.[44] But for our purposes here, the primary context of disagreement lies in the understanding of what it is to be a person, and there the Maori and Pakeha versions and variations provide us with an accessible, concrete, and fascinating example of two philosophically profound yet clearly different conceptual schemes.

It is often said, with increasing contempt, that the Western conception of self is "individualistic," perhaps excessively so. But insofar as this refers only to the obvious—namely, the physical discernibility of individual human beings and some rudimentary awareness that "I feel this and you don't" (and vice versa)—it is hard to understand what all the fuss is about. How could people *not* be individualistic? But here Hegel and the German idealists (as well as Spinoza) give us an armchair-bound clue, the idea that what weight one gives to merely physical individuality, and how one construes the peculiar notion of what philosophers call "privacy" or "privileged access," make all the difference. The Maori, to be sure, have just as firm a grasp of their physical individuality and the privacy of their own pains as any individualistic Western *Übermensch*. But the significance of any meaningful action or experience can be properly described only in collective, or we might say "corporate," terms.[45] An offense perpetrated by any member of a group or family is rightly blamed on the whole group or family. An offense suffered by any member of a group or family is felt equally by the whole group or family, and revenge (*utu*) may rightly be taken by any member of the offended group on any member of the offending group.[46] An individual is thus wholly caught up in kinship relations. Indeed, the death of an individual is in an important sense not death at all.[47]

One's real self is the "kinship self," and the kinship self survives. The Western idea that the group exists to serve the interests of its members is considered utter and dangerous nonsense.[48]

Of course, in the two hundred years of Maori and Pakeha joint tenure of New Zealand, the two conceptions of self have become entangled, although the influence has been, as one would expect, rather one-sided (at least until recently). Maoris have become more comfortable with the idea of individual choice and, indeed, in a society where a large percentage of the population is of "mixed blood," being a Maori becomes a matter of choice and commitment.[49] But what one also sees is a progressive infiltration of Maori concepts and language into the culture at large. The ongoing disputes are a fascinating case study of how cross-cultural conflicts can proceed in the cautious, incremental steps that are necessary to bring about mutual understanding. To assume that what is involved in such understanding is simply the translation of one language into the other, or the acceptance by one or both parties of the conceptual scheme of the other, is to miss the point of the whole discussion. Personal identity is not just the question of who one is (as an embodied being with thoughts, feelings, and memories). It is a much larger question of who *we* are, where "we" refers to any number of groups of which we are members and with which we identify, including groups that insist on the story that we are all "independent individuals."

Personal Identity in Love

> How do I love thee? Let me count the ways.
> Elizabeth Barrett Browning, *Sonnets from the Portuguese*

Love seems to be an awkward topic for philosophers, despite the enthusiasm displayed for both the sexual and the nonsexual varieties by Plato and Aristotle, respectively. But in such emotions there is much to be learned, particularly on the subject of personal identity. Amelie Rorty begins her essay "The Historicity of Psychological Attitudes" thus: "There is a set of psychological attitudes—love, joy, perhaps some sorts of desire—that are individuated by the character of the subject, the character of the object, and the relation between them."[50] I am not so sure about joy, and desire is too mixed and exciting a bag for me to get into here, but love surely is just of this kind. Erotic or romantic love might seem to be the first and in any case most titillating example of love, but Rorty perhaps wisely focusses her attention on the love of friendship or friendship–love.[51] She does not assume that the love is reciprocated or symmetrical. Indeed, it is important for the concept she calls "permeability" that the sense of self it embraces includes the other but is, nevertheless, a "psychological attitude," that is, a feature of the person who loves rather than a relationship between the lover and the beloved, however one might hope or expect that the one will accompany the other. The "object" of love, however, must nevertheless be a person, not a thing, and not just one or another aspect of a person.[52] To say that love is permeable is to say that "the lover is affected, changed not only by loving but by the details of the character of the person loved."[53] Such changes in turn affect the actions of the lover and become part of a whole "narrative history" in which the all-too-often highlighted ephemera of love—the pangs, stabs, twinges, and thrills—can be identified as "feelings of love" only by virtue of their (small) place in this narrative history.[54] What concerns Rorty is the continuity or "constancy" of love, a question that does not concern me here. But insofar as the concept of "permeability" seems to me to capture an essential feature of love (both erotic and friendly), and this feature has essentially to do with self and personal identity, I want to explore that conception here, however briefly.[55]

Ever since Plato, philosophers who have been concerned to analyze the essential features of love have had what I would consider to be an obsession with the object. Against a background of misunderstandings in which emotions and their like are taken to be mere "feelings" or physiological disturbances, this point of view can be quite healthy, one might even say therapeutic. In 1963, Anthony Kenny summed up the not-so-new emphasis on the fact that emotions are necessarily directed toward objects—their "intentionality"—by distinguishing between two kinds of feelings, those with and those without objects. Love (like virtually all emotions) was decidedly of the former variety. Before Kenny, Brentano had argued a similar thesis, which was picked up by Freud, who initiated a particularly vulgar series of coinages, such as "the love object." But long before Freud, Plato had taken a similar route to understanding love when he had Socrates, in the *Symposium*, suggest (among other things) that love is a longing for beauty, or rather Beauty (the Form and not any particular instantiation). But that focussed all the attention on the brilliance of the true object of love, which, not surprisingly, by the twelfth century turned out to be God. What got neglected, I would argue, is the importance of the subject and, as Rorty rightly insists, the dynamic relation between the lover and the beloved.

But this relation is not simply, I repeat, the relationship *between* the lover and the beloved so much as it is the relation *as perceived* by the lover, the "subject." And whatever else that perception might consist of (including the beauty and charms of the beloved), it includes perceiving/conceiving of one's self, one's identity, in terms that are dictated with, through, and/or by the beloved. In an actual relationship, that is, where the two people in question are actually talking to, listening to, looking at, touching, and otherwise communicating with one another, the sense in which their identities are mutually (re)constituted is fairly obvious. He says to her, "I like your hair that way," and that becomes her preferred way of viewing herself. She says to him, "I don't know how you can stand to read Heidegger," and his interest, perhaps immediately, starts to flag. It is no deep philosophical insight, nor does it require a quasi-paranoid notion of "Being-for-Others," to recognize that we are affected, often deeply and permanently, by the opinions and judgments of others, especially if they are people we care about very much, whom we wish to please, and whom we wish to think well of us. But this is not merely a consequence or effect of love, nor is it merely a symptom of that psychological attitude. It is part of what makes love *love*, as opposed to mere admiration, adoration, sexual or other acquisitive or self-interested desire, mutual enjoyment, companionship, or shared interests (including an interest in one another).

Where the permeability or shared identity of love becomes more complicated and phenomenologically interesting, however, is where it is unreciprocated—indeed, where the beloved may not even know of the existence, much less of the *amour*, of the other. In such an instance, the dialogue exemplified above goes on, in effect, within the psyche of the lover, but the exchange is not all that different for that change of venue. Of course, unrequited love has its freedoms, not least is the ability to conjure up unrefuted flattery on the part of the beloved and a conception of oneself that is entirely to one's liking (and within one's control). Thus unrequited love becomes a spectacular aid to self-deception as well as a wonderful forum for the imagination. Stendhal defiantly stated the superiority of unrequited love on this basis, and Goethe is said to have declared, what must be one of his best lines (out of millions), "I love you, but what business is that of yours?" But whether or not reciprocated love essentially involves taking the (real or imagined) preferences and judgments of the beloved "to heart," it nevertheless involves remaking one's own sense of self with the other in mind.

The picture is further complicated when we consider the historical–cultural variations and the various ontological presuppositions of love. If love is a sharing of selves, the culturally determined nature of the self is going to be an important determinant of love and its kinds. In other words, one can experience certain sorts of love only if one has a certain sort of self and a certain conception of his or her personal identity. Friendship, as described by Aristotle in the *Nicomachean Ethics*, does not involve exactly the same concept of friendship that is available to us, although we obviously are capable of picking out the similarities and applying them to our own purposes. Eros, as described by the various speakers in the *Symposium*, is not the same as our conception of "romantic" love. Indeed, that conception took another two thousand years to develop fully, with dramatic changes in the relations between men and women, the status of women, the concept of marriage, the concept of "passion," and, most important for our purposes here, the concepts of self and personal identity.

The story told by Aristophanes in the *Symposium* is an ideal if not literal model for "shared identity," although it is obvious to what extent that model is limited, not only by its fanciful nature but also by the overly determinate concept of identity that it presupposes. We are not, as in the Aristophanes story, "two halves of an original whole." Love alone does not "complete" us. And with reference to the *Symposium* as a whole, we do not see ourselves as an integral part of a more or less harmonious polis. Quite the contrary, we (and the scope of this "we" would have to be very carefully circumscribed) see ourselves as individuals, more or less but contingently connected to others through bonds of kinship or affection.

Romantic love attempts to combine the individualistic, independent self and the interdependent, shared self in what would have to be a rather unstable, tentative fusion. This is, indeed, just the portrait of love (and much more) that we get out of some of the Romantic philosophers of the nineteenth century, and it is quite specific, I would argue, to a certain kind of culture. But what this tentatively shared self amounts to, and in what sense we are "permeable" to the other, is a subject that deserves careful but kindly attention, neither the tweezers of overly thin conceptual analysis nor the usual rubber gloves of psychology. What other conceptions of love there might be, particularly in cultures with a quite different and already interdependent conception of self, is an extremely important and by no means easy investigation. In some such societies (among the Maori, for example) there seems to be no special conception of love similar to that which we designate "romantic." And what is true of this one very special emotion may be true as well of the entire range of our emotional life. If emotions are not merely intrusions into the self, barbarians of the Freudian "id" banging on the gates of the ego, then much of what we should say of the self must also be said of our passions. The self, as Hume suggested more than two centuries ago, may be constituted not in thought but in our passions, and the nature and narrative of our passions in turn may involve nothing less than the nature and narrative of our whole way of life.[55]

Recovering Personal Identity

We do not need to strain our imagination, our intuition, or our understanding of neurology in order to find philosophical problems of self and personal identity that should occupy our best philosophical minds and begin a long and fruitful conversation. We do not need highly improbable if not impossible examples of confused personal identity when our lives are so rich with confusions, confrontations, and questions that urgently demand discussion and attempts at mutual understanding. Questions of self and personal identity now hold the key to peace in the world, and mutual understanding is no longer an exotic exercise but a quotidian necessity. If a seemingly classic (but in fact fairly recent) philosophical puzzle has become thin and "desiccated," then let's let it go and turn to matters more rich and rewarding. And when the subject is the self as person, we do not have to look very far.

8

DECEPTION, SELF, AND SELF-DECEPTION IN PHILOSOPHY

"I have done that," says my memory. "I cannot have done that,"
says my pride, and remains inexorable. Eventually, memory
yields.

Friedrich Nietzsche, *Beyond Good and Evil*

If the self and personal identity are to be characterized in terms
of a "(partially true) narrative," then what looms before us, as
evidenced by its frequent mention in the preceding chapter, is the familiar but
paradoxical matter of self-deception, our fooling ourselves, in particular, about
who we are. But because the narratives we tell about ourselves and about
others are so closely and often confusingly linked to the narratives others tell
about us and themselves, deception and self-deception cannot be easily separated, and both have much to do not only with who we are (and who we
think we are) but with one of those all-embracing philosophical concerns,
the search for the *truth*.

Why Truth?

Nietzsche once asked, "Why must we have truth at any cost anyway?"[1] It was
an odd question, coming from the philosopher who prided himself, above all,
on his brutal honesty, and it is an obscene question, in any case, for the
profession that sees itself as solely seeking the truth. Even those philosophers
who challenge the very idea of truth, not just Nietzsche and Nagarjuna but

Jacques Derrida and Richard Rorty as well, are scrupulous and unforgiving when it comes to deception, misrepresentation, and "creative misreadings," at least of their own work.[2] Philosophers in general insist on the truth even if they do not believe in "the Truth." They despise deception and they ridicule the self-deception of the "vulgar," which it is their mission to undo.

Australian philosopher Tony Coady probably speaks for most philosophers when he writes, "Dishonesty has always been perceived in our culture, and in all cultures but the most bizarre, as a central human vice. Moreover the specific form of dishonesty known as lying has generally been scorned, and the habitual liar treated with contempt. There are perfectly good reasons for this." But, he adds, "We should note that this perception is consistent with a certain hesitancy about what constitutes a lie and with the more than sneaking suspicion that there might be a number of contexts in which lying is actually justified."[3] Plato defended "the noble lie," and the ultrarespectable English ethicist Henry Sidgwick suggested that a "high-minded lie" in the direction of humility might do us all a good deal of good.[4]

Philosophers have often fantasized whole cultures composed of liars, if only as a possible counterexample to the categorical imperative or as a source of deliciously self-referential paradoxes. The neo-Marxist notion of "false consciousness" and one common use of the word "myth" have reinforced the idea that a whole society could be in self-deception. But the possibility of such pervasive self-deception already presupposes some ideal and independent criterion for the truth while at the same time giving considerable recognition to the legitimacy and the necessity of deception. In this chapter, I want to further muddy these already treacherous waters without denying what I take to be obvious: that in general—indeed, more than just in general—we have to trust what people tell us, and that lying, without some further specification, is wrong.[5] Whatever the pronouncements of the philosophers, the case against deception both in and out of philosophy is clouded, not only by questions about consequences but also by questions of culture and the intricacies of self-deception.

We could, of course, limit the use of "deception" and especially the use of "lying" to just those cases in which an untruth is knowingly and maliciously told with the intention to deceive. In other words, we could saddle this rich set of questions, as others, with an intolerable "thinnness." But this would eliminate a good deal of the subject matter. In particular, it would eliminate what I shall suggest is a very large proportion of cases in which deception and self-deception function together and support one another. It would also eliminate all of those cases in which cultural considerations clearly dictate deception in the name of politeness, or appropriateness, or for the sake of face or feelings, whatever the unvarnished and possibly rude truth may be. To define lying as wrong or to limit "lying" to cases of wrongful deception begs important questions, one of which is Nietzsche's "Why must we have truth at any cost anyway?" And as we already noted, Nietzsche is not alone. Plato and Sidgwick both defend the high-minded lie, and one of the beliefs advocated for novice monks, I am told, is the obvious falsehood "I am the worst person in the world." In Buddhism, the demand for truth and truthfulness seems to include acquiescence in the face of such astounding precepts, all in the name of their salutary effects. Nietzsche is pursuing a very different program, of course, defending desirable untruths that are inspiring and conducive to creativity, self-realization, and the "Will to Power." But the point, it seems to me, is the same. Truth is in the service of ethics, not the other way around.

"Dishonesty is a form of injustice, a vice," Coady says, echoing the harsh condemnations of Augustine and Kant. "It deforms the liar and debases the currency of language." But not all untruths are malicious, and not all deceptions are lies. The truth hurts, and sometimes it destroys. Lies can protect and inspire, and deception can serve noble ends. Self-deception sustains the illusions that sustain us, and though conducive to pathological dysfunction it is self-deception, and not the truth alone, that shall set us free.[6] Indeed, in many if not most cases of self-deception (and deception, too), the question of truth can be a source of considerable consternation, not just for the perplexing reasons long advocated by epistemological skeptics but also because of the self-fulfilling (and sometimes self-denying) features of our beliefs about our selves and those aspects of the world that matter most to us. A saintly man considers himself wicked. What is the truth of the matter? A mass murderer with strong political beliefs, a "terrorist" in the eyes of the press, considers herself a noble freedom fighter. Who is right and who is wrong? A lover trusts and defends the beloved, no matter how hideous the evidence to the contrary. Is this self-deception, or is it just—love? The truth in such matters is rarely a matter of "the facts" alone.

Truth and Lie in the Philosophical Sense

Call me a truth-seeker, and I will be satisfied.
                    Ludwig Wittgenstein, letter to his sister

When it comes to the larger questions of philosophy—the meaning of life, the nature of morality, the existence and personality of God, and the teleology of nature—it is by no means clear what it means to seek "the truth," whatever the established rhetoric. Philosophical doctrines seem to be more like professions of faith, perspectives on reality, interpretations, conceptual sculptures, an art form, rather than hypotheses or claims about truth as such. It was Hegel, following Plato, who clearly distinguished Philosophical Truth ("the Truth") from the ordinary truths of science and everyday life, defending the peculiar status of the former.[7] And yet, for over two thousand years, both East and West, the peculiar nature of philosophical truth seems only rarely to have thrown into question the status of truthfulness as a definitive moral and intellectual virtue in philosophy.

If this is a paradox, it is not a very interesting one, but it gives rise to a fascinating if neglected set of questions about the self-aggrandizing language of philosophy and the variety of deceptions and self-deceptions among philosophers. There is no doubt, for example, that philosophers have almost always deceived themselves, if not others, about the importance of philosophy, a fact made manifest only occasionally by some iconoclast such as Nietzsche or Wittgenstein or a Zen master like Dōgen. On a more parochial level, philosophers generally deceive themselves and try to deceive others about the superiority of this school or method as opposed to that one, typically ripping one thread out of a fabric and defending it alone as the whole, the truth. More personally, philosophers often deceive themselves about their supposed love and pursuit of the truth—not to mention wisdom—when ignoring the centrality of such concerns as their reputation in the agora and their status in the profession. Plato's bully in the *Republic*, Thrasymachus, has in fact remained as much of a presence in philosophy as Socrates, though he is rarely recognized as who he is.

Throughout the history of philosophy, deception has been assumed to be a vice and honesty a virtue. Of course, one might tactfully suggest that the very nature of the subject, namely, the articulation of profound truths, requires such a commitment. If philosophers didn't seek and tell the truth, what would distinguish them from poets and mythmakers, apart from their bad prose and uninspiring examples? Philosophers seek and tell the truth, the *whole* truth, and nothing but the truth. Or so they would have us believe. Diogenes strolled the city looking for an honest man, not expecting to find another but never doubting that he himself was one. He would not have fared much better, we suspect, if he had toured the philosophers' hall of fame. His immediate predecessor Socrates insisted that he was telling the truth when he claimed to know nothing, an argumentative strategy that was doubly a lie. Many philosophers and scientists, too, readily recognize that the search for truth may be something of a cover, a noble facade for working out personal problems, pleasing their parents, or pursuing personal ambition. Nietzsche suggested that every great philosophy is "the personal confession of its author and a kind of involuntary and unconscious memoir."[8] But unconscious revelation is hardly the same as telling the truth, and when philosophers such as Nietzsche go on to argue that there is, in fact, no truth, refusing to tell the truth then becomes a kind of truthfulness and insisting on the truth becomes a philosophically venal sort of lie.[9]

And yet, Socrates, we are told, died for the sake of his honesty. Epictetus, an early Stoic, defended above all the principle "not to speak falsely." In more modern times, Immanuel Kant took the prohibition against lying as his paradigm of a "categorical imperative," the unconditioned moral law.[10] There could be no exceptions, not even to save the life of a friend. Even Nietzsche took honesty to be one of his four "cardinal" virtues, and the "existentialist" Jean-Paul Sartre insisted that deception is a vice, perhaps indeed the ultimate vice.[11] Sartre argued adamantly on behalf of the "transparency" of consciousness, which enabled him to argue (against Freud) that all deception is in some sense willful and therefore blameworthy. And today one reads American ethicists, such as Edmund Pincoffs, who insists that dishonesty is so grievous a vice that its merits cannot even be intelligibly deliberated.[12] In this, unlike many other matters, philosophy and common sense seem to be in agreement. And whether philosophy merely follows and reports on the zeitgeist or actually has some hand in directing it, it would be safe to say that the philosophical championing of honesty is an accurate reflection of popular morality. Lying, for philosophers and laymen alike, is wrong.[13]

But what does it mean to insist that lying is wrong? And how wrong is it, really? The blanket pronouncements of the philosophers typically conceal more than they reveal, and the best questions are left under the covers. Is a lie told to embellish an otherwise tedious narrative just as wrong as a lie told in order to cover up a misdeed and avoid punishment? Is a lie told in desperation any less wrong than a calculated, merely convenient lie? Is a lie told out of self-deception more or less wrong than a clearheaded, tactical lie? (Is the former even a lie?) Are all lies wrong—is lying *as such* wrong?—or do some lies serve an important function not only in protecting people from harm (especially emotional harm) but also in developing and protecting one's own sense of individuality and privacy? One might better think of lying as diplomatic, as fortification, as essential protection for a necessarily less than candid self. Or one could just think of honesty as merely one among many of the virtues, not a fundamental virtue at all.

It is worth noting that Aristotle, in his catalog of moral virtues, lumped "truthfulness" together with "friendliness" and "wit," important traits to choose in a friend or colleague, to be sure, but hardly the cornerstone without which the entire edifice of morality would fall down. Moreover, what Aristotle meant by "truthfulness" primarily concerned the telling of one's accomplishments, "neither more nor less"—in contemporary terms, handing in an honest résumé.[14] He did not seem at all concerned about social lies, "white lies," or, for that matter, even political lies except insofar as these contributed to injustice or corruption.[15] Critics have often challenged Kant's analysis of honesty as a "perfect duty," appealing to our natural inclination to insist that it is far more important to save the life of a friend than it is to tell the truth to the Nazis who are after him. But if there is even one such case in which it is right to lie and honesty can be overidden, then the "perfect" status of the duty not to lie is compromised, and the question is opened to negotiation.

It is in the light of such dogmatic (a priori) condemnation, too, that we can understand the perennial controversy surrounding the seemingly innocent "white lie," the lie that saves instead of causing harm. And, to say the obvious (though it is often neglected or disdained by philosophers), lies can also entertain, as theater and as fiction, and not only on the stage or on the page. Indeed, lies can also be useful and fascinating in philosophy. Not only do they provide promising heuristic goads to further thinking, they provide some of the essential subject matter as well. How many dozens of professors are now employed because some Cretan, years ago, supposedly declared that "all Cretans are liars" and thus generated the most basic paradox in logic and philosophy. (If he told the truth, then he was lying, but if he was lying, then . . .). Is there anything wrong with a lie when it causes no harm? And is it always true that we should tell the truth "even when it hurts"?

Behind the blanket prohibition on lying we can discern the outlines of a familiar philosophical metaphor, the truth as light, as bright, plain, and simple, shining as the Holy Grail of Rationality, while dishonesty, on the other hand, is dark and devious, the ill-paved path through irrationality and confusion. In revealing the truth, we think of consciousness as transparent through and through; in deception we detect an opacity, an obstacle, a wall within consciousness. The honest man and the true philosopher know all and tell all (except in Socrates' case, since he insists that he does not know anything). Nevertheless, Socrates' student Plato offers to lead us out of the shadows and into the light, even at great peril. The philosopher illuminates that which the liar and the layman leave in the dark, including his or her own inner soul.[16] Truth and light are good; deception and darkness are bad or evil, leading not only to ignorance and harm but also to the degradation of rationality, the abuse of language, and the corruption of the soul. But philosophy, one begins to suspect, has overrated these metaphors of clarity and transparency. The obvious truth is that our simplest social relationships could not exist without the opaque medium of the lie.

In his novel *The Idiot*, Fyodor Dostoyevsky gave us a portrait of a man who had all of the virtues, including perfect honesty.[17] He was, of course, an utter disaster to everyone he encountered. More recently, Albert Camus presented us (in *The Stranger*) with an odd "antihero," "a hero for the truth" who was incapable of lying.[18] It is not surprising that he comes off as something of a monster, inhuman, "with virtually no human qualities at all" (as the prosecutor points out at his trial for murder). On a more mundane and "real life" philosophical level, one cannot imagine getting through an average budget meeting or a cocktail party speaking nothing but the truth, the whole truth, and nothing but the truth. If one wished to be perverse, he or she might well hypothesize that deception, not truth, is the cement of civilization, a cement that does not so much hold us together as it safely separates us and our thoughts. We cannot imagine social intercourse without opacity.

Steve Braude, a philosopher who works extensively in parapsychology, illustrates the utter importance of deception with a simple experiment. He asks his audience if anyone would take a pill (which he has supposedly invented) that will allow him or her to read the minds of everyone within a hundred-yard radius. Not surprisingly, no one accepts the offer. We can all imagine the restless thoughts flickering through a friend's mind as we describe our latest trauma or the adventure of the day, the distracted and hardly flattering thoughts of our students as we reach the climax of the lecture two minutes before the bell rings, the casual and not at all romantic thoughts of a lover in a moment of intimacy. "What are you thinking?" is an extremely dangerous and foolish question, inviting if not usually requiring the tactical but flatly deceptive answer, "Oh, nothing."

The threatening nature of the truth has long been whitewashed by philosophers, often under a pseudo-secularized version of the religious banner "The truth shall set you free."[19] But, against the philosophers, we all know that sometimes the truth hurts and the harm is not redeemed, that the truth is sometimes if not often unnecessary, that the truth complicates social arrangements, undermines collective myths, destroys relationships, incites violence and vengeance. Deception is sometimes not a vice but a social virtue, and systematic deception is an essential part of the order of the (social) world. In many societies, social harmony is valued far more than truthfulness as such, and to tell the other person what he or she wants to hear rather than what one might actually feel or believe is not only permitted but expected. In such circumstances, do we still want to speak of "deception" at all? And could we not begin to see our own enlightened emphasis on "seeking the truth at all costs" (as Ernst Jones wrote admiringly of Sigmund Freud) as one more ethnocentric peculiarity, another curious product of our strong sense of individual autonomy and a particularly unsociable conception of "the truth"?

Deception, Self-Deception, and the Self

The difficulty making such distinctions [between real and only apparent truthfulness] is almost as great for liars as for their dupes, because self-deception enters into such estimates to such an extraordinary degree. Hypocrites half believe their own stories, and sentimentality makes fraud take on the most innocuous tints.

Sissela Bok, *Lying*

It takes two to lie, one to tell and one to listen.

Homer Simpson

The roles of deception and self-deception in philosophy are not unrelated to the ways that deception and self-deception have been discussed by philosophers. It is often assumed, for example, that deception is a peculiarly linguistic activity having to do with the assertion of false propositions, and that self-deception is therefore a paradoxical if not impossible lie to oneself.[20] But I can effectively deceive someone by driving or walking off in the wrong direction, without saying a word, and there is good evidence that many animals systematically practice deception.[21] And it is wrong to suppose that self-deception is simply the application of deception to oneself, not because that view generates paradoxes but because it represents a serious misunderstanding of the phenomenon. If one explores the strange realm of self-directed psychological attitudes (and various "self-" prefaced ascriptions of psychological attitudes), what immediately becomes evident is that rarely are self-ascription and ascription to others just different applications of the same psychological description. (Consider, just as a small sample, self-love, self-pity, self-respect, and self-loathing.) Indeed, if one were to think of self-deception as deception *about* the self as well as deception directed *to* the self, there would be less temptation to assimilate the first-person cases to the third person.[22]

What this also means is that the nature of the self is again part of our inquiry, along with the various conventions and conceptions concerning deception. Insofar as the self is a social being and not merely a locus of self-reference, the character of both the self and self-deception depends on the character of the society or culture in question. What we are depends only in part on what we think of ourselves, and what we think of ourselves is rarely free of the opinions of others and of the ethical values of our society. We want to think well of ourselves, and so the need to convince, as well as the strong temptation to deceive others about ourselves and also to fool ourselves, is always with us. The various social conventions that dictate the rules about lying and deception are the same conventions that dictate the acceptable nature of one's self. What gets praised as good character and what gets condemned as deception are by no means the same in different contexts and cultures. In the pages that follow, part of my concern will be some of those connections between contexts, cultures, deception, and the self.

The connection between deception and self-deception is much more common and convoluted than philosophers, focussing on transparency, tend to suppose. It is one thing to self-consciously and intentionally tell what one knows to be a falsehood, but it is something quite different to tell what one sincerely believes but is false especially if this is not a case of mere misinformation. Thus the phenomenon of self-deception further muddies the supposedly transparent waters of truth-telling and knowledge. In what sense does one know otherwise? And what if one doesn't seem to know but nevertheless *ought* to know the truth, for example, because the ample evidence is right before one's eyes? The presence of that "ought" suggests that both self-deception and deception have a normative as well as a factual basis. Furthermore, when we are taught that the truth is of primary importance, more important than social harmony, isn't this is itself a normative judgment, cultivated in some societies and not in others. What of those many societies (and is ours so obviously excepted?) in which saying what one is supposed to say is deemed more important than saying what one believes to be the truth? An honest answer to "How are you?" or "How do I look?" is usually inappropriate (even assuming that that is what is actually being asked). "Honest criticism" is as often as not a violation of social propriety. Conversation, as J. L. Austin pointed out a half century ago, is not for the most part concerned with asserting truths.

In so many discussions of deception and, especially, self-deception, it is simply assumed that in lying, one is clear about the truth and then purposefully and directly misleads the other about its nature. Lying, accordingly, is fully intentional and malicious, at least insofar as it willfully deprives another of something extremely important, the truth. But this presupposes a degree of autonomy, rationality, and transparency that just doesn't hold up to scrutiny. There are, of course, cold-blooded, self-interested lies, knowingly false answers to such direct questions as "Where were you last night?" and "Who ate all the cookies?" But one might consider the claim that such lies are the special case rather than the rule, like cold-blooded murder-for-profit in the bloody complex of accidental, negligent, desperate, and passionate homicides. Our fascination with lying and deception will not be satisfied by the straightforward cases. What we are after is a drama of truth and falsehood in the complex social and emotional webs we weave, compared to which what is often singled out as "the lie" tends to become of little philosophical interest just because its status is so obvious.[23]

Self-deception, like deception, is a dynamic social phenomenon, not just an internal drama or a pathological condition. The "social" nature of the phenomenon, however, is often less than obvious, but part of the reason for this is that philosophers tend to think of self-deception as an odd and even paradoxical version of deception, as a "lie to oneself" not involving other people in any way at all. Of course, the lie may well be "about" other people— as in a lover's self-deceptive vision of his or her beloved, and other people may be affected by one's self-deception, as they themselves are deceived in turn. But a conception of self-deception that begins with the idea that the dynamics of self-deception are individually self-contained will lose the essential thread, which is not merely terminological, between deception and self-deception, namely, their shared role in our social and personal relationships. So, too, it is important to get away from the static "knowing and not knowing" conception that characterizes many philosophical studies of self-deception.[24] As an integral part of an ongoing relationship, both deception and self-deception are necessarily dynamic, unstable (or, perhaps, "metastable"[25]), and a continuous effort of enormous complexity.[26]

Deception and self-deception, I want to argue, are conceptually distinct but thoroughly entangled phenomena. Superficially, one essentially involves other people, the other does not. But to treat them as different versions of the same phenomenon in two very different settings or to treat them wholly differently (as lying and lying to oneself, respectively) is to miss the dynamic that motivates both (and to miss the very important differences between them). To fool ourselves, we must either fool or exclude others; and to successfully fool others, we best fool ourselves. Philosophical discussions of lying too often take as the paradigm example the straightforwardly cynical, self-interested lie and ignore the more common species of lying that includes some degree of self-deception as well. Transparency to ourselves can be just as intolerable as transparency to others, and for the same reason. The self, with its flaws and failings, is too much in evidence.

The recognition of one's own motives and the significance of one's own thoughts can be devastating to one's self-image and sense of self. Part of the self is self-presentation and self-disclosure, but an aspect of equal importance is the need to disguise, to hide, not to disclose, those facets of the self that are less than flattering, humiliating, or simply irrelevant to the social context or interpersonal project at hand. To a certain extent, this is merely a matter of attention, of editing, of selective self-presentation, but it is not just (or even for the most part) in our own hands. The self is essentially a social construct, and our sense of ourselves depends on other people, or what Jean-Paul Sartre called (with more than a touch of paranoia) "our Being-for-Others."[27] One can hide or refuse to disclose oneself to oneself in many ways, notably by ignoring or distracting oneself, but none of these ploys has a ghost of a chance if others cannot be distracted or fooled—or at least put off—as well. Deception and self-deception are intimately intertwined. We fool ourselves in order to fool others, and we fool others in order to fool ourselves. And to make it more complicated (as it should be), we do not always know which is which, who is self and who is other.

Deception between persons is rarely so cynical that it does not involve more than a trace of sincerity and belief, in most cases the belief that even if this particular "fact" is false, the truth that the lie is protecting is far more significant than the act of lying. Thus we have the lover who lies to protect his love, or the scientist who fudges her results to "prove" a hypothesis she just "knows" to be true. Sissela Bok rightly suggests that there is a thin line at best separating the lie for the sake of the truth and the lie that marks one a liar. Lying for the sake of the truth is a paradox that already requires a considerable amount of self-deception. Deception between persons is rarely if ever unmotivated, and even a mischievous lie "for its own sake" (the familiar "shaving" of one's age, for example) is typically a cover-up for other lies, insecurities, and distrust. Thus Samuel Johnson wrote, of self-deceptive men who would be virtuous, "Having none to recall their attention to their lives, they rate themselves by the goodness of their opinions, and forget how much more easily men may shew their virtue in their talk than in their actions."

As we start to understand deception and self-deception as an essential aspect of self-consciousness and not as willful violations of principle or antisocial acts, we begin to lose that sense of blanket condemnation of "lying as wrong," and to understand deception and self-deception as part of the matrix of human relations, neither good nor evil as such but open to sympathy and understanding rather than blame. Amelie Rorty recites the touching case of a talented young doctor who refuses to recognize in herself all of the evident symptoms of cancer. Her behavior makes it obvious that, in some sense, she does know of her condition, but the explicit recognition would be devastating. And so she pretends, to herself and others, convincing no one but herself, perhaps, but maintaining the desperate deception without which she could not keep up her practice. Is there anyone at all who would call such behavior blameworthy?[28]

People tell lies not only to avoid punishment or to impress others but also because they need to define and protect themselves (their selves) and cope with difficult social situations. Within the limited realm of self-knowledge, in particular, deception is almost always a matter of coping rather than a celebration of falsehood as such. Indeed, what it means to be false to oneself is a rather complex ethical problem; both ourselves and our knowledge of ourselves are not only incomplete but also undergoing continuous revision, often along the lines of ideals and ambitions that are themselves ill-conceived, inappropriate, or merely borrowed. It is within this continuing coauthorship of self, self-esteem, and self-knowledge that both deception and self-deception must be appreciated, and even the most cynical interpersonal intrigues are first of all shared productions of the self, involving a mix of conspiracy and vulnerability. Consider, for example, the web of affections and deceptions in Choderlos de Laclos's *Liaisons dangereuses*, which deceptively presents itself to us as an aristocratic game but soon reveals itself as a life-or-death theater of mutual self-deception.[29] And as in *Liaisons dangereuses* (whose author felt it necessary to produce a lengthy preface morally denouncing and distancing himself from the psychology he so insightfully represented), what is too often presented as a morality tale becomes a study in interpersonal psychology and the mutual, surreptitious, social construction of the self. It is not as if ethics is (or should be) absent from such a study, but our evaluations can no longer be of the Manichaean "truth is good, deception is evil" variety.

In self-deception, telling the truth can easily become a vice parading as a virtue. In the name of integrity, one can use truth as a weapon and honesty as a strategy. Children and lovers, as authors on the subject often point out, frequently tell the truth precisely in order to hurt and to humiliate. Such truth-telling can be manipulative, even vicious. In Camus's last novel, *The Fall*, an extremely devious character named Clamence confesses to an acquaintance (the reader, of course) the truth about his life, including first and foremost the many lies he had always been telling himself.[30] What becomes obvious, however, is that he is still deceiving himself by way of seducing the other, and even his truths are only a ploy. What Clamence is after, we learn in the last pages, is neither truth nor total disclosure but a subtle vengeance, and his confession is a subversive expression of a deeply felt resentment.

But who is the victim, and who is the villain, in such tales of deviousness? Why do we think that victims and villains must be part of the structure of deception? As often as not, deception and self-deception combine to form the most sincere belief among coconspirators, not victim and villain. Virtually every faith and religion is a large-scale example of such belief, but so, too, is almost everyone's self-image and every society's sense of itself, including the scientific and philosophical communities as well as every ethnic group or culture. Nietzsche, and later Jung, wrote extensively on our need for myths and warned against an age that would try to do without them. But what is a myth if not an elaborate, self-defining, collective self-deception? And if all such deceptions are wrong, then would there be any truth that is ultimately worth defending?

The Tangled Web: Duplicity as a Holistic Phenomenon

O, what a tangled web we weave
When first we practice to deceive.

Sir Walter Scott, Lochinvar

If deception and self-deception are to be understood first of all as interrelated dynamic interpersonal and social phenomena, then it is a mistake to try to understand them in terms of one or another artificially isolated aspect of the relationship. For example, in most modern discussions of lying, much of the focus has been on the alleged victim, the person who is misled or betrayed by the lie. The evaluation thus tends to trace out the obvious and not so obvious effects of even the "whitest" lie, its ability to undermine trust and render the victim helpless when the truth might well have allowed some significant action. Sissela Bok, for example, pursues such a quest in wonderful detail, tracing the consequences of professional lies, political lies, loving lies, paternalistic lies, therapeutic lies, experimental lies, and so on.[31] Bok discusses at length the complications of authoritarian deception and the manufacture of excuses, including the notorious slippery slope from the very plausible claim that "the whole truth" is impossible to tell down to the insidious thesis that the truth is not necessary.

That is the challenge and the fun of "thick" philosophical investigations of lying; first we recognize the obvious immediate consequences: hurt feelings, a tragically un- or ill-informed patient (client, friend, public). Then the devastating penalties for an unsuccessful cover-up become evident. Finally, there are the more subtle implications of spreading distrust, increased cynicism and consequent withdrawal, a corruption of language and public discourse. What gets left out of many of those discussions of deception, however, is the need to focus on the psychology of the liar and not just the consequences facing the liar. For if deception and self-deception are so intimately involved, then the assumption that the perpetrator of the lie is not also its victim becomes less plausible. The lie is a matter of mutual engagement and not just a malevolent act perpetrated by one person upon another.

Alternatively, when philosophers have fixed their gaze on the nature of the lie instead of its consequences, they have tended to deny even further the interpersonal and social nature of deception. Kant in particular was adamant about the logical inconsistency of the "maxim" of any and every lie, established by the fact that one could not universalize the allowability of lying without undermining the very possibility of language (assuming, that is, that the primary purpose of language centers on such activities as describing true facts and making promises). Of course, because lying is (by definition) the *intentional* telling of a falsehood, some attention must be focussed on the liar who has and exercises that intention. But Kant quite explicitly dismisses and ignores the motives and the character who stand behind the lie, preferring to emphasize the immorality of lying rather than to understand the psychological and social dynamics. But even as ethics, it is certainly not unimportant what motivates lying and what kind of characters we are dealing with when we point our fingers at liars.

Here is where "virtue ethics" gains its hold. It is a conscientiously thick examination not only of this lie or falsehood but also of the context in which it is told, the aims and intentions behind its telling, and, most important, the personality and character of the prevaricator. But to overemphasize the character of the liar is just as misleading as an isolated emphasis on the lie or its consequences. Deception is, to employ that overused and much abused word again, a *holistic* phenomenon. One cannot break it up into parts and expect to understand its vital organic unity. One cannot try to understand or evaluate the lie, the liar, the victim, and the consequences, and then put these together in some "multidimensional" analysis that adds up to an adequate understanding.

One of the most distinctive and most neglected features of lying is that it is surprisingly hard to do. As anyone who has tried to protect even a small, casual lie can tell you, the amount of thought and care required to keep in mind all of the logical implications and possible contradictions ("If I was at Sam's place, then I couldn't have seen Thelma at the Casino, but if I didn't see Thelma, how could I have known about the party at Shelby's house?"). It is always easiest, the old adage tells us (with considerable truth), to tell the truth. But next easiest is to believe your own lie, to become so submerged in its network of details and implications that the continuation of the lie—as Aristotle argued for honesty—becomes second nature, without further thought or deliberation. In either case, however, neither ease nor difficulty is a dependable mark of morality, and one might (like a novelist or any other storyteller) delight in the intrigue and self-conscious tension that artful lying requires. Part of the pathology of compulsive liars may well be the high-adrenaline challenge of holding a number of lies together as a high-risk acrobat might juggle a number of brightly lit torches or razor-sharp knives—along with the sometimes psychotic need to cover up not just something but (by logical implication) almost everything.

Here, of course, there may be considerable temptation to scissor off the liar from any particular lie or any particular audience, but a moment's reflection makes it clear that this, too, is a distinctively and often compulsively public performance, part of a possibly rich and probably very deep pattern of self-deception as well as a way of relating to other people, despite the fact that the nature of the relationship may be quite puzzling or offensive to them. So, too, with more innocent and straightforwardly strategic lies. Lying involves a complex logic that reaches across and cuts through our various social relationships, and sometimes with great difficulty weaves a portrait of the self and its relations. And even in self-deception, it is the inconsistencies in our stories discovered or discoverable by other people that motivate our continued efforts at duplicity. After all, if self-deception were a matter of mere internal consistency, would anyone but a logician feel compelled to avoid inconsistency at all costs? Would "cognitive dissonance" ever become an issue, much less a motivational force, if it did not also become subject to the scrutiny of others?[32]

No matter what the challenge or the logical complexity of the lie or the effects of the lie on the liar and his or her social entanglements, the primary concern always seems to be the benign or harmful effects of the lie on the listener. But here again there are a social matrix and a set of interpersonal presumptions that generally go unnoticed. What renders most lies odious is that they occur in a context in which one expects the truth, most obviously, in response to a direct inquiry. But even there the odiousness of the lie depends on the context and the nature of the question ("What are you think-ing?"), and there are circumstances in which only a Kantian or a paranoid would insist that the truth is essential and lying is immoral. Imagine yourself on a intercity bus or a short plane ride next to a somewhat tedious fellow passenger who insists on knowing "What do you do?" One can readily imagine offering up the most truthful but boring answer as an alternative to an utterly offensive reply, or, alternatively, one can with slightly more effort imagine constructing a fascinating but wholly false account of one's life as a K.G.B. double agent or a Texas Ranger. By rebuffing the query, one gets a chance to read or sleep, but by lying imaginatively, there seems to be no harm done but rather a welcome entertainment for both of you during an otherwise tedious voyage. There is, of course, the odd chance that one's fellow passenger may (contrary to all expectations) show up again, wreaking the sort of havoc that only old movies and *Seinfeld* can fully appreciate; and it is true, no doubt, that every lie opens one up to possible complications of this sort. But this is hardly a moral objection to lying, and in the absence of harm, such elaborate lies seem unobjectionable. (So, too, one could argue, for the "big lies" that hold most cultures and religions together—myths of origin, shared fantasies of moral right and manifest destiny, illusions of favored status in the eyes of the divine, delusions of grandeur.[33] But here, of course, the question of harm emerges on a global and often tragic scale.) In any case, the attention should be on the social context and the relationship—including global relationships—and not exclusively on the lie or the consequences of the lie.

It is a mistake to think about and condemn deception and self-deception sui generis. Not only are there legitimate lies in literature, heuristics in sci-ence, myth in religion and philosophy, but these are not just isolated fictional frames with at most metaphorical connections to considerations of self or extremely tenuous "expressions" of ourselves and our relations with other people. Quite the contrary, these are the "myths and metaphors we live by," according to many authors from the ancients to our contemporaries.[34] Once we give up the philosophical tendency to generalize about deception and self-deception in the abstract and focus instead on the whole phenomenon of lying—the intentions and motives behind it, the context as well as the con-sequences and the interpersonal relationship between the participants—it becomes increasingly obvious that most lies are not merely lies but also self-deception, and are part of a larger matrix of beliefs and emotions that define not only this relationship but also a community or a culture.

The lies of love (or pretended love) depend for their credibility on a re-markable institution that defines and gives structure as well as elaborate dis-course to a seemingly "primitive" emotion.[35] Consider how much cultural apparatus goes into a simple but vicious lie "I love you" (when one does not). And how often is the felt truth uttered with the knowledge (or in many cases a host of doubts) that it may in fact be a lie? Self-deception, like deception, is motivated not by self-interest, cold and calculating, but by our engagement in an emotionally charged world in which things matter to us, in which the truth is by no means clear, and wishful thinking and the expectations of others matter more to us than that abstract metaconception known to us as "the Truth."

Deception and self-deception are part and parcel of our engagements in the world, including, not least, the development and maintenance of our image and sense of ourselves. Deception is first of all a way of relating, a not entirely accurate presentation of self to others and to oneself. There is no single point where presentation becomes deception, where pretense becomes sincerity, where play becomes the real thing. Self-presentation is always deception, but whether or not it counts as deception, or whether or not it is blameworthy, depends on the context, the performance, the expectations.[36] Some deception is harmful and even immoral, but some of it is neither. Indeed, an extremist might even argue that there is no such phenomenon as lying as such, only various ways in which we relate to one another as insecure social creatures surrounded and infiltrated by an inevitably equivocal language. We are, perhaps, not only capable of lying but virtually incapable of not doing so.[37] Deception and self-deception, according to such a kinky view, may not be perversions so much as they are the very stuff of human intercourse.

The Duplicitous Self and the Self of Self-Deception

Hypocrisy is the homage that vice pays to virtue.

La Rochefoucauld

It has often been pointed out, in current Continental philosophy, with various degrees of obfuscation that the self is double. This can be put in a number of ways, beginning with the obvious: that we see ourselves "from the inside" but can also be seen (and sometimes see ourselves) "from the outside," from a second- or third-person (misleadingly called "objective") point of view. But the complex relations between these two (or three) viewpoints gives rise to some deep suspicions and the seemingly outrageous charge that the self is intrinsically duplicitous, not only double but, as we say, "two-faced." In *The Fall*, Camus has his character Clamence confess this ambiguity, which he goes on to demonstrate in his progressive seduction of his almost mute interlocutor and the reader. The face presented to the world is at odds with the face that smiles knowingly inward. But, then again, perhaps the face that smiles inward is itself an illusion, only a reflection of the looks it absorbs from others.[38]

With this in mind, let me distinguish between two different models of self-deception, which in turn depend on two quite different models of the self. In dull analytic jargon, the two have been referred to as the internalist and the externalist models of self-deception, and they are based, respectively, on similarly internalist and externalist accounts of the self. An internalist views self-deception as a relation between a person and a set of beliefs (broadly construed, which may or may not involve the contradictory "believing p and not-p" paradox that preoccupies so much of the analytic literature). Accordingly, internalist models of self-deception tend to be concerned with the internal structure or architecture of the self. Thus Freud divides the self into consciousness and the unconscious, a troubled house with an inaccessible basement, and later into "agencies." Amelie Rorty ingeniously suggests that the self is something like a medieval city, a virtual labyrinth of pathways and neighborhoods functioning independently and without knowledge of the others.[39] Less architectural theorists look for ways of gerrymandering belief or bypassing belief altogether, by way of "avowals" or other acknowledgments.[40] The problem for the internalist, perhaps but not necessarily made more intractable by paradox, is to understand how one can in some sense "know and not seem to know." Self-deception, in other words, is first of all an epistemological problem.

The externalist, on the other hand, sees self-deception as a social phenomenon. It has to do less with a person and his or her beliefs than it has to do with a person and his or her roles and relationships. Self-deception is a consequence of wanting to be thought of and treated in certain ways, and not others, by other people. One's self-conceptions are the product and not the source of the opinions of others, and self-deception is thus an attempt to manipulate those opinions and not just one's own. I think the idea that we fool ourselves in order to fool others more often than not gets it backward, and the idea that in self-deception we first of all lie to ourselves is just plain wrong. Self-deception begins and continues by playing a part, by acting the good husband, the responsible citizen, the competent, healthy professional. This may or may not be accompanied by self-avowal. It may or may not be accompanied by rationalization or denial. Self-deception is therefore first of all a performance, if sometimes a performance enjoyed only by oneself. Thus Sartre argues that Being-for-Others is an essential ingredient of the self, even when others are not around.[41]

It is also within the perspective of Being-for-Others that we can understand why Sartre comes down so hard on "sincerity," which is only a "display" of the truth, a show, another self-presentation, a mode of deception, and not genuine self-reflection.[42] Here, too, we can understand why Roger Ames claims that the Chinese have no conception of self-deception.[43] He is appealing to the clearly externalist model of the Chinese self, and with it an externalist account of self-deception. But, then, why should we assume that the internalist model so accurately portrays the European self, or that the externalist view is all that foreign to us? On the externalist model, self-deception is contextual, and the context is paradigmatically a social context. But isn't this ultimately true of our Western conception of self and self-deception? At one end of this view, there is no self without others.[44] Or, as St. Exupery writes, "Man is but a network of relationships, and these alone matter to him."[45] According to this externalist model, one might say, half tongue in cheek, that the "inner self" is social.

I want to endorse a version of this view. What does it mean, however, to say that the self is social? I mentioned earlier that it is one thing to claim that the self is socially construed, another to insist that it is socially constructed, and still another to maintain that it is socially constructed as a social self, three claims often conflated. To say that the self is socially contrued is by far the weakest of the three, the one understandably adopted by most social scientists, and it leaves entirely open to what extent the nature of the self is determined, for example, by biological and noncognitive social forces and attitudes. To have a construal of the self is to adopt a perspective, to look at it in a certain way, but this has minimal ontological commitments. It might be, for example, that as a teacher I construe the selves of my students as "student selves," that is, defined in terms of their behavior, preparation for, and performance in class. I do not pretend that they do not have other, most likely more pressing conceptions of self themselves, as I find out when I meet them in the local pub. To claim that different cultures construe the self in different ways is to make a minimal claim, one that is just as true of various subcultures in our own culture. Self-deception, so understood, would consist in part of adopting an inappropriate construal of self in certain contexts.

To say that the self is socially constructed, by contrast, is to make a much more radical claim. It is to insist that there is no self apart from its construction in particular social contexts (although one might distinguish here between a very general claim that one will have no concept of self at all unless he or she grows up in some society or other, and the more particularist claim that a person learns to cultivate a particular self—a Texan or a Chuang Chou or Maori self, for example—only by growing up in Texas or Chuang Chou or Aotearoa [New Zealand][46]). To insist that the self is constructed, however, is not yet to claim that the construction is of any particular typology, in particular, it does not mean that the self so constructed is a social self. The American "rugged individualist" is a socially constructed self, as are the selves of the infamously antisocial Ik.[47]

To say that the self is socially constructed *as* a social self is to make a very particular kind of claim, which must be distinguished from the other two. The Chinese self is socially constructed as a social self, an interdependent self;

but, again, we need to make at least one further problematic distinction. The social construction of self proceeds in part by way of a language, a language that includes a certain vocabulary of selfhood. In this language we learn to talk about ourselves in certain ways. A self-consciously individualist culture will naturally emphasize the importance of such notions as individuality, autonomy, and independence. A self-consciously communitarian culture will naturally emphasize the importance of such notions as community, loyalty, duty, and kinship. But how we *talk* about ourselves is only a partial indication of how we *think* about ourselves and how we actually behave. The social construction of self also proceeds without language, without self-description, by way of ten thousand nonverbal cues and examples: everything from a mother's refusal to leave her infant alone even for a minute and the fact that people tend not to look each other in the eyes, to the waging of war and the celebration of religious rituals. It is perfectly possible, therefore, for a culture to cultivate a way of talking about themselves and the self that is somewhat at odds with the ways in which they actually conceive of themselves and their relationships to each another. Indeed, in times of social tension or dislocation, or in order to distinguish oneself from an alien culture, such divergence of self-conception from practice may be extremely common.[48]

The resultant complexity of the self—as opposed, say, to the thin Cartesian model of the self—obviously invites self-deception, deception *about* the self. If there is no self other than that which is construed, socially constructed, and constructed as social, it might be thought dubious in what sense there is a self to be deceived about. There are, of course, any number of logical and deconstructionist tricks to inflate these generalized schemes into seemingly intractable paradoxes, but that is not where the interest in self and deception lies. It is rather in the increasingly rich web of personal and mutual conceptions of self that we now all must navigate in our dealings with the rest of the world. It is a bewildering but absolutely essential learning experience, but, from the available evidence, we are not doing terribly well. Ever more fanatic individualism and retreat seem to be spreading as a global response, even in societies that once were models of social harmony, in philosophy as well as in fact. The current fantasies with extraterrestrial visits and invasions, I would suggest, is not an extension of our multicultural challenge but a somewhat pathological distraction from that challenge. (How often those extraterrestrials are either "just like us" or so viciously hostile that no interaction is possible.[49])

Deception, I have argued, is one of the many ways in which we navigate our way in the social world. Self-deception is also one of those ways—one might say that it is a way that we attend to our navigating—and in an increasingly complex world, it is by no means clear that deception and self-deception—understood as mechanisms for getting along in the world—are always vices. That, too, is one of the joys of philosophy. It comes from realizing that our ideas about ourselves and even about truth are not truths, but experiments whose outcome is by no means obvious. It is in terms of these ongoing experiments that we find ourselves living a philosophical and a fascinatingly reflective life, defined not by paradoxes but by our continuing interactions with others and with ourselves.

AFTERTHOUGHT

Has "Analytic Philosophy" Ruined Philosophy?

Philosophy reduced to 'theory of knowledge,' in fact no more
than a timid epochism and doctrine of abstinence—a philosophy
that never gets beyond the threshold and takes pains to deny
itself the right to enter—that is philosophy in its last throes.
Friedrich Nietzsche, *Beyond Good and Evil*

I hear it now, all the time. Not as a question but as a verdict: "Analytic philosophy has ruined philosophy." I hear it from my friends
in anthropology, in literature departments, in cultural and women's studies
programs. I hear it from people in business who, thinking back to their college
liberal arts degrees, retain some dim concern for the state of the discipline.
And, of course, I hear it from nonanalytic philosopher friends, who have an
ax of their own to grind. The fact that I am known for my work in "Continental" philosophy supposedly makes me a sympathetic ear. But I am deeply
troubled by this widespread misunderstanding of what is happening in philosophy as well as by what is happening in philosophy. Still, as Mark Twain
said on listening to Wagner, "It's not as bad as it sounds."

Much too much is made today of the contrast and supposed conflict between what is called "analytic" philosophy, on the one hand, and "Continental" philosophy, on the other. The contrast is a false one. "Analysis" refers to
a *method*, a method that, superficially at least, concentrates on the nature of
language. "Continental" refers to a *place*, namely, continental Europe. Apart
from the fact that "the Continent" so referred to often includes only Germany
and France, and the often ignored fact that "analytic philosophy" includes a

fair number of contrasting and competing methodologies, it should be clear to even a casual reader that the basic contrast is mistaken or misleading.[1] While there are many twisted and interwoven schools, methods, and styles of philosophy, these are rarely so easily distinguished by such a narrow body of water as the English Channel.

"Analytic philosophy" is often defined in terms of its interest in logic and language, but that interest emerged first in Germany (with Frege in particular) and was fully shared by the progenitor of the twentieth century's "Continental" movements, Edmund Husserl. The most influential philosopher of the century, Ludwig Wittgenstein, who was twice the definitive philosopher of the "analytic" tradition, came to England from Austria, never leaving his "Continental" roots behind him. He was particularly interested in the limits of language, but so are postmodernists, the nemeses of most analytic philosophers. There are analytic philosophers who, like their peers on the Continent, talk and write about sex, gender, death, and the meaning of life. Analytic philosophy is not necessarily as "thin" as it sometimes seems. Despite the more narrow pronouncements of some of its more illustrious practitioners, it need not be just logic, devoid of concern for content. It need not be only concerned with arguments, regardless of substance. It is not "scientific," as Hans Reichenbach crowed at the peak of the movement fifty years ago.[2] It need not be devoid of interest in history, context, empirical content, and etymology. If Bertrand Russell misrepresented the case against the Hegelians at Oxbridge in his day, he was, nevertheless, the very model of an engaged and popular philosopher, with a geat deal to say to ordinary people about immensely important issues. There are so many excellent philosophers today who are using analysis (which means no more, ultimately, than trying to be clear) to address real problems. What a shame, then, that analytic philosophy has saddled itself with such a "thin" paradigm and reputation as obsession with logic and language, to the disdainful exclusion of everything else.[3]

The paradigm comes from Russell, who with Alfred North Whitehead set the pace for the century in their *Principia Mathematica*, which argued that the basic principles of arithmetic could be derived from even more fundamental principles of logic. That "manly" paradigm set the standard for "real" philosophy, as anything less than logical came to be more or less dismissed as "not philosophy."[4] Russell went on to pursue the more general notion that there are "simple" sentences (or, more accurately, propositions) that correspond to discrete and "simple" facts in the world. The resulting philosophy of "logical atomism" eschewed context and what Bradley had called "internal relations," and focussed instead on the logical analysis of propositions and their compounds. The "logical form" of a sentence, Russell argued, was not the same as its ordinary grammatical form. So began a century-long search for an "ideal language," one that would consist of all and only the proper logical forms. This was true minimalism in philosophy, predating (and outlasting) the short-lived minimalism in the arts. But the problem with minimalism is that it is so minimal, so thin and ultimately uninteresting.

It was not as if the paradigm ever went unchallenged, even from within the small circle of distinguished analysts. The search for an all-embracing formal theory hit a devastating snag in the logic of Kurt Gödel, who in 1931 formulated an "incompleteness proof" showing that there will always be some unprovable sentence in any formal system powerful enough to do what the linguistic philosophers wanted it to do. The philosophical consequences of that proof are still being debated, but several leading mathematicians and philosophers abandoned the search for an ideal formal language as a result of it. At the very least, Gödel's proof was a warning shot within the inner sanctum. Then Russell's most brilliant student, Wittgenstein, turned against his own *Tractatus Logico-Philosophicus* (the pretentious title was borrowed from Spinoza) and the "logical positivist" movement it inspired. In his *Philosophical Investigations*, Wittgenstein rejected the decontextualized logic of Russell's (and his own) early atomism. "Analysis," accordingly, took on a new meaning. It was no longer the analysis of the proper logical form of simple sentences but the investigation of the many uses of language ("language games") in everyday "forms of life."

One theme of the *Investigations* has had a particularly deleterious effect on philosophy. Whereas the *Tractatus* maintained a healthy respect, even reverence, for philosophy, the *Investigations* tended to diagnose philosophy as a kind of intellectual malady for which, fortunately or unfortunately (depending on how you look at it and who pays your salary), only more philosophy is the cure. Philosophy, writes Wittgenstein, is "language going on a holiday," language transgressing its ordinary contexts and the "games" in which it normally functions. Philosophy traps us by allowing us to misuse the language, mistaking one application for another, thinking that because a certain question makes sense in one context or in one form of life, it must therefore make sense in another or in no context at all. But if context and use are everything, then the technical tools developed by Frege, Russell, and (early) Wittgenstein may be of no use at all.

Even the positivists, however, were not nearly as "thin" as they are usually thought to be. They were, for the most part, German and Austrian left-wingers and freethinkers who were appalled by Hitler's rise to power and the pervasiveness of Nazism. With their insistence on scientific and logical rigor, the positivists were rejecting the German Romanticism they blamed for the horrors they saw and experienced. They were champions of sanity in a world going insane. Like Husserl, who also was writing in Germany at about the same time, the positivists' reaction was first and foremost a defense of rationality against fascism and National Socialism. The problem was that, in their insistence on scientific and logical rigor and their rejection of German Romanticism, the logical positivists tended to push ethics and other nonscientific subjects out of philosophy. Like Wittgenstein at the end of the *Tractatus*, they seemed to insist that nothing meaningful could be said about such matters. But that left the status of ethics dubious or, at best, dangling. If philosophers were not in a position to chastise the sins of the world, then who would be? The logical positivists fought to keep the Enlightenment alive, despite its damage in World War I and its eclipse by the Nazis. Unfortunately, they also threatened to put an end to ethics and rich philosophy in general and reduce philosophy to a conceptual janitorial service for science.[5]

If Russell's influence on analytic philosophy was a mixed blessing, so, too, was the influence of Wittgenstein. (It is worth noting with some alarm that today it is the *Tractatus* and not the *Investigations* that is once again the focus of analytic attention.) Wittgenstein's self-styled revolution in philosophy was aided by the fact that he was a charismatic, mesmerizing teacher, more of a guru than a professor. His students—and then the students of his students—emulated his intensity and (sometimes rather ludicrously) learned to imitate his tortured mannerisms and his neurotic seriousness. But to hear it reported by those who sat at his feet, to be in Wittgenstein's presence was without doubt to be present at the painful birth of something most profound. The problem is that no one, including Wittgenstein, could say very clearly what it was.

But Wittgenstein's idea that philosophy was a kind of intellectual disease took hold, and the idea that only more philosophy is the cure was not greeted with enthusiasm outside of the small circles being paid and paying to subject themselves to the malady. And if the technical tools developed by the great analytic philosophers turn out to be of no use except to cure such self-imposed distress, then the whole field is faced with an acute loss of purpose, punctuated by occasional fits of defiance. Some analytic philosophers who don't know what else to do with their lives admit that philosophy is an addiction, an ultimately meaningless activity in which tenured professors justify their jobs by passing the disease on to their students. The result is frustration for everyone involved. Protecting their hard-earned tools and techniques, defensive philosophers cut themselves off from the world. The most joyful of all intellectual disciplines has given birth to bitterness and *ressentiment*. What is now called "pragmatism," in both analytic and Continental circles, ultimately amounts to the view that one shouldn't waste time with philosophy. Some of the most influential writings in current philosophy have as their theme "We have been wasting our lives with these questions." The old James–Dewey notion of pragmatism, namely, that ideas should really *matter* for something, remains for them an abstract and merely self-serving gesture.

The forced fanaticism and defensiveness is even more ruinous than the bitterness. Philosophy is the one academic discipline that tends to naturally emerge in everyone's life, in times of turmoil or traumatic change or simply in quiet moments of reflection. That would seem to indicate a special and continuing role for philosophers. But the idea of simply having a conversation with ordinary people, without the need for special skills or privileged knowledge, strikes many philosophers as demeaning—or, worse, as the inevitable step toward unemployment. Embarrassed by pedestrian translations of their ideas, which can sound, in the vernacular, like warmed-over grandmotherly wisdom, philosophers retreat to obscurity. This is not new, of course. Heraclitus did it quite consciously, two and a half millennia ago, and Hegel did it, equally consciously and in order to make himself seem worthy of an academic post, two centuries ago. Heidegger famously followed the same obscurantist strategy, and so, more recently, did Michel Foucault. The idea of carrying on an intelligent conversation with ordinary intelligent people terrifies most philosophers, and so they prefer to converse only with one another in a language and regarding perplexities that only they comprehend.

In Anglo-American–Australasian philosophy, formalization provided the means to do this. Even the simplest formula is sufficient to terrify or turn off virtually all "untrained" readers.[6] How often I have seen an interesting topic obliterated by utterly unnecessary but supposedly impressive acronyms, formulas and equations? (Indeed, how often is the topic itself mistranslated, distorted, and consequently misunderstood and misdirected by formalization?[7]) But the virtue of formalism isn't clarity; it is exclusiveness. The exclusivity of such techniques produces a kind of tribalism in philosophy. A good anthropologist would be fascinated. It is the "training" that holds the tribe together, where this includes not only analytical skills but also a distinctive style of dress ("frumpy academic" with a few self-consciously well-dressed deviants), predictable rituals (for instance, the insistence on referring incessantly to one another and to no one else), and a commitment to using the same tired examples employed by Frege and Russell a century ago.

As in every tribe, there is an enormous gap between those who are members and those who are not. Membership is a matter of bloodlines (academic connections)—the same teachers, the same graduate program. This produces a debilitating inbreeding, not unlike the proverbial two-headed babies in Kentucky and Tasmania. It absolutely kills any but the most nominal interest in diversity. In this tribal society, there is a place reserved for anyone who is simply smart and, of course, willing to play the game, follow the rules, consider him or herself as one of the tribe. (Wittgenstein, without English connections, skyrocketed to prominence on the basis of his intelligence alone.) As such, analytic philosophy has come to look a lot like Mensa, an organization of self-consciously smart people quite apart from any substance or content, devoid of reference to any virtues but one. But the initiation (like graduate studies) is designed to destroy all previous learning, common sense, and ordinary philosophical interest. Within the tribe, there remains the appearance of real dissension, of course. ("I completely disagree with him.") But heaven forbid that any outsider should raise an ill-formed, heartfelt objection, no matter how right on target. Magazines and *The New York Times* are full of now-routine outrage against the impoverishment of philosophy. The ritual response from the tribe is, if anything, a rude guffaw.

What has threatened to ruin philosophy, in other words, is not analytic philosophy but the tribalism of too many well-placed analytic philosophers. They have built a wall of formal jargon around what should be readily accessible ideas. They adopt the posture of the harsh, hardheaded critic even when (especially when) it would be more appropriate to listen and be sympathetic. And they have thinned the subject and restricted, redefined, or reduced their interests to a small number of technical concerns that are consequently of no interest to anyone else. As the better departments get thinner and thinner, their graduate students spread out across the country to reinforce this deadening image of philosophy. The best departments in the country are doggedly committed to reproducing and defending their own narrow specialty. But do such spectacular collections of philosophical technicians have anything to offer to the hundreds of undergraduates who want to study or at least get an acquaintance with philosophy? Or all of those buyers of New Age books, hungry for some philosophy? The thin technicalities of the subject may be a matter of pride, not embarrassment, in the tribe, but it is only a matter of time before more parents, taxpayers, readers, and administrators start to ask, Why should we pay for this? Is this what our kids should be learning? Is this philosophy?

Analytic philosophy, like Husserl's phenomenology, began with an emphasis on rigorous thinking, and throughout its vicissitudes continues to provide an important and often amiable complement or corrective to the flights of speculation and the tendency to obfuscation that also lie at the heart of philosophy. But it need thereby be neither inaccessible, overly technical, limited in its interests, nor socially insensitive. It can and must become rich and thick and jargon-free. Formalization (outside of the formal disciplines) should be seen as a slip into obscurity rather than a contribution to clarity. Tribalism should be seen as an embarrassment, not a source of security. Professionalism should be reserved as a virtue for doctors, lawyers, and business executives, and eschewed by academics (except, perhaps, in their role as teachers and administrators).

The bright hope lies in the rich array of inter- and cross-disciplinary and multicultural studies that are opening up, first at the margins but now near the center of philosophy. Philosophers, at least some of them, are no longer embarrassed to use techniques from literary criticism and anthropology in reading their own texts. More astounding, they are increasingly willing to read other disciplines' texts and write quite seriously about philosophy of/ and/in literature, philosophy of quantum physics, philosophy and management, philosophy, neurology, and cognitive science, philosophy and the arts, philosophy and fashion. Philosophers now teach in medical schools, business schools, art schools, and it is no longer a one-way path of communication. Nearly every major philosophy department now has links with women's studies and cultural studies. As philosophy becomes more and more "impure," it may also learn to talk to and share with other people.

The debate between "analytic" and "Continental" philosophy should now be over. Philosophers have much better things to do than to pursue old misunderstandings. Like so many disputes in the academy, this one is significant for what it leaves out, namely, the rest of the world. It is as if only philosophical methods that have their origins in Europe and in the foundations of mathematics and ontology—as both of these did—are candidates for "philosophy" at all. Both analytic philosophy and Continental philosophy have been ethnocentric and stubbornly closed to approaches that do not suit their methods. There are philosophies in Asia and Latin America, Africa, and our own Native American culture. If they do not fit into philosophy's narrow paradigm, then that may be good enough reason to junk that outmoded exclusivist paradigm. There are all of those other disciplines, from fetal embryology to marketing to narratology, brimming with philosophical questions that have been all but ignored by philosophers in their quest for pure abstraction and thinness. But if philosophy departments, and that presumptuous and exclusivist mode of philosophy that Richard Rorty refers to as "Philosophy with a capital P," were to disappear tomorrow, philosophy would not go away. It would be found in every part of the university and everywhere else. It would lose only its pretentiousness and, unfortunately, its unique claims to useless employment.

Analytic philosophy continues to be a healthy corrective to the sometimes excessive romanticisms of our day. But this does not mean that we should look at excessive romanticism and analytic philosophy as poison and antidote, respectively. They are two parts of a dialectic that, at its best, allows us to articulate some stunning visions and insights. Analytic philosophy, when it doesn't insist on being the only voice in the room, opens up (rather than closes down) the world. It need not be exclusive or reductionist or materialist or overly formal or self-absorbed in its own techniques. Nor need it be oblivious to content, context, culture, and history. Indeed, the best analytic philosophy has always consisted of an uneasy tension between the need to speculate and the urge to clarify. But why call it "analytic," except to put people on the defensive? Indeed, why call it anything at all? Thinking carefully about the perennial problems of life, striving for both clarity and enlightenment and enjoying the process, that's what Pythagoras had in mind when he hesitantly (and ironically) described himself as a "philosopher," a lover of wisdom.

NOTES

Preface

1. Pablo Neruda, "On Impure Poetry," in *Selected Poems.* (New York: Grove Press, 1961)

Introduction

1. "My Mental Development," in P. Schilpp, ed., *The Philosophy of Bertrand Russell* (La Salle, IL: Open Court, 1975). In fact, Russell was responding to some British "Hegelians," who were very different from their German predecessor.

2. Many philosophers insist that their way of doing philosophy—reductionist, thin, and logical—is the only real philosophy. Indeed, several of us have discussed the plausibility of forming subdepartments of "real philosophy" (one of my colleagues, an excellent logician, self-mockingly calls it "manly philosophy"), leaving the rest of us in the appropriately touchy-feely role of talking about the messy richness of life.

3. My campaign against "thinness" here is by no means limited to "analytic" philosophy. The poststructuralist formalism, say, of Gilles Deleuze is every bit as enervating and joyless, despite the nihilist rant, as anything that analytic philosophy has produced.

4. John Rawls, *Theory of Justice* (Cambridge, Mass.: Harvard University Press, 1971), p. viii.

5. Indeed, even ordinary experience has long been the object of derision and suspicion in philosophy: "But isn't that an *empirical* question?" This is often followed by (or at least implies) "That's not philosophy!"And so the subject gets thinner and thinner until it loses so much mass that it has virtually no weight at all.

6. A similar sentiment has been expressed by Robert Nozick in virtually all of his recent books: *Philosophical Explanations*, Cambridge, Mass.: Harvard University

Press, 1981 *The Examined Life*, (New York: Simon and Schuster, 1989) and *The Nature of Rationality* (Princeton, N.J.: Princeton University Press, 1993). But after elegantly stating his conversion from the combative "put-down" mode of philosophy to a new more congenial approach, he cannot restrain himself from showing off the combat skills he has honed so well. I know the problem.

7. A. L. Herman, "The Pleasures of Philosophy," paper presented at meeting of Society for Asian and Comparative Philosophy, Honolulu, January 5–9, 1998.

8. The logical positivists considered themselves empiricists, but only because they treasured science. "Experience" itself was an abstraction to them, part of their thin, purely logical discussion about the concepts of evidence and verification. The phrase "nothing but" comes from James, who contrasted the "nothing but" attitude of empiricism with the "something more" attitude of rationalism. James himself, "radical empiricist" though he may have been, was nothing of a "nothing but" philosopher.

9. I am thinking primarily of Russell's attack on idealism, of course, but similar attacks have been emanating from the ranks of the postmodernists, Gilles Deleuze in particular. A good chunk of his overcelebrated book on Nietzsche is, in fact, an oddly perverse attack on Hegel and Hegelianism. *Nietzsche and Philosophy*, trans. H. Tomlinson (New York: Columbia University Press, 1983).

10. There are postmodernists and Postmodernists, of course, but I am thinking of the ultrathin self-styled "nihilism" of George Bataille as well as Deleuze and Lyotard.

11. In postmodern philosophy, this avoidance of taking a stand has itself been elevated to a philosophical principle. The latest French superstars now make sport of accusing their elders (notably Sartre) of being too subjective, in the sense of overemphasizing the subject. (Sartre, recall, insisted that the subject of consciousness was nothing at all, but that was still, evidently, too much, according to Jean-Luc Nancy, for instance.)

12. John Rajchman and Cornell West, *Post-Analytic Philosophy* (New York: Columbia University Press, 1985).

13. Here we are not just talking about postmodern flakes. This is the position argued by Donald Davidson in "The Folly of Trying to Define Truth," *Journal of Philosophy*, 93, no. 6 (June 1996): 263–278.

14. In analytic philosophy, one can trace this weight-loss from early works by Sidney Shoemaker and John Perry to Derek Parfit and some of the latest work in cognitive science. (Owen Flanagan bravely pleads for its continued usefulness in *Self Expressions* [New York: Oxford University Press, 1996].) In Continental philosophy, one might similarly track the collapse of the concept of the self from Sartre's comparatively substantive claim that consciousness is "nothingness" to the utter dismissal of subjectivity in Foucault, Deleuze, and Jean-Luc Nancy.

15. See, for example, his *Essays on Heidegger and Others*, vol. 2 of his *Philosophical Papers* (New York: Cambridge University Press, 1991), 22ff. Rorty himself talks for the most part only about the problems that other philosophers have created, but he insists that the real problems of human life—poverty, political oppression, economic exploitation, cruelty, and racism, for example—are nonphilosophical. But this, too, is due to an overly thin conception of what philosophy

is and can do. Between starting a revolution and mentally masturbating there is that rich conversation in which Rorty himself has so been successfully engaged.

16. Socrates famously insisted that the unexamined life is not worth living, but it is by no means clear in exactly which of many senses Socrates did and did not examine his own life. Clearly he did not have in mind the notion of "introspection" that is so prevalent in modern notions of self-examination. Nor did he seem to see the truly examined life as anything resembling an ordinary life with its ordinary engagements. Thus Peggy Noonan, referring to her former boss Ronald Reagan, remarked that he had shown that the unexamined life *was* worth living. Beneath that joke lay an enormous set of philosophical questions.

17. Paul Woodruff, "Plato on Education," in *Philosophers on Education*, ed. Amelie Rorty (New York: Routledge, 1998).

18. See the underappreciated but brilliant piece of muckraking by the great independent journalist, I. F. Stone, *The Trial of Socrates* (Boston: Little Brown, 1988).

19. Of course, many of those puzzles rather cavalierly invoke death—what to do in the lifeboat, whether to torture the terrorist who knows the location of the doomsday bomb, and so on. But talking about death is quite a different matter than facing death, as Socrates did, and the seriousness of contemporary philosophy can hardly be thought of (with a straight face) as a response to life-or-death issues.

20. The phrase "deep thinker" will always carry with it the sneer of contempt bestowed upon it by Rod Steiger in the 1954 film *On the Waterfront*. But then, again, my borrowed irony should be balanced by Wittgenstein's own deathbed comment, worthy of Socrates: "Tell them I had a wonderful life." Quoted in Rush Rhees, ed., *Recollections of Wittgenstein* (Lanham, Mo.: Rowman Little field, 1981). See also M. O'C. Drury, "Notes on Conversations," ibid., 76–171; and Terry Eagleton and Derek Jarman, *Wittgenstein* (London: British Film Institute, 1993), a screenplay.

Chapter 1

1. The classic text here is A. J. Ayer's *Language, Truth and Logic* (New York: Dover, 1952).

2. Bernard Williams, *Shame and Necessity* (Berkeley: University of California Press, 1997).

3. Sam Keen, *The Passionate Life* (New York: Harper & Row, 197x).

4. For example, see my essay "A More Severe Morality: Nietzsche's Affirmative Ethics," in my *From Hegel to Existentialism* (New York: Oxford University Press, 1988); and Lester Hunt, *Nietzsche and the Origin of Virtue* (New York: Routledge, 1991).

5. I owe this clarification to a good question by George Sher.

6. The "burn" and "rust" metaphors are from Neil Young. Versions of them can be found in the Old Testament, Alexander the Great, the English and German Romantic poets, and Walter Pater.

7. There is, no doubt, some neurophysiological explanation of such behavior,

probably in terms of such exotic brain stem spots as the locus coeruleus and the deficiency or excess of such chemicals as norepinephrine/seratonin. I do not doubt that a good deal of "the passionate life" is chronic rather than cultivated, but the question—if we are not to beg such questions as whether a virtue must be something "under one's control"—is whether the passionate life can be considered virtuous and, if so, what its virtues might be.

8. Some of these themes were anticipated by Bernard Williams in his "Morality and the Emotions," in B. Williams, _Problems of the Self_ (Cambridge: Cambridge University Press, 1973), but long before that, of course, by Plato and Aristotle, and subsequently by Nietzsche.

9. I should sharply distinguish this vision of the virtues from a contentious contemporary use of that term. A century before Bill Bennett's _Book of Virtues_, Nietzsche had this to say: "Then again there are those who consider it a virtue to say, 'virtue is necessary'; but at bottom they believe only that the police are necessary." _Thus Spoke Zarathustra_, trans. W. Kaufmann, (New York: (Viking, 1954), part II, "On the Virtuous," 207.

10. Philippa Foot, "Virtues and Vices," in F. Foot, _Virtues and Vices and Other Essays_ (Berkeley: University of California Press, 1978). This view of Aristotle seems to have far-reaching influence, for example, in David Steward Nivison's comparison of Aristotle and Mencius in his excellent article on "Mencius and Motivation," _Journal of the American Academy of Religion_, special issue on classical Chinese philosophy (September 1979): 419.

11. Notably in _Daybreak_, trans. R. J. Hollingdale (Cambridge: Cambridge University Press, 1982).

12. Amelie Rorty, _Explaining Emotions_ (Los Angeles: University of California Press, 1980).

13. Bernard Williams, _Ethics and the Limits of Philosophy_ (Cambridge, Mass. Harvard University Press, 1985), 9. Cf. Aristotle, _Nicomachean Ethics_, trans. David Ross (London: Oxford University Press, 1954), book III. William Frankena, no friend of virtue ethics, has suggested that the virtues are no more than the disposition to obey rational principles, thus eviscerating the topic as worth study in its own right.

14. Gilbert Ryle, _Concept of Mind_ (New York: Barnes and Noble, 1949).

15. E.g., O. H. Green, "Emotions and Belief," _American Philosophical Quarterly Monograph_, no. 6 (1972).

16. Of course, a new and different "character" may be revealed by or emerge from that lapse, as when one falls in love or is overwhelmed emotionally by the birth of a new baby. Nevertheless, the virtue lies in the having of the emotion, not the disposition of character that may follow. ("I didn't know he had it in him.")

17. Barbara Herman, _The Practice of Moral Judgment_ (Cambridge: Cambridge University Press, 1983).

18. Here I would include not only the great Scottish moralists, notably David Hume and Adam Smith (who placed far more emphasis on emotions than did their colleagues Francis Hutcheson and Lord Shaftsbury), but also Jean-Jacques Rousseau, who in his educational works (e.g., _Emile_) stressed the importance of

the natural sentiments as opposed to those "unnatural" and "corrupt" calculations often called reason. An interesting contrast might be made here between this familiar Western view and classical Chinese thought. Thus Confucian scholar Tu Wei-ming distinguishes cultivated human sentiments from mere "natural" feelings, thus reversing the Scots' emphasis on the naturalness of the moral sentiments. Tu Wei-ming, *Centrality and Commonality* (Albany: SUNY Press, 1989).

19. If love is a virtue, for instance, there may yet be instances in which love is folly, although one would balk at the idea that love could sometimes be vicious. There are such passions, of course, but perhaps they should not be called "love" (but rather "obsession")—for example. Heathcliff's destructive passion for Cathy in *Wuthering Heights* would seem to be like this. We might insist that love is a virtue even when it is foolish or destructive, however, just as we insist on calling justice a virtue even when the results are disastrous, or just as we insist on calling honesty a virtue even when the outcome is much worse than it would be with a simple "white" lie. But then, I think, we would want to draw some careful distinctions within the arena of virtuous behavior, adding some other measures that are independent of virtue-talk. I owe this clarification to a good question by Robert Audi.

20. Confucius, in emphasizing what we would call "the unity of theory and practice," repeatedly stresses the "virtuosity" of the virtuous person (*jen-ze*). It is no coincidence that this is also a familiar term in music, and, given Confucius's sense of the centrality of music in life, "virtuosity" is not a mistranslation.

21. Alexander Nehamas, *Nietzsche: Life as Literature* (Cambridge, Mass.: Harvard University Press, 1985).

22. The heavy, and I would say unwarranted, emphasis on "the Will to Power" comes largely from Heidegger, who had little or no respect for the texts he used so freely. On the American and Anglophone scene, Walter Kaufmann gave the notion considerable attention in his *Nietzsche* (Princeton, N.J.: Princeton University Press, 1953), the book that made Nietzsche at least respectable in a still bitterly anti-Nazi, positivistic philosophical world. The primary texts for such interpretations, however, are to be found in Nietzsche's unpublished notes, which ought to be treated with considerable suspicion. The concept itself smacks of too much of that Schopenhauerian willfulness that Nietzsche struggled through much of his career to shrug off. To be sure, Nietzsche utilizes the metaphors of strength, health, and power throughout his ethical works, and he does use the assertion of power to correct certain obvious flaws in hedonism and answer certain psychological mysteries about extreme forms of religious behavior, particularly asceticism. But I believe that it is a serious mistake in interpretation to conceive of Will to Power— or anything much like it—as the germ from which Nietzsche's entire philosophy grows. (For an ingenious attempt to "reconstruct" just such a "system," see John Richardson, *Nietzsche's System* [New York: Oxford University Press, 1996]. Regarding doubts about the overuse and abuse of Nietzsche's book (put together by others) called *The Will to Power*, see Bernd Magnus, "Author, Writer, Text: *The Will to Power*," *International Studies in Philosophy*, 22, no. 2 (1990): 49–57.

23. Francisco Goya, *Caprichos* (1797) (New York: Dover, 1970).

24. *Observations on the Feeling of the Beautiful and the Sublime*, trans. John T.

Goldthwait (Berkeley: University of California Press, 1960). Contrast this early sentiment with his drippingly sarcastic phrase, *schmelzender Theilnehmung* ("melting compassion") in the quote that begins this section.

25. Bernard Gert, *The Moral Rules* (New York: Oxford University Press, 1978).

26. The shift of attention from action and character to feelings can be argued to have occurred in Europe in the eighteenth century, in the works of Rousseau, most obviously, but also in the work of the Moral Sentiment theorists. There is an ancient argument against the passions, raised by Julia Annas, that holds that passion leads to excess. But what is meant by "excess," and is it not the desirability of such "excess" that is brought into question here? If "excess" means bad behavior, then there are plenty of arguments, in utilitarianism and in virtue ethics, to condemn such behavior. But if "excess" refers to the passions themselves, the ancient argument begs the question. My argument is that being passionate is, in a qualified sense, good in itself. And if that is so, then an "excess" of passion is impossible in just the same way that an excess of any virtue is impossible, according to Aristotle.

27. This is not to deny, however, that love might take inappropriate objects. Plato anticipates this possibility when he insists that love (eros) cannot be merely desire but must be desire for the Good. I take it, in a pedestrian illustration, that this means that one cannot love a person for features that are evil. This conflicts with some current popular wisdom, for instance, in the many too many movies in which one morally perverted character supposedly "loves" another precisely because of his or her moral perversions (for instance, in the several movie versions of Choderlos de Laclos's epistolary novel, *Dangerous Liaisons* (*Liaisons dangereuses*), for example in 1988, with Glenn Close and John Malkovich, directed by Stephen Frears). I owe this clarification to a difficult question from Robert Audi.

28. Edward Sankowski, "Responsibility of Persons for Their Emotions," *Canadian Journal of Philosophy*, 7 (1977): 829–840.

29. Arthur Danto, "Basic Actions," in his *Analytical Philosophy of Action* (Cambridge: Cambridge University Press, 1973).

30. Nietzsche takes this view to the extreme by arguing that not only are virtues particular—that is, they have particular objects—but they are also particular in kind, that is, they are unique to the virtuous person.

31. E.g., Williams, "Morality and the Emotions."

32. Rorty, *Explaining Emotions*.

33. This is not an a priori argument, and it is subject to obvious empirical counterexamples, such as the soaring divorce rate. But the fact that love often ends does not undermine the thesis that love is an emotional process that is (or can be) intensified and "deepened" with protracted intimacy, familiarity, knowledge, understanding, and shared experiences. The most poetic description of this process is Stendhal's description of "crystallization," as the beloved accrues more and more charms and virtues. Stendhal (Marie-Henri Beyle), *On Love*, trans. C. K. Scott-Moncrieff (New York: Liveright, 1947), 28–34.

34. Kant, *Lectures on Ethics* trans. L. W. Beck (Indianapolis: Bobbs-Merrill, 1963), 164.

35. Sartre rather messes up this neat claim by insisting that, nevertheless, in

sex we try to turn the other into a purely sexual subject—indeed, even into a purely sexual object—but, necessarily, we are unsuccessful. *Being and Nothingness*, trans. Hazel Barnes (New York: Simon and Schuster, 1956), part III, "Concrete Relations with Others."

36. Alan Goldman, "Plain Sex," *Philosophy and Public Affairs*, 6, no. 3 Alan Soble discusses the ontology of love at length in his *The Structure of Love* (New Haven: Yale University Press, 1990).

37. John Milton, "On Marriage and Divorce," in *The Philosophy of (Erotic) Love*, ed. Robert C. Solomon and Kathleen M. Higgins (Lawrence: University Press of Kansas, 1991), 79–84.

38. See my *About Love* (Lanham, Md.: Rowman & Littlefield, 1994), chapter 2.

39. The term "intensity" is overly one-dimensional and quantitative, and is often confused with (and then measured by) physiological arousal. But the most powerful passions may be "calm" (Hume's term) and the most petty irritations can become "violent" (also Hume's term).

40. This is defended in detail in my *About Love*, 194ff.

41. In the *Tao Te Ching*, distinction is made between those who love life and live it fully, those who love life and fail to live it fully, and those who love life too much, and thereby overemphasize death. Lao-tzu might interestingly be compared with Epicurus in this regard. Lao-tze, *Tao Te Ching*, trans. Stephen Addis and Stanley Lombardo (Indianapolis: Hackett, 1993).

42. In *The Secret Life of Dogs*, Elizabeth Marshall Thomas reflects on a familiar finding of comparative neuroscience, that while the brains of dogs are homeostatically "wired," allowing them the peaceful restfulness and Zenlike stare that those of us who live with them have come to know and love, the brains of primates are "wired" in the sense that the term has taken on in the counterculture, "wired" as in overstimulated, "wired" as in perpetually restless, "wired" as in—human. Freud was wrong when he suggested the homeostatic model for the human psyche (although he would have been right about dogs). Elizabeth Marshall Thomas, *The Hidden Life of Dogs* (Boston: Houghton Mifflin, 1993).

43. Kathleen M. Higgins, *Nietzsche's Zarathustra* (Philadelphia: Temple University Press, 1987), ix–x.

44. The phrase come from a letter from Nietzsche to Paul Rée. See my "A More Severe Morality: Nietszche's Affirmative Philosophy" in my *From Hegel to Existentialism*.

45. E.g., "The only critique of a philosophy that . . . proves something, mainly trying to see whether one can live in accordance with it, has never been taught at universities: all that has ever been taught is a critique of words by means of other words." Nietzsche, "Schopenhauer as Educator," in *Untimely Meditations*, trans R. J. Hollingdale (Cambridge: Cambridge University Press, 1982), §**8**, 187.

46. Bernd Magnus, Stanley Stewart, and Jean-Pierre Mileur, *Nietzsche's Case: Philosophy as/and Literature* (New York: Routledge: 1994); Nehamas, *Nietzsche: Life as Literature*. My own argument is elaborated in my "Nietzsche *Ad Hominem*, Perspectivism, Personality and *Ressentiment*," in *The Cambridge Companion to Nietzsche*, ed. Bernd Magnus and Kathleen M. Higgins (Cambridge: Cambridge University Press, 1996).

47. The phrase comes from Pindar. Quotes from *Gay Science*, trans. W. Kaufmann (New York: Random House, 1968).

48. In fact, the *Übermensch* appears only at the beginning of *Thus Spoke Zarathustra* and plays virtually no role in Nietzsche's philosophy.

49. Notably in "Skirmishes of an Untimely Man," in *Twilight of the Idols*, trans. W. Kaufman (New York: Random House, 1968), esp. §§49–50.

50. Homer, *Iliad*, xv, 348–351; Aristotle, *Nicomachean Ethics*, book III, chapter 8 (1116). Ross (in a footnote to his Aristotle translation) points out that the quotation more likely resembles Agamemnon than Hector (*Ethics* 17. 68); but see Aristotle (1117): "passion is sometimes reckoned as courage; . . . for passion above all things is eager to rush on danger. . . ." Hence Homer's "put strength into his passion." Aristotle goes on to say that men who act from passion are not truly brave but more akin to beasts. They do not act "for honor's sake nor as the rule directs" (ibid.). Nevertheless, he adds, "they have something akin to courage."

51. See, for example, T. M. Scanlon's *What We Owe to Each Other* (Cambridge, Mass.: Harvard, 1999) and Simon Blackburn's excellent review in *The Washington Post* Book Section, Feb. 21, 1999: p. 24.

52. Aristotle, *Nicomachean Ethics*, book II, chapter 5.

Chapter 2

1. Joel Feinberg, "Sentiment and Sentimentality in Practical Ethics," in *Proceedings of the American Philosophical Association*, (March 26, 1982).

2. For a good and detailed examination of the proper place of emotion in argument, see Douglas Walton, *The Place of Emotion in Argument* (University Park: Pennsylvania State University Press, 1992). He discusses in some detail arguments *ad populem* (appeals to popular prejudice), *ad miseracordia* (appeals to pity), *ad baculum* (appeals to fear and anger), and ad hominem (personal attacks).

3. Jerome Shaffer, "An Assessment of Emotion," *American Philosophical Quarterly*, 20, no. 2 (April 1983): reprinted in G. Myers and K. Irani, eds., *Emotions* (New York: Haven, 1983).

4. In Myers, op.cit. 202–203.

5. Ibid., 220.

6. For an informed counter to this supposition, consider Gavin de Becker's practical self-help book, *The Gift of Fear: Survival Signals That Protect Us from Danger* (Boston: Little Brown, 1997). De Becker is a security guard (specializing in "threat assessment and risk management") who protects the lives of Hollywood stars, and is thereby far better attuned to the virtues of fear than most of us. Fear, he writes, is a gift because it is an intuitive survival response. More often than not, people who get into trouble do not take heed of their own fearful intuitions. (In America, 80 percent of violent acts are perpetrated by aggressors known to their victims.) Fear may or may not be pleasant, but it is, without a doubt, a desirable response. One might here compare it with pain, which is (for most of us, most of the time) unpleasant, but without it, we would lose fingers and limbs, would burn and strain ourselves to death. It is not that a life without pain is no longer a life, as some masochists might argue; rather, a life without pain would be a danger to life itself.

7. For example, Jonathan Bennett, one of the most prominent recent commentators on this great book, ends his commentary after book II. But see, by way of contrast, the sensitive treatments of Spinoza by Jerome Neu, *Emotion, Thought and Therapy* (Berkeley: University of California Press, 1977); by Yirmiyahu Yovel, *Spinoza and Other Heretics* (Princeton, N.J.: Princeton University Press, 1989); and by Amelie Rorty, in *The Philosophy of (Erotic) Love*, ed. Robert Solomon and Kathleen Higgins (Lawrence: University of Kansas, 1991).

8. See, e.g., Catherine Z. Elgin, *Considered Judgment* (Princeton, N.J.: Princeton University Press, 1996).

9. William James, "What Is an Emotion?" *Mind* (1884). Reprinted in Cheshire Calhoun and Robert Solomon, eds., *What Is an Emotion?* (Oxford: Oxford University Press, 1984).

10. The startle response has been defended as a paradigm of emotion by Jenefer Robinson, "Startle," *Journal of Philosophy*, Vol. xcii, no 2, 1995. The "jerks and winces" view of emotions is at least suggested by Gilbert Ryle in his halfhearted treatment of them in his classic, *The Concept of Mind* (New York: Barnes and Noble, 1949).

11. One is tempted to say "the quest for truth," but this is a hard line to hold in these postmodern times. Both honest and cynical scholars will tell how much "ego" and the quest for fame and fortune evoke this passion, including the relatively modest recognition that this or that claim or position is "mine!" In the wake of Foucault, virtually all quests for knowledge can expect to be accused of being instead a covert grab for power. Nietzsche raised, as a tantalizing question (in *Beyond Good and Evil*), what the "Will to Truth" really amounted to, admitting that in some cases, at least, it did seem to serve as an autonomous motive in desperate need of an accounting. Perhaps the most interesting cases, however, are the most ironic, those in which we see such scholars as Jacques Derrida, Richard Rorty, and Stanley Fish arguing, passionately, that "there is no truth." But without some such passion, it is difficult indeed to imagine any argument at all.

12. A good and comprehensible Heideggerian account of how practices and theories work together in social intercourse is Charles Spinosa, Fernando Flores, and Hubert Dreyfus, *Disclosing New Worlds* (Cambridge, Mass.: MIT Press, 1997).

13. W. B. Cannon, *Bodily Changes in Pain, Hunger, Fear and Rage* (New York: Appleton, 1929); John Dewey, *The Theory of Emotion* (1894), in *Early Works, 1882–1898* (Carbondale: Southern Illinois University Press, 1967).

14. E.g., in *The Passions* (New York: Doubleday/Anchor, 1976; Indianapolis: Hackett, 1993). But this must be distinguished from those quasi-behaviorist views in which considerations of responsibility and the social situation simply enter into the description of the emotion, without any particular tie to the subject's own perspective. See, e.g., Errol Bedford, "Emotions," *Proceedings of the Aristotelean Society*, Vol. 57, (1957).

15. George Lakoff and Mark Johnson, *Metaphors We Live By* (Chicago: University of Chicago Press, 1980). Freud was an advocate of neurological reductionism in his early days (see his "Project for a Scientific Psychology" [1895] in *Standard Works*, trans. J. Strachey (London: Hogarth Press, 1953) vol. 2). Even after giving up this view, he continued to employ hydraulic imagery, for example, in terms of

pressure, blocking, filling (cathexis), releasing (catharsis), channelling (sublimation), and the like for much of his career. See my "Freud's Neurological Theory of Mind," in my *From Hegel to Existentialism* (Oxford: Oxford University Press, 1988). But also consider this comment by Alasdair MacIntyre on Homer: "All psychology in Homer is physiology." In his *After Virtue* (Notre Dame, Ind.: (Notre Dame University Press, 1981), 18.

16. William James, *The Principles of Psychology* (New York: Dover, 1950), vol. 1, p. 5; Freud, "Project for a Scientific Theory," 295.

17. See Paul Griffiths, *What Emotions Really Are* (Chicago: University of Chicago Press, 1997).

18. I have defended this sociocultural view in "The Cross-Cultural Comparison of Emotions," *Emotions in Asian Thought*, ed. R. Ames, J. Marks (Albany: SUNY Press, 1994).

19. William James, "What Is an Emotion?" in Calhoun and Solomon, *What Is an Emotion?*, 128.

20. *Rhetoric*, 1378–1380, trans. Jon Solomon for Calhoun and Solomon, *What Is an Emotion?*.

21. Daniel Dennett, *Consciousness Explained* (Boston: Little, Brown, 1991); John Searle, *Rediscovering the Mind* (Cambridge, Mass.: MIT Press, 1994); David Chalmers, *The Conscious Mind* (Oxford: Oxford University Press, 1996) and Searle's review of Chalmers in the *New York Review of Books* (February 1997). For a compendium of articles covering the twentieth century, see William Lyons, *Modern Philosophy of Mind* (London: Penguin, 1996) and my review, *Philosophy East and West*, 46, no. 3 (July 1996).

22. René Descartes, *The Passions of the Soul*, trans. S. H. Voss (Indianapolis: Hackett, 1989). In fact, one might say (without absurdity) that Descartes was no "Cartesian." See, notably, G. Baker and K. Morris, *Descartes's Dualism* (London: Routledge, 1996).

23. Descartes, *Passions of the Soul*, para XXV.

24. Specifically, *The Passions* (New York: Doubleday, 1976; rev. ed., Indianapolis: Hackett, 1993); more recently, "On Emotions as Judgments," *American Philosophical Quarterly*, 25, no. 2 (April 1988).

25. See, for example, Paul Ekman, *Darwin and Facial Expression* (New York: Academic Press, 1973) and his "Biological and Cultural Contributions to Body and Facial Movement," in *The Anthropology of the Body*, ed. J. Blacking (London: Academic Press, 1977).

26. Nico Frijda, *Emotions* (Cambridge: Cambridge University Press, 1987).

27. Frijda also argues this in his book, a multidimensional account of emotions.

28. Ryle, *Concept of Mind*, esp chapter 4; Ludwig Wittgenstein, *Philosophical Investigations* trans. G. E. M. Anscombe, (Oxford: Blackwell, 1953).

29. Not so much in Sartre's early monograph, *The Emotions: Sketch of a Theory*, trans B. Frechtman (New York: Citadel, 1948), where he characterizes emotions as "magical transformations of the world," a subjective form of "escape behavior," as throughout his monumental *Being and Nothingness*, trans H. Barnes (New York: Philosophical Library, 1956).

30. There is a bit of perversity that needs a note here. Continental philosophers since Nietzsche, notably Heidegger and, following him, Sartre, insist on denying that they are doing "ethics." This is nonsense, a misleading way of indicating their disapproval of what Sartre disdainfully calls "bourgeois ethics," and it is clearly a Kantian model that they have in mind. Immanuel Levinas, in opposition, takes the "priority of the ethical to ontology" as the hallmark of his philosophy.

31. The difference here bears on my disagreements with "social construction theory" (e.g., Rom Harré, James Averill). Part of the disagreement focuses on the existence of some natural or rudimentary emotion responses that precede social-ization, although, to be sure, such responses are greatly modified and embellished by society. But, more to the point here, it is not so much that the emotions are constructed by society as that emotions both define and are defined by the rela-tionships and the societies in which they play an essential role. Love, for example, is not just a "feeling," nor is it biology (or, as Freud put it, "lust plus the ordeal of civility"). It is, to be sure, both of these, and also "socially constructed." But it is not as if the "relationship" is something entirely distinct from the mutual emo-tions (including, of course, much more than love), nor can the emotions be readily distinguished from the relationship. There are many cases, of course, of "unre-quited" love, and, needless to say, it makes perfectly good sense to speak of "one person's feeling for another." But the love, to put it crudely, is *in the relationship*; it is not, as some famous poets have tended to suggest, two parallel but wholly distinct sets of inner vibrations in happy harmony.

32. Sartre, *The Emotions*, 36.

33. See, for example, Daniel Dennett, *The Intentional Stance* (Cambridge, Mass.: MIT Press, 1987); and *Consciousness Explained*.

34. Ryle, for example, in *Concept of Mind* fudges the issue with the idea of "multi-track dispositions," making clear that the number of such hypothetical tracks might be, for any given emotion, indefinitely large.

35. Frijda, *Emotions*.

36. Solomon, "Emotions and Choices," *Review of Metaphysics* vol. 28, no. 1, Sept. (1973).

37. Errol Bedford, "Emotions," *PAAS*, vol. 57 (1957).

38. Nico Frijda, "The Politics of Emotion," in *ISRE Proceedings* Storrs, CT: ISRE, 1994.

39. Nietzsche, *Daybreak*, trans. R. J. Hollingdale (Cambridge: Cambridge Uni-versity Press, 1982).

40. Ronald de Sousa, *The Rationality of Emotion* (Cambridge, Mass.: MIT Press, 1987).

41. Ibid., 182, with reference to the research of Daniel Stern, *The First Rela-tionship: Mother and Infant* (Cambridge, Mass.: Harvard University Press, 1977), 45.

42. Among the more sophisticated of such attempts is Michael Stocker, "The Schizophrenia of Modern Ethical Theories," in his *Valuing Emotions* (Cambridge: Cambridge University Press, 1996). See also Paul E. Griffiths, *What an Emotion Really Is* (Chicago: University of Chicago Press, 1997), for a critique of all such attempts.

43. Such cynics include La Rochefoucauld, Albert Camus, and W. C. Fields.

44. Jean Briggs, *Never in Anger* (Cambridge, Mass.: Harvard University Press, 1970). See my "Getting Angry: The Jamesian Paradigm in Anthropology," in *Culture Theory*, ed. A. Levine and R. Schweder (Cambridge: Cambridge University Press, 1984).

45. Robert Levi, *The Tahitians* (Chicago: University of Chicago Press, 1973).

46. See my "In Defense of Sentimentality," *Philosophy and Literature*, vol. 14, Fall pp. 304–323 (1990).

47. See, for example, Stephen P. Stich, *From Folk Psychology to Cognitive Science* (Cambridge, Mass.: MIT Press, 1983); and Alvin I. Goldman, "The Mentalizing Folk," in *Metarepresentation*, ed. D. Sperber (Oxford: Oxford University Press, 1998).

48. "Emotions and Choice," *Review of Metaphysics*, 28, no. 1 (September 1973): Repr. in *Explaining Emotions*, ed. Amelie Rorty (Berkeley: University of California Press, 1980). pp. 251–282.

49. Introduction to the present book, p. x. For an egregious example of such glib dismissive philosophizing, I refer the reader to chapter 3 of my book *The Passions*, "The Emotions Objectively Viewed: The Psychologist's Puzzle," 72–77, for which I apologize in the 1993 edition.

Chapter 3

1. For example, Allan Gibbard suggests in *Wise Choices, Apt Feelings* (Cambridge, Mass: Harvard University Press, 1990), 10, that "the most sophisticated theory of rationality [for action] might be called the *Hume-Ramsey theory*," which "in short, demands no more than a formal coherence of preferences, in a way that can be expressed by a set of axioms."

2. Hume, *Treatise of Human Nature*, book. 2, III.iii.

3. Ibid.

4. In many current discussions of ethics, there is a general confusion of what Kant called "practical reason" with practical reasoning. The latter may be instrumental, but the former is far richer and more complex, concerned with ends as well as means.

5. There are whole schools of philosophy that dispute the privileged position of rationality in mainstream philosophy, notably the Taoists in ancient and contemporary China, Nagarjuna, a Buddhist in second century India, and, in our own time, Nietzsche.

6. Chuang Tzu, *Chuang Tzu* (London: Allen and Unwin, 1961), 65. Confucius said, "If you look at them from the point of view of their differences, then there is liver and gall, Ch'u and Yuéh. But if you look at them from the point of view of their sameness, then the ten thousand things are one." It is worth noting that the Chinese equivalent of "reason" is *li shen*, which means, roughly, "seeing patterns." One might therefore hypothesize that the Chinese conception of rationality is "right-brained," and the Western conception of rationality as reasoning is "left-brained."

7. Robert Nozick's *Nature of Rationality* (Princeton, N.J.: Princeton University Press, 1993), currently the most sophisticated and readable book in the field, begins by lamenting the inaccessibility of most current philosophical work on ra-

tionality—which he insists is a perennially important topic for public discussion: "Until recently, questions about rationality had been the common possession of humankind, largely accessible to intelligent people, . . . part of the general culture. . . . for the intellectual health of our society, the fundamental ideas must stay public." He then proceeds to present a thin logical account in which his wizardry is fully in evidence, transforming the study of rationality into a technical subject "sprinkled with, when not wholly engulfed by, forbidding formulas in unfamiliar symbolic notations that are elaborated into mathematical structure" (xiii–xvi). Cf. note 6, introduction to the present book.

8. Max Weber rejected instrumental, merely "procedural," rationality because he thought that such bureaucratic emphasis on efficiency had co-opted rationality as such. Although he became one of the dominant theoreticians of rationality in the twentieth century, he favored the distinctively emotional, the nonrational, and perhaps even the irrational powers of spirituality.

9. I have in mind, in particular, the stream of philosophers following Bataille in France, including Kojeve, Lacan, Deleuze, and Irigaray. (It is always worth noting how, in the land of Descartes, the French have so single-mindedly rejected what is most "enlightened" about Descartes's thought.) But similar sentiments, though rarely so "irrationalist," can also be found in analytic philosophy, in the long tradition of skepticism that begins with Hume, and in the very limited notion of rationality as argument that has become the centerpiece of analytic methodology. When rationality becomes tediously boring, a game of one-upmanship in which only specialized skill and cleverness count, one should expect irrationalism to rear its head.

10. Courtesy of Jay Garfield at the University of Tasmania.

11. Lewis Rowell, *Thinking About Music* (Amherst: University of Massachusetts Press, 1983), 202.

12. Ibid.

13. Ibid.

14. Eliot Deutsch, "Reflections on Some Aspects of the Theory of *Rasa*" in his *Studies in Comparative Aesthetics*, vol. 2 (Honolulu: University of Hawaii Press, 1975), 16.

15. I think it was Leibniz who said, "A well-ordered desk is a sign of a sick mind." (Just joking.)

16. Nietzsche is often quoted and discussed in terms of his occasional suggestions that "there is no truth" and the like. Much closer to his heart are questions about *kinds* of truth and the comparative worth of scientific versus other kinds of perspectives. See, for example, Alexander Nehamas, *Nietzsche: Life as Literature* (Cambridge, Mass.: Harvard University Press, 1985).

17. This is best known in the rationalists, Spinoza and Leibniz, but it is clearly assumed even by the most skeptical empiricists—for instance, by Hume, who insists that there could not be miracles because they would violate this principle.

18. E.g., Keith Lehrer, *Self-Trust* (New York: Oxford University Press, 1997).

19. Schlomo Biderman and Ben-Ami Scharfstein, eds., *Rationality in Question: On Eastern and Western Views of Rationality* (Leiden: E. J. Brill, 1989), 219.

20. The great genius of Erving Goffman's minute descriptions of everyday

practices lies precisely in the fact that this is beyond the abilities of virtually all of us, despite the fact that we engage in those practices and perform the relevant activities all of the time, displaying obvious (implicit) knowledge of the rules and finely refined qualifications. What is remarkable, in other words, is just how *abnormal* such descriptions of normal behavior are. So, too, I would argue, the Goffmanian descriptions of the usually rather self-centered and selfish everyday practices of Jerry Seinfeld and his gang are often the funniest part of the show, *Seinfeld*, not because the behavior is at all unusual but rather because the ulterior motives and procedures for such behavior are rarely if ever articulated.

21. This is by no means simply a philosophical matter. The justification for mistreating and slaughtering animals has long been their lack of rationality, in one or another of these rather sophisticated senses. Similar arguments, of course, have supported racism, exploitation, and even slavery ever since Aristotle. Jeremy Bentham answered such self-serving claims over two centuries ago: "The question is not, can an animal think, but can it suffer?"

22. Jonathan Bennett wrote: "It is possible to swallow in such a greedy and undigested lump the Kant-Wittgenstein stress upon language that one sees it as just obvious that there cannot be judgments where there is no language; but this is not obvious at all, and those who say that it is are merely substituting intellectual fashions for arguments." *Rationality* (London: Routledge and Kegan Paul, 1964, reiss. with new preface, Indianapolis: Hackett, 1989), 2.

23. Nietzsche, *Gay Science*, no. 360. Cf. David Glidden, who in a fit of populist rage once argued that "many in our profession are successful reasoners precisely because their emotions are defective." An accomplished Plato scholar, he argued that "many of us follow Plato's path because we are far more comfortable with our reasoning than we are with our own feelings." "Philosophers on a Train," paper read at the American Philosophical Society meetings in Portland, Ore., 1988).

24. E.g., Lehrer, *Self-Trust*.

25. This, I take it, is what is behind much of Martin Heidegger's posturing in *Being and Time*, in particular. See, for a clear elaboration, Hubert Dreyfus, *Being-in-the-World* (Cambridge, Mass.: MIT Press, 1991); and Hubert Dreyfus, Charles Spinosa, and Fernando Flores, *Disclosing New Worlds* (Cambridge, Mass.: MIT Press, 1997).

26. *Principia Mathematica*, written with Alfred North Whitehead in 1905. For a good description of the notorious difficulties of the field, see Adam Morton's introduction to A. Morton, ed. *Paul Benacerraf: Philosopher Meets Critics* (Oxford: Blackwell, 1997).

27. Paradigm cases of such views would be found in Taoism and some forms of Buddhism. Such views also permeate a good deal of Western ethics, notably in the philosophy of Nietzsche but also in radical versions of virtue ethics, in which rational principles are viewed as irrelevant or deleterious to the good life.

28. The phrase "the action itself" has been an invitation to thinness, designating only the slimmest possible behavioral description of the action, perhaps only a bodily movement or, at the farthest extreme, a mere volition, an "act of will." (Pritchard, "Does Moral Philosophy Rest on a Mistake?" *Mind* 21 (1912): 21–

37.) But "the action itself" should be inclusive rather than exclusive, including the intentions that precede it as well as the circumstances in which it is performed. For some purposes, the motives, the background, the history, and, especially, the meaning of the behavior may all count as part of "the action itself." Occasionally, "the action itself" may indeed be little more than a bodily movement, but this would barely count as an action at all, I would think, and is of little interest except to physiologists, the few remaining behaviorists in the world, and philosophers.

29. Compared with what I suggested in chapter 1, I may seem overgenerous with utilitarianism here. But what I appreciate in John Stuart Mill's version of that ethic, in particular, is precisely its emphasis on detail and richness—sometimes disguised as "quality." I have suggested elsewhere that Mill might more fruitfully be compared not with Bentham but with Aristotle. Indeed, despite Nietzsche's mockery ("Man does not live for pleasure; only the Englishman does"), I would suggest that Mill, too, is a good Aristotelean, at heart a virtue ethicist. See my *Ethics and Excellence* (New York: Oxford University Press, 1991).

30. I am thinking, for example, of the considerable literature on the problem of comparing different desires or preferences, and the suggestion that rationality might best be served not by the satisfaction of preferences but by the "satisficing" of preferences within the larger sphere of overall well-being. See, for example, Michael Slote, *Beyond Optimizing* (Cambridge, Mass.: Harvard University Press, 1989). The conclusion is what I am promoting here, but the route of argument— and the fact that the point requires such an argument—is very different.

31. One might say that my project here is the reverse of that in Jonathan Bennett's wonderful little book, *Rationality*. He begins with honeybees and proceeds, by way of various thought experiments, to ask how much more than their admittedly fascinating behavior is needed for rationality. I am beginning with philosophers' rather sophisticated self-attributions in order to ask, "How much less?"

32. There is continuing debate about exactly what Aristotle took to be the role of reason in ethics. The reason that we (as philosophers) employ when trying to describe the features of the flourishing life—not to mention the reason we employ when trying to understand Aristotle—is not the reason that is embedded in the "life of reason." Aristotle's famous but confusing "practical syllogism" in book VII of the *Nicomachean Ethics* is by no means obviously a model or a procedure for deliberation, nor is it clearly the structure of intentional action, as G. E. M. Anscombe once argued. See, e.g., John Cooper, *Reason and in Aristotle's Ethics* (Indianapolis: Hackett, 1986).

33. For a more sympathetic view of Kant, see Barbara Herman, *The Practice of Moral Judgment* (Cambridge: Cambridge University Press, 1983).

34. Thomas Nagel, *The View From Nowhere* (New York: Oxford University Press, 1986).

35. See ibid., 186.

36. David Gauthier, *Morals by Agreement* (New York: Oxford University Press, 1986).

37. "Business Ethics and Game Theory," *Business Ethics Quarterly*, vol. 9, no. 1 January 1999:11–30. But research by Robert Frank, one of our more humanistic

economists, suggests that people who believe such theories (e.g., his economist colleagues) in fact tend to act more selfishly than their "less rational" brethren.

38. It is worth noting at exactly what point philosophers themselves dispense with argument and insist on simply "seeing" the point. Indeed, one common claim for rationality—dating back to Plato's nous—is that beyond procedural rationality (clarity and careful use of evidence and argumentation, for instance) there is that sort of rationality that "sees" veridical or apodictic certainty. Edmund Husserl gives us elaborate "phenomenological" procedures, but ultimately, he tells us, if we do not "see" the truth, there is nothing more to be said. Bloomsbury philosopher G. E. Moore is said to have reacted to anyone who did not share his intuitions of the Good with a withering stare. As clever in argument as he was reputed to be, Moore was famous among philosophers for his moral dogmatism. In this light, too, we might want to pay close attention to the actual role of what John Rawls variously calls "intuitively appealing accounts," "various reasonable and natural presumptions," and "initial convictions" in his discussion of "reflective equilibrium." To what extent is the rationality of this most painstakingly methodical theoretician just a well-argued but nevertheless unsupported assertion of his own political preferences? (Rawls has as much as admitted such, in his subsequent works, especially *Political Liberalism*, in which he restricts his once universally rational claims quite explicitly to the claims of rationality inherent in his own—liberal democratic—way of seeing things.)

39. The best discussion of this problem is Patricia Greenspan, *Emotions and Reasons* (London: Routledge, 1988), 111ff.

40. Allan Gibbard, *Wise Choices, Apt Feelings* (Cambridge, Mass.: Harvard University Press, 1990), p. 10.

41. Solomon, *The Passions* (New York: Doubleday, 1976). See also Robert Gordon, *The Structure of Emotions* (New York: Cambridge University Press, 1987).

42. Nietzsche, *Beyond Good and Evil*, trans. W. Kaufmann (New York: Random House, 1967), §62.

43. Ronald de Sousa, *Rationality of Emotions* (Cambridge, Mass.: MIT Press, 1987)

44. Gordon, *Structure of Emotions*.

45. See Michael Stocker, "The Schizophrenia of Modern Ethical Theories," *Journal of Philosophy*, 73 (1976):

46. Heidegger, *Being and Time*.

47. For a very positive view of the Stoics, see Martha Nussbaum, *Therapy of Desire* (Princeton, N.J.: Princeton University Press, 1994). On the Persian philosopher al-Kindi, see L. E. Goodman, "Medieval Jewish and Islamic Philosophers," in Biderman and Scharfstein, *Rationality in Question*, 95–99. On Schopenhauer, by all means read Schopenhauer.

48. Friedrich Nietzsche, *On the Genealogy of Morals*, trans. W. Kaufmann (New York: Random House, 1967), essay III.

49. Nico Frijda, *The Emotions* (Cambridge: Cambridge University Press, 1986).

50. For a good study of the "distance" problem in caring, see Michael Slote, "The Justice of Caring," in *Virtue and Vice*, E. Paul, J. Paul, F. Miller, eds. (New

York: Cambridge University Press, 1998): 171–195. See also Virginia Held, *Feminist Morality* (Chicago: University of Chicago Press, 1993).

Chapter 4

1. Socrates dismisses any appeal to the sentiments in the *Crito*, for example.

2. Rawls, *A Theory of Justice* (Cambridge, Mass.: Harvard University Press, 1971.)

3. Again, "schmelzender Theilnehmung." Kant, *Grundlegung*, in *Werke*, vol. IV, 399); Kant, *Grounding of the Metaphysics of Morals*, trans J. W. Ellington (Indianapolis: Hackett, 1981), 12 ("melting compassion" is Paton's translation; "tender sympathy," Lewis White Beck's and Ellington's). Kant's account of retribution is in his *Philosophy of Law*, trans. W. Hastie (Edinburgh: Clark, 1889), see chapter 1.

4. Curiously, there seems to be no proper word in modern English for the emotion(s) constitutive of vengeance. "Vengeance" itself is not the name of an emotion but refers to the intended (or actual) outcome. So, too, one desires revenge but revenge is the aim and not the desire itself. "Vengefulness" comes closer to describing the psychological state, but it tends to describe a trait of character rather than a specific emotion or psychological episode. "Wrath" is a good biblical word that actually does name the vindictive emotion in question, but it is, perhaps tellingly, virtually out of use except in biblical threats and phrases. Here, accordingly, I will treat "vengeance" and its cognates as the name of an emotion, with the understanding that this is not literally proper. I assume, however, that there is such an emotion (or functional set of emotions) and that the problem here is nominal rather than substantial.

5. Robert Nozick, *Anarchy, State and Utopia* (New York: Basic Books, 1974), pp. ix–x.

6. Rawls's method of "reflective equilibrium" is intended to resolve such conflicts, but the paucity of examples in *A Theory of Justice* (Cambridge, Mass: Harvard University Press, 1971) suggests that even our "intuitions" and "initial convictions" are insufficiently concrete to provide the dialectic that would be required for a real confrontation. Nor is there reason to think that all such conflicts are resolvable, that there is, in fact, an "equilibrium" point.

7. David Miller, *Social Justice* (Oxford: Oxford University Press, 1976).

8. Michael Walzer, *Spheres of Justice* (New York: Basic Books, 1983).

9. See my *Passion for Justice* (New York: Addison-Wesley, 1990; Lanham, Md.: Rowman and Littlefield, 1993).

10. Rawls recognizes this in *Political Liberalism* (New York: Columbia University Press, 1993), but what then gets lost is the attempt at global reach.

11. It is not hard to see Rawls's "original position" and the traditional "state of nature" allegories in this light, as techniques for shearing away as much particular reference and context as possible. Then, of course, there is the less circuitous route of simply speaking for God, in effect, from the all-knowing perspective.

12. Agamemnon to Menelaus, concerning the fate of their prisoners: "Let us not leave even one of them alive, down to the babies in our mother's wombs." And Homer, commenting, tells us that "he turned his brother's heart, and urged

justice." The Iliad, trans. R. Lattimore, 2nd ed. (Chicago: University of Chicago Press, 1975), 6.51–65.

13. *The Republic*, book I. If this is translated into the obfuscating language of Michel Foucault instead of the openly roughhouse vernacular of Thrasymachus, the thesis that "the just is nothing but the advantage of the stronger" sounds more plausible to modern ears. I will not pursue this suggestion here.

14. I think that the best contemporary defense of this thesis is Michael Walzer's *Spheres of Justice*, though I prefer the more Hegelian notion of context to the rather Leibnizian image of a sphere just because contexts so often and readily overlap and cause conflict, whereas a sphere (and many of Walzer's examples) seems overly self-contained.

15. I have in mind the *Symposium*, for example, where it seems clear that Plato is giving Socrates more than a run for his money and challenging Socrates even within the confines of the dialogue. The very personal speech of Alcibiades, for instance, provides a direct counterpoint to Socrates' overly philosophical account of eros according to Diotima's ethereal wisdom. See, e.g., Martha Nussbaum, "The Speech of Alcibiades," in *The Philosophy of (Erotic) Love*, ed. Robert Solomon and Kathleen Higgins (Lawrence: University Press of Kansas, 1991), 279–316.

16. In addition to the traditional accounts of the origins of the so-called social contract and Rawls's original position, there are, for example, Bruce Ackerman's spaceship scenario, Nozick's somewhat different game theoretical account of the growth of protective associations, and the Marxist abstractions about class and forces of production. There is a great deal of literature about why these models aren't as "neutral" as they pretend to be, but I want to start at the other end and complain that they ignore or rule out of order all of those preexisting personal relationships and affections without which any claims to justice would be irrelevant or hollow.

17. A riveting discussion of this courtroom locution is Susan Jacoby's description of the post–Nuremberg Nazi trials, in which concentration camp victims and the families of victims were instructed to testify, almost robotlike, "We don't want vengeance; we want justice." What they wanted, of course, was revenge. Susan Jacoby, *Wild Justice* (New York: Harper & Row, 1983).

18. One of the best, though admittedly not clearest discussions of the "Evil for Evil" formula as a deep misunderstanding of retribution can be found in Hegel's *Philosophy of Right*, Para 218–20 Hegel, in turn, takes his cue from Kant, who defends punishment as "equality," but as a matter of purely practical reason, of course, not of nasty and irrational vengeance. For a defense of the role of vengeance in prosecuting the death penalty, see also Ernst van der Haag, "Deterrence and Uncertainty," *Journal of Criminal Law, Criminology and Police Science*, 141 (1969), reprinted in just about every book on the subject, eg. Robert C. Solomon and Mark Murphy, *What is Justice?* 2d ed. (New York: Oxford University Press, 1999).

19. This is ambiguous, of course. Vengeance is particularly personal in that it involves an offense or injury to oneself or someone very close to oneself. Not all emotions are personal in this sense. Some emotions are "impersonal" in that they have as their object truth (in the case of curiosity, for example), or moral principle

(in indignation) or—justice. I do not want to defend the (mistaken) position that all emotions are about the self or self-involved, but they are, nevertheless, personal in that one takes the matter in question personally. Thus curiosity reflects one's interest, and moral indignation reflects one's commitment to the violated principle in question. Robert Nozick, in *Philosophical Explanations* (Cambridge, Mass.: Harvard University Press, 1981), suggests that we distinguish retribution from revenge insofar as the first is impersonal and, according to certain standards, justified, while the latter is strictly personal, and therefore not justified at all. In the pages that follow, I want to undermine that distinction.

20. In P. Marongiu and G. Newman's *Vengeance* (Lanham, Md.: Rowman & Littlefield, 1987), for example, the Sardinian code of "vendetta" is discussed in some detail as exemplary of a culture in which personal retaliation is considered not only acceptable but also obligatory. But it is the aggrieved party, not the state, that has the responsibility for punishment.

21. It may be worth noting that Camus's Sisyphus has two very different, and I would say opposed, responses to the injustice and absurdity of the world. First and foremost, he throws himself into his task ("his rock is his thing") and survives by engaging himself in the moment. ("Each atom of that stone, each mineral flake of that night-filled mountain, in itself forms a world. The struggle itself towards the heights is enough to fill a man's heart. One must consider Sisyphus happy.") Such an attitude (what Nietzsche called "amor fati") seems to eclipse considerations of justice. But Camus's other reaction, which informs much of his later work, is Sisyphus's "scorn and defiance" of the gods and his "rebellion"—which might better be understood as sheer *ressentiment*. But resentment, as Nietzsche had pointed out a half-century earlier, can be a powerful even "objective" demand for justice. Camus, *The Myth of Sisyphus*, trans. Justin O'Brien (New York: Vintage, 1960); Nietzsche, *On the Genealogy of Morals*, trans. Walter Kaufmann (New York: Random House, 1967).

22. David Miller, in his *Social Justice*, distinguishes three very different social contexts and three competing conceptions of justice to explain, with a fair amount of anthropological data, why there is no single "correct" theory of justice. Context is the determinant of theories (or, more generally, conceptions) of justice. One might also consult, with some trepidation, Jean-François Lyotard's obscure but similar "antitotalizing" thesis in his *The Postmodern Condition* (Minneapolis: University of Minnesota Press, 1984).

23. Cheshire Calhoun, "Justice, Care and Gender Bias." *Journal of Philosophy*, Vol. LXXXV, 9 (Sept. 1988) pp. 451–55. Nell Noddings, *Caring: A Feminine Approach to Ethics and Moral Education* (Berkeley: University of California Press, 1984).

24. "One is tempted to say that ethics has so far been guided by Logos, the masculine spirit, whereas the more natural and, perhaps, stronger approach would be through Eros, the feminine spirit." (Noddings, *Caring*).

25. "One of the saddest features of this picture of violence [in the world today] is that the deeds are so often done in the name of principle. . . . This approach through law and principle is not, I suggest, the approach of the mother. It is the approach of the detached one, of the other. The view to be expressed here is a

feminine view. . . . It is feminine in the deep classical sense—rooted in receptivity, relatedness, and responsiveness." Ibid., 1–2, 5.

26. There are, however, larger social and cultural factors that seem to me to explain this move in philosophy, for example, the "sophisticated" reaction against growing women's literature in the eighteenth century and, more recently, a widespread bias against all emotion as "sentimentality." See, for example, Jane Tomkins, *Sensational Designs* (New York: Oxford University Press, 1985) and my "In Defense of Sentimentality," *Philosophy and Literature*, (Fall, 1990. 14: 304–323).

27. Jean-Jacques Rousseau is an interesting paradigm here. Although he is more often discussed in philosophy as one of the authors of social contract theory, he is also the philosopher who defended the benevolence of human emotion and influenced generations of Romantics to follow. He is also the philosopher who is responsible for a particularly pathological, if not paranoid, notion of freedom that is, I would argue, a much more pervasive influence on contemporary conservative thought than most conservatives would ever allow. I would argue that he is also a more flattering model for Rawls's theory of justice than Kant, who provided Rawls with much of his methodology. In temperament, Rawls's *Theory of Justice* (140, 264, and esp. 463 and 540) seems to me more in the spirit of *Emile*. Of course, Rousseau was also the inspiration for Kant's moral philosophy, a fact that too often gets lost in a casual introductory paragraph and is ignored in formal analyses of Kant.

28. For Hume, but not Smith, justice was an "artificial"—as opposed to a "natural"—sentiment, for it consisted of the calculated attempt to organize society on the basis of utility. But Hume was willing to recognize that, insofar as it had the ability to move us, justice was not just a set of utilitarian calculations but a cultivated sentiment that could be as spontaneous and heartfelt as his much celebrated sympathy. For Smith, justice was nothing more than our horror at seeing others harmed, and thus went hand in hand with sympathy, which was the ability to perceive such harm in others.

29. Arthur Schopenhauer, *On the Basis of Morality*, trans. E. F. Payne (Indianapolis: Bobbs-Merrill, 1965).

30. *Random House Dictionary* (New York: Random House, 1980).

31. *Theory of the Moral Sentiments* (TMS), I.i.15.

32. Ibid., I.i.2. "As we have no immediate experience of what other men feel, we can form no idea of the manner in which they are affected, but by conceiving what we ourselves should feel in the like situation." Ibid. See Patricia Verhane, *Ethics and Economics: The Legacy of Adam Smith for Modern Capitalism* (New York: Oxford University Press, 1990), esp. 32ff. For the best if not last words on disgust, see William Miller's brilliant *Anatomy of Disgust* (Cambridge, Mass.: Harvard University Press, 1996), esp. chapter 8, Conn.: 179ff.

33. Hume, *Treatise of Human Nature*, 235.

34. Ibid., 577, 579.

35. TMS, III.2.6.

36. Ibid., III.2.7.

37. A. MacIntyre, *Whose Justice? Which Rationality?* (Notre Dame: University of Notre Dame Press, 1988) 268.

38. I am indebted to Annette Baier for letting me see some of her then unpublished work on Hume, and to Patricia Werhane for letting me see some of her then unpublished work on Adam Smith. Their books have since been published as *A Progress of Sentiments* (Cambridge, Mass.: Harvard University Press, 1991) and *Adam Smith and His Legacy for Modern Capitalism* (New York: Oxford University Press, 1991) respectively.

39. The term "negative emotions" has been effectively employed by Laurence Thomas, for instance, in "Grief and Guilt," in *Emotion*, ed. G. Myers and K. Irani (New York: Haven, 1983). His basic list of "negative" emotions includes grief, guilt, envy, and hatred. The idea is that these are distinctively unpleasant and undesirable in themselves (unlike joy and love, for instance) but are to be valued for the "support" they give to the "positive" emotions. My argument here is somewhat different, but the overall point is much the same.

40. Laurence Thomas, *Living Morally* (Philadelphia: Temple University Press, 1983).

41. Martha Nussbaum has argued similarly with regard to "love and the moral point of view." She notes that Adam Smith, who defended the importance of all sorts of emotions, nevertheless denied love the status of a moral sentiment on the grounds that it was too exclusive and particular. See her *Love's Knowledge* (New York: Oxford University Press, 1990), esp. 338f. Nussbaum also makes the astounding claim that recent theorists of emotion have virtually ignored "the connection between emotions and beliefs about what is valuable and important" (293 and n. 15).

42. Helmut Schoeck, *Envy* (New York: Harcourt Brace Jovanovich, 1970).

43. Nietzsche, *On the Genealogy of Morals*, II.

44. On the first claim, see Jean Briggs, *Never in Anger* (Cambridge, Mass.: Harvard University Press, 1975); on the second, see, e.g., Daniel Callahan, *Setting Limits: Medical Goals in an Aging Society* (Washington, D.C.; Georgetown University Press, 1995).

45. It is instructive that one of Nietzsche's best critics, Max Scheler, never took Nietzsche to task for being unfair to resentment; he only wanted to insist that Christianity and Christian morality were not necessarily based on this admittedly repulsive emotion. See Scheler's *Ressentiment* (New York: Free Press, 1961).

46. G. W. F. Hegel, *Phenomenology of Spirit*, trans. A. V. Miller (New York: Oxford University Press, 1977), chapter 4. See L. Rauch and D. Sherman, *The Drive for Self-Mastery: Hegel's Phenomenology of Self-Consciousness*. (Albany: SUNY Press, 1999); and Francis Fukuyama, *The End of History and the Last Man* (New York: Free Press, 1992) and his acknowledgment of unyielding nationalism in Europe, in *The Economist* (June 1992).

47. For a good discussion of group emotions of justice, see Andrew Sharp, *Justice and the Maori* (Auckland, N.Z.: Oxford University Press, 1990).

48. Sartre comes dangerously close to this conclusion in his *Critique of Dialectical Reason*, in which it is a shared sense of oppression alone that forges a true sense of community or *Mitsein*.

49. Smith, TMS, I.:5.5.

50. Exodus 21:24–25.

51. Jeffrie G. Murphy and Jean Hampton, *Mercy and Forgiveness.* (New York: Cambridge, 1988).

52. Aristotle, on the other hand, treats anger and the urge to revenge as one. *Rhetoric* 1378A20–1380A4.

53. See, again, Sharp, *Justice and the Maori* (Auckland, N.Z.: Oxford University Press, 1990); and also Marongiu and Newman, *Vengeance.* To be sure, one might insist that what rationality and "measure" are to be found in vengeance are ingrained in various social practices rather than in the emotion itself, but this, I think, is a fruitless distinction. The social practice is, among other things, the cultivation of the emotion, and the emotion is, in part, the internalization of the social practice. The more general thesis that hovers here is "the social construction of emotions," the thesis that an emotion is constituted by social norms and concepts. For good statements of the social constructionist position, see Rom Harré, *The Social Construction of Emotions* (Oxford: Blackwell, 1986); and James Averill, "The Social Construction of Emotions," in *The Social Construction of the Person*, ed. K. J. Gergen and K. E. Davis (New York: Springer-Verlag. 1985).

54. Robert S. Gerstein, "Capital Punishment: A Retributivist Response," *Ethics*, 85 (1985): 75–79.

55. Jacoby, *Wild Justice.*

56. Robert Axelrod, *The Evolution of Cooperation* (New York: Basic Books, 1984).

57. I do not want to make it sound, as in the *lex talionis* ("eye for eye, tooth for tooth) and in Gilbert and Sullivan's *Mikado* ("an object all sublime/make the punishment fit the crime"), that this notion of "fit" is always all that obvious, even in the case in which it is most often taken as paradigm, the taking of a life for a life. As Albert Camus argued against the death penalty, "For there to be equivalence, the death penalty would have to punish a criminal who had warned his victim of the date at which he would inflict a horrible death on him and who, from that moment onward, had confined him at his mercy for months. Such a monster is not encountered in private life." "Reflections on the Guillotine" in *Resistance, Rebellion, and Death*, trans. J. O'Brien (New York: Knopf, 1960).

58. Most movie plots assume the existence of such a point of satisfaction, and it is perhaps a sign of our bad taste that most revenge films involve only the most extreme kinds of wrongs calling for only the most extreme forms of vengeance. Most comedies, however, identify the point of satisfaction as something less than death and destruction, and the subtleties of humiliation constitute much of the plot as well as the satisfaction that follows. Perhaps the point is most evident when such satisfaction is withheld from the audience, for example in Woody Allen's acclaimed "black comedy" *Crimes and Misdeameanors* (1989). See also William Miller's remarkable *Humiliation* (Ithaca, N.Y.: Cornell University Press, 1993).

59. Steven Feld is professor of anthropology at New York University and the author of *Sound and Sentiment*, (Phila: University & Pennsylvania Press, 1982) a study of the Kaluli of Papua New Guinea. It is important to note that this concept of "satisfaction" is not necessarily equivalent to Kant's "equality." One can "buy off anger" precisely because one need not pay back in kind, and even in cases in which a return of like for like is appropriate, it may be judged offensive and simpleminded, as if we were to repay a friend who gives us a birthday present by

giving in return a present that is exactly the same. It is also important to note that such exchange is first of all a way of fostering and tightening the community. It is not the fulfillment of any real or implicit contract. Indeed, the very idea of retribution is reestablishing and strengthening ties in the community, not pursuing individual grievances.

Chapter 5

1. Whatever else one may want to say about pain, for instance, first there is feeling. Suffering, whatever else it may be, is first of all experience and only secondarily the subject of such evaluations as "harm" or "dammage" (Hobbes). Note the banality of such phrases as "the least advantaged" and "the worst off" in current philosophical discourse. On the empirical side, statistics on malnutrition, disease, and poverty are always much easier to stomach than the plight of any individual sufferer. One can always argue, for instance, about the statistical methods themselves, effectively distracting us from the awfulness of the suffering.

2. "The horrible stuff will happen," says the Danny Glover character in the film *Grand Canyon*. Indeed, this is so obvious that it usually need not be said. Nor do people want to hear it. Despite critical acclaim, the movie quickly died at the box office.

3. Miguel de Unamuno, *The Tragic Sense of Life*, trans. A. Kerrigan (Princeton, N.J.: Princeton University Press, 1974, 29. Unamuno (1864–1936) was perhaps the greatest philosopher of Spain, and he took great pride in the fact that his philosophy was distinctively Spanish, which may explain his neglect by French, German, English, and American philosophers. He wrote elegant poetry, novels, and literary commentary as well as philosophical essays.

4. See Peter Koestenbaum's essay on Unamuno in *The Encyclopedia of Philosophy*, ed. Paul Edwards (New York: Macmillan, 1967), vol. 8, 182–185. See also J. J. Ellis, *The Tragic Pursuit of Being: Unamuno and Sartre* (Tuscaloosa: University of Alabama Press, 1988).

5. "[Man] philosophizes either in order to resign himself to life or to seek some finality in it, or to distract himself and forget his griefs, or for pastime and amusement." *The Tragic Sense*, 29.

6. Don Quixote was Unamuno's paradigm example of the existential hero, but there was nothing mock-heroic about Unamuno. He supported the Allies against Germany in World War I and opposed Franco's fascist regime. He was put under house arrest in 1936 and died a short time later.

7. One can, of course, have meaningless responsibilities, but this makes sense only within a larger context of commitments and responsibilities that one does endorse and embrace. Cynicism, we might say, is the global idea that *all* responsibilities are meaningless.

8. But, as Camus came to realize in his retelling of the Sisyphus story, eternal life is no answer to the meaninglessness of life, the Absurd. Of course, if life is thought to be without meaning because of death, then this would be an appropriate antidote. But if life is without meaning because of the inevitability of suffering, then a life of eternal suffering is surely without meaning.

9. The prime example here, of course, is the great pessimist Arthur Schopenhauer, *World as Will and Idea*, trans E. F. Payne (New York: Dover, 1966).

10. See, for example, the story that begins Chapter 6.

11. Spinoza, *Ethics*; Leibniz, *Monadology*; Schopenhauer, *The Fourfold Root of the Principle of Sufficient Reason*.

12. Peter Huber, *Liability* (New York: Basic Books, 1988).

13. But Camus too urges us to confront the universe with "scorn and defiance," in other words, blaming and sticking up for our rights (*Myth of Sisyphus*). Ultimately, he, too, refuses to accept the Absurd, and "facing" it does not amount to acceptance.

14. For example, Roderick Chisholm, "The Problem of Evil," in *The Problem of Evil*, ed. M. M. Adams and R. M. Adams (Oxford: 1990) and Alvin Plantinga, *Freedom and Evil* (London: 1975).

15. Rabbi Harold S. Kushner, *When Bad Things Happen to Good People*, (New York: Schocken Books, 1981); Bill McKibben, *The End of Nature* (New York: Random House, 1989).

16. Bernard Williams, *Shame and Necessity*, (Berkeley: University, California Press, 1993), 68.

17. Current tort law shares in this ancient sense of collective responsibility. Punishing the innocent may be an idea that seems to us intolerable in questions of criminal law (so, too, guilt by association), but in tort law and civil proceedings, the intentional punishment of the innocent is simply given another name: "strict liability." It is, in fact, a version of punishing a person or an organization for merely being associated with or otherwise connected to a person who has done something wrong. And when that associate has "deep pockets," the unjust practice of punishing the innocent can become lucrative indeed. Huber, *Liability*, esp. 98ff.

18. C. G. Jung, "Job" in *The Portable Jung*), ed. J. Campbell (New York: Viking, 1971 See also John Wilcox, *The Bitterness of Job* (Ann Arbor: University of Michigan Press, 1989); and Zuckerman, *Job the Silent* (New York: Oxford University Press, 1991).

19. "Karma" literally means "residue." John Rawls has distinguished what he calls "the plain truth," that which is evident in straightforwardly earthly and ethical terms, and "the comprehensive truth," the metaphysical and theological beliefs—for example, in reincarnation—that may be brought in to undergird this evidence. I owe this connection to Dean Chatterjee, with reference to John Rawls, *Political Liberalism* (New York: Columbia University Press, 1993) at the conference on South Asian Philosophy, Eastwest Center, Honolulu, January, 1998.

20. Nietzsche's own classic study is his first book, *The Birth of Tragedy*, trans. W. Kaufmann (New York: Random House, 1966). For a good general account of the amazing influence of the ancient Greeks on nineteenth-century Germans intellectuals and literati, see E. Butler, *The Tyranny of Greece over Germany* (Boston: Beacon Press, 1958).

21. Socrates, in the *Symposium*, argues rather that tragedy and comedy are one. But the more profound view here belongs to Milan Kundera, who thus explains the concept of kitsch in his wonderful novel, *The Unbearable Lightness of Being* (New York: Harper and Row, 1984), and more recently "Kitsch is the trans-

lation of the stupidity of received ideas into the language of beauty and feeling. It moves us to tears for ourselves, for the banality of what we think and feel." Lecture delivered in Jerusalem, printed in *Mishkenot Sha'ananim Newsletter*, no. 3 (July 1985): 5.

22. Cecil M. Bowra, *Sophoclean Tragedy* (Oxford: Clarendon Press, 1945); Cedric H. Whitman, "Irrational Evil," in *Sophocles* (Cambridge, Mass.: Harvard University Press, 1951); Marjorie Barstow, (*Classical Weekly*, 6, no 1 (October 5, 1912). An excellent and original discussion of the changes in the notion of tragedy from the early Greek tragedians to the later philosophers Plato and Aristotle is Martha Nussbaum's, *The Fragility of Goodness* (Cambridge: Cambridge University Press, 1986).

A similar attempt to squirm out of tragedy can be identified in the familiar treatments of *Hamlet*. The play is a tragedy of accidents, coincidences, misfortunes. There is only one definitive, unquestionable, intentionally evil act, and that is Claudius's murder of his brother, the king. But for Hamlet, it is an impossible situation to begin with—a college student advised by his dear dead father to avenge his death upon his uncle, who is now his mother's husband. And so he is driven to distraction. How could he not be? But the standard interpretations insist that the source of the tragedy is that "he couldn't make up his mind." Here, again, is the tragic flaw theory. And if it was all Hamlet's fault after all, then it is not the sort of situation that we in our innocence could possibly have to worry about. Dr. Sanford Weimer, Los Angeles psychologist with a side interest in Bayesian decision theory, has demonstrated that all of Hamlet's decisions, especially those not to act at a particular time (for example, to kill Claudius while he is praying), are in fact perfectly reasonable, not at all a matter of "he couldn't make up his mind."

23. Nussbaum, *The Fragility of Goodness*.

24. The classic source is Kant's third antinomy: "*Thesis*: there are in the world causes through freedom. *Antithesis*: there is no freedom, but only natural causes." *Critique of Pure Reason*, trans. N. K. Smith (New York: Macmillan, 1966), B472

25. Jean-Paul Sartre, *Being and Nothingness*, chapter 2.

26. Kurt Vonnegut, *Slaughterhouse Five* (New York: Delacorte, 1969).

27. Aristophanes' lovelorn half-creatures serve as a metaphor here. The concrete sense in which they are two halves of a former whole gives a literal twist to the "meant for" or "made for" imagery.

28. Robert Nozick offers us a catalog of "invisible hand" explanations in his *Anarchy, State and Utopia* (New York: Basic Books, 1974), 20–21.

29. But even strict interpretations of evolutionary theory, in terms of random mutations, natural selection, and so on, follow "invisible hand" type patterns of emergence. J. Crow and M. Kimura, *An Introduction to Population Genetics Theory* (New York: Harper & Row, 1970).

30. Bernard Williams sometimes suggests that this notion of necessity is bound up with a notion of teleology or purposiveness (e.g., *Shame and Necessity*, 141). I do not quite see this. The notion of fate does indeed have everything to do with the future, but I do not see that it is thereby teleological. (The bullet with my name on it does not necessarily serve any purpose, although one could, of course,

add a teleological thesis to the notion of necessity.) That one judges (in retrospect) that this was indeed a good thing does not imply that it happened "in order to. . . ."

31. See ibid.

32. Sartre, interview in 1970.

33. "Chance" is usually converted to "indeterminism," a purely scientific, more neutral notion. See e.g., Robert Kane, *The Significance of Free Will* (New York: Oxford University Press, 1997).

34. Kant, *Grounding for the Metaphysics of Morals*, trans. James W. Ellington (Indianapolis: Hackett, 1981), Section, I, 7. (How much goodwill will a good will will, if a good will will will goodwill? Thanks to Rob Pennock.)

35. Nussbaum, *The Fragility of Goodness.*

36. Wittgenstein inherited the question "Why is there something rather than nothing?" from the German Romantics, especially Friedrich Schelling, who most certainly did not have mere chance on his mind. Schelling's philosophy, like that of Hegel, reveled in the notion of necessity.

37. See, e.g., Robert T. Pennock, *Tower of Babel: Science, Philosophy and the New Creationism* (Cambridge, Mass.: MIT Press, 1998).

38. "Is this a game of chance?" asks the sad-sack sucker in the poker game in *My Little Chickadee*. The W. C. Fields character answers, "Not the way I play it."

39. Whether people who believe that "everything ultimately happens by chance," lead meaningful or meaning-impoverished lives depends on how seriously they take their stochastic model of life. I know one excellent physicist who gets incensed by people who do not accept the "everything is chance" model, but that is only because he does not for a moment think that their accepting it is in fact a matter of chance. He is, as it turns out, a deeply religious man. Indeterminism is only a theory (a good one indeed), but not a philosophy of life.

40. It is with some irony that one observes some of the most brilliant and best-paid moral philosophers of our time dismiss such obvious social advantages as intelligence and good upbringing as utterly irrelevant to considerations of merit and, by the logical extension of the same argument, dismiss merit itself as irrelevant to considerations of justice. Surely there is some informal inconsistency here, though one hesitates to put a name to it.

41. Even so sophisticated a philosopher as Robert Nozick, for example, talks metaphorically about the "light and the dark." *The Examined Life* (New York: Simon and Schuster, 1989), chapter 18, 205ff.

42. Jane Brooks, "Pondering an Act of God," *Newsweek*, April 29, 1991, 10.

Chapter 6

1. Martin Heidegger, *Being and Time*, trans. Joan Stambaugh (Albany: SUNY Press, 1996), esp. division II, section I, 213–246; cf. Boethius, *The Consolation of Philosophy*, (Arundel; Centaur, 1963).

2. But again, to give credit where it is due, I would mention Thomas Nagel's essay "Death," in his *Mortal Questions* (New York: Cambridge University Press, 1979); Roy Perrett's *Death and Immortality* (The Hague: Martinus Nijhoff, 1987); Fred Feldman's *Confrontations with the Reaper* (New York Oxford University Press,

1992), Herbert Fingarette's *Death* (LaSalle, IL: Open Court, 1996); and Jay Rosenberg's *Thinking Clearly about Death* (Indianapolis: Hackett, 1998).

3. Robert Solomon, "Is There Happiness After Death?" *Philosophy*, 51 (1976): 189–193.

4. Aristotle, *Nicomachean Ethics*, trans. W. D. Ross (Oxford: Oxford University Press, 1948), book I, chapter 10. I argued this in "Is There Happiness After Death?"

5. As of 1998, 70 percent of Americans claim to endorse the death penalty "for some crimes," despite the overwhelming evidence that such punishment does not deter crime. My own adopted state of Texas, to its shame, leads the American bloodbath and in fact ranks high in the world—just behind China, Iraq, and Iran—in state executions. For Gary Gilmore's story, see Norman Mailer, *The Executioner's Song* (Boston: Little, Brown, 1979).

6. Sydney Carton's dramatic gesture, at the end of Dickens's *Tale of Two Cities*, may have been a "far, far better thing than [he had] ever done," but, for most of us, a good death can come only at the end of a life well lived.

7. The French *mort* (*fin*), like *merde*, seems more matter-of-fact. The German *Tod*, like so much of German, has the sound of a heavy footstep.

8. For example, Feldman's *Confrontations with the Reaper*, esp. "Puzzles" in part II.

9. Except, notably, those nasty questions about consciousness, which play an integral part in philosophical questions about death.

10. Stephen Covey has a well-known quadrant, "Important and Urgent," "Unimportant but urgent," "not urgent but important," and "Unimportant and Not-Urgent," pointing out, correctly, that many of us, much of the time, find ourselves moved by the urgency rather than the importance of things to do. *The Seven Habits of Highly Effective People* (New York: Simon and Schuster, 1989).

11. Paul Edwards, *Heidegger on Death: A Critical Evaluation* (La Salle, IL: Monist Monographs, 1979); *Reincarnation: A Critical Evaluation* (Amherst, N.Y.: Prometheus, 1996).

12. Alasdair MacIntyre, *After Virtue* (Notre Dame, Ind.: University of Notre Dame Press, 1981), 120.

13. James Miller, *Michel Foucault* (New York: Simon and Schuster, 1993); Susan Sontag, Introduction to Antonin Artaud, *Selections* (Berkeley: University of California Press, 1976); Arthur Rimbaud, *Works*, trans. Paul Schmidt (New York: Harper and Row, 1975).

14. Heidegger, *Being and Time*, 46–49.

15. MacIntyre, *After Virtue*.

16. Notably, *The First Man*, published posthumously, unpolished, by Camus's daughter (New York: Knapf, 1995).

17. The outline of this argument is similar to Sartre's argument in *Being and Nothingness*, trans H. Barnes (New York: Philosophical Library, 1986) 680–707.

18. One can too easily imagine a crypto–Heideggerian accountant perpetrating the concept of *Dasein* (aka *Homo economicus*) as Being-unto-Taxes, for whom all of life's practices should be sorted into such existential categories as "tax deductible," "employee business expenses," and "capital gains." (Unfortunately, that

sounds not unlike the lives that the IRS imposes on most of us good citizens already.)

19. It is still called the "last will and testament," but it is rare that we find much of a testament—a creed, a credo, a covenant with the living, a personal reflection on the meaning of life. A will, these days, is not expected to be anything other than a legal directive for the distribution of property (including, typically, the "property" of one's corpse).

20. "Letter to Menoeceus," in Epicurus, *Letters, Principle Doctrines and Vatican Sayings*, trans. Russell M. Geer (Indianapolis: Bobbs-Merrill, 1981), 54.

21. "Wei Boyang and his loyal disciple, together with their dog, revived, became real immortals, and went away." *Shenxian Zhuan* (fourteenth century).

22. Betty Sue Flowers, in "Death, the Bald Scenario" *Death and Philosophy*, ed. Jeff Malpas and Robert Solomon, (London: Routledge, 1998).

23. One could mention, briefly, not only Hume's philosophical "indifference" to death but also his pronounced atomism, his atheism, and his qualified hedonism, not to mention the fact that, from all available evidence, both Epicurus and Hume were great guys.

24. David Hume, *Dialogues Concerning Natural Religion*, ed. Norman Kemp Smith (Indianapolis: Bobbs-Merrill, 1962), 77.

25. Thomas Nagel, *Mortal Questions* (Cambridge: Cambridge University Press, 1979), "Death," 7.

26. Ibid.

27. Ibid., 8

28. See David Lewis and Stephanie Lewis, "Holes," in David Lewis, *Collected Essays* (New York: Oxford University Press, 1983).

29. I say "concrete" only to allow for the dim vision of my great-grandparents, who no doubt anticipated having great-grandchildren sometime in the future.

30. See Jeff Malpas, "Death and the Having of a Life," in Malpas and Solomon, *Death and Philosophy*.

31. *It's a Wonderful Life*, directed by Frank Capra (1946).

32. Jeffrey Masson, *When Elephants Weep* (New York: Dell, 1995). There is some confusion, however, when it comes to talking about what animals fear or fight for when, for instance, "they fight for their lives." Such behavior is observable even in some of the "lowest" forms of animal life and, in a slower time frame, in many plants as well. But it is not at all clear that "fighting for one's life" is about life at all, which is to say, it is not at all obvious that such behavior in any way involves the awareness of death as a possibility. So, too, it would seem that the phenomenology of a drowning person is that the person fights for the next breath, not for his or her life. In all living things, there is perhaps this instinctual drive for self-preservation, but this is not necessarily about death. What is most confused, however, is the identification of this instinctual drive for self-preservation with some sort of basic right, as Hobbes notoriously suggests. Whether or not one thinks that there is a right to life, this right is not to be derived from either biology or phenomenology.

33. Too much is made, I fear, of the pain of dying. To be sure, the way many people die today—of protracted diseases such as cancer—is frightening in part,

but only in part, because of the pain. But anyone who has ever suffered a serious trauma—a high-speed automobile crash or the quick mutilation of the body with a sharp and dangerous implement—knows that the pain is negligible in such instances. Sometimes, as in severe burns, the pain comes considerably later. But in fatal injuries, like being decapitated with a sword, the pain is not even an issue, and to think that it is, is to confuse the death issue. So, too, I find the arguments surrounding the "cruel and unusual" techniques of capital punishment to be misleading, at least. The pain of being (successfully) executed, whether by guillotine, hangman, firing squad, electric chair, or lethal injection, is usually brief and minimal.

34. Homer, *Iliad* 22: 438; See MacIntyre, *After Virtue*, p. 120, for a discussion of the meaning of desecration of the body.

35. So, too, the proper burial of the dead forms the core of the plot of the tragedy of Antigone, for whom the need to bury her dead brother is more important to her than her life.

36. William Miller, *An Anatomy of Disgust* (Cambridge, Mass.: Harvard University Press, 1997), 49. See also Caroline Bynum, *The Resurrection of the Body in Western Christianity* (New York: Columbia University Press, 1995).

37. Edmund Spenser, *Faerie Queene*, I.I.21.

38. One could argue that Socrates was seriously self-deceived on this point. Reading all or any of Plato's dialogues, it is clear that what Socrates loved most was to talk with other people, not think by himself.

39. Spinoza, *Ethics*, 4th ed., trans. W. H. White and A. H. Sterling (London: Oxford University Press, 1930), 235.

40. One might object that surely my pain and anxiety are for me, and for me alone, a concern apart from empathic friends and relatives and the medical staff who must figure out how to deal with them. But, again, I think pain and anxiety management are issues quite separate from death, not in the analytic sense of "separateness" that I have been questioning but in the more obvious sense that these are features of our experience that are unpleasant in any situation, and more so when the prospect is unending rather than terminal. Death and dying are not necessarily painful, and the anxiety must be understood, I am arguing, in a much broader and more social frame than "Being-unto-Death."

41. Pluto (Mickey Mouse's dog) whizzes from puppyhood through bones and Frisbees as he faces death by drowning in an old Walt Disney comic book.

42. Again, this is not to deny that one might "fight for his or her life," but that one does not do so, except on reflection, to avoid death. Animals, accordingly, "fight for their lives" but not for "self-preservation." They do, however, fight (to their deaths) for the safety of their offspring or cohorts.

Chapter 7

1. For example, see Bernard Williams, "The Self and the Future," *The Philosophical Review*, 79, no. 2 (April 1970):

2. Ibid. Cf. David Wiggins, "Personal Identity," in his *Sameness and Substance* (New York: Oxford University Press, 1980); Peter van Inwagen, *Material Beings*

Ithaca, N.Y.: Cornell University Press, 1987); Sydney Shoemaker, *Self-Knowledge and Self-Identity* (Ithaca, N.Y.: Cornell University Press, 1963), and "Persons and Their Pasts," *American Philosophial Quarterly*, (1970); David Lewis, "Survival and Identity," in *The Identities of Persons*, ed. Amelie Rorty (Berkeley: University of California Press, 1976); Bernard Williams, "Bodily Continuity and Personal Identity: A Reply," in his *Problems of the Self* (New York: Cambridge University Press, 1973); Derek Parfit, *Reasons and Persons* (New York: Oxford University Press, 1984); Mark Johnston, "Human Beings," *Journal of Philosophy*, 84, no. 2 (February 1987). And, of course, Steve Martin and Lilly Tomlin in *All of Me*, directed by Rob Reiner (1984).

3. Parfit, *Reasons and Persons*.

4. Johnston, "Human Beings," 60.

5. E.g., Shoemaker, *Self-Knowledge and Self-Identity* and "Persons and Their Pasts; Lewis, Survival and Identity"; Williams, "Bodily Continuity and Personal Identity: A Reply"; and Parfit, *Reasons and Persons*.

6. See, e.g., Owen Flanagan, *Self Expressions* (New York: Oxford University Press, 1996).

7. Jacqueline Trimier, "African Philosophy," in *From Africa to Zen*, ed. R. Solomon and K. Higgins (Lanham, Md.: Rowman & Littlefield, 1993).

8. For an intricate analysis of these different concepts, see Charles Taylor's majestic *Sources of the Self* (Cambridge, Mass.: Harvarrd University Press. 1989). There is also a rich history of the self to be told in conjunction with (as well as in opposition to) the passions in Western philosophy. See Amelie Rorty, "The Coordination of the Self and the Passions," in *Self as Person in Asian Theory and Practice*, ed. Roger Ames (Albany: SUNY Press, 1994), 35–56.

9. David Hume, *Treatise of Human Nature*, 2d ed., Selbe-Bigge, ed. (Oxford: Clarendon, 1973): p. 252.

10. Heine on Fichte, in *Reflections of Philosophy and Religion in Germany*. Trans. John Snodgrass (Boston: Bencon, 1959).

11. Mark Johnston, "Human Beings," 62. The phrase "peculiarly philosophical" is his.

12. For example, in his *English Letters* Voltaire defended Locke as the great defender of reason, apparently all but indifferent to the ferocious philosophical battles that were being carried on *within* the new Enlightenment tradition. He rejected Cartesian metaphysics, which he had been forced-fed as a student, but not Descartes's rational method.

13. See, for example, P. F. Strawson's relatively conservative discussion of Kant and Hume on the "soul" in his *Bounds of Sense* (London: Methuen, 1966), 162–170.

14. I have tried to do so in my "Hegel's Spirit of *Geist*," *Review of Metaphysics*, vol. 23, no. 4, (1971) and in my book *In the Spirit of Hegel* (New York: University Press, 1983). Those credentials stated, I hope I can avoid unnecessary obscurity without seeming the coward, but I will return to this difficult chapter in the history of philosophy nonetheless.

15. E.g., H. A. Markus and S. Kitayama, "Culture and the Self: Implications for

Cognition, Emotion, and Motivation," *Psychological Review*, 98, no. 2 (1991): 224–253.

16. The hyperbole is not merely of the local speech-on-the-mall and comment-to-the-press variety. It is also promulgated by some very influential philosophers, many of them French—Michel Foucault and Jean-François Lyotard, for example—and any number of domestic French wannabees. Much of the charm of Jacques Derrida and what, despite his frail protests, has come to be known as "deconstruction" is the fact that it calls the notion of selfhood into serious question and raises such "multicultural" questions. Of course, Derrida is as fond of mere "puzzles" as any post-Moorean analytic philosopher, many of the puzzles puzzling precisely because of their obscurity and self-undermining presentation. But which set of puzzles—A's brain in B or the "logocentric" imperialism of the Western tradition—seems to me a matter of profound indifference.

17. Aristophanes in Plato's *Symposium*, trans. A. Nehamas and P. Woodruff (Indianapolis: Hackett, 1989), 25–31; Robert C. Solomon, *About Love* (New York: Simon and Schuster, 1988; Lanham, Md.: Rowman & Littlefield, 1994), 185ff.

18. Philosophers who write about personal identity rarely seem to appreciate the effects on selfhood of even minor bodily changes. Physical incompetence, for example, can devastate one's sense of self. (One remembers the existential anxieties of six weeks in a leg cast.)

19. One might well compare Kafka's story with other tales of transformation in which the subject knowingly *willed* or even delighted in the change. Zeus seemed to specialize in such (temporary) transformations. More down to earth, the identity ruptures in transsexuals is a case in point. All too often, problematic paradigms of personal identity are presented without any such specification of choice or agency. From the transcendental point of view, perhaps, it is supposed not to make a difference. From the perspective of real life identities, it sometimes makes *all* the difference.

20. Jean-Paul Sartre, *Being and Nothingness*, trans. Hazel Barnes (New York: Philosophical Library, 1956): pp. 303ff.

21. *The Phenomenology of Spirit*, trans. A. V. Miller (New York: Oxford University Press, 1977), part B, chapter 2, 109ff. In the dialectic of the *Phenomenology*, the "master–slave" chapter follows the very short chapter "Self-certainty," which, along with much else, entertains and rejects as question-begging the Cartesian "certainty" of self. Hegel also considers, with equal brevity, the importance of the notion of "desire" in self-consciousness and, echoing Fichte, the ultimate awareness of oneself as "*life*." These more rudimentary forms of self-consciousness are then carried over (and *aufheben*'d) in the parable of "master and slave." (There is also a short discussion of the "I" as a matter of immediate acquaintance in the first chapter of the book, "Sense-certainty.")

22. These are Stoicism and skepticism, respectively, but eventually the dialectic turns to an entirely different sense of personal identity that involves group identification (*Sittlichkeit* or "ethical substance") rather than the dubious independence of a competitive "state of nature." I have defended the idea that Hegel's discussion constitutes his contribution to the ongoing "state of nature" debate (and the na-

ture of the "social contract" that is formulated therein) in my *In the Spirit of Hegel*, chapter 7.

23. Schopenhauer argues the curious view that all non-human animals are instantiations of the same idea, but every human being has his or her own distinctive character. *World as Will and Idea*, trans. E. F. Payne (New York: Dover, 1966): Book IV, 55. It seems that Schopenhauer never had a dog.

24. Sartre's character Garcin in *Huis clos* again provides us with an example. But his allegedly "out of character" behavior is a fatal blemish on his virtue. In the popular movie *Back to the Future* (directed by Robert Zemeckis in 1985), a single spontaneous act, totally out of character, changes the future father of the hero into an entirely different person (though he is still the father of the somehow unchanged son).

25. See, for a protracted discussion of this contextualization of self and character, Flanagan, *Self Expressions*.

26. (E.g., Michael Slote, *Virtues* (New York: Oxford University Press, 19xx).

27. My colleague Jaime Pennebaker (Department of Psychology, University of Texas) has studied the correlation between people's use of key emotion and character words in storytelling and their explicit self-ascriptions. He found virtually no correlation whatever.

28. Hegel, *Phenomenology*, part C, BB VI, B, II, 342ff.

29. Aristotle, *Nicomachean Ethics*, trans. W. D. Ross, (London: Oxford University Press, 1954) book IV, chapter 9, 104.

30. For a particularly insightful and sensitive discussion of Augustine and Pascal in this regard, see Bas van Frassen, "The Peculiar Effects of Love and Desire," in *Perspectives on Self-Deception*, ed. Amelie Rorty and Brian B. McLaughlin (Los Angeles: University of California Press, 1988), p. 136f. What did perplex the Greeks, however, was the related problem of *akrasia* or incontinence. But *akrasia* presumes knowledge of what one should do even though one fails to do it, while self-deception involves a denial of what one should do.

31. A protracted study of such a split, focusing on the difficulties of loyalty and integrity in corporate life, is Robert Jackall's *Moral Mazes* (New York: Oxford University Press, 1988).

32. The ongoing battle between Freud and Sartre and their followers often fails to take note of the similar complexity of these two great thinkers. Their opposing languages of "mechanism" and "bad faith," and their supposedly antagonistic views on the existence of "the Unconscious," tend to distract from their mutual concern, undercutting the "transparency" of Cartesian self-reflection. See also Amelie Rorty's "Deception, Liars, and Layers," in *Perspectives on Self-Deception*, ed. Amelie Rorty and Brian B. McLaughlin (Los Angeles: University of California Press, 1988).

33. See, for example, Thomas Nagel, "Brain Bisection and the Unity of Consciousness," in his *Mortal Questions* (Cambridge: Cambridge University Press, 1979); and George Graham, ed., *Philosophical Psychopathology* (Cambridge, Mass.: MIT Press, 1994).

34. The phrase is from Mark Johnson ("Human Beings"), who rejects the relevance of any such consideration.

35. Markus and Kitayama, "Culture and the Self," 224.

36. Ibid.

37. In particular, to Kant's "Paralogisms of Rational Psychology." I have examined and defended this connection between Kant and Hegel in "Hegel's Concept of *Geist*." in R. Solomon *From Hegel to Existentialism* (New York: Oxford University Press, 1988).

38. M. Mauss, "A Category of the Human Mind: The Notion of Person, the Notion of Self," trans. W. D. Halls, in *The Category of the Person: Anthropology, Philosophy, History*, ed. M. Carrithers, S. Collins, and S. Lukes (Cambridge: Cambridge University Press, 1985), 1–25.

39. E.g., A. Bloom, *The Linguistic Shaping of Thought* (Hillsdale, N.J.: Erlbaum, 1981), discussed in Markus and Kitayama, 233–234. According to Bloom, 97 percent of Amerian subjects indicated that they saw no consequential difference in moral education between punishing a child for "immoral" behavior and rewarding a child for "moral" behavior. Only 55 percent of Taiwanese and 65 percent of Hong Kong respondents agreed. Cf. Jerome Bruner, *Actual Minds, Possible Worlds* (New York: Plenum, 1986).

40. Johnston, "Human Beings," 60; italics and bracketed qualification added.

41. Donald Davidson, "On the Very Idea of Alternative Conceptual Schemes," in his *Essays on Actions and Events* (New York: Oxford University Press, 1980). Davidson's famous and very influential article has always struck me as a paradigm of philosophical "thinness." One of the richest problems in the philosophical realm is reduced to a paradox. But there is nothing in the notion of "alternative conceptual schemes" that requires the total incommensurability Davidson uses as his foil. It is quite sufficient that there be systematic mutual misunderstanding. But if one "raises the ante" such that total incommensurability becomes the criterion for alternative schemes, then of course it could make no sense to speak of such schemes, and the pressing problems of multiculturalism evaporate into an abstract debate about the sources of just one more philosophical confusion.

42. For an excellent account of the Maori–Pakeha disputes, see Andrew Sharp, *Justice and the Maori* (Auckland, N.Z.: Oxford University Press, 1990). The standard history of the nineteenth-century "Maori Wars" is Keith Sinclair, *The Origins of the Maori Wars* (Auckland, N.Z.: Oxford University Press). Several good philosophical accounts of the controversial Treaty of Waitangi of 1840 are in G. Oddie and R. Perett, eds., *Justice, Ethics and New Zealand Society* (Auckland, N.Z.: Oxford University Press, 1992).

43. Sharp, *Justice and the Maori*, chapter 2.

44. See, for example, articles by Moana Jackson and John Patterson in *Justice, Ethics and New Zealand Society*;

45. John Patterson, "A Maori Concept of Collective Responsibility," in *Justice, Ethics and New Zealand Society*, 11–26. While the term "corporate" suggests a perfectly plausible analogue to the "loss of identity" (or, more positively, the acquisition of a collective identity) in adopting a role in the modern corporation, the term has a much wider meaning not (yet) wholly consumed by the embrace of entrepreneurial economics.

46. The problem of translating *utu* is itself symptomatic of the conceptual

differences encounteed at every stage of such cross-cultural comparisons. *Utu* is more than mere "getting even," and includes reparations and "setting matters right." While *utu* is a function of group pride or dignity (*mana*, another term that defies simple translation), vengeance is usually restricted to the individual offended. (One can avenge another, but one gets revenge for oneself.) And, of course, *utu* is considered not only legitimate but also obligatory, whereas revenge is dismissed as mere irationality by most Western theorists of retributive justice. See Chapter Four. 85 (1985): 75–79.

47. "Kairangatiura, when alone and surrounded by his enemies about to slay him, is reported to have said: 'you will kill me, my tribe will kill you and the country will be *mine*.'" Quoted in Roy Perrett, "Individualism, Justice and the Maori View of the Self," in *Justice, Ethics and New Zealand Society*, 29.

48. Thus the awkwardness of the debates about whether or not the Treaty of Waitangi is a "social contract." The very idea of the social contract, at least in the Hobbesian version that is the subject of much of the philosophical discussion, relies on a strong notion of individual interests and group formation as a means to satisfy those interests. Or one could take as the "individuals" in question tribes or whole cultures rather than individual persons, but then it is not at all clear if the psychology—as opposed to the logic—of contract goes through. See *Justice, Ethics and New Zealand Society*, esp. articles by Stephen Davies, R. E. Ewin, Jindra Tichy, and Graham Oddie.

49. Sharp, "Being a Maori," in *Justice and the Maori*; and Richard Mulan, *Maori, Pakeha and Democracy*, quoted in Perrett, "Individualism . . . Self," 31.

50. Amelie Rorty, "The Historicity of Psychological Attitudes: Love Is Not Love Which Alters When It Alteration Finds," in her *Mind in Action* (Boston: Beacon Press, 1990), 121.

51. Ibid., 122.

52. Ibid., 123.

53. Ibid.

54. Ibid.

55. I have pursued the kindred concept of what I call "shared identity" in love at greater length in *Love: Emotion, Myth and Metaphor* (New York: Doubleday, 1981; New York: Prometheus Books, 1990) and *About Love* (New York: Simon and Schuster, 1988; Lanham, Md.: Rowman & Littlefield, 1994).

56. See Rorty, "The Coordination of the Self and the Passions."

Chapter 8

1. Nietzsche, *Beyond Good and Evil*, trans. W. Kaufmann (New York: Random House, 1966).

2. Consider Nietzsche's late lament, "Has anyone understood me?" (*Ecce Homo*). Consider, too, Derrida's indignant response to widespread criticism of his work when he was offered an honorary degree at Cambridge in the spring of 1992: "I have never written any such thing!" he insisted to the press and against his critics, hardly indifferent to the truth of the matter. This is not, of course, a refutation of the position (any more than the perils of Pyrrhus constituted a

refutation of ancient skepticism). But it is a pragmatic paradox of considerable interest, embodying what Bernd Magnus (following Stanley Fish) calls a "self-consuming concept."

3. C. A. J. Coady, "The Morality of Lying," in *To Tell a Lie: Truth in Business and the Professions* (Sydney: St. James Ethics Center, 1992), 7–12, repr. in *Res Publica* (Melbourne: Center for Philosophy and Public Issues, 1992).

4. Indeed, Sidgwick further suggested that philosophers might be well instructed to lie systematically to their readers. While he firmly believed in the truth of the doctrine of utilitarianism, he also believed that public knowledge of that doctrine might have results that would be disastrous. Accordingly, the promotion of the utilitarian doctrine in practice required systematic deception.

5. For example, one might deny that a person has a *right* to the truth in question. Do Nazis have a right to know where their innocent victim is hiding? Does an eavesdropper have the right to overhear only truths? Did Special Prosecutor Kenneth Starr have a right to ask or hear the truth about his quarry's private sex life? It is said that dishonesty is a form of injustice, but in that case greater injustices may excuse or override the injustice of a lie. One might even refuse to call such lies "lies." This maneuver would presumably eliminate jokes and fictions as lies, at least where the audience does not expect to hear the truth. One critical concern here, of course, is the case of "white lies," often based on social conventions. See C. A. J. Coady, *Testimony* (Oxford: Clarendon Press, 1992). Even more interesting are those cases and cultures in which social convention is considered mandatory and "trump," even at the expense of what we would consider an outright lie.

6. Amelie Rorty, "Adaptivity and Self-Knowledge" in her *Mind in Action* (Boston: Beacon Press, 1990) and "The Hidden Politics of Self-Deception" (in R. Ames and W. Dissanake, eds. *Self and Deception* (Albany: SUNY Press, 1996): pp 73–90.

7. Or, as Oxford philosopher J. L. Austin later put it, "*In vino veritas*, perhaps, but in a sober symposium, *verum*."

8. Nietzsche, *Beyond Good and Evil*. para. 6.

9. Nietzsche, "On Truth and Lie in the Extra-Moral Sense" (1873), in *The Portable Nietzsche*, ed. W. Kaufmann (New York: Viking Press, 1954).

10. Kant, *Grounding of the Metaphysics of Morals*, trans. J. Ellington (Indianapolis: Hackett, 1981).

11. Jean-Paul Sartre, "Bad Faith," in *Being and Nothingness*. trans. H. Barnes (New York: Philosophical Library, 1956), 86–116.

12. Edmund Pincoffs, *Quandaries and Virtues* (Lawrence: University Press of Kansas, 1986).

13. Nor should this be assumed to apply only to "advanced" and philosophical cultures. I mentioned (in the preceding chapter) that the ancient inhabitants of the island of Maui used to throw the umbilical cords of their newborn infants into the (then active) crater of the volcano Haleakala to assure that their children would grow up to be honest. On my way to an East–West Center conference on self and deception, I was struck by the fact that, of all the virtues, honesty was singled out as exemplary in Hawaii (and keeping one's surfboard polished).

14. Aristotle, *Nicomachean Ethics*, trans. W. D. Ross (Oxford: Oxford University Press, 1944).

15. Aristotle, *Politics*, trans. B. Jowett, in *The Works of Aristotle*, ed. R. McKeon (New York, Random House, 1941).

16. Plato, *Republic*, trans. G. M. A. Grube (Indianapolis: Hackett, 1974), book VII.

17. Fyodor Dostoyevsky, *The Idiot*, trans. Henry Carlisle and Olga Carlisle (New York: New American Library, 1969).

18. Albert Camus, *The Stranger* trans. S. Gilbert (New York: Random House, 1946). Camus's own commentary on his novel and his character Meursault ("a hero for the truth") was published in the preface to Germaine Greer's 1955 edition. Camus's judgment is compromised by the fact that Meursault does lie in the novel—indeed, commits outright perjury—and his obliviousness to matters of morals makes it highly unlikely that he can be said to "refuse to lie."

19. It is perhaps not without intentional ambiguity that this originally religious injunction (John 8:32) is engraved on the administration building of the University of Texas at Austin.

20. This is the formulation discussed in the analytic literature, for example, in Brian McLaughlin, "Self-Deception and the Structure of the Self," in *Self and Deception*, 31–52. And it is the point of departure even for those who reject the paradox, e.g. Herbert Fingarette in his excellent little book *Self-Deception* (Highlands NJ-Humanities Press, 1969). It is also used by Jean-Paul Sartre at the beginning of his famous discussion of "bad faith" (*mauvaise foi*) in *Being and Nothingness*. This is unfortunate, as bad faith is clearly a much broader and richer concept than self-deception. In fact, Sartre uses the paradox only to set up a show trial against Freud's psychological determinism and to attack his notion of "the Unconscious." The "knowing p and not-p" paradox plays virtually no role in either his examples or his subsequent arguments. I would suggest that the examples in the early (part I) chapter "Bad Faith" might better be looked at in the light of the concepts of Being-for-Others and the all-important notions of freedom and responsibility, in parts III and IV, respectively. Indeed, I would argue that Sartre's attack on Freud and his casual treatment of the paradoxes of self-deception are at most secondary, if not incidental, to his overall aim, which is to attack what Kathleen Higgins has called the "atmosphere" of irresponsibility that he perceived in Parisian society. (Of course, as so often, the same charge has been leveled in turn against Sartre himself by Herbert Lottman, in his detailed chronicles of the actual (lack of) involvement of Sartre and his comrades in the French Resistance during World War II.)

21. E.g., Carolyn Ristau on broken wing displays by waterbirds: "Aspects of the Cognitive Ethology of an Injury-Feigning Bird, the Piping Plover," in *Cognitive Ethology: The Minds of Other Animals*, ed. C. Ristau (Hillsdale, N.J.: Erlbaum, 1991). See also D. Cheney and R. Sefarth, *How Monkeys See the World* (Chicago: University of Chicago Press, 1990), on deceptive monkeyshines among our fellow primates.

22. I owe this tentative suggestion to Annette Baier.

23. This is not to say, of course, that such lies are not abominable or fascinating in their consequences. Anyone who has ever lived or worked with a ha-

bitual liar knows all too painfully the psychological damage such a person inflicts on others. Having worked for eight years with a colleague who was unable or unwilling to tell the truth, I almost found myself becoming a Kantian. See also Judy Govier, *Social Trust* (Montreal: McGill University Press, 1997).

24. Robert Audi, "Self-Deception, Rationalization, and Reasons for Acting," in *Perspectives on Self-Deception*, ed. B. McLaughlin and A. Rorty, (Berkeley: University of California Press, 1988).

25. A term that Sartre borrows from chemistry in *Being and Nothingness*, 99f. Metastability has a tentative stability, an appearance of stability, but the slightest intrusion or misstep brings total disaster. Consider a waiter carrying an overly full tray of cups of hot coffee. All goes smoothly until the first jiggle, and a single boiling-hot drop touches his bare skin. He flinches slightly, and. . . .

26. Sartre, *Being and Nothingness*, 112ff.; cf. Marcia Baron, "What Is Wrong with Self-Deception?" in McLaughlin and Rorty, *Perspectives on Self-Deception*.

27. Sartre, *Being and Nothingness*, part III. Philosophers too often talk as if our sense of personal identity were just an internal affair (of self-revelation or memory or the transcendental unity of consciousness). Indeed, Sartre's analysis of the self in *Being and Nothingness* too readily appears to be what some philosophers call an "internalist" account. (Even the term "for-Itself" has obvious Cartesian credentials.) But in our obligatory reading of Sartre in the context of discussions of self-deception, I would like to urge that three textual points be kept in mind: (1) that the famous, often-reprinted chapter "Bad Faith" is one (remarkably short) early chapter in an 800-page book, and the subject is rarely mentioned again; (2) that Sartre insists "Being-for-Others" is on an "ontological par" with the other two modes of being, "Being-for-Itself" and "Being-in-Itself." He is not, therefore, a traditional Cartesian dualist and his concept of self is not an internalist account. In fact, Sartre's argument and his examples are quite at odds with the ontological apparatus he provided for us in that early chapter of his huge book. The examples, which have been rightly criticized as inadequate by both Allen Wood (in Rorty and McLaughlin, *Perspectives on Self-Deception*) and by Kathleen Higgins (in Ames and Dissanoyake, *Self and Deception*) involve "Being-for-Others" as well as the categories of "facticity" and "transcendence" he explicitly employs there. Thus construed, they escape many of Wood's (but not Higgins') objections; (3) in an earlier work, *The Transcendence of the Ego*, Sartre insists that the self is not "in" consciousness but is "outside of us in the world, like the consciousness of another." His is therefore an "externalist" account of the self, not a Cartesian account at all.

28. Amelie Rorty, "The Deceptive Self, Liars, and Layers," in Rorty and McLaughlin, *Perspectives on Self-Deception*.

29. Choderlos de Laclos, *Liaisons dangereuses* trans. P. W. K. Stone (New York: Penguin, 1961).

30. Camus, *The Fall* trans. J. O'Brien (New York: Vintage, 1956). In many ways, *The Fall* is the opposite of *The Stranger*. Meursault (the "stranger") is the very portrait of transparency, all experience and virtually no reflection or self-consciousness. Clamence, by contrast, is all reflection and painful self-consciousness. One tells the truth because he is too simpleminded to lie; the other,

because—full of self-deception himself—he needs to seduce and deceive his listeners. In what sense might either of them be said to be "not lying"?

31. Sissela Bok, *Lying* (New York: Random House, 1978).

32. Leon Festinger, *Cognitive Dissonance* (Evanston, Ill.: Row, Peterson, 1957).

33. In Fiji, before the arrival of the British, Viti Levu was considered, with some reason, the center of the earth, its largest landmass, surrounded by ocean and a few hundred modest islands. When confronted with a map of the world, nineteenth-century Fijians reacted first with predictable denial, then humiliation. It was then that the story of the great African canoe Kannitow became established among the Fijians, despite its dubious veracity. Our British commentator scoffs. But then thinking of the standard stories of our own culture (Columbus's "discovery," the conquest of the West, the USA as the beacon of democracy and freedom in the world), are our stories any more reasonable, given what we know about history and the world?

34. George Lakoff and Mark Johnson, *Myths We Live By* (Chicago: University of Chicago Press, 1980).

35. Roland Barthes, *A Lover's Discourse* (New York: Farrar, Straus and Giroux, 1977).

36. This is the point where proposition-minded philosophers too readily isolate false verbal self-ascriptions of such presentations and point to them as the paradigm of deception—lying, in effect, about who one is. (Aristotle treats "truthfulness" this way, *Ethics*, book iv, chapter 9.) But a more typical and more interesting case is the person with some, but still quite limited, knowledge who acts as if he or she is an expert without ever claiming to be one. As casual conversation and social self-presentation, this is innocent enough. But in a context in which a real expert is or becomes urgently needed, it becomes not only deception but also fraud and betrayal. So, too, it is not deception to "act friendly" with a person for whom one has no special affection. Nor is it even obvious that proclaiming one's friendship in such circumstances, as encouragement or a friendly gesture, for example, is deception or in any way blameworthy. It is only when the expectations of the so-called friend (or in rare cases, other people) are such that the true devotion of a friend is called for and not forthcoming that, in retrospect, the entire performance gets indicted.

37. Nietzsche, "Truth and Lie in the Extra-Moral Sense"; Jean Baudrillard, *Selected Writings* (Palo Alto, Calif.: Stanford University Press, 1988).

38. Suggestions of this sort abound in the wonderful work of Erving Goffman, notably *The Presentation of Self in Everyday Life* (New York: Doubleday, 1959).

39. Rorty, "The Deceptive Self, Liars, and Layers."

40. Fingarette, *Self-Deception*.

41. Sartre, *Being and Nothingness*, part III, chapter 1, esp. Section iv, "The Look." So, too, Nietzsche, who suggests that "herd morality" gets internalized by the individual, who mistakes it for practical reason. *Twilight of the Idols*, sect. 5.

42. Ibid., 110–111.

43. Roger Ames, "The Classical Chinese Self and Hypocrisy," in Ames and Dissanayake, *Self and Deception*, 219–240.

44. E.g., Hegel "Lordship and Bondage," in the *Phenomenology of Spirit* trans.

A. V. Miller, (New York: Oxford University Press, 1977), P. F. Strawson, in *Individuals* (London: Methuen, 1959); and grudgingly, even Sartre, in "The Reef of Solipsism," in *Being and Nothingness*, 303ff.

45. *Pilote de guerre* quoted by Maurice Merleau-Ponty in *The Phenomenology of Perception* trans. C. Smith (London: Routledge and Kegan Paul, 1962).

46. Both the general and the particularist claim are deveoped, for example, by Clifford Geertz in his *Interpretation of Cultures* (New York: Basic Books, 1966). Both are suggested, at least, by Hegel in *Phenomenology*.

47. Colin Turnbull, *The Mountain People* (New York: Simon and Schuster, 1974).

48. For two good philosophical discussions of this, see Alasdair MacIntyre's *After Virtue* (Notre Dame, Ind.: University of Notre Dame Press, 1981), especially the opening chapters, and Nietzsche's classic discussion of the Greeks in his *Birth of Tragedy*, trans. W. Kaufmann (New York: Random House, 1967).

49. *E.T.* and *Independence Day* are two "blockbuster" examples.

Afterthought

1. In a famous and but still embarrassing exchange, the French phenomenologist Maurice Merleau-Ponty turned to Ryle at a conference and asked, "But are we not doing the same thing?"—to which Ryle, in full Oxonian sarcasm, bellowed, "I hope not!" And yet, Ryle had in fact read and reviewed Husserl and Heidegger, and Merleau-Ponty had been steeped in the work of the behaviorists with whom Ryle has always (against his objections) been associated. Thus the beginning of a long and often hypocritical misunderstanding, "analytic" and "Continental" philosophy at one another's throats, one standing for rigor and science, the other standing against logocentrism and scientism. See, for a continuation of this unfortunate tradition, the exceptionally divisive entry by Anthony Quinton, "Continental Philosophy," in *Oxford Companion to Philosophy*, ed. Ted Honderich (Oxford; Oxford University Press, 1996)

2. Hans Reichenbach, *The Rise of Scientific Philosophy* (Berkeley: University of California Press, 1951).

3. To be fair, one should say that Continental philosophy, beginning at least with Kant and his followers (Fichte, Schelling, Hegel), has done as much to make philosophy "professional," incomprehensible, and inaccessible to the ordinary intelligent reader as anyone in the analytic tradition. Husserl, whatever his other merits, was a writer utterly devoid of charm. Heidegger, rather famously, took the obscurity of his work to be one of its greatest virtues. Jean-Paul Sartre imitated the very worst in the German tradition, though happily he was saved by his practical (and impractical) interest in politics, his literary skills, and his flair for examples. Of the structuralists and the poststructuralists and other postmoderns, I leave the reader to make his or her own judgment, except to relate a single anecdote, if I may. Michel Foucault, when he was visiting at Berkeley, was asked by John Searle how he could think and argue so clearly but write so badly. He answered, without irony, that no one would take him seriously otherwise.

4. So exited ethics, aesthetics, and the philosophy of religion, along with every sort of "applied" philosophy. Russell himself seemed to be of two minds about his

"popular" works, including *Why I Am not a Christian* and a defense of extramarital sex, *Marriage and Morals*. He suffered imprisonment and abuse as a pacifist, and was unjustly refused a position in New York because he was a "libertine and a pervert." With Jean-Paul Sartre, he set up a tribunal to judge American "war crimes" in Vietnam. Analysis or no analysis, Russell surely lived up to the Nietzschean adage that "a philosopher should be an example."

5. Wittgenstein himself never thought that ethics, aesthetics, and religion were unimportant. For him, these subjects were *too important* for the logical language of science.

6. Stephen Hawking's editor wisely pointed out to him that he would lose half of his readership for *each* mathematical symbol he used in his *Brief History of Time*.

7. Larry Wright, an analytic philosopher and logician with impeccable credentials, has been arguing not only that deductive reasoning is not the basis for philosophy (a heretical view in iteself) but also that deduction is not basic to reasoning, which requires only partly articulate competence in dealing with the world. Harsher views hold that analytic philosophy is founded on a mistake, namely, decontextualization. See, e.g., Hans Sluga's introduction to his book *Gottlob Frege* (London: Routledge, 1980).

INDEX

veil of ignorance, 88–89
virtue ethics. *See* ethics, virtue
Vonnegut, Kurt, 134–35

Waugh, Evelyn, 151
Wealth of Nations, 135

West, Cornel, 10
Whitehead, A. N., 219
will to power, 22–23, 31–35
Williams, Bernard, 17, 20, 24, 125, 176
Wittgenstein, Ludwig, 5–7, 18–9, 75, 139–40, 219–22